CHURCHILL

CHURCHILL

MILITARY GENIUS OR MENACE?

STEPHEN NAPIER

The
History
Press

For Sophie and James

First published 2018

The History Press
The Mill, Brimscombe Port
Stroud, Gloucestershire, GL5 2QG
www.thehistorypress.co.uk

© Stephen Napier, 2018

The right of Stephen Napier to be identified as the Author
of this work has been asserted in accordance with the
Copyright, Designs and Patents Act 1988.

British Library Cataloguing in Publication Data.
A catalogue record for this book is available from the British Library.

ISBN 978 0 7509 8684 7

Typesetting and origination by The History Press
Printed and bound by CPI Group (UK) Ltd

CONTENTS

INTRODUCTION

Before the outbreak of the Second World War, the Conservative MP Winston Churchill was regarded as a maverick politician past his prime with a reputation as a political opportunist that he had earnt by changing parties from the Conservatives to the Liberals – a man not to be trusted. As Home Secretary in 1911, Churchill had called out the Army to restore order as coal miners rioted in Tonypandy in Wales which also made him a lifelong enemy of the socialists and trade unions. Churchill was a member of the English aristocracy and stoutly defended the retention of the British Empire, opposing any form of independence for India. His military career had been greatly tarnished by the catastrophe of the poorly planned Gallipoli campaign of the First World War. At the end of that conflict and despite the British being heartily sick of the bloodshed, Churchill, having resumed his political career in 1917, enthusiastically supported the White Russians while the Secretary of State for War by sending British troops to Russia. This was a determined effort to destroy the infant Bolshevik regime of Lenin which Churchill regarded as a threat to the old establishments that ruled the world.

With the recent centenary of the First World War and renewed interest in the Second World War, Churchill today is regarded as one of the greatest leaders and politicians that Britain has ever had in its 2,000-year history. He stands alongside legends such as King Arthur and royal leaders such as Henry VIII and Elizabeth I who fought to save Britain in the hour of its greatest danger of invasion. Churchill has even been called the greatest human being ever to occupy No.10 Downing Street by one biographer.[1]

The popular image that endures to this day is of Churchill when he was appointed Prime Minister in 1940 – a rotund figure in a bowler hat, bow tie, coat and tails and trademark fat cigar in his mouth or hand, strolling through the streets of Whitehall. Churchill is equally renowned for the famous V for Victory gesture adapted from the two-fingered salute of the bowmen of Agincourt that came to symbolise the strength and will of the British people to resist, survive and go on to victory over Germany and the leader of the Nazi Party, Adolf Hitler.

It is indisputable that Churchill's inspirational speeches and broadcasts, when Britain had little else to fight with and invasion was threatened, roused the nation and convinced his political colleagues that Britain should fight on alone, even after Hitler's armies had conquered France and dominated most of Europe. Churchill saw that America was the only source of salvation for Britain and gambled that it would enter the war – and won. Churchill also found an unlikely ally in Stalin when Germany invaded Russia, a country which Britain had risked going to go to war with over Finland only a year earlier in 1940.

Churchill worked ceaselessly to build what he called a 'Grand Alliance', regularly leaving England to meet with his new allies and to co-ordinate aid and military strategy between them against, firstly, Germany and then Japan. Churchill tried by the force of his personality to develop relationships with Roosevelt and Stalin with varying degrees of success in order to be able to influence strategic decisions.

With the leaders of the United States and Russia, Churchill presided over the redrawing of the frontiers of Europe as the powerful Red Army worked its way westwards, steamrolling all in its path as Germany began to collapse in the last twelve months of the war. Since early 1944, Churchill and some Americans had been alive to the dangers posed by the Russian military machine as political discussions between the Allies regarding the borders and new governments of countries previously occupied by Germany were rendered redundant by the advances of Soviet tanks and infantry. The euphoria following victory over Germany was replaced by concerns about the ambitions of Stalin and his massive army. The British Chiefs of Staff even drew up plans for a possible outbreak of war with the Russians (Operation Unthinkable) and Churchill described to the incoming President Truman how an iron curtain had been drawn across the German front line.[2] A year later, in March 1946, Churchill would for the first time publicly describe the limits of Soviet occupation as an 'iron curtain' across Europe.[3]

As a political and inspirational leader, Churchill remains hugely relevant today for the enormous impact he made on the history of the world. Although the Cold War has ended and the Iron Curtain and its component Berlin Wall have now been consigned to history, the boundaries and political systems of most east European countries were settled at the end of the Second World War and remained unchanged until the collapse of communism in 1989 and the break-up of Yugoslavia in the 1990s.

The Second World War gave one last great opportunity to a complex man. Churchill was an adventurer, an aristocrat, an artist, a romantic, a devoted family man and often a brilliant orator. A keen historian and prolific author, Churchill had written more words than anyone at that time on British history and this gave him a unique perspective that helped sustain him in his leadership throughout the war. Given this background and the fact that Churchill was half American himself, it was almost destiny that he should be the man chosen to become leader of Britain in the hour of its greatest need. Churchill was the one person capable of persuading America to enter the war to defeat the territorial hegemony of Hitler's Nazi Germany by utilising Britain as a military springboard into Europe before it too was forced to surrender.

The war went on for six years, and in its first three years Britain lurched from crisis to crisis, evacuation after evacuation. Thousands of soldiers, sailors and airmen were killed, wounded or taken prisoner, with millions of tons of equipment lost, requiring replacement after each new military setback. Churchill, as the Prime Minister and self-appointed Minister of Defence, was at the centre of the direction of the war and the strategic military decisions taken by the British War Cabinet and the Chiefs of Staff.

As the Prime Minister and the British Commander-in-Chief, any close scrutiny of the success or otherwise of his strategies for the conduct of the war have largely been glossed over by the ultimate Allied victory. Churchill himself famously said, 'For my part, I consider that it will be found much better by all Parties to leave the past to history, especially as I propose to write that history myself.'[4]

True to his word, Churchill wrote his six-volume history of the Second World War which, along with the official government histories, remained a standard reference for many years, although historians have long been aware of some discrepancies in Churchill's version of events. The last two decades have seen greater scrutiny of Churchill by authors such as David Reynolds in his *In Command of History*.

Historians are often accused of having perfect hindsight while failing to take into account all the relevant factors behind important historical decisions. Certainly only Winston Churchill knew what was in his mind at critical points in the war but enough accounts and observations have been left by the man himself and those working closely with him to be able to understand how and why certain decisions were made. The strategic planning process is an essential part of the functioning of any organisation, be it commercial or government, as is a subsequent review of the outcome or 'lessons learnt' following the implementation of those plans. The plans of the British government and its Prime Minister during the Second World War affected many millions of civilians and soldiers around the world and are therefore not exempt from any such scrutiny.

This is a full account of the background to Churchill's strategic decisions and how their outcomes affected Britain and the progress of the war.

I

CHURCHILL AND BRITAIN PRE-WAR

It was the sombre, weary voice of British Conservative Prime Minister Neville Chamberlain that brought the tidings of war to the British people on 3 September 1939:

> This morning the British Ambassador in Berlin handed the German Government a final Note stating that, unless we heard from them by 11 o'clock that they were prepared at once to withdraw their troops from Poland, a state of war would exist between us.
>
> I have to tell you now that no such undertaking has been received, and that consequently this country is at war with Germany.
>
> You can imagine what a bitter blow it is to me that all my long struggle to win peace has failed. Yet I cannot believe that there is anything more or anything different that I could have done and that would have been more successful …

All over the country, those families lucky enough to have a wireless huddled around their sets while the aromas of Sunday roast lunches wafted through the homes of those who could afford them. People were anxious for news to end a national state of tension and foreboding that had persisted since Germany had invaded Poland on 1 September despite the threats by Britain and France to come to the aid of their ally. It had only been just over twenty years since the end of the last war with Germany, a horrendous struggle that lasted four years and had been described as 'the war to end all wars'. Those who had fought in it and lived, and those who could remember it, looked in speechless horror at each other. Families across the nation now faced once more a threat to their own survival and the potential loss of family members, relatives and friends. Some mothers began to sob quietly, to be comforted by their grim-faced husbands. Across the nation, the eerie quiet was suddenly dispelled by wailing air raid sirens and the people's fearful mood was replaced by one of terror. Those who already had an air raid shelter or had dug trenches rushed into them for cover, while others ran to the windows to try to see the approaching German planes; everyone scrambled to find their newly issued gas masks. Anti-aircraft crews manned their guns purposely for the first time around London as ground crews struggled to launch their giant silver barrage balloons in time. Fortunately, it was a false alarm but nevertheless provided a harbinger of the war to come.

Despite their fears of war, most people (even those of a religious calling) believed that the declaration of war by Britain was right in the circumstances. The Reverend Dabill:

> I have always been a pacifist and have laboured incessantly for peace but there seems to be no alternative. I would rather have war with its vast threat to the future than we should go back on our promise to Poland. There is not room in the same world for our way and the Nazi way. One or the other has to go.[1]

War had nearly come in 1938 when Germany had threatened Czechoslovakia and had only been averted by Chamberlain's last-minute negotiations in Munich with Adolf Hitler. On Chamberlain's return to England, hundreds of people had gathered at Croydon airport to spontaneously express their relief to the Prime Minister who famously waved a document signed by Germany and declared 'peace in our time'.

Following the ascendancy of Hitler to power in Germany on 30 January 1933, Germany had begun systematically flaunting the limitations of the Treaty of Versailles imposed on it after the First World War. This took the form of a massive rearmament programme from March 1935 to both build up the armed forces and stimulate German industry after the disastrous effects of the Great Depression. Emboldened by the lack of an Allied response to these violations, Germany set about taking back the territories of the old Austro-Hungarian Empire taken away from it in 1919.

These events in Europe were watched from the United States of America by Franklin D. Roosevelt, who had been elected President on 4 March 1933.

Roosevelt defeated the incumbent Republican President Herbert Hoover and was elected after pledging a 'New Deal' for an America suffering acutely in the Great Depression. Despite being strongly focussed on restarting the national economy and creating employment, Roosevelt was not removed from international politics. While Winston Churchill's warnings during the 1930s about German territorial ambitions are well known, Roosevelt's interest and actions in international politics are not so apparent in a country that prided itself on its isolationism and a stance of non-intervention in the 1920s and 1930s after the United States had become involved in the last year of the First World War.

As early as May 1933, Roosevelt had outlined his proposed programme of world security and disarmament, which was endorsed by Hitler, but both Germany and Japan subsequently left the League of Nations that year. In 1934, Roosevelt made a declaration at the Geneva disarmament conference appealing for global disarmament, for member countries to adhere to current treaty obligations and asking that no country should send troops across its own borders. In an address to the closing session of the Geneva conference, the US delegation declared, 'In effect, the policy of the United States is to keep out of war, but to help in every possible way to discourage war.'[2]

The Great Depression of the early 1930s posed many challenges for the industrialised nations of the world, both domestically and in their international relations. With the rise to power of Hitler, some countries, especially France, were concerned by Germany's new agenda ,while on the other side of the world a war was in progress between Japan and China. Japan, a mountainous series of islands with few natural resources, had wanted to make up for lost time compared with the European powers in becoming a colonial power. This expansion started with the seizure of Manchuria in September 1931. In response to this Japanese aggression, Roosevelt approved an increase in budget funding for new US Navy ships in 1934 on the basis that warships took a long time to construct and that a US Navy fleet would eventually be likely to come into conflict with Japan in the Pacific Ocean. Roosevelt also asked Edgar Hoover at the FBI to investigate all possible Nazis and their sympathisers in the United States.

In the years 1935 to 1939, the US Congress passed four Neutrality Acts, the last three altering the conditions and duration of the original Act of August 1935 which was designed to keep the United States out of a possible European war by banning the shipment of armaments to belligerents. The demand for this legislation arose from the belief of many Americans that the entry of the US into the First World War had been a mistake. Japan subsequently withdrew from the Washington naval treaty in December 1934, claiming it was biased against Japan. When Italy invaded Abyssinia in 1935, Roosevelt invoked the 1935 Neutrality Act recently passed by Congress and banned the sales of arms to both belligerent countries. Such was the Democratic Party's majority in Congress that the Neutrality Act gave the President the necessary powers to invoke the Act without having to refer to Congress.

Having denounced the Treaty of Versailles as unjust and announced the introduction of conscription and a rearmament programme in March 1935, Hitler declared two months later that he was 'for peace' and would abide by the Treaty of Locarno, provided other nations did the same. His Foreign Minister, von Neurath, signalled to European diplomats Germany's intention to reoccupy the demilitarised Rhineland bordering France in order to gauge their likely reaction. The justification given by von Neurath was that it was in response to a Soviet–French pact which Germany saw as a violation of the Locarno Treaty. The British were not unsympathetic to Germany's position and had planned to begin discussions with Germany in order to reach a general negotiated settlement to resolve many of Germany's territorial issues and grievances. In mid 1935, Britain and Germany had signed a Naval Agreement which restricted Germany's navy to a third the size of Britain's. While favourable to Britain, this treaty actually undid all the naval restrictions of Versailles and permitted the Germans to start a massive shipbuilding programme which included submarines. France was not consulted and strong protests by Winston Churchill in the House of Commons were ignored. Churchill also pointed out that a resurgent German Navy would compel Britain to keep a large part of its fleet in the North Sea, which would limit the Royal Navy's capacity to counter any Japanese moves in the Pacific.[3]

On 7 March 1936, a token German force reoccupied the Rhineland. The British did not formally protest (the view was in fact taken by Lord Lothian, the future British Ambassador to the United States, that Germany was reoccupying its backyard) while the French government, which was going through its own financial and political crisis, decided not to mobilise its troops in view of the expense of such an operation. The Germans had been instructed to withdraw in the event of any opposition but none came; nevertheless Hitler is reported to have said:

The forty-eight hours after the march into the Rhineland were the most nerve-racking in my life. If the French had then marched into the Rhineland we would have had to withdraw with our tails between our legs, for the military resources at our disposal would have been wholly inadequate for even a moderate resistance.[4]

It is notable that the German General Staff were aghast at this blatant act of brinkmanship by Hitler as the German forces were totally unprepared for war. In order to gain combat experience with their newly developed aircraft and tanks, the German Luftwaffe (the Condor Legion) and two armoured units had become involved in the Spanish Civil War on the side of the Nationalist leader, General Franco, to ensure that Franco emerged victorious. A communist or socialist Spain or France would have presented a threat to Germany in Western Europe. England, France and the United States officially refused to support the opposition Republicans but this did not stop volunteers travelling to Spain to fight for them. American companies did, however, continue to sell trucks and oil to Franco until this loophole was closed by Roosevelt with the revised Neutrality Act of January 1937.

The reoccupation of the Rhineland came as no surprise to Churchill, who had foreseen this eventuality and had warned of the dangers of Germany's rearmament and territorial ambitions for many years from the Conservative Party back benches. Churchill had resumed his political career after his stint in the trenches in 1916 but this had been largely unsuccessful. Following the ascension of David Lloyd George as Prime Minister in December 1916, he had been appointed Minister of Munitions in July 1917. After becoming Secretary of State for War in January 1919, Churchill was instrumental in the next few years in the despatch of British troops to Russia and arms to Poland in an effort to prevent the rise of Bolshevism. Losing his seat in the general election of 1922, such was Churchill's feeling against the socialism of the new Labour Party that he re-joined the Conservatives and was duly elected in 1924 as the MP for Epping in Stanley Baldwin's government, being made Chancellor of the Exchequer. Churchill served in this position for five years and presided over Britain's disastrous return to the Gold Standard, which caused deflation, widespread unemployment and industrial unrest that started with the coal miners and culminated in the General Strike of 1926. The Conservative Party was defeated in the general election of 1929 and although Churchill retained his seat he was not offered any senior positions in either the Conservative Party or the National Government formed by Ramsay McDonald in 1931, which left plenty of time for Churchill to write and tour overseas.

To many commentators, however, Churchill was a spent force and increasingly irrelevant. For nearly two years from the spring of 1933, Churchill had doggedly peddled his views on India to the few Conservative MPs left after the election, alienating many in his own party and diminishing his standing in the House of Commons as a whole. Churchill refused to countenance India being granted the status of a dominion or even limited independence. From 1935 onwards, Churchill subjected firstly his own re-elected Conservative government under Baldwin and then the Chamberlain government to a barrage of memoranda, questions and amendments from the back bench, most concerned with the dangers of the rise to power of Hitler in Germany and German rearmament compared with the paltry state of the British armed forces, which had been only slowly rearming since 1934. Churchill described himself as the voice in the wilderness, warning against Hitler and his National Socialism.

After the reoccupation of the Rhineland, Churchill warned on 16 March in the House of Commons:

> ... here is the Fuehrer, the great leader of the country, who has raised his country so high – and I honour him for that – able to bring home once again a trophy. One year it is the Saar, another month the right of Germany to conscription, another month to gain from Britain the right to build submarines, another month the Rhineland. Where will it be next? Austria, Memel, other territories and disturbed areas are already in view ...
>
> We cannot look back with much pleasure on our foreign policy in the last five years. They have been disastrous years ...
>
> We have seen the most depressing and alarming changes in the outlook of mankind which have ever taken place is so short a period of time. Five years ago all felt safe ... The difference in our position now! We find ourselves compelled once again to face the hateful problems and ordeals which those of us who worked and toiled in the last great struggle hoped were gone for ever.[5]

Churchill worked hard behind the scenes to cultivate a network of contacts and political friends in England and abroad during this time. However, he severely undermined these moves and his reputation with ill-judged support for Edward VIII and Mrs Simpson in a hostile Parliament on 8 December 1936.

The German reoccupation of the Rhineland, the Japanese invasion of China and Italian aggression in Abyssinia led to Roosevelt making a speech in October 1937 regarding the need to economically quarantine aggressor nations. This speech, which reflected a change in position from that of the Geneva disarmament conference three years previously, was not well received domestically in the United States and in certain newspapers. Unlike Churchill, who was on the political sidelines, Roosevelt was able take action by passing legislation such as the Neutrality Acts and make plans in anticipation of future conflicts such as expanding the US Navy's shipbuilding programme. It is clear that Roosevelt, from early in his presidency, identified an 'axis of evil' that existed between Germany, Italy and Japan. His suspicions were no doubt confirmed by the November 1936 Anti-Comintern Pact between Germany and Japan which Italy joined a year later.

Following years of agitation and interference in Austrian affairs by Germany and the Austrian Nazi Party for a union or 'Anschluss' with Germany, the Austrian Chancellor, Schussnigg, ordered that a referendum be held. Rather than waiting for any unfavourable results, Hitler demanded that all government positions of power be given to members of the Nazi Party under its leader, Seyss-Inquart. Schussnigg resigned and Seyss-Inquart promptly invited the Germans to come and restore order, which they did the next day, 12 March 1938. Hitler followed his Army into Austria and was met by jubilant crowds everywhere; in Vienna three days later, Austria was declared a part of Germany. There was little reaction from Britain and France.

The unopposed union with Austria provided the incentive for Hitler to attempt to reunite other German people living in the new modern nation of Czechoslovakia, which had been created after the First World War. In the north of the country in the Sudetenland was a sizeable German population which had been agitating since 1934 for an autonomous region with the formation of a German Home Front Party. Stories of alleged atrocities against the Sudeten Germans were broadcast by Nazi propaganda whilst Hitler publicly intimidated the Czech President, Dr Benes.

The day after the occupation of Austria, Churchill predicted the next German threat would be towards Czechoslovakia:

> To English ears, the name of Czechoslovakia sounds outlandish. No doubt they are only a small democratic State, no doubt they have an army only two or three times as large as ours, no doubt they have a munitions supply only three times as great as that of Italy, but still they are a virile people, they have their rights, they have their treaty rights, they have a fine line of fortresses, and they have a strongly manifested will to live, a will to live freely.
>
> Czechoslovakia is at this moment isolated, both in the economic and in the military sense. Her trade outlet through Hamburg, which is based upon the Peace Treaty, can, of course, be closed at any moment. Now her

communications by rail and river to the South, and after the South to the South–East, are liable to be severed at any moment. Her trade may be subjected to tolls of a destructive character, of an absolutely strangling character.[6]

Britain and France were largely apathetic and certainly did not want war. Chamberlain flew to meet Hitler twice in September but Britain and France decided that Benes had no alternative but to accede to German demands. At the second meeting, Hitler informed Chamberlain (much to his frustration) that other territories belonging to Hungary and Poland should also be returned to Germany. Hitler gave an ultimatum to Czechoslovakia that unless all his demands were met by 2 p.m. on 28 September, Germany would invade on 1 October. The deadline came and went. Chamberlain then proposed another meeting in Munich on 29 September to which Czechoslovakia was not even invited, and Britain and France again acceded to Germany's demands. Benes immediately resigned on hearing of the agreement and on 1 October German troops entered the Sudetenland.

Given Churchill's public warnings of events that had become reality, the Czechoslovakian issue saw him being invited to participate in informal meetings with the Foreign Secretary, Lord Halifax, and Chamberlain. However, while both listened to Churchill, neither took his advice, which was to threaten Germany with immediate war if it entered Czechoslovakia. In a speech of 5 October in Parliament during a motion to approve the policy adopted by Chamberlain at Munich, Churchill expressed his view that Czechoslovakia could have negotiated a better solution without the intervention of Britain and France, much to the embarrassment of his own party and Chamberlain, who was still basking in post–Munich approbation:

I will begin by saying what everybody would like to ignore or forget but which must nevertheless be stated, namely, that we have sustained a total and unmitigated defeat, and that France has suffered even more than we have …

… All is over. Silent, mournful, abandoned, broken, Czechoslovakia recedes into the darkness. She has suffered in every respect by her association with the Western democracies and with the League of Nations, of which she has always been an obedient servant. She has suffered in particular from her association with France, under whose guidance and policy she has been actuated for so long. The very measures taken by His Majesty's Government in the Anglo-French Agreement to give her the best chance possible, namely, the 50% clean cut in certain districts instead of a plebiscite, have turned to her detriment, because there is to be a plebiscite too in wider areas, and those other Powers who had claims have also come down upon the helpless victim.

... I venture to think that in future the Czechoslovak State cannot be maintained as an independent entity. You will find that in a period of time which may be measured by years, but may be measured only by months, Czechoslovakia will be engulfed in the Nazi regime. Perhaps they may join it in despair or in revenge. At any rate, that story is over and told. But we cannot consider the abandonment and ruin of Czechoslovakia in the light only of what happened only last month. It is the most grievous consequence which we have yet experienced of what we have done and of what we have left undone in the last five years – five years of futile good intention, five years of eager search for the line of least resistance, five years of uninterrupted retreat of British power, five years of neglect of our air defences. Those are the features which I stand here to declare and which marked an improvident stewardship for which Great Britain and France have dearly to pay.[7]

Following this speech, relations between Churchill and Chamberlain deteriorated considerably and a mysterious campaign began in Churchill's own constituency of Epping to have him deselected as an MP. With the occupation of the rest of Czechoslovakia in March 1939 and the Italian invasion of Abyssinia in April 1939, Churchill felt vindicated enough to resume writing to government ministers again, including Chamberlain. As the sound of war drums got nearer, Churchill's salvoes of advice to Ministers gained intensity, as did a campaign by some newspapers for Churchill to be given a Cabinet position.

That winter, Hitler exploited the differences between the Czechs and Slovaks, further ratcheting up tensions in the country. Encouraged by Hitler, the Slovaks declared an autonomous state on 14 March 1939 and the next day German troops occupied the remaining Czech provinces of Bohemia and Moravia; Slovakia then promptly surrendered its 2-day-old independence to become a protectorate of Germany. Thus the fledgling state of Czechoslovakia ceased to exist, dismembered not only by Germany but also Poland and Hungary, which also seized territory; these events were exactly as foreseen by Churchill.

Even Chamberlain could no longer ignore German territorial ambitions and belatedly realised that Hitler's word and promises meant nothing. British public opinion began to swing against Hitler following the dissection of Czechoslovakia. Knowing that the last territorial 'injustice' inflicted on Germany by the Treaty of Versailles was in Poland, on 31 March Britain and France offered Poland and Rumania a guarantee of safety which was also extended to Greece and Turkey. In the Treaty of Versailles, Poland had been granted a land corridor to the Baltic Sea near Danzig which had isolated East Prussia from the rest of Germany and given Poland the German states of Posen, West Prussia and Upper Silesia. The city of Danzig had been made a free city. Hitler wanted all these German states returned and was determined to pursue his territorial ambitions in the east. Poland would provide large extra areas for agriculture, slave labour and access to the lands further east – the '*lebensraum*' that Hitler had dreamt of for Germany in his book *Mein Kampf*. Poland had been partitioned several times in the eighteenth century and immediately after the First World War, in a short war with Russia, it had managed to extend its eastern boundary into the Russian Ukraine as well as incorporating Lithuania.

Following the guarantees by Britain and France to Poland, a round of frantic diplomacy began in Europe. Germany tried to isolate Poland and eventually formed the Pact of Steel with Italy on 22 May 1938. Russia, irritated by British guarantees to Poland that it believed were impossible for it to honour, also began negotiating with Britain and France, who concluded pacts with Rumania, Greece and Turkey. Just as the protagonists in the First World War had roped themselves together by a series of treaties and alliances before the outbreak of war so that when one member slipped and fell the others were dragged into the conflict, so did the same countries seek to tie themselves together after the Munich crisis, hoping for peace, deterrence and security.

The most significant outcome of this diplomatic activity was the German–Soviet non-aggression pact of 23 August 1939, which came like a bombshell to the international diplomatic community and left-wing communist sympathisers around the world, particularly a certain group of Cambridge undergraduates. Britain and France were left floundering in their negotiations with Russia, while Japan actually recalled its Ambassador from Germany as Japan at that time was fighting a losing battle on the Manchurian–Mongolian border against Soviet and Mongolian troops at Khalkhin Gol. Meanwhile, other flashpoints were developing around the world. Italy had invaded Albania in April 1939 and the British settlement at Tientsin in China had been blockaded by Japan, which itself had been involved in a renewed conflict with China since July 1937 following the Japanese provocation at the Marco Polo Bridge near Peking. In Poland, members of the local Nazi Party in Danzig continued to manufacture 'incidents' with Polish customs officers at the borders of the city.

Roosevelt's views, privately at least, on the aggressive behaviour of certain countries threatening peace very closely mirrored those of Churchill's, yet the two men had very little contact before the war, despite each knowing of the other. Theodore Roosevelt's father had written to his son in 1908 and described Randolph Churchill as 'sharp' and Winston as a 'cheap character' – observations that Theodore as President may well have passed on to his cousin, Franklin. The two men did meet at a dinner in 1918 in London when Roosevelt was Assistant Secretary of the Navy and Churchill apparently snubbed Roosevelt, who later referred to Churchill as a 'stinker'.[8] Roosevelt was then too busy to see Churchill eleven years later during a private trip to New York by Churchill after Roosevelt had been newly elected as Governor. However, Roosevelt's son did stay for a while at Churchill's Chartwell residence and Churchill had written several newspaper articles praising Roosevelt's efforts to stimulate the American economy. In 1933, Churchill sent Roosevelt a copy of his first volume on the Duke of Marlborough in an opening gambit. Churchill's constant blasts against appeasement in Parliament were reported throughout the world in newspapers and radio broadcasts, and some of his lectures were even broadcast in their entirety on America radio, so Roosevelt was familiar with Churchill's politics. Both men had naval backgrounds and had an interest in the intrigues of spies and intelligence work, so they had much in common. Perhaps the far-ranging aspects of deploying naval fleets globally gave both men their strategic insights and vision for waging economic warfare on an enemy by their cutting lines of supply on either land or water.

British Rearmament

There is a popular misconception that Britain did not begin rearming until immediately prior to the outbreak of war. From 1919, British strategic thinking was dominated by the 'ten-year rule' (no war for ten years) and concerns about Japanese intentions. The fears about Japan were well founded but at the same time misguided as Japan invaded Manchuria in 1931 and not any part of the British Empire.

The British national budgets before 1933 were made against the background of the Great Depression and necessary cuts to military expenditure. While defence expenditure reached a nadir in 1932, from that point on there were steady increases in the annual budgets, which particularly benefited the RAF and Royal Navy. The rise to power of Hitler was the stimulus for a Defence Review Committee, which in February 1934 recommended that the RAF increase its strength to eighty-four squadrons and the base at Singapore be strengthened. One of the major obstacles to any increase in defence spending was the then Chancellor of the Exchequer, Neville Chamberlain.[9]

The RAF further benefited from an unintended admission by Hitler that the Luftwaffe had already achieved parity with the RAF in terms of numbers of planes. In a reply to a question in Parliament from Churchill, the government had stated that it had a comfortable margin of numbers over German aircraft and so, with this admission, the government was forced to introduce a new programme of aircraft production on 22 May 1935. This programme was then superseded in February 1936 by Scheme F, which called for 8,000 new aircraft in three years and saw the development of modern monoplanes including the Hurricane (wooden-framed and canvas-covered like biplanes) and the first aluminium plane, the Spitfire. In March 1938, a new programme, Scheme L, was launched for 12,000 aircraft to be built in two years with an emphasis on fighter aircraft and the development of a radar network along the coast of southern England. It should be noted that neither of the previous programmes actually met their targets as production was limited at that time in British factories that were still working on a peacetime footing.

To increase production capacities, government-backed 'shadow factories' – privately owned factories which were subsidised by the government – were established, particularly for the manufacture of aircraft and engines. The Royal Navy too suffered from budget restrictions and international naval treaty obligations until 1936, when a new programme of shipbuilding was approved. By 1938 the Royal Navy had an effective tonnage of 2 million tons, almost 25 per cent of which had been added since the level of 1935.[10] The Royal Navy acquired five new battleships of the King George V class and modernised existing battleships by varying degrees. Ships such as HMS *Renown* and HMS *Warspite* were completely modernised but others such as HMS *Hood*, HMS *Barham* and HMS *Repulse*, as well as the Nelson and Royal Sovereign classes, were not modernised and lacked improvements to horizontal deck armour, fire control systems and machinery. Most importantly, aircraft carriers of the Illustrious class and a series of large cruiser classes were ordered and expedited. Churchill was greatly involved in the Parliamentary debates about increased budgets for the Royal Navy and was keen to express his views on naval strategy in a future conflict. In March 1939, Churchill wrote a memorandum on sea power which he forwarded to many Cabinet ministers including

Chamberlain in order to further his ambition of being given a ministerial position. In this memorandum, Churchill declared that the threat from submarines
had been neutralised and that aircraft would not prevent modern warships
from exercising their sea power. Churchill also indicated that the most vital sea
battle would be that fought in the Mediterranean against the Italian Navy to
keep the sea lanes to the Suez Canal open and that the Japanese were unlikely
to attack the fortress of Singapore.[11]

Churchill also expressed his views on modern warfare in published articles
he wrote for the *News of the World* in April 1938 and *Colliers* magazine in January
1939. In the former article, Churchill derided the future of tanks: 'The tank has
no doubt a great part to play; but I, personally, doubt very much whether it will
ever see again the palmy days of 1918.'[12] Churchill believed that in the technological battle between tanks and anti-tank guns, advances in the firepower of
anti-tank guns and rifles would overcome the armoured skins of the tanks.[13]

In *Colliers* magazine, Churchill declared that following recent improvements
in anti-aircraft armament:

> Even a single well-armed vessel will hold its own against aircraft; still more
> a squadron or a fleet of modern warships, whether at sea or in harbour, will
> be able to endure aerial attack.[14]

In the same article, entitled 'Let the Tyrant Criminals Bomb' in reference to
Hitler and Mussolini, Churchill wrote that attempts to terrorise civilian populations by mass bombing would only encourage the spirit of resistance and
'fury' among the people.

The British Army was considerably neglected compared with the other two
services and has been aptly described as the 'Cinderella' service. In 1933, the
Army consisted of five regular and twelve Territorial divisions and remained at
this level until one division was expanded into two armoured divisions and an
extra Territorial division created in 1938. The provision of modern anti-aircraft
guns for home defence was a major drain on the Army budgets and only modest
upgrade programmes were implemented. On 19 April 1939, a thirty-two Army
division programme was approved and at the Land Force Committee meeting
on 7 September, after the declarations of war, Churchill argued successfully
for an Army of at least fifty-five divisions. This was duly incorporated into a
Land Forces Committee report approved by the Cabinet on 9 September.[15]
This target was to be met within two years (twenty divisions in the first twelve
months) with the dominions' assistance in supplying the necessary formations.

For the inhabitants of Britain, preparations for what now seemed like an inevitable war after the failure of the Munich talks to save Czechoslovakia began in earnest with the issuing of gas masks to every person in early 1939. Families queued up at local town halls to receive the appropriate adult, toddler or baby masks. Images at the cinema of the destruction wrought by the German Luftwaffe in the Spanish Civil War instilled a fear of German bombing into many people – a fear also cultivated by a government publicity campaign. From the occupation of Czechoslovakia and the outbreak of war, nearly 1.5 million Anderson air raid shelters were issued to households with a garden. These were at no charge if the household income was less than £5 a week; otherwise there was a charge of £7. The Anderson shelters were made of corrugated iron and were installed in a rectangular hole 4ft deep dug in the garden. People equipped them with what comforts they could in the form of temporary beds and lamps but in winter they were particularly cold and damp. Neighbours sometimes competed with each other to disguise the appearance of the shelters by covering them with banks of earth for extra protection and planting flowers or vegetables on top of them or nearby.

Germany had a false start in its invasion of Poland when on 25 August German troops were mobilised but Italy suddenly declared itself unready for war without further massive German supplies. After hasty German and Italian discussions, at 4.45 a.m. on 1 September 1939, German troops entered Poland after fabricating a border incident and two days later Britain and France declared war on Germany.

The German refusal to heed the British and French ultimatums regarding Poland came as no surprise to Churchill, whose stance and warnings of German aggression had been completely vindicated. Chamberlain, having been proven utterly wrong about German intentions and given the pro-Churchill sentiments in some quarters of the press, had no option but to offer Churchill an unspecified position in the War Cabinet on the day Germany entered Poland. On 3 September after the British declaration of war, Chamberlain met briefly with Churchill again. Afterwards, Churchill got into the back of the car where his wife, Clementine, was anxiously waiting.

'It's the Admiralty,' he said, adding with a pleased chuckle, 'That's a lot better than I thought.'[16]

2

THE PHONEY WAR AND NORWEGIAN OVERTURE

The day after Germany invaded Poland, the evacuation of children and mothers with babies began from the all the major cities in England. Some families were reluctant to send their children away in the unfortunately named Operation Pied Piper, and by the end of the month only half the designated children had been evacuated. A total of 827,000 children between the ages of 5 and 14 and 524,000 mothers and children under school age were eventually billeted out with foster parents or in lodgings, the government paying 10s 6d to each billetor for the first child and a further 8s 6d for subsequent children.[1] A total of nearly 1.4 million people were evacuated and relocated in the first week of the war.[2]

The billeting experience was often a cultural shock for both parties; billetors were frequently horrified by the lack of hygiene of the children staying with them, who were often treated as unpaid servants. The more fortunate children got to enjoy a higher standard of living than they had in the cities but most naturally missed their family and friends:

We were marched in a crocodile with our gas masks slung round our necks and a label on our coats giving our names and the name of our school to the nearest railway station and we travelled to Paddington station in London to start our journey. Nobody had any idea where we were going and we ate our sandwiches packed by our mothers that morning, and tried to keep quiet and well behaved. Our teachers went from carriage to carriage talking to us and answering questions.

It was about 8pm at night when we arrived at Locking Rd station in Weston-Super-Mare and were again marched to a local school where we sat around in a circle and people came in who had volunteered to take in an evacuee, or two. We were tired, hungry and rather lost and I remember I was one of the last of the children to be picked out and taken away. The better looking and the better clothed certainly went first.[3]

Following the declaration of war in September, the five regular divisions and five additional territorial divisions were transported to France as the British Expeditionary Force (BEF), which lacked a lot of equipment including anti-aircraft guns. The Royal Ordnance factories were equipped to produce munitions on a large scale when producing at maximum capacity but were initially unable to meet the necessary production targets of munitions and small arms even with the assistance of the newly created 'shadow' agency factories.

After his appointment as First Lord of the Admiralty at the meeting with Chamberlain on 3 September, Churchill attended his first War Cabinet at 5 p.m. and then went to the Admiralty where he occupied the very same office he had used in the First World War; the Admiralty had signalled to every ship in the fleet, 'Winston is back.' Churchill immediately threw himself into his duties, galvanising his immediate reports and all the staff at the Admiralty. While the first nine months of the Second World War has been described as the Phoney War, it was certainly not for the Royal Navy, which found itself battling U-boats and German warships from the first day of hostilities. On 3 September, the steamship *Athenia* was sunk by a U-boat with the loss of 112 lives. The merchant ships that normally plied the trade routes carrying Britain's essential food and raw materials from the Empire and America had to be protected by organising them into more easily defended convoys. The convoy system was a valuable lesson learnt from the First World War and was a priority for Churchill as twenty-eight merchant ships had already been sunk in the first two weeks of the war.[4] Churchill ordered as much intelligence as possible on the dispositions of the German warships and submarines to be gathered and plotted on Admiralty charts fixed to the walls. The Royal Navy, for its part, also attacked or tried to capture German merchant ships wherever it could find them in international waters. Churchill also instigated comprehensive reviews of the Navy's shipbuilding programme, armaments and new technologies, including anti-submarine detection equipment. At that time British warships had not yet been equipped with radar. President Roosevelt also wrote directly to Churchill in October and invited Churchill to stay in touch in what was their first contact of the war. This letter may well have been prompted by a reissue that month of Churchill's book *Great Contemporaries*, which contained a largely favourable essay on Roosevelt. This contact with Roosevelt was exactly what Churchill had hoped for when he sent the first volume of his Marlborough biography to Roosevelt in 1933.

Churchill's position in the War Cabinet gave him access to reports and a voice in the discussions on the prosecution of the whole war, not just naval matters. Following debate about sending British warships into the Baltic Sea and engaging or blockading the German fleet, the importance of Swedish iron ore to German industry and the fabrication of weapons became apparent. Churchill at once seized on the possibility of interrupting or halting altogether the shipment of these raw materials as a way of waging economic warfare on Germany. At the War Cabinet of 19 September, Churchill described how vital the iron ore was to Germany and how German cargo ships remained within the 3-mile territorial waters limit of neutral Norway, from where the Swedish iron ore was shipped in winter. The Royal Navy had put in place a blockade around the Norwegian coast which the German ships were able to evade by steaming within the Norwegian territorial limits. Churchill reminded the War Cabinet that these territorial waters had been mined by the Royal Navy previously in the First World War to stop a similar traffic and there was an urgent need to do this again, despite being in breach of international conventions and Norway's neutrality. The War Cabinet at this time merely took note of Churchill's proposal as there were other more pressing matters such as the parlous state of Britain's air defence systems and the situation in Poland.[5] From the start of this new world war, Churchill continuously urged for aggressive action in exactly the same way he had done at the start of the First World War against, for example, Turkey, which had led to the disastrous Dardanelles campaign.

On 4 October, the German campaign in Poland having been successfully concluded, Hitler gave a speech in the Reichstag suggesting that peace negotiations could now take place. However, no concessions were offered while Poland was declared a 'part of Germany' and as such was no longer an item for negotiation. The British reply was given by Chamberlain on 12 October in a speech to Parliament which listed Hitler's broken promises and territorial gains but did not completely close the door on future talks:

> The issue is, therefore, plain. Either the German government must give
> convincing proof of the sincerity of their desire for peace by definite acts

and by the provision of effective guarantees of their intention to fulfil their undertakings, or we must persevere in our duty to the end. It is for Germany to make her choice.[6]

Chamberlain spoke of Britain as not embarking on the war for vindictive purposes but as being the defender of the freedom of nations around the world. For Hitler, this response to his vague overtures was enough to for him to resolve that a negotiated peace in Europe was not possible and that Germany should attack France at the earliest opportunity. While Hitler's territorial ambitions lay to the east and Russia, he could not countenance a campaign against Russia while there was a hostile nation bordering Germany.

An English housewife summed up this international diplomacy in her diary:

October 13th 1939
According to Berlin, Mr Chamberlain has insulted Hitler, who says 'now that Britain so obviously wishes to wage war she shall feel the power of Germany's air, naval and military strength'. It's all so hateful as no doubt Hitler can justify (and does) his position as absolutely as Mr Chamberlain can justify his.[7]

An outline plan of attack on France had been prepared by Germany before Hitler's Reichstag speech but now detailed planning began, again much to the reluctance of the chiefs of the three armed forces. The German rearmament programme then in progress had factored in a major conflict from 1942 onwards and the forces, in particular the German Kriegsmarine, were unprepared. The dates of the attack were repeatedly postponed during November and December due to the Army not being ready after its campaign in Poland and because of bad weather. A build-up of German troops began along the French, Belgian and Dutch borders while the ten divisions of the British Expeditionary Force that had landed in France from 10 September moved up alongside the three French Army groups on opposite sides of the borders. On 10 January 1940, a German plane carrying a staff officer with documents regarding the attack (Case Gelb – Yellow) was forced to crash land in Belgium and the Germans assumed their plans had been exposed. The British War Cabinet was, however, dismissive of this apparent intelligence windfall, regarding it as 'suspicious'.[8] Hitler ordered revisions to Case Gelb along with a deception campaign with the object of making the Allies think the original plan was still being followed.

Churchill took time out from his work at the Admiralty to host dinner parties for various political allies, and this included Chamberlain and his wife on 13 October. Their meal was interrupted three times by a messenger bringing the news of the sinking of a U-boat each time. An astute Mrs Chamberlain commented that if the sinkings went on at the same rate, the war would be soon won. Was it not all invented, she asked? By Churchill's standards, it was not a late night and he was evidently on his best behaviour. This type of staged incident would be repeated by Churchill later in the war. He later admitted that the reports of the U-boats could not be confirmed and any prestige he may or may not have earnt that evening was quickly dispelled the next morning when news broke of the sinking of the old battleship HMS *Royal Oak* at anchor in Scapa Flow when the naval base's anti-submarine defences were boldly penetrated by a U-boat.[9]

On 5 October 1939, Stalin invited the government of Finland to talks in Moscow. The Russians were particularly concerned about the vulnerability of the city of Leningrad given its close proximity to Finland and made various demands, including the abandonment of the Mannerheim Line fortifications that Finland had constructed opposite Leningrad and the ceding of the peninsula controlling the approaches to the northern Finnish port of Petsamo, which was uncomfortably close to the Russian port of Murmansk on the other side of the peninsula. For neutral Finland, these demands were completely unacceptable and the negotiations unsurprisingly collapsed. On 30 November 1939, Russian troops invaded Finland. Despite being massively outnumbered, the small Finnish Army was well equipped, experienced at fighting in winter conditions and initially resisted the Russian attacks.

Churchill's standing at the Admiralty and in public opinion received a considerable boost with the sinking of the German raider, *Graf Spee*. On 13 December 1939, the pocket battleship was spotted and engaged by three British cruisers off the coast of South America. Despite being outgunned, the three cruisers bravely pressed home their attacks and forced the *Graf Spee* to take refuge in the Uruguayan port of Montevideo. Four days later, after considerable diplomatic intrigue, the *Graf Spee* was scuttled, its captain believing that a superior British fleet was waiting outside the port. Several South American countries protested to the United States that this naval action had violated the 300-mile safety belt around the United States and South America, which had been declared by Roosevelt at the pan-American conference in October 1939.

The question of stopping the iron ore shipments was never far from Churchill's mind and in the War Cabinet meetings of 30 November and

10 December he raised it again without any success. Churchill also asked Ambassador Joseph Kennedy to privately sound out Roosevelt's attitude to the mining of Norway and Churchill duly reported his concurrence to the War Cabinet on 11 December; Roosevelt was just as much in favour of aggressive action as Churchill. That same day, Churchill stated in a note to the War Cabinet that it was in Britain's interest if Norway and Sweden were forced into a war with Germany: 'We have more to gain than lose by a German attack upon Norway or Sweden.'[10]

The possibility was also raised in Churchill's note that the despatch of British troops to Norway and Sweden would have the additional benefit of being able to control the iron ore trade. Churchill attempted to force a decision for immediate action at the War Cabinet of 22 December but he was overruled by Cabinet concerns about Sweden being alienated by any attempt to land British troops at Narvik. Churchill was not concerned by this, reasoning that if Germany invaded Scandinavia as a result of British landings, then Sweden and Norway would then have to fight and would naturally look to Britain and France for aid. On 31 December, the Chiefs of Staff recommended an operation proceed to occupy Narvik to stop the export of iron ore to Germany as long as the approval of Sweden was forthcoming; it was noted that this operation would be the first British offensive of the war and 'might well prove decisive' as there was 'no prospect of an equal chance being afforded us elsewhere'.[11] However, Sweden was determined to remain neutral and not do anything to antagonise Germany, which at that time was even replacing the armaments that Sweden had sent to the Finns.

Many British civilians sympathised with the plight of Finland:

January 1 1940
Can 1940 bring us the blessing of just a European peace? The year starts with Finland battling against Russia in a most extraordinary manner. After a whole month the Russians have scarcely gained anything except the disgust of the world.[12]

Debate within the Cabinet continued for over a week, stoked by regular papers from the Chiefs of Staff. At the War Cabinet of 12 January 1940 it was decided that no action would be taken, to Churchill's apparently visible anger. This frustration was further evident in his radio broadcast to the nation on 20 January, when Churchill was critical of the neutral European countries that expected to remain free while not contributing to the war and leaving

Britain and France to fight for them. Lord Halifax did not appreciate having to weather the subsequent negative diplomatic reactions from Denmark, Holland, Switzerland and Norway and instructed Churchill not to make any more foreign policy speeches without first referring the speech to him.[13] Another Scandinavian paper was written by the Chiefs of Staff with much subsequent discussion and the French General Gamelin then advised the Secretary of State that France wished to mount an expedition to Scandinavia to support Finland, causing several more days to be lost in devising plans for such an operation.

Finally, at the Supreme War Council of 5 February, it was decided to send troops to aid Finland via Norway regardless of the consequences, provided Finland sent an appeal for help. This was confirmed at the War Cabinet meeting of 7 February and British troops earmarked for the operation began to assemble at various ports. This operation would not only provide military support to Finland but would also gain control of the iron ore mines, thus killing two birds with one stone, as Chamberlain put it to Édouard Daladier, the French Prime Minister.

Churchill was then handed another public relations coup. Following the *Graf Spee* episode, the pocket battleship's supply ship, the *Altmark*, which was believed to be carrying British prisoners (crews of merchant ships sunk by the *Graf Spee*), was spotted in Norwegian territorial waters on 16 February by a British destroyer. At the request of the British, the *Altmark* was challenged and searched three times by officers from its escort of Norwegian motor torpedo boats. The British destroyer HMS *Cossack* then tried to intercept the *Altmark*, which was forced to take refuge in a fjord, protected by the torpedo boats, which trained their torpedo tubes on the destroyer. Churchill, with Halifax's approval, personally ordered crew from HMS *Cossack* to board the *Altmark* and to return any fire from the Norwegians. The boarding action next day was successful and 299 seamen were liberated. Churchill's bold action was lauded across the country and by the King himself in a congratulatory message.

The plans for landing British and French troops in Norway continued to be developed but not until 17 February did the Chiefs of Staff offer 20 March as the earliest date for the operation, provided the green light was given by the War Cabinet no later than 11 March. Norway and Sweden were, however, still not supportive of any direct action to assist Finland or of regular foreign troops traversing their territories to fight in Finland against Russia.

Meanwhile, throughout these weeks of deliberations, the Finns had been battling the Russians and despite inflicting heavy casualties were slowly being pushed back from the Mannerheim Line by sheer weight of numbers. Finland made belated demands to the Allies for 50,000 men and 100 bombers, which were impossible to provide from the relatively weak resources then available. As the military situation in Finland worsened, peace negotiations began on 12 February, although fighting continued around Vyborg. On 4 March, the Chief of Staffs concluded that any Scandinavian operation to help Finland was by that time pointless because of the peace negotiations already in progress. A week later, the Chiefs of Staff changed their position again and decided that troops should be landed in Norway to stop the shipments of iron ore after all. This was approved by the War Cabinet on 12 March and thus, more than two months after such an operation was first discussed seriously, the debate came full circle and the first British offensive of the war would be to land troops in neutral Norway. This was more than six months after Churchill had first suggested the operation in September 1939. Next day, Finland signed a truce with Russia and was forced to cede more territory to Russia than had been originally demanded by Moscow.

Churchill meanwhile, ever keen to mount offensive action, came up with another scheme to drop mines in the River Rhine to disrupt river traffic and destroy bridges, but the French were also wary of possible German reprisals and did not immediately approve the plan.

Chamberlain, in view of the end of the Finnish–Russian Winter War, on 14 March then suspended plans for a landing altogether. In so doing, a possible war with Russia was avoided as British and French prevarication for two months before finally reaching a decision to take action in Scandinavia was overtaken by the ceasefire. Chamberlain had ordered a 'standstill' to the operation to consider the direct access Russia now had across Finland to Norway and Sweden. Once again, plans were placed on hold and the troops already assembled at various ports began to disperse. Finland expressed its disappointment that the proposed Allied support would have arrived too late and was inadequate anyway, while public opinion was of the view that Finland's predicament could have been prevented if the Allies had acted more quickly and thoroughly.[14] As a consequence of the Allied failure to act, the French government under Daladier collapsed and a new Prime Minister, Paul Reynaud, was appointed.

A report from Sweden on 26 March that Germany was concentrating troops for a possible invasion of Norway again stirred the Allies into action. At the British-French Supreme War Council meeting of 28 March, the mining of Norwegian territorial waters on 5 April was finally agreed, with mines to be dropped into the River Rhine the day after. Then, to Churchill's astonishment, the new French government decided that the mining of the Rhine should be postponed for three months. Churchill flew to Paris to take up the matter directly with Reynaud and Daladier (now the Minister of Defence) but returned to London convinced by Daladier's arguments that French factories were indeed vulnerable to German reprisals for the next three months until French air defences could be built up.

Following the Supreme War Council meeting, the War Cabinet decided a day later that plans contingent on possible German reactions to the mine laying should be devised, the Chiefs of Staff issuing orders for these plans on 31 March.[15] As the plans were for a proposed response to German actions, they were dependent on receiving adequate warning of German intentions. The Chiefs of Staff believed on 4 April that they had such a warning system in place to enable a series of pre-emptive conditional landings to be made in Norway under what was then known as Plan R4.[16]

A special mine-laying naval force to lay two minefields sailed from England on 5 April, only for reports two days later of German naval forces converging on Norway to force the cancellation of the planned southern minefield; the northern minefield was laid as planned. By noon, it became clear that German naval forces were heading for Narvik. The Norwegian government was not informed until 8 April of the British minelaying action.

Using paratroops and assault troops carried by warships, the simultaneous occupation of Narvik, Trondheim, Oslo and Bergen and Stavanger was executed by six German divisions on 9 April 1940, achieving almost total surprise. After months of procrastination by the Allies, the Germans had finally beaten them to occupying Norway.

Hitler had not planned an invasion of Norway, although Admiral Raeder had been keen to see Norway occupied to construct submarine bases and to prevent the British from threatening the Baltic Sea, where Germany's main naval bases were located. Although preliminary plans to occupy Norway were first drawn up in response to meetings between Hitler and the Norwegian National Union Party leader Quisling in December 1939, the decision to invade was only taken immediately following the *Altmark* incident, from which Hitler divined that Britain was ready to infringe Norwegian neutrality whenever it suited.[17] From this, Hitler reasoned that the threat to German ore supplies over winter would be unreasonable. Given the intense diplomatic activity between Britain, Norway, Finland and Sweden, it is also possible that the Germans got wind of Allied intentions to land troops in Norway from a Nazi sympathiser. Churchill's speeches and radio broadcasts about the misuse of Norwegian territorial waters that would not be tolerated forever also strongly hinted at possible future Allied actions. The public expressions of Allied support for Finland that could only be realised by land forces moving through Norway and Sweden also served to signal potential Allied plans to both the Germans and the Russians. The executive order for the invasion was signed on 1 March by Hitler with the first proposed date of the invasion being 20 March; because of ice in the Baltic the operation had to be postponed to 9 April.

Thus the German invasion of Norway was triggered directly by Churchill's pursuit of the *Altmark* and indirectly by the poorly concealed intentions of the Allies. In his history of the Second World War, Churchill claims that the decision was taken in December 1939 after the talks between Hitler and Quisling.

Churchill's workload was then increased significantly when he was appointed chairman of the Military Co-ordination Committee from 4 April in a War Cabinet reshuffle. Following the news of the German landings in Norway, the War Cabinet was thrown into a state of confusion. There were reports of many German warships on the move off the Norwegian coast but little information from Norway itself. In view of the numbers of German ships on the move, the British decided to wait until the naval situation was resolved before sending any troopships. Churchill immediately despatched as many ships as he could to the North Atlantic fearing a German naval breakout, including two cruisers at Rosyth with the troops of the 146th Brigade designated for operations in Norway already aboard. These troops were hurriedly offloaded but their equipment was not. When the brigade was subsequently re-embarked on different ships and then diverted to Namsos by Churchill (who had prior approval from the committee for this if the situation warranted it) it had no equipment as this had gone to Narvik.

Plans for landings that had been in existence for several weeks then had to be changed as new information was received as to which parts of Norway the Germans had occupied. The British and French had assumed their forces would be making unopposed landings in friendly Norwegian ports before any German invasion and accordingly ordinary merchant ships had been allocated to transport the force. The end result of these deliberations was a further delay of three days before the first troops left England.

Two infantry brigades, the 24th Guards and the 146th Brigade (from the 49th Division of territorial troops), were sent to Narvik on 12 April. Believing Narvik was unoccupied, the Narvik force was split by Churchill on 13 April with the 146th Brigade to go south to land at Namsos. The original plans to land troops at Stavanger and Bergen in the south of Norway were abandoned as they were already in German hands and alternative landings were planned at Namsos and Andalsnes, north and south of Trondheim. These diversionary landings were surprisingly successful and faced little opposition. The 146th Brigade got ashore at Namsos on 16 April (without its equipment) and two battalions of the 148th Brigade plus 600 marines at Andalsnes two days later. Narvik was subsequently found to be occupied by the Germans, and as the weather deteriorated a base for operations was made at Harsted, on an island offshore from Narvik. Two companies of Scots Guards were landed on the mainland to the north of Narvik near Sjovegan and a battalion of Irish Guards was landed on the opposite side of the fjord to Narvik in order to set up artillery positions to bombard Narvik. Further landings to capture Trondheim directly by the 15th Infantry Brigade (Hammer Force) were cancelled by the Chiefs of Staff on 19 April because of the risk to Royal Navy ships from the dominant Luftwaffe and the belief that Trondheim could be taken by the troops already landed.[18] While the Navy and Army commanders at Narvik debated what to do and awaited reinforcements, the forces at Namsos and Andalsnes were directed to capture Trondheim in a pincer movement from the north and south. Having originally intended to occupy unopposed ports in southern Norway, these weak forces were given the new objectives of capturing German-occupied Trondheim as well as stopping the German northward advance to Narvik. Norwegian troops unsuccessfully battled German troops advancing from Oslo and the 148th Brigade troops at Lillehammer were also unable to halt them. With no air cover and little artillery, the poorly trained and equipped Territorial troops were pushed back towards Andalsnes.

Churchill did not help matters by setting up personal radio links to the naval Narvik force commander, Lord Cork, who was also having difficulties working with the Army force commander, General Macksey, in the traditional joint Army–Navy model of command. While Lord Cork was keen to begin operations to capture Narvik as soon as possible, Macksey felt that his orders were to make landings only if they were unopposed.[19] Following the diversion of the 146th Brigade to Namsos, Macksey requested reinforcements for the Narvik operation, only to be told to 'press on' by the Chiefs of Staff following a note critical of Macksey from Churchill.[20] After receiving details of the plan made by Lord Cork and Macksey for assaulting Narvik, Churchill was asked in the Military Co-ordination Committee meeting of 19 April to produce the relevant telegram so that it could be examined by the Admiralty and the War Office.[21] Churchill took the lead on briefing the War Cabinet at most meetings as he was receiving copies of all signals from the Allied forces in Norway through the Admiralty and was very much in control of the Allied forces in Narvik through Lord Cork. The War Office went as far as to complain about the poor communications, reminding Churchill and the Air Ministry on 12 April that copies of all signals had to be forwarded to the War Office for the preparation of intelligence bulletins for the use of the Chiefs of Staff and the Military Co-ordination Committee.[22]

As a consequence of the disharmony between the Narvik force commanders, Lord Cork was put in overall command on 20 April by the War Office at Churchill's specific request. Churchill claimed in the War Cabinet of 21 April that:

> We had taken a risk with our eyes open, knowing that it was a very hazardous operation to throw lightly equipped forces ashore without proper maintenance facilities. This, however, had been the only way possible of bolstering up the Norwegians, and as a result of what we had done the Norwegians were still holding out.[23]

Macksey further incurred Churchill's ire when he refused to use the Royal Navy ships to bombard the town of Narvik because of concerns about the civilian casualties. Churchill signalled Lord Cork on 22 April, 'If this officer appears to be spreading a bad spirit through the higher ranks of the land force, do not hesitate to relieve him or place him under arrest.'

On 25 April, the War Cabinet approved Churchill's suggestion of mining neutral Sweden's territorial waters between Sweden and Denmark in a further attempt to hinder German iron ore shipments.

The piecemeal arrival of the 15th Brigade also failed to halt the Germans, who had complete air superiority after a squadron of Gladiator fighters deployed at a newly built temporary base at Lake Lesjaskog was destroyed on the ground the day after its arrival. There was no fuel at the base for the Gladiators to refuel and get airborne. Intermittent air cover for the British forces in Norway could only be provided by aircraft operating from the aircraft carriers HMS *Ark Royal* and *Glorious*.

The Military Co-ordination Committee on 26 April then did an about-turn and decided that even if Trondheim was captured, it would need strong air defences and the Royal Navy to maintain supplies in the face of German aerial dominance. Accordingly, plans to capture Trondheim were abandoned and preparations were authorised for the evacuation of the central Norway forces. The press would be briefed that the landings in central Norway were only a diversion for the real objective, which had been Narvik all along.[24]

The Andalsnes force, faced with its destruction or capture, was evacuated on the night of 30 April; the Namsos force, which had made no progress in its attempts to capture Trondheim even when reinforced by three battalions of French ski troops, was forced to do the same two days later. These two evacuations left no Allied troops to block the German advance northwards to Narvik to relieve their own troops in the town.

Narvik now became the focus of Allied plans as its capture had become of paramount political and military importance. Churchill advised the War Cabinet on 6 May of the repercussions of a defeat at Narvik:

> It would show that our will to win and our fighting capacity were less than those of the enemy. The difficulties of the Germans in the Narvik operations were no less than our own, and if we accepted defeat without a bitter struggle, it would have a devastating effect on world opinion.[25]

General Claude Auchinleck was appointed as Commander-in-Chief of the Norwegian Expedition Force on 21 April and arrived in Narvik on 13 May to take overall command of the Allied forces. Auchinleck did not immediately meet with General Macksey, who was apparently ill. Auchinleck sent an appreciation of the situation on 16 May offering hope for a successful Allied attack on Narvik, but by 21 May the Chiefs of Staff had already raised the likelihood of a potential evacuation after the capture of Narvik because of the turn of events in France.[26] Auchinleck's reply held little prospect for success, indicating that it would be difficult to successfully carry out his orders without further reinforcements of anti-aircraft guns and aircraft.[27]

The Narvik forces were eventually reinforced by a French brigade of ski troops, a Foreign Legion brigade, two Norwegian Army brigades and a brigade of Polish troops. Britain had no more troops available and any further reinforcements would have had to come from units in France.

However, even as limited landings were made to the south to block the German advance of reinforcements to Narvik and the numbers of available British aircraft were built up, Auchinleck was ordered on 24 May to evacuate the Narvik forces. Auchinleck decided to launch the attack on Narvik anyway to ensure the destruction of the iron ore facilities and provide cover for the evacuation, which was not announced to the troops. The attack went ahead on 27 May and Narvik was finally captured within twenty-four hours.

Six days later, the evacuation of the troops involved began, the last of which were embarked on 8 June. The French troops were evacuated as well as those Norwegians that wanted to go to England.

Of the Allied force, British casualties totalled 1,869 killed, wounded or missing with a further 2,500 casualties lost at sea in naval battles. The French lost 530 men killed, wounded or missing.[28] The Norwegians had about 1,700 casualties, including 860 men killed plus 400 civilians. German casualties were similar.[29]

The whole operation can only be described as a fiasco. The initial plan was amateurish and entirely reactive in nature, handing the initiative to the Germans on the assumption that Anglo-French forces would have adequate advance warning of German moves and be landed before the arrival of the Germans. Insufficient numbers of British troops were landed, with the Allies sending brigades to fight the same number of German divisions. No proper air cover was planned or provided and the Luftwaffe was able to capitalise on its superiority when the weather permitted. Many of the British troops were poorly trained Territorials, all were poorly equipped for winter warfare and there was little in the way of artillery, anti-aircraft guns or armour to support them. Supply bases for each of the landings had to be built from scratch following the failure to capture the port of Trondheim and the distribution of supplies to units was hampered by a lack of suitable small craft and by German aircraft attacks. Churchill behaved like a Commander-in-Chief trying to co-ordinate the campaign rather than leaving it to the commanders on the ground, an example being his decision regarding the diversion of the 146th Brigade from Narvik to Namsos while its equipment went to Narvik, which only caused complete confusion. The Military Co-ordination Committee also made other poor decisions and was then forced to change them, such as the decision not to attack Trondheim after troops had already been landed, which only necessitated their subsequent evacuation.

While the Allied ground forces had been comprehensively defeated, substantial damage was inflicted on the German Navy. Their losses included ten destroyers lost or damaged plus two heavy cruisers and two light cruisers sunk, which represented a substantial portion of the entire Kriegsmarine. Two major ships, the *Scharnhorst* and *Gneisenau*, were damaged for the loss of the aircraft carrier HMS *Glorious*, which had been caught unescorted and was subsequently sunk by the *Scharnhorst*.

The port of Narvik was, however, badly damaged in the fighting. The ore-crushing plant was totally destroyed along with the loading facilities and wooden quays, which would take an estimated twelve months to rebuild; the Allies had succeeded in their objective of stopping the iron ore exports, albeit temporarily.[30] As it was nearly summer, German shipments would continue by means of the usual warm weather route through the Gulf of Bothnia while the Narvik facilities were repaired.

One consequence of the invasion was that Britain lost Sweden as a source of iron ore. Germany took 70 per cent of Swedish iron ore and Britain took 13 per cent, which meant that the 700,000 tons of ore imported into Britain in 1939 now had to be found elsewhere. In fact, 10 per cent of all Britain's imports came from Scandinavia – iron ore, butter, fish, bacon and eggs – and these were soon in short supply. A trade agreement struck between Britain and Sweden had attempted to fix exports of iron ore to Germany and Britain at 1938 levels but this was rendered redundant by the invasion.

A further consequence of the German invasion of Norway was the simultaneous occupation of Denmark. Again, this was not something planned by Hitler, but in order to mount air operations over Norway the Luftwaffe required the strategic airfield at Aalborg in northern Jutland. Denmark itself would also become, later in the war, the northernmost component of Germany's air defence system. In response, British troops occupied bases in the Faroe Islands and Iceland.

Churchill's chairmanship of the Military Co-ordination Committee during the Norwegian crisis in April proved to be so chaotic after only a week that Chamberlain was forced to resume the chair for three days from 16 April and occasionally later on, much to the relief of all, including Churchill himself who later sent a note to Chamberlain thanking him for stepping in. The note was also critical of the structure of the committee as having too many voices with no overall responsibility for the creation and direction of military policy, which was the sole preserve of the Prime Minister. The meetings had been characterised by clashes of personality between Churchill and the Chiefs of Staff and a 'first class political row' was brewing over the abortive plans to attack Trondheim.[31] The War Cabinet had also complained to Chamberlain about not being kept informed and a lack of papers to consider on proposed operations.

Churchill himself would later describe the Norwegian campaign as 'ramshackle', but this was entirely due to its planning in which Churchill was heavily involved and the comment does not reflect well on the Allied soldiers and airmen who died in the campaign. Ambassador Kennedy recognised the part Churchill had played in the fiasco, in a telegram to Roosevelt: 'Mr Churchill's sun has been caused to set very rapidly by the situation in Norway, which some people are already characterising as the second Gallipoli.'[32]

As the Phoney War dragged on, more and more evacuees began to return to their homes. The main reason for this was that the feared German heavy air attacks had not developed, but another contributing factor was the decision by the government on 4 October 1939 to recover 6s of the weekly cost of evacuation billeting from all parents through the local councils.[33] With the average weekly wage being only about £5, this was an expense that not many could afford. After only four months of war, 88 per cent of mothers, 86 per cent of pre-school children and nearly half the school children had returned home.[34]

Most people were convinced, however, that Britain was correct in standing up to Germany, as one English woman wrote to her American penfriend:

> I think France and Britain are doing the right thing in trying to wipe out Nazism and all its horrors, don't you? I wish your country would help us but I suppose it is wiser to keep out of the war.
>
> We are fully prepared to meet Hitler and I am firmly convinced God is on our side as we are fighting a people who have been made to forsake him.[35]

During the Phoney War, RAF bomber planes flew missions over Germany and dropped propaganda leaflets rather than bombs:

> September 28th 1940
> Everyone is talking about the income tax but taking it very calmly, 7/6d in the pound! The Daily Telegraph reported that the pilot of one of our 'leaflet planes' reported back at headquarters two hours before he was due. His astonished Commanding Officer asked for an explanation. 'Well Sir,' the young officer replied, 'I flew over enemy territory as instructed and tipped out the parcels over the side.'
>
> 'Do you mean you threw them out still wrapped in their bundles?' said the CO in an anxious voice.
>
> 'Yes, Sir.'
> 'Good God, man, you might have killed somebody!'[36]

Daily life in Britain was also becoming more difficult. On 28 October 1939, the Cabinet proposed that meat, sugar, butter and bacon be rationed.[37] Rationing was then introduced once a system of ration books was in place from 11 November with initially just bacon and butter affected. With the reduction in merchant shipping and its wholesale conversion to carrying war material, the amount of fresh fruit reaching England dropped sharply. Oranges and bananas became a rarity, as did chocolate. Cigarettes and coking coal were also rationed:

> January 17th 1941
> Mother heard that her money which used to bring in 5% then 3½% is now 2%! Everyone is grumbling about their drop in income and no wonder and for what? Other direct effects of war are the rationing of food and petrol, increase in the cost of living (it's gone up 12½% at least), unemployment amongst certain trades, especially among building and flower growing concerns in Worthing.[38]

Air raid precautions and the blackout were a new way of life that had to be got used to. Streetlights were turned off and getting about after dark could be hazardous for pedestrians and motor traffic alike. In the last four months of 1939, 4,133 people were killed on the roads compared with 2,497 people in the same period in 1938. In December alone there were 1,155 fatalities and the problem became so serious that limited dim street lighting was permitted in February 1940, when the speed limit for motor vehicles was also reduced to 20mph.[39]

Walls of sandbags had transformed the entrances to public buildings in the cities, while some shop owners boarded up their windows to leave only a small viewing window for shoppers in order to lessen potential injuries from flying glass.

Plans for limited conscription applying to single men aged between 20 and 22 were given Parliamentary approval in the Military Training Act in May 1939. This required men to undertake six months' military training, and some 240,000 registered for service. It became difficult for people to plan their lives as the government legislated more and more for the war. Attendances at universities dropped and young people did not know whether to marry or not as they could be asked to relocate for essential war work or required to join the armed forces.

Another act of Parliament was necessary to increase the numbers of personnel in the armed forces. The National Service (Armed Forces) Act passed on 3 September 1939 made all able men between the ages of 18 and 41 liable for conscription; as part of the legislation it was decided that single men would be called up before married men. Men aged 20 to 23 were required to register on

21 October 1939 – the start of a long and drawn-out process of registration by age group which saw 40-year-olds only registering in June 1941. By the end of 1939, more than 1.5 million men had been conscripted to join the British armed forces. Of those, just over 1.1 million went to the British Army and the rest were split between the Royal Navy and the RAF. From January 1940, all men between the ages of 19 and 27 were to be progressively conscripted.

Before the Norwegian operation had concluded but after the first two evacuations of troops, Chamberlain faced a debate in the House of Commons on 7 May on the conduct of the war. With the troops still in Norway in a precarious position, the mood in the House was one of rebellion against Chamberlain after his failed promotion of peace at Munich and his ineffective leadership in the war so far. Churchill managed to avoid any censureship or responsibility for the Norwegian fiasco and spoke in support of Chamberlain, making no reference to his own part in the affair. A different spin on the evacuations was also offered by Churchill, who said that the British Army had been saved from having to defend the Norwegian coastline. Chamberlain's government defeated the motion along party lines but the Prime Minister was mortally wounded; Chamberlain left the chamber with cries of 'Go! Go! Go!' ringing in his ears. Next day, 9 May, there was much coming and going at Downing Street as Chamberlain knew he could not continue as Prime Minister. There were only two candidates for the position, Churchill and Halifax. Churchill was by far the most popular choice both inside Parliament and outside, and, perhaps in view of this, Halifax was reluctant to press his case, citing the fact that as he was a member of the House of Lords he could not be an effective Prime Minister, as he did not come from the centre of power that was the House of Commons. The last Prime Minister to come from the House of Lords had been in 1902, and following the 1909 Parliament Act the balance of power had shifted further to the House of Commons as the House of Lords could no longer veto any proposed legislation. Chamberlain believed this was not an insurmountable problem but Halifax would have had to renounce his seat in the House of Lords and stand for election in the lower house, which would have taken time. This meant there was only one genuine candidate for the position of Prime Minister – Churchill. Later that afternoon, Chamberlain attempted to form a National Coalition government but the Labour Party was lukewarm and deferred the decision to its National Executive Committee, which happened to be gathering in Bournemouth that weekend for its annual conference. Churchill and his supporters that evening were very confident of forming a government the next day, and with good reason.

Churchill later wrote in his history of the conclusion to the Norwegian debacle, 'Failure at Trondheim, Stalemate at Narvik … Considering the prominent part I played in these events … it was a marvel that I survived and maintained my position in public esteem and parliamentary confidence.'[40]

While this reflection is poignant and honest, only the War Cabinet and a few generals knew the full extent of Churchill's involvement with Norway and the trigger for the invasion of Norway, the *Altmark* incident, would not become clear until after the war.

3

FALL OF FRANCE

At dawn on Friday 10 May 1940, the Phoney War came to a sudden end when German paratroops landed in Holland and Army units crossed the frontiers from Germany into Holland, Belgium and Luxembourg. The attack was not that unexpected as both sides had observed the build-up of each other's forces along their common borders for many months, during which there had been several false invasion alarms.

The situation was confused for most of the day with little accurate information coming from the Continent. In London that day, the Military Co-ordination Committee met twice and the War Cabinet three times, and only at its third meeting did the War Cabinet consider the unresolved political issue of government and who was to lead the nation. The Labour Party leadership had met that afternoon and at 5 p.m. telephoned to confirm its decision that the party would support a National Coalition, but refused to serve under any government led by Chamberlain. Halifax, still concerned about being a member of the House of Lords, refused to be nominated for the position of Prime Minister, which he believed would rapidly become untenable if Churchill was Minister of Defence at the same time. Chamberlain promptly went to Buckingham Palace to resign and offer King George VI his recommendation as to his successor. At 6 p.m., Churchill was summoned to see the King and duly became Britain's Prime Minister at the age of 65. Churchill was not the first choice of King George because of his previous support for Edward VIII and Mrs Simpson in 1936, and the Halifaxes were frequent visitors to Buckingham Palace. However, through their regular meetings during the war, the two men eventually came to respect one another.

On the return journey to the Admiralty, Churchill was apparently more pensive than usual and said to his bodyguard, Inspector Thompson, 'God alone knows how great it is. I hope it is not too late. I am very much afraid that it is. But we can only do our best, and give the rest of what we have ...'[1]

Churchill spent a hectic evening making Cabinet appointments and receiving congratulations from well-wishers. One of those to telephone was the American Ambassador, Kennedy, who joked about being partly responsible for helping Churchill become Prime Minister after Roosevelt (code name Eunice) had approved Churchill's decision to mine Norwegian territorial waters: 'Eunice went to the party. Hence Norway, hence Prime Minister.'[2]

In reply, Churchill grumbled that Eunice should have gone to the party three months earlier and Kennedy retorted that 'she' had been willing to.[3]

Churchill finally went to bed in the early hours of the morning a very contented man, despite Europe being once again embroiled in war:

> I was conscious of a sound sense of relief. At last I had the authority to preside over the whole scene. I felt as if I was walking with destiny, and that all my past life had been but a preparation for this hour and for this trial. Eleven years in the political wilderness had freed me from ordinary Party antagonisms. My warning over the last six years had been so numerous, so detailed and were now so terribly vindicated that no-one could gainsay me. I could not be reproached either for making the war or with want of preparation for it. I thought I knew a good deal about it all, and I was sure I should not fail. Therefore although impatient for the morning, I slept soundly and had no need for cheering dreams.[4]

Churchill had a lifelong fascination with the military and history. He had played with soldiers as a child, had joined the Army cadets at Harrow and went to Sandhurst Military College at the age of 19 before a short spell in the Army. In 1900, Churchill began a career in politics when elected as MP for Oldham for the Conservatives, which ended with his dismissal as First Lord of the Admiralty in a Liberal government after the Dardanelles campaign of 1915. As a form of self-imposed penance, Churchill had himself put on the Army's active list and served in the trenches of Flanders for just over five months in 1916. Widely read, an experienced politician and an avid student of the strategies and tactics of the great battles of history, Churchill believed he was uniquely qualified to lead the British Isles in a time of war.

Although Churchill's appointment as Prime Minister was not initially welcomed by many of his political colleagues, he did enjoy widespread public support. Churchill was greeted by cheering crowds outside Downing Street and his appointment was celebrated in a famous political cartoon 'All behind you, Winston', published in the *Evening Standard* newspaper on 14 May, although only Cabinet members were depicted in the cartoon and the ordinary people were just a faceless mob in the background.

In his diary, however, the Foreign Office Permanent Undersecretary, Lord Cadogan, said he was not at all sure of Winston.[5] Lord Davidson, in a letter to Baldwin, said that the Tories did not trust Winston and that after the first clash of war had passed it may well be that a sounder government may emerge. Other civil servants in Whitehall were not enthused either, believing Winston would be a complete failure and that Neville would return.[6] Halifax, Churchill's only rival candidate, later wrote, 'I don't think WSC will be a very good PM though … the country will think he gives them a fillip.'[7]

One British housewife, however, was more impressed by Churchill becoming Prime Minister and recorded in her diary:

> If I had to spend my whole life with a man, I'd choose Mr Chamberlain but I think I'd sooner have Mr Churchill if there was a storm and I was shipwrecked.[8]

A number of people greeted Churchill enthusiastically two days later on a walk from Downing Street to the Admiralty and on reaching the building, Churchill apparently dissolved into tears. 'Poor people,' he said. 'They trust me and I can give them nothing but disaster for quite a long time.'[9]

Three days later, Churchill told the House of Commons in his first speech as Prime Minister that he had no policy or strategy for the defeat of Germany and 'nothing to offer but blood, toil, tears and sweat', declaring that the British aim was:

> Victory. Victory at all costs. Victory in spite of all terror. Victory, however long and hard the road may be, for without victory there is no survival.

Chamberlain was given a hero's welcome in the House, while the reception for Churchill was far more reserved. Unfazed by this, Churchill immediately plunged himself into the business of running and winning the war. As well as selecting a new War Cabinet, Churchill created a new Defence Committee in place of the previous Military Co-ordination Committee with himself as head and the Minister of Defence. This streamlined the strategic decision-making process but left the responsibility for strategic thinking solely with Churchill. The Defence Committee had two levels, one for Operations and the other for Supply matters, and Churchill presided over both. The Chiefs of Staff Committee, where the strategies for war were drawn up and evaluated, reported to the Defence Committee and Churchill through Lord Ismay, Churchill's Chief of Staff. Ismay and a small secretarial staff had previously reported to Churchill as the chairman of the Military Co-ordination Committee and this was maintained in the new structure.

In May 1940 the Chiefs of Staff were:

Chief Imperial General Staff (CIGS) – General Edmund Ironside
Chief of Air Staff – Air Chief Marshal Sir Cyril Newall (and Chairman)
Admiral of the Fleet – Sir Dudley Pound

At the end of the month Churchill replaced Ironside with Sir John Dill. Responsible for the day-to-day direction of the war, the Chiefs of Staff took a largely passive role in terms of overall strategy development, directing the activities of the Joint Planning Staff and evaluating plans from commanders in the field largely as directed by Churchill, who was almost the single source of strategic ideas for the conduct of the war. The Chiefs of Staff saw their role as supporting their political masters; the actions of the armed forces were the ultimate extension of international politics and therefore the Chiefs of Staff left politics to the Foreign office and Churchill. As the war progressed, both the Defence Committee and the War Cabinet were consulted less and less, being only involved in the approval of major operations and contributing very little in the way of strategic ideas or discussion.

On the European Continent, the Allied armies had amassed 135 divisions in the field as follows:

Belgium 22
Holland   8
Britain   10
Poland   1
France   94[10]

While the French Army was the largest of the Allies, only sixty-seven of the divisions deployed were regular infantry, the balance being static fortress divisions manning the Maginot Line of defences along the border with Germany. The Allied armies were all at different states of training and readiness, for example only five divisions of the British Expeditionary Force (BEF) were regular troops, the other five being part-time Territorials. The divisions suffered from a shortage of anti-aircraft guns and artillery as production in Britain was still in a transition to a war footing and many units did not have their full establishment of other equipment. The Allies also had problems of command and control because of the many different languages spoken by the various Army generals.

The Germans, for their part, had eighty-nine divisions deployed in three army groups as follows:

Army Group B 28 divisions (including 3 Armoured and 1 motorised) (von Bock)
Army Group A 44 divisions (including 7 Armoured and 3 motorised) Luxembourg Ardennes (von Rundstedt)
Army Group C 17 divisions

Additionally, the German Army command, OKH, had a further forty-five divisions in reserve. In order not to antagonise the Germans, the Belgians had not permitted any foreign troops to enter their country. Therefore with the invasion of Belgium on 10 May, the BEF, which had been in prepared positions in France since the end of 1939, immediately advanced into Belgium to the proposed line of defence along the River Dyle, to which the Belgians were expected to fall back. Unfortunately this was exactly as the Germans had predicted, and as the British troops moved forward in the north, the Panzer divisions of Army Group A further south struck on 11 May from the reoccupied Rhineland through the Ardennes and straight at the junction of the French First and Second Army Groups, bypassing the Maginot Line of fortresses with the objective of cutting the Allied armies in two. By 13 May, the German Panzer divisions had crossed the River Meuse between Sedan and Dinant and established bridgeheads on the opposite bank.

That day, the French Prime Minister, Reynaud, appealed to the British for more fighter aircraft to combat the German air superiority. In view of the numbers of German aircraft, this was not unreasonable, given that the French had put into the field the bulk of the Allied infantry and armour resisting the Germans. However, the War Cabinet declined to send any more aircraft in order to not weaken its own fighter and bomber forces. With rearmament programmes still in progress, the Chief of Air Staff said that Britain required sixty squadrons for its own defence and only had thirty-nine at that point in time, ten already being in France.

The main point of German attack was not yet apparent to the Allies, who suffered a further blow when Dutch resistance ended on 14 May, allowing the Germans to quickly occupy the rest of Holland and concentrate more forces against Belgium and the BEF. The BEF did not reach the line at the River Dyle until that day and found the planned defences either unfinished or non-existent. With the collapse of Holland, there was little time to prepare new defensive positions before the Germans attacked. Reynaud asked for ten more British fighter squadrons on 14 May and next day expressed panic in a telephone call to Churchill when the Germans broke through at Sedan.[11]

The two French armies at the Ardennes directly in the path of the Germans, the 2nd and 9th Armies, were of low-grade troops as the French thought the Ardennes were impassable to wheeled vehicles. Two French armoured divisions were rushed to the area to mount a counter-attack but these were delayed by a lack of fuel and the roads being clogged by fleeing civilians. The 2nd Army directly in the path of the Germans began to disintegrate under concentrated air attacks and fell back southwards towards the Maginot Line, leaving a 10-mile gap in the French front line. The 9th Army received permission to fall back as well and this opened the flood gates to the German advance. On 15 May, the German armoured and infantry divisions began to exploit a gap nearly 40 miles wide and drive for the coast of northern France. At the point of the attack by the Panzer divisions were Luftwaffe dive-bombers, which knocked out strongpoints and acted as mobile artillery. Heavier bombers in turn pounded the rear areas and communications of the French divisions, causing co-ordination difficulties and morale to plummet. The Allies, particularly the French, had been expecting a static battle to quickly develop and the rapid advances of tanks supported by aircraft came as a devastating shock. While the French possessed almost as many tanks as the Germans, they were dispersed throughout the infantry divisions and could not be concentrated for an attack.

Following a suggestion from the British Ambassador in France looking at the acquisition of obsolete destroyers for France, Churchill on 15 May sent a telegram to Roosevelt (his first as Prime Minister) asking for the loan of fifty destroyers that he knew had been mothballed by the US Navy at the end of the First World War. In addition, Churchill asked for new aircraft already on order to be supplied from existing US stocks rather than having to wait for them to be built. Supplies of steel were also requested as stocks of iron ore were depleted following the Norwegian venture. Churchill's last request in his telegram was regarding the Japanese: 'Sixthly, I am looking to you to keep that Japanese dog quiet in the Pacific, using Singapore in any way convenient.'[12]

On 16 May, the War Cabinet agreed at a morning meeting to send to France four additional fighter squadrons in eight flights or half squadrons.[13] Churchill then flew to Paris to see for himself what was happening as the decision by French forces to withdraw when their lines had been penetrated by a reported mere 120 German tanks seemed unacceptable to him. In Paris, Churchill found the French government largely defeatist and civil servants already burning secret papers. The French blamed a lack of British fighter aircraft to protect their troops from the German dive-bombers while they were trying to engage the attacking German tanks, so Churchill agreed to provide extra fighter cover over France.

In England, Air Chief Marshal Dowding was horrified at what he saw as the frittering away of the RAF squadrons in France. Dowding wrote a ten-point memorandum to the Chief of Air Staff, Newall, pointing out that a revised minimum of fifty-two squadrons were required for the defence of Britain and he was now reduced to just thirty-six squadrons. Nevertheless, on Churchill's return from France, the War Cabinet agreed later that night to a further six squadrons, based in England, to be rotated for operations in France with three squadrons in the morning and three in the afternoon. That night, the BEF began to withdraw in a movement that continued until the line of the River Escaut was reached on the night of 18–19 May. The need for this withdrawal was blamed by the BEF's commander, Lord Gort, on the collapse of the French 1st Army on their right under General Blanchard.[14] This movement by the BEF exposed the Belgian Army on their left, which had no option but to conform to the movements of the British, and this greatly unsettled them.

On 17 May, Roosevelt declined to supply Britain with any destroyers on the grounds that the approval of this loan would require the authorisation of Congress and Roosevelt was reluctant to press the issue 'at this moment'. The message was delivered by Kennedy, who explained that Roosevelt could not 'go ahead of his public'. Kennedy had been pro-Chamberlain and was not a supporter of Churchill. Kennedy had written in his diary on 15 May:

I couldn't help but think as I sat there talking to Churchill how ill-conditioned he looked and the fact that there was a tray with plenty of liquor on it alongside him and he was drinking a scotch highball, which

I thought indeed not the first one he had drunk that night, that, after all, the affairs of Great Britain might be in the hands of the most dynamic individual in Great Britain but certainly not in the hands of the best judgement in Great Britain.[15]

On 18 May, apparently while shaving in the morning, Churchill discussed the war with his son, Randolph, and came up with the notion that the only way to win the war was to 'drag the United States in'.[16] Exactly when this idea became a deliberate strategy of Churchill's remains to be seen, but certainly on this day the first doubts about the situation in France began to materialise with the rapid advances of the Germans across France.

A day later, the situation had worsened, with the spearhead of the German armoured thrust across northern France reaching Cambrai and Peronne. The Allied armies in northern France were increasingly in danger of being cut off and for the first time Chamberlain in the War Cabinet spoke of holding out until America 'could be induced to come to our help'.[17] Churchill asked for reports to be drawn up on the consequences of the fall of Paris and the problems associated with the complete withdrawal of the BEF from France altogether. On 19 May, Gort ordered a further withdrawal to the south towards Amiens via Arras to maintain contact with the French forces on his right flank. Regarding French appeals for more aircraft, Churchill instructed the same day that no more RAF fighter aircraft be sent out of England to France as they might be needed to cover an evacuation of the BEF.[18]

Churchill expressed his disappointment in Roosevelt's refusal to lend the destroyers in a peeved reply by telegram dated 20 May, warning of the dangers of his government falling and Germany potentially acquiring the Royal Navy in negotiations conducted by 'others'. The telegram was concluded in a more moderate fashion with the sentiment that '… happily no need at present to dwell upon such ideas.'[19] That day, elements of German units reached the English Channel near Abbeville and began to push northwards along the coast behind most of the BEF, cutting off two divisions of the 2nd Corps further south.

After a failed joint British and French counter-attack at Arras on 21 May, Churchill commented while waiting for a phone call to Reynaud that:

In all the history of war, I have never seen such mismanagement.[20]

Churchill flew next day once more to France to meet with Reynaud and his new Commander-in-Chief, General Weygand. Not content with managing

Britain's war, Churchill could not resist trying to direct the efforts of the French as well as a sort of de facto Supreme Commander. Weygand appeared to be more confident than his predecessor and had a plan which was agreed for the Allies to attack simultaneously from the north and south to cut off the German Panzer divisions. Churchill seized on this plan as the only offensive action that might have a chance of halting the German advance. Others within the War Cabinet that night were more sceptical of the French fighting abilities and that the proposed operation might fall between two stools.[21] The Chief of Staff of the BEF in France, Lt General Pownall, was incredulous at the orders for the Weygand Plan and later railed bitterly against Churchill for this order, 'Can nobody prevent him from trying to conduct operations himself as a super Commander in Chief? He can have no conception of our situation – How is an attack like this to be staged involving three nationalities at an hour's notice? The man's mad.'[22]

When queried on 23 May as to the progress of the planned counter-attack, Weygand said it was in progress from the south when evidently it was not; Weygand also reported incorrectly that French troops had retaken Amiens.[23] The counter-attack was delayed on 23, 24 and 26 May, and ultimately the French did not participate at all. Recriminations between British and French began after the evacuation of British troops from Boulogne during the night of 22–23 May. The communication lines of the BEF were now threatened and the men were put on half rations; an additional 800,000 iron rations had to be flown in from England. Calais was surrounded on 24 May but the troops holding the port were not evacuated and were told to fight for as long as possible in a telegram by Churchill to the garrison commander on 26 May. Despite this message, Calais fell the next day and Dunkirk remained the only port in northern France still in Allied hands.

With the battle in France going badly, the War Cabinet decided on 24 May to abandon Narvik once it had been captured as the troops and equipment in Norway were needed more urgently back in Britain.

The beleaguered French and British soldiers in France then received an unexpected reprieve, although they did not know it as the situation was still very confused. The German commander of Army Group A, von Rundstedt, called a halt on 24 May for the Panzer divisions partly because of concerns about his forces being overextended and partly out of the need for essential maintenance to be carried out on the tanks. Hitler condoned this order to halt and the advance was not resumed until 26 May.

In light of the German advances and the emerging threat to the rear of his army, Gort decided on 25 May that he could no longer wait for the planned

French counter-attack and began a retreat to the coast of his own initiative. The Germans were planning a major attack at the junction of the British and Belgian troops at Courtrai; the Belgian troops by this time were completely demoralised by news of their King planning to leave the country. Gort moved British troops scheduled for the Weygand attack to the south next day back to the north in order to protect Dunkirk and his line of withdrawal. At the Defence Committee meeting on the same day, Churchill had independently arrived at same decision regarding the BEF, although he made it contingent on the outcome of a meeting with Reynaud next day. At that meeting on 26 May in London, Reynaud warned that Marshal Pétain, who had recently been appointed as his deputy, would seek an armistice and claimed that fifty French divisions deployed from the Maginot Line to the sea had been unable to stop three times the number of German divisions. Churchill asked Reynaud to instruct Weygand to give the official order for the withdrawal of the BEF, which he duly did. Later that day, the withdrawal of the BEF and its evacuation by sea (Operation Dynamo) was authorised by the War Cabinet, planning having been in progress since 20 May.[24]

The first troops were evacuated from Dunkirk on the night of 27–28 May and the operation continued for another five days. Luftwaffe aircraft hampered the operation, forcing naval activity to be largely restricted to night operations, but did not achieve the destruction promised to Hitler by its commander, Göring. Damage to the harbour jetties meant that the larger naval vessels could not approach the shore so an armada of smaller boats was requisitioned to ferry men from the beaches to the larger ships waiting off shore.

Soon after my brother and I went to bed, we became excited when a large, by river standards, grey boat came alongside the 'Diana Mary'. A naval officer looked her over then came up to the house. He was greeted by my sister, my brother and I with some trepidation. He asked to see my father and, when he was told my father was not at the house, the officer left a telephone number and told us to tell our father to telephone the number immediately he returned.

When my father called the number, he was instructed to deliver the 'Diana Mary' at Teddington by 08:00 the following morning. The whole family went to deliver her and, when we arrived at the dock, she was immediately refuelled and my father was asked if he wanted to take her over to France. He replied that he did, but my mother intervened and insisted that he change his mind. Whereupon, three sailors jumped aboard, cast off and we watched as the 'Diana Mary' disappeared down river. There was a great sense of urgency and only a few minutes passed from the time we came alongside to the time she sailed away. My mother had lost her first husband during the First World War, less than a month before Armistice Day, and I believe she did not wish my father to be exposed to a risk that could make her a war widow for the second time.

The 'Diana Mary' proudly played her part in the evacuation from Dunkirk but, when she was returned to us, she was badly damaged and had to be scrapped. The amount of compensation was minimal and nowhere near enough to buy a replacement. Unlike many other boat owners in similar situations, my father left all equipment in place in the belief that it would be useful during her voyages but, when it was returned, nothing remained on board. There were several souvenirs in the boat such as ammunition, parts of uniforms and similar military paraphernalia. Some of it was French so it must have rescued French troops as well as our own.[25]

The last men were picked up at midnight on 2 June. The BEF had lost 68,111 men killed, wounded or missing and all its heavy equipment such as artillery, anti-aircraft guns, armoured vehicles and lorries. A total of 335,490 men were evacuated, including 110,000 Allied troops, but up to 40,000 men of the French rearguard were taken prisoner.[26] The number of men that returned to England was nothing short of a miracle as far as the War Cabinet was concerned; Operation Dynamo had been expected to evacuate no more than 50,000 men and the additional troops would be a significant extra force of defenders in the projected invasion of Britain by Germany. However, the remnants of 2nd Corps, the entire 51st Division and a part of the 1st Armoured Division remained in France, having been cut off by the German advance.

The arrival of troop trains into London carrying the soldiers evacuated from France brought home the realities of war to many people:

It was a hot evening and the crowd on the platform were listless, seemingly resigned to misfortune. Suddenly a train drew in. It was full of soldiery, unkempt, unshaven and in tattered uniforms. Some of them were bandaged – all of them looked exhausted. The people on the platform suddenly realised the significance of this apparition. The refreshment room was rushed and everything eatable or drinkable was purchased and thrust into the hands of the weary passengers. Scarcely a word was spoken on either side. When the train drew out, there was not a dry eye to be seen on the platform.[27]

As word got around, more and more civilians descended on the stationary trains from nearby houses:

> The trains stopped in the cutting while awaiting dispersal to various main line stations for the troops to be directed back to what remained of their units in various parts of the country, or to hospitals. Local people brought tea and sandwiches and cigarettes to the troops while they were stopped at the North Pole. My parents and I went and saw them there. We climbed down the grassy bank and one soldier gave me his RA (Royal Artillery) badge. Some wore tattered uniforms, some only had on odd articles of borrowed mufti and yet others had arms in slings, head bandages or crutches. All had days of beard growth. All looked exhausted, and dishevelled, yet they managed cheery grins and showed typical cockney wit and grit as they gratefully accepted the sustenance on offer, thankful no doubt to be alive and back on British soil, thanks to the heroism of our indomitable Navy, Air Force cover, and the courage of the skippers and crew of all the 'little ships'.[28]

As the French situation became more desperate, Roosevelt became more involved, sending a telegram to Mussolini urging Italy to stay neutral. At the War Cabinet on 26 May, Churchill and Halifax disagreed on the question of seeking peace terms, with Churchill adamant that Hitler would not offer favourable terms to Britain.[29] Halifax was of the opinion that Hitler would be prepared to offer reasonable terms to France and Britain and sent a telegram to France suggesting that the United States be requested to approach Italy to broker peace negotiations. Later the same day, Roosevelt offered to mediate between Britain, France and Italy to quickly resolve Italy's territorial grievances in order to forestall the possible entry of Italy into the war.

Churchill asked the Chiefs of Staff to consider the question of whether Britain could survive the war and an invasion alone and they duly reported that they believed that Britain would hold out as long as the Navy and Air Force were intact, and that the good morale of the British people and its armed forces would ultimately counterbalance the superiority and material advantages of Germany.[30] Having witnessed the collapse of morale in France, Churchill was determined that the same rot would not set in within Britain and wrote a minute to his Cabinet colleagues and senior civil servants urging them to maintain high morale and express confidence in the ability of Britain to 'defend its Island, Empire and Cause'.[31]

Belgium finally surrendered on 28 May and its King fled to England, which only increased the German pressure on the British and French troops in northern France.

The War Cabinet now became very concerned with the future disposition of the French fleet in the likely capitulation of France and the entry of an opportunistic Italy into the war. During War Cabinet discussions on seeking terms on 28 May, Churchill was still strongly opposed to negotiations on the basis that Hitler was unlikely to offer very favourable terms given the German success so far. That day, France also proposed that Britain and France use Italy as an intermediary to seek terms from Germany but again Churchill resisted this:

> The PRIME MINISTER thought that the chances of decent terms being offered to us at the present time were a thousand to one against.[32]

Churchill was determined that Britain should not surrender and somewhat illogically believed that Britain would receive no worse terms if it fought on for the next few months and was defeated in the coming battle for Britain; this was against all the historical lessons of nations being forced to accept worse terms when finally defeated, Finland being the most recent example.

Roosevelt's approaches to Italy did not receive a positive response and this was confirmed by Mussolini on 31 May when he spoke of Italy honouring its alliances; it was then clear to the British and Americans that Italy was planning to enter the war.

With northern France now occupied, the German Army forces turned southwards and the French sought to establish a new defensive line north of Paris. The French again requested more British air support and ground troops to support this new front but Britain was in no position to meet the demands for aircraft. Incredibly, despite the reverse suffered by the BEF at Dunkirk, Churchill agreed to send two more divisions to France to bolster the two divisions of 2nd Corps commanded by Lt General Alan Brooke. On returning to England at the end of May to organise these replacement divisions, Brooke was ordered by the Chiefs of Staff to return to France and form a new BEF with the addition of the 52nd Division and the 1st Canadian Division, which were to be sent to France to reinforce the British units still there. Churchill still held out hopes of forming a redoubt in Brittany and wanted to do all he could to keep the French fighting; Brooke was astonished: 'The mission I was being sent on from a military point of view had no value and no possibility of accomplishing anything. Furthermore we had only just escaped a major disaster at Dunkirk and were now risking a second such disaster.'[33]

Marshall Pétain told the French government on 5 June that France must seek peace with Germany. For the British public, the rapid ejection of the British forces from France came as a further shock after the defeat in Norway, although the number of men evacuated was presented as a success by the government:

June 5th 1940
The Prime Minister made an important speech yesterday about the Dunkirk withdrawal and the events leading up to it. It seems miraculous that over 300000 men were able to escape the terrific German onslaught. Some people think it was God's answer to the National Day of prayer last Sunday week. I feel very loath to draw God's name into this ghastly affair.[34]

Buoyed by the success of the Dunkirk evacuation, even though an invasion was imminent, Churchill's thoughts had turned to resuming the offensive by any possible means against Germany. On 5 June, Churchill requested in a minute that the Chiefs of Staff examine ways to land both troops and tanks on the Continent from flat-bottomed boats in 'butcher and bolt' raiding operations. This minute started the development of the landing craft capable of carrying tanks and the Combined Operations force which was first headed by Admiral Keyes and then later Louis Mountbatten. A few weeks later, on 16 July, Churchill ordered that Europe be set ablaze with the formation of the Special Operations Executive for clandestine missions on the Continent. Other ideas by Churchill for Britain to resume the offensive were more bizarre. These included a plan for the RAF to firebomb the Black Forest, which was nevertheless approved by the War Cabinet on 11 June. Operation Razzle to destroy German field crops with incendiary bombs was also approved on 2 July; neither operation was successful.[35] Another idea to use balloons to carry incendiary bombs into Germany was also abandoned.

A second evacuation of British troops began immediately after Dunkirk, this time from Norway where only the men of Narvik Force remained to be evacuated after having captured the town; the last troops left Norway on the night of 7–8 June.

On 10 June, Italy entered the war, thus realising the worst fears of the British and French. France was now being attacked from two directions with the entry of Italian troops into the south of France, while Britain faced the additional threat to its maritime security from the large Italian surface fleet and submarines. The fate of the French fleet became even more pressing for the British. In desperation, Churchill again pleaded with Kennedy on the 12 June for the loan of the fifty mothballed destroyers, some of which were already being reconditioned by the US Navy. Kennedy passed the message to Roosevelt, who remained silent on the issue. Churchill has been criticised for requesting these ships but these were the only vessels that could be quickly supplied by the US Navy. The British requirement was only short term until ships currently being constructed could be launched.

With the Italian declaration of war, in North Africa General Wavell immediately ordered a series of raids across the Libyan border from Egypt in order to deter the Italian forces from invading Egypt. There were twelve Italian divisions based in Libya to defend the colony from any French aggression from Tunisia. The first raid took place on 11 June and further successful raids culminated in the capture of Fort Capuzzo on 14 June. Thus the first shots in what would become the Desert Campaign were fired by the British. For its part, the Italian Air Force bombed the island of Malta that week.

Churchill's main objective at this stage was to keep France fighting in the war as long as possible. Reynaud cabled Roosevelt on 10 June, thanking him for the offers of American aid but requesting that the United States make a public declaration of its intention to send aid and material support to the Allies by all means 'short of an expeditionary force'. Mussolini and consequently Hitler knew from Roosevelt's telegrams to Italy that the United States was working with the Allies. Reynaud leaked details of this message to some press correspondents and the telegram's contents were reported in America, much to Roosevelt's discomfort.[36]

Churchill went to France again on 11 June, this time to Briare, for another meeting with Reynaud and Weygand; the latter now believed the French could not resist for much longer and that Britain would soon succumb to Germany as well. Churchill was anxious that new plans be made for an offensive and that the French keep fighting until the United States came in, which was thought to be likely when the Germans began to attack Britain. The offer by Churchill of new and strong British divisions on the way and further fighter aircraft seemed to give the French renewed hope. In another attempt to keep the French fighting, Churchill asked the French commanders to plan the formation of a redoubt of resistance in Brittany from which future Allied action could be launched, but the French were not enthusiastic.[37] Next morning, Churchill again queried why the French could not keep fighting until the United States came in, to which Reynaud's response was that only the industrial resources of the United States could provide a solution to the problems confronting Britain and France and immediate American support was essential.[38] Reynaud and Churchill promised to send appeals to Roosevelt, and with that the meeting concluded and the

British flying party flew back to England. Soon after their return a copy of Roosevelt's reply to Reynaud's message of 10 June arrived, which stated that efforts to aid France would be redoubled but made no other commitments. However, this was seized on by Churchill as an indication of American intentions as 'the President could hardly urge the French to continue the struggle, and to undergo further deprivations, if he did not intend to enter the war to support them'.[39] Churchill immediately sent an optimistic cable to Reynaud:

> If France on this message of President Roosevelt's continues in the field and in the war, we feel that the United States is committed beyond recall to take the only remaining step, namely, becoming a belligerent in form as she already has constituted herself in fact.[40]

Churchill also wrote a telegram as promised to Roosevelt asking for permission to publish the President's message of support. However, in the early hours of the morning, having taken Roosevelt's reply merely at face value, Reynaud asked for another meeting with Churchill that day so Churchill and his entourage immediately flew back to France, this time to the village of Tours. Before they left, a message arrived from America stating that Roosevelt did not want his telegram published. As his actions in sending military supplies to Britain and France were potentially embarrassing, Roosevelt added a handwritten instruction to the draft telegram that his message was not for publication.[41]

At the meeting in Tours, a frantic Reynaud wanted proof that the United States was going to enter the war, claiming that he had Roosevelt's approval to publish his appeal to Roosevelt of 10 June.[42] Reynaud went on to say that the French Cabinet wanted to know what Britain's position would be if France was to seek peace terms, as under the conditions of the Franco-British alliance neither country could seek peace without the permission of the other. Churchill repeated his view that time must be gained to allow America to make a pledge of support but declared that Britain would go on alone to either victory or death. At this, Weygand reportedly said to Reynaud that Britain would have 'her neck wrung like a chicken'.[43]

Churchill did manage to convince Reynaud to make another appeal to Roosevelt, and with this the meeting ended, Churchill leaving to return to England. This would be the last meeting of the Supreme War Council. The British received one piece of good news when Admiral Darlan, the Commander-in-Chief of the French Navy, gave Churchill on 12 June a solemn promise that the French fleet would not fall into the hands of the Germans.

The fighting continued for the British units still in France, although the French armies were completely demoralised. The 52nd Division arrived and took its place in the line on 12 June, but after only four days of fighting, as other French forces began to withdraw to Brittany, the 52nd Division was ordered by Brooke to retire to Cherbourg and re-embark for England. The leading brigade of the Canadians arrived in France on 14 June and while still entrained moving inland received instructions to re-embark. Unlike at Dunkirk, these divisions did not lose all of their equipment. Churchill telephoned Brooke when he heard about the evacuation that had been ordered and the two men argued for half an hour before Churchill approved Brooke's decision. Brooke later commented that Churchill, '… was interfering with a commander in the field, and without sufficient knowledge of conditions prevailing on that front at that time, he was endeavouring to carry out his wishes against that commander's better judgement'.[44]

After German attacks broke through the new French defensive line, Paris was declared an open city on 13 June and occupied by German troops the next day. Roosevelt's reply to the entreaties of both Britain and France was a promise of more aid but he emphasised that this was not a military commitment as 'only the Congress could make such commitments'.[45]

Churchill's efforts to keep France in the war had failed and with the receipt of Roosevelt's final telegram, the last traces of any fighting spirit in the French evaporated. Haunted by the spectre of adverse public opinion, Roosevelt had gone further than he intended and had been forced to finally commit to a neutral position by Cordell Hull, the US Secretary of State.[46] On the morning of 16 June, Churchill received a telegram from Reynaud seeking Britain's permission to begin talks with Germany, which Churchill agreed to only on the basis that the French fleet be directed to British harbours. Several diplomats and a French general who had fled to England by plane, General de Gaulle, then came up with a proposal for a declaration of the union of France with Britain which would be announced by de Gaulle in order to give heart to Reynaud in a last-ditch attempt to keep France in the war. However, this ploy failed as, after a confused informal vote on the proposed union by the French Cabinet which Reynaud lost by a mere two votes, Reynaud resigned and Pétain became Premier.

The French ceased fighting on 17 June and an armistice was signed four days later. Bitter about the British withdrawal and failure to provide more fighter aircraft, the French largely blamed Britain for their defeat.

De Gaulle broadcast an appeal via BBC radio on 18 June for the French to resist the German occupation and Churchill made him head of the French

National Committee in Britain. On 28 June, the War Cabinet declared that de Gaulle was the leader of the Free French, an impetuous decision that would have consequences in the relationships between the Allies for the rest of the war.[47]

To increase the rate of building and re-equipping the growing British Army, orders had been placed in the United States before Churchill became Prime Minister for large quantities of war material such as copper, explosives, artillery and aircraft engines. Roosevelt was ready to assist Britain and was happy to accept the orders (which helped enormously to stimulate American industry) despite the provisions of the Neutrality Act, which forbade the sale of arms to belligerents. In mid June, the first major shipment from the United States was made after Roosevelt had approved the sale by declaring that the US would export surplus or obsolete weapons to private firms as a way of circumventing the Neutrality Act in order for the weapons to be sold to the British government. On 3 June, General Marshall, the US Army Chief of Staff, declared a list of items as being surplus or obsolete to US Army requirements and the British immediately purchased nearly everything on the list plus extra items.[48]

Emboldened by the relative security of the Russo-German pact, Russia also flexed its military muscles to acquire previously disputed lands or new territories. While the world was preoccupied with France and the fall of Paris, on 15 June 1940 Soviet armies marched unopposed into the Baltic states of Latvia, Estonia and Lithuania, setting up pro-communist governments in each state without protest from the West. The British War Cabinet took the view that Russia was only bolstering its defences against Germany.[49]

Although the British Army had been defeated, the Royal Navy and the RAF were largely intact and Churchill considered how the war could be taken to Germany. On 8 July Churchill wrote to the new Minister for Aircraft Production:

> But when I look round to see how we can win the war I see that there is only one sure path. We have no continental army which can defeat the German military power. The blockade is broken and Hitler has Asia and probably North Africa to draw from. Should he be repulsed here or not try invasion, he will recoil eastward and we have nothing to stop him. But there is one thing that will bring him back and bring him down, and that is an absolutely devastating, exterminating attack by very heavy bombers from this country upon the Nazi homeland. We must be able to overwhelm them by this means, without which I do not see a way through. We cannot accept any lower aim than air mastery. When can it be obtained?[50]

This minute was credited by Air Chief Marshal Harris as being the origin of what became the British and American bombing offensive against Germany.

The Royal Navy was fully preoccupied defending the coastline of England against invasion and with protecting convoys from German surfacer raiders and U-boats. The fate of the French fleet now became a major issue for Britain and Churchill as it was vital that Germany should not acquire it following the entry of Italy into the war. Admiral Darlan signalled the fleet on 20 and 24 June with orders that ships were to stay in French or colonial ports and that in the event of any German attempt to seize them preparations for self-destruction should be made.[51] Darlan went further and ordered ships to leave for the US or scuttle themselves if the terms of the armistice terms were changed.

Rather than demand a complete surrender, the terms of the armistice with France demanded by Germany cleverly allowed southern France to continue to exist as a sovereign state that became to be known as Vichy France. This strategy allowed France to retain her overseas colonies and a neutralised naval fleet, thus ensuring both did not fall into Britain's hands. It also meant that a wedge was driven between Britain and France diplomatically. However, in adopting this strategy, Germany had foregone the opportunity to dramatically increase the strength of its own navy at the stroke of a pen.

On 24 June, Halifax sent an ultimatum to the new Vichy government regarding the French fleet. British action against the fleet, particularly the four largest and most modern ships, was discussed in the War Cabinet. Tension quickly arose between France and Britain; French ships in Portsmouth, Plymouth and Alexandria were interned and France demanded their immediate release. Another French ship carrying gold bullion was intercepted and seized after previously having been allowed to proceed.

Finally, on 27 June, Churchill proposed an attack on the French naval base at Oran in Algeria; the same day, he received confirmation of Roosevelt's refusal to supply the requested destroyers. Having been prompted by Churchill to consider the future disposition of the British fleet if Britain was forced to sue for peace in his telegram of 15 June that pleaded for the destroyers, Roosevelt did precisely that in a conversation with Lord Halifax in Washington on 2 July. Roosevelt, clearly believing that Britain might be in a difficult position soon if Gibraltar was lost, suggested that Anglo-American technical discussions needed to be held to plan for the future naval situation as soon as possible in London – without any publicity because of the impending American election.[52]

On the morning of 3 July, a British fleet arrived off Oran where two of the most powerful French ships, the *Dunkerque* and the *Strasbourg*, were in harbour. Elsewhere, simultaneous operations were carried out against French ships in Alexandria, Plymouth and Portsmouth; there was only resistance aboard one submarine in Plymouth, where a member of the crew and the British boarding party were killed. At Oran, the French admiral refused to surrender or join the British fleet and tense negotiations continued for several hours, during which time the French ships in the harbour prepared to get under way. British aircraft laid mines across the entrance to the harbour while a destroyer kept an anti-submarine watch close to the harbour entrance. The Vichy government, being closely monitored by the Germans, ordered that the ships at Oran should not surrender and that all available French naval forces should proceed to Oran. This message was intercepted by the British and Churchill personally ordered the attack: 'Settle the matter immediately or you may have French reinforcements to deal with.'

At 5.55 p.m. the Royal Navy opened fire on the French ships still in harbour in a bombardment that lasted only nine minutes but was devastating in effect. The stationary French ships were easy targets, unable to manoeuvre in the harbour. One ship exploded, the *Dunkerque* ran aground and 1,250 French sailors were killed. Having first believed that the British ships had come to join them, the French sailors were stunned when the British opened fire – a betrayal which has not been forgiven to this day. The Royal Navy were not enthusiastic about their distasteful task either and under cover of the bombardment the *Strasbourg* and two destroyers managed to leave the harbour and escape the British cordon, steaming at high speed to Toulon.

Churchill feared that the Vichy government would declare war on Britain but this did not eventuate, although a retaliatory air raid was made on Gibraltar. The Vichy government finally broke off diplomatic relations with Britain on 5 July after a French cruiser was 'accidentally' sunk in the Mediterranean.[53] To Churchill's surprise, he was given a standing ovation in the House of Commons when he reported on the Oran action next day. There was also favourable public reaction from around the world including India, Spain and the United States. Ruthlessness was a vital leadership attribute that Britain needed to ensure its survival and Churchill demonstrated to the world that he possessed that quality in abundance.

Roosevelt had been kept informed by Lord Lothian, the British Ambassador to the United States, of the proposed actions regarding the French fleet, of which Roosevelt strongly approved. Lothian reported:

I asked him whether that meant that American opinion would support forcible seizure of these ships. He said, 'Certainly.' They would expect them to be seized rather than that they should fall into German hands and that he would do everything in his power to help this solution. He said that he had offered to buy the Fleet from the French before the Reynaud Government fell but that there was nobody from whom he could buy it today.[54]

Roosevelt was finally convinced by Churchill's ruthless action at Oran that Britain would continue the fight and would not surrender. A report to Roosevelt by his emissary, Colonel Donovan, in London had also helped further convince Roosevelt of this rather than the pessimistic telegrams from his Ambassador, Kennedy. A way was found to bypass Congress and on 2 September Roosevelt approved the lease to Britain of the mothballed destroyers requested by Churchill. With an election due in early November, this was a bold move by Roosevelt because of the prevailing anti-war sentiment in America. The trade-off for the destroyers was the lease of nine British strategic bases in the Atlantic and Caribbean to the Americans on ninety-nine-year leases as these were deemed vital to securing America's Western Hemisphere defence. The deal was a poor one for England and the arrangement was seen by some as the loss of part of the Empire. Churchill had little choice but to accept the offer and towards the end of the year the reconditioned destroyers began to arrive in England. Of dubious sea-keeping abilities, the destroyers had no anti-aircraft armament and had to be refitted with anti-submarine equipment before they could even begin escorting convoys. What was immeasurable was Roosevelt's firm belief that Britain would survive in 1940 and the only way to defeat Nazi Germany was for the British Isles to be used as a base by the Allies for taking the fight back to Germany.

On 3 July, having received rather alarming reports of poor British morale following the French surrender and in order to raise spirits for the coming battle for Britain, Churchill wrote another minute to all senior civil servants and military leaders in the same vein as the previous minute in May, urging them to always display steadfastness and resolution in public and be ruthless in stamping out negative opinion from their staff. This minute was also published as a letter in the newspapers of the day.

Lord Ismay later wrote of the first year of war:

If in August 1939 the Chiefs of Staff had reason to think this was going to be the situation after less than twelve months of hostilities, I believe they would have unhesitatingly warned the Cabinet that to go to war would be to invite overwhelming disaster and that somehow or other, time must be bought to put our house in order, even at the expense of humiliating concessions.[55]

After only six weeks of being Prime Minister, the strain began to show on Churchill, forcing his wife, Clementine, to write to him about his rough and overbearing manner.[56] Churchill had long warned of the dangers of war and suddenly he had been given the authority to lead Britain, but perhaps Britain could not be saved. Germany had dealt Britain and France a salutary lesson in warfare and now controlled most of Europe. France, Belgium, Holland and Luxembourg had been invaded as a result of the French and British declarations of war on Germany over Poland and Britain was now facing its own imminent invasion. The neutral countries of Norway and Denmark had also been invaded as a consequence of British and French actions while Poland, the *casus belli*, had received no assistance whatsoever from Britain and France and had been conquered by Germany and Russia in a few weeks. The one consolation for Britain and Churchill was that, thanks to the 'halt order' of von Rundstedt and Hitler, the Dunkirk evacuation succeeded beyond the wildest dreams of the Chiefs of Staff and Churchill. The sizeable evacuated force, although lacking much equipment, allowed Britain with the RAF and Royal Navy intact to continue the war against Germany without the need to enter peace negotiations.

As he had done in Norway, Churchill had again interfered directly in the Battle of France in an effort to influence the fighting, much to the irritation of the French and British commanders such as Weygand, Brooke and Pownall. Churchill's decision to send more troops to France after Dunkirk in an effort to keep France fighting had to be reversed, but fortunately the entire 2nd Corps was evacuated without loss of valuable men and equipment.

Churchill's pre-war ideas on the dominance of anti-tank guns over tanks were rudely dispelled by the Germans' employment of combined tank and aircraft tactics, which became known as Blitzkrieg, or lightning war. The 'palmy' days for tanks in 1918 had been completely overshadowed by the German Panzer divisions of 1940.

Most importantly, a seed of thought that Britain could only survive with the entry of the USA into the war had been planted in Churchill's mind and was clearly being discussed by the War Cabinet, at least unofficially.

4

THE BLITZ

Following the invasion of Poland on 1 September 1939, Roosevelt had sent a message to all the belligerent countries involved, pleading for civilian targets to not be bombed:

> The ruthless bombing from the air of civilians in unfortified centres of population during the course of the hostilities which have raged in various quarters of the earth during the past few years, which has resulted in the maiming and in the death of thousands of defenceless men, women and children, has sickened the hearts of every civilized man and woman, and has profoundly shocked the conscience of humanity.
>
> If resort is had to this form of inhuman barbarism during the period of the tragic conflagration with which the world is now confronted, hundreds of thousands of innocent human beings who have no responsibility for, and who are not even remotely participating in, the hostilities which have now broken out, will lose their lives. I am therefore addressing this urgent appeal to every Government which may be engaged in hostilities publicly to affirm its determination that its armed forces shall in no event, and under no circumstances, undertake the bombardment from the air of civilian populations or of unfortified cities, upon the understanding that these same rules of warfare will be scrupulously observed by all of their opponents. I request an immediate reply.[1]

At the start of the war, the War Cabinet had decided that as long as the German Luftwaffe attacked military targets, the RAF would do the same. Before the

French campaign in 1940, the RAF had both targeted the Kriegsmarine and dropped a considerable amount of propaganda leaflets over Germany. With the invasion of France, from 15 May the RAF bombed railway yards, troop concentrations and oil-producing plants in the Ruhr. The Germans mounted similar but not very effective night-time raids on airfields and industrial targets in England.

After the conclusion of the French campaign marked by the new French government at Vichy signing an armistice on 22 June, various covert approaches were made by the Germans to the British about a peace settlement. On 1 August, King Gustav of Sweden wrote to Hitler and King George offering to facilitate peace negotiations between Germany and Britain. The offer was discussed at the War Cabinet meeting of 8 August and a reply sent along the lines of Chamberlain's speech in Parliament in 1939, when the British asked for positive actions by Germany to right the wrongs committed in Europe. No reply was received. Earlier in June, Churchill had ordered the seizure of four Swedish destroyers in the Faroe Islands on their way to Sweden, much to the astonishment of the Royal Navy. Churchill possibly had plans for pressgang-ing them into the Royal Navy but, perhaps fearful of this being a pretext for Germany to occupy Sweden, Churchill ordered their release a few days later.[2] The Foreign Secretary, Halifax, observed of Churchill after a War Cabinet dis-cussion of these events, 'It is the most extraordinary brain, Winston's, to watch functioning that I have ever seen. A most curious mixture of a child's emotion and a man's reason.'[3]

Another discreet approach was made by the German embassy in Washington to Lord Lothian. The German-controlled Dutch radio also broadcast a plea for Roosevelt to mediate.[4] In September, the British embassy in Stockholm was approached by an intermediary for someone claiming to represent Hitler. The German proposals were examined but no subsequent meetings took place.[5]

Hitler himself had appealed for peace in a speech in the Reichstag on 17 July but any peace initiatives were firmly rebuffed by British diplomats on Churchill's instructions. Now resigned to the need to continue the war with Britain, Hitler on 1 August ordered the destruction of the RAF as the necessary prerequisite to an invasion of Britain; operations were to begin on 13 August with an estimated three days being required to knock out the RAF. Hitler made a final attempt the next day to start peace negotiations when German bombers dropped leaflets over southern England with details of his peace proposals. In the coming aerial offensive, the Luftwaffe crews were under strict instructions not to bomb London, as revealed to Churchill by the code breakers at Bletchley Park who had broken some low-grade Luftwaffe cyphers. However, even as plans for the attacks on Britain were being finalised, senior German staff at the Ober Kommandant Wehrmacht (OKW – High Command) had already been directed by Hitler on 1 July to make plans for the invasion of Russia.

The Luftwaffe had amassed some 3,000 aircraft in three Air Groups of which 1,100 aircraft were the Me 109 fighter, roughly equivalent to the Spitfire. The RAF, frantically rebuilding since the losses in France, had some 700 Spitfires and Hurricanes with a further 290 in reserve. Fighter Command had established an integrated air defence system with radar stations and Observer Corps positions reporting to a regional fighter control centre, Britain having been divided into four regions or sectors. Fighters could be scrambled to meet specific German raids rather than flying continuous patrols, which reduced the number of flying hours each day for pilots. Fighter Command's No. 11 Group in the south-east of England would bear the brunt of the battle, which began in earnest on 12 August with the main German offensive, code-named Eagle Day, scheduled for a day later. German dive-bombers struck at the coastal radar stations, damaging five but only putting one out of action until 23 August (Isle of Wight), and at airfields as fighters for both sides struggled for aerial supremacy over the skies of England. Initially focusing on coastal airfields, the Luftwaffe in mid August changed its tactics and began to attack targets further inland in an attempt to lure more British fighters up into the battle. Although the RAF shot down twice as many planes as it lost, the supply of replacement pilots could not keep up with casualties and a crisis was looming towards the end of the month. Then, on the night of 24 August, a German bomber that was lost or forced to jettison its load dropped its bombs on central London. Churchill, having discussed a plan to bomb Berlin previously with Air Marshal Portal, rang Bomber Command himself to order the retaliatory mission. The attack was nearly cancelled by the Chief of Air Staff, Newall, but following discussions with Harris, who was deputising for Portal, Bomber Command agreed to the Berlin mission and the RAF began missions that day.[6] A total of forty-three aircraft raided Berlin, the first of several raids over the next week. Later, at the end of October, Churchill would replace Newall on the Chiefs of Staff Committee with Portal, who served there for the rest of the war.

At the War Cabinet meeting of 29 August, Churchill claimed that the RAF pilots were showing restraint in not bombing civilian targets.[7] There is no record of any discussion in the War Cabinet or Defence Committee of a change of RAF bombing policy until a memorandum written by Churchill dated 3 September was circulated. Again, the paper was apparently not discussed or endorsed at a War Cabinet meeting:

> The Navy can lose us the war, but only the Air Force can win it. Therefore our supreme effort must be to gain overwhelming mastery in the Air. The Fighters are our salvation, but the Bombers alone provide the means of victory. We must therefore develop the power to carry an ever-increasing volume of explosives to Germany, so as to pulverise the entire industry and scientific structure on which the war effort and economic life of the enemy depends, while holding him at arm's length in our Island.[8]

This paper outlined to the War Cabinet the offensive bombing strategy proposed by Churchill that would ultimately be a war-winning one but have devastating effects on the German civilian population. Unable to fight the German Army directly in any theatre because of the comparative weakness and losses of the British Army, while the Royal Navy struggled against the U-boats and raiders to keep the sea lanes open, the only offensive action possible against Germany was to use RAF bombers to try to destroy the German war industry and economy. Mounting losses of aircraft and crews in daylight raids had forced the RAF to conduct these missions at night from mid 1940 onwards.

While Churchill seems to have made the decision to attack Berlin more motivated by a desire for revenge and to go on the offensive against Germany rather than because of the cumulative losses of RAF pilots and aircraft, the Berlin raids prompted a change in German strategy that gave the weakened RAF time to recover just when it was close to collapse. Hitler had been told by Göring that the bombing of Berlin could never happen and he was apparently enraged by the raids, threatening in a Reichstag speech on 4 September to retaliate 100-fold to the tonnage of bombs dropped on Berlin. On 7 September, 300 German bombers escorted by 600 fighters attacked the East London Docklands, causing extensive damage, huge fires and killing 306 people in the area. That night, more German aircraft using the warehouse fires as navigation beacons caused even greater destruction. The Blitz had started.

What came to be known as 'Black Saturday' was a huge shock for Londoners. The Luftwaffe had arrived in the late afternoon of a fine day when many people were out and about enjoying the warm weather. The sirens first started at just after 4 p.m. and the attack lasted for twelve hours. More than 430 people were killed London-wide and more than 1,600 were seriously wounded; hospitals simply could not cope with the sudden influx of casualties. On a tour of the bomb damaged docklands the day after the air raids, Churchill remarked to Ismay, 'What fellows they are! Do you hear them? They cheered me as if I had given them a victory, instead of getting their homes bombed to bits.'[9]

On that Saturday, the German planes had operated in daylight and had encountered British fighter aircraft. For subsequent raids between 7 September and 13 November (London being bombed every night except for one) the Luftwaffe changed its tactics to night raids, which meant that Fighter Command could do little to stop them as British night fighter aircraft were only at a very primitive stage of development at this stage of the war.

On Black Saturday just ninety-two anti-aircraft guns had protected London. Churchill immediately ordered a major improvement to the capital's defences and within four days the number of anti-aircraft guns around London had more than doubled. The crews that manned these guns were ordered to fire at the attackers whether they could see one or not as this gave the impression that they were doing an efficient job defending London and this was considered good for morale.[10]

The Luftwaffe redoubled its efforts in mid September to subdue the RAF but was ultimately unsuccessful. Dowding's anguished memorandum about sending further planes to France that was reluctantly accepted by Churchill permitted the RAF to retain just enough pilots and planes to win the Battle of Britain. Whether Churchill realised it or not, his decision to bomb Germany also gave the RAF precious time to recover from the attacks by the Luftwaffe, which ultimately saved England from invasion. The other consequence of this decision was that British and German civilians were now very much in the firing line as collateral damage from the exchanges of inaccurate blows by the air forces of the two nations.

The subject of civilian casualties was not mentioned in any bombing policy papers. Churchill forbade publication of air raid casualty numbers and, perhaps mindful of public opinion both in Britain and America, advised Halifax in a minute of 13 October to discourage the International Red Cross from monitoring the British and German air offensives:

It would simply result in a committee under German influence or fear, reporting at the very best that it was six of one and half-a-dozen of the other. It is even very likely they would report that we had committed the major breaches. Anyhow, we do not want these people thrusting themselves in, as even if Germany offered to stop the bombing now, we should not consent to it. Bombing of military objectives, increasingly widely interpreted, seems at present our main road home.[11]

Churchill also believed American public opinion would change when reports of cities of the same names as in the United States being bombed in England reached the Americans.[12]

The German air raids were extended to Cardiff, Bristol, Liverpool and Manchester. The invasion of England was repeatedly postponed by Hitler, first from 15 September to 21 September and then ultimately altogether just when the RAF was on the verge of defeat. The Kriegsmarine had been severely weakened in the fighting in Norway; that September the Germans only had five destroyers, one battlecruiser and three cruisers operational, and the Kriegsmarine doubted its ability to prevent the Royal Navy from intercepting any invasion force. The failure of the Luftwaffe to subdue the RAF was no doubt ultimately greeted with relief by the Kriegsmarine. Without realising it, the Royal Navy by its bold actions in the Norwegian campaign had played a major part in forcing Hitler to abandon his plans to invade Britain.

However, the Luftwaffe continued to wage war against English cities in an attempt to destroy the industrial towns and ports of Southampton, Birmingham, Liverpool, Bristol, Plymouth and Portsmouth. Even Belfast, Cardiff, Swansea and Glasgow became targets of the bomber offensive. Hitler and Churchill were evidently pursuing the same strategy of using air power to destroy their enemies' economies and will to fight.

One Portsmouth family described being bombed:

It started fairly early in the evening. All I know is that we had hours with an unholy pounding. It really was absolutely frightening. An air raid warden came in and started screaming that my mother had left a light on upstairs in the end bedroom. It wasn't – the top of our house was alight. It was an incendiary bomb. As we were leaving the house there was another one, caught in the rafters. We had to run out of the house – my mother, my father, my brother, my aunt, my cousin and my grandmother. As we came out of the house it was like broad daylight, we were in a ring of fire. The Guildhall was burning, everywhere you looked you were literally surrounded by fire.

We had to leave in exactly what we stood up in. That raid lasted until 5 or 6 the following morning. We had to leave our house to go to a shelter in Somers Road, in the grounds of St Peter's Church, but the shelter in the grounds was full, so we had to go down into the bowels of the church. That absolutely petrified me because we were going deeper and deeper underground. We were lucky because we hadn't been in there long when there was a mighty explosion which shook the boiler room where we were. The explosion was a direct hit on the shelter in the grounds which we had tried to get to previously. We were down there for five or six hours; the raids were continuous all night – ten to twelve hours on Portsmouth that night.

When we eventually came out of the church, there was devastation all the way round, complete and utter devastation. There was no electricity, no gas, no water. It was like a scene of a movie. You would have to live through it to be able to imagine what it was like.

We made our way back to our house; we were tired, cold, hungry – it was January – and we hadn't even been able to stop to get a coat, we just ran. When we got back to the road where we lived, our house was just gutted. We had nothing. Nothing left. My father decided to try to go to another aunt's of ours in Fratton Road, but when we got to the top of Fratton Bridge, you could see very little remained of Fratton Road. So we didn't know what to do, we just stood on the bridge. Don't forget we had no money. A cattle truck came along and he offered to take us all as far as Barnham (my father had relations in Bognor Regis). The truck took us to Barnham Station, where we caught a train to Bognor – only one stop along the line as I remember. Then we descended on my uncle, my father's brother – the whole lot of us.

We had only the clothes we stood up in. I had slippers on my feet, which were sodden because of walking through all the water in the streets in Portsmouth which were awash with water and debris. We wanted something to eat and drink. My aunt Rose offered to make us some cocoa. We were all sitting bunched together, all dejected and still terrified, and she had a whistling kettle which made a sound like when the bombs came down and we all dived under the table.

I have no idea where we got help from, all I know is that my mother got £75 compensation from the government for the loss of everything. I don't know whether there was any insurance but all the places, buildings, were demolished. The £75 enabled us to buy clothes and we had to live in rented accommodation in Bognor. Eventually all the family, the other relations who were in Portsmouth who we hadn't been able to contact, came to Bognor and we all lived there until we came back to Portsmouth in 1945.[13]

Some people suffered stoically:

> I have the greatest admiration for the Eastenders. They were marvellous.
> How they stuck the war I don't know. I heard this from a fireman:
>   A fireman went to a very badly bombed area where an old lady was stand-
> ing outside a house. And he said: 'Look Mum, you really ought to get away
> because this street is not safe. They are bombing this area all the time.'
>   'Yes, son,' she said. 'I quite agree with you. I ought to move.' So that was that.
>   Two nights later the street was bombed again and he went back and there
> was the old lady standing on the pavement and he said: 'Mum! Why didn't
> you move as I said?'
>   She said: 'Yes, son. I have moved. I've moved next door.'[14]

The government in 1939 initially refused to allow the London Underground
stations to be used as shelters so as not to interfere with the running of trains
and out of the fear that people taking shelter might develop a bunker mentality,
refusing to leave. At first, Underground officials locked the entrances to the
stations during raids but in the second week of heavy bombing the government
relented and ordered the stations to be opened. Each day, orderly lines of people
queued until 4 p.m., when they were permitted access. In mid September 1940,
about 150,000 people a night slept in the Underground, although by the winter
and spring months the numbers had declined to 100,000 or fewer. The noises
of the battle overhead were muffled and sleep was easier in the deepest stations,
but many were still killed by direct hits.[15] Underground stations and public
shelters did not ever house more than 15 per cent of Greater London residents,
however.[16] Peak use of Underground stations as shelters was 177,000 on
27 September 1940 and a November 1940 census of London found that about
13 per cent of residents used the Underground and other large communal
shelters, 27 per cent used their outdoor Anderson shelters at home and the
remainder (nearly 60 per cent) stayed at home indoors:[17]

> By September the Germans had changed to night bombing. Every night they
> came so everything had to be done before 6pm, as you knew they would
> arrive soon after. We made sandwiches and filled Thermos flasks and moved
> our bedding into the shelter and slept there. When it was bad we took it in
> turns to sleep. On the opposite side of the road to our house lived the coal
> man who had two big horses and we all took turns to keep watch. The main
> problem apart from the bombs was shrapnel from the anti-aircraft shells which,

after exploding, fell to the ground – jagged pieces of metal up to 10 inches long. They could cause a very bad injury if they hit you. Our nearest bomb was about 200 yards away. It demolished 3 houses and badly damaged the two on either side. Some of the people had gone to spend the night in one of the deep underground stations and some were in the shelters. Neighbours and the rescue service dug those who still remained in the houses out. They were injured, but nobody died. It was the most awful mess. We lost our front windows and a lot of plaster came down from the bedroom ceilings and shrapnel came through the roof on to the beds. More people were going to the tube stations each night or stayed where they felt safest – under a heavy kitchen table, or in the cupboard under the stairs, a cellar if you had one, or a shelter like ours. You had to tell the warden where you were so they knew where to look for you if you got a direct hit. Most important was your shelter bag – everybody had one – which contained your rent book, ration books, identity cards, photos of the family, birth and marriage certificates and any special keepsake. And most important – the Insurance Policies! Even very poor people paid insurance, 1 penny per week for each child and 2 pence each for Mum and Dad. No Londoner would let any member of their family have a pauper's funeral. This bag was taken everywhere at this time.

It was a fact that although you were up most of the night, perhaps only getting 1 or 2 hours sleep, nobody thought to stay home. When the 'all-clear' sounded, as daylight came, you had a wash and put on your day clothes, got ready and went to work. Being so close to the gas works, the Shell-mex depot (one of the largest petrol depots in London), the Fulham power stations and behind all of them the railway and the river Thames, we certainly got our share of bombing. A big problem was when the main water or gas pipes were hit, leaving everyone without gas or water for cooking, etc. Uncle Bill got a big tin bucket and knocked holes in the bottom, stood it on two bricks and lit a fire in it. We always kept buckets and saucepans full of water, so we were able to make tea on the fire. We could only have the fire in daylight. As Autumn came on, if the weather was bad with fog or rain, it was great, as the bombers could not come so we got a night in bed.

When you see anything on TV about the London blitz, they always show the city of London burning, with hose pipes and firemen everywhere and maybe a big hole in the ground with a bus in it. Well, it wasn't the only place. That same night (the Sunday after Christmas) we, in Fulham, had many hundreds of incendiary bombs. They were 12 inch cylinders and I think about one hundred were packed in a container which the plane dropped. When the container hit a hard surface such as a road or a roof, it burst and showered the bombs everywhere and where they fell they started burning. If you got to them quickly with a shovel of sand or earth or pumped some water on it they were extinguished. The difficulty was that when they fell on a roof, you could go up a ladder and pull them off into the garden with a rake but once the roof caught fire you could do nothing.[18]

About this time, disparities in the air raid protection for different levels of British society began to emerge. Ordinary people were dependent on the public shelters, their Anderson shelters if they had one, cellars, cupboards under the stairs or even beneath the dining room table. The Underground stations were wet, damp and smelly with no toilet facilities or washrooms. These conditions were a far cry from the furnished shelters beneath the Dorchester or Savoy hotels where the senior civil servants, politicians and aristocracy went during air raids, few of them paying guests of the hotel. Those more fortunate to have motor vehicles (and a petrol ration) were also able to leave the cities at any time. Churchill decided that the reinforced rooms of 10 Downing Street were not safe and he moved to the Annexe at Storey Gate. There was also a purpose-built shelter at Dollis Hill for the War Cabinet (which was only used once) and Churchill regularly withdrew to countryside retreats such as Chequers, where his whole family congregated at weekends. Believing that Chequers was too well known to the Germans and therefore a likely target, Churchill and his entourage started using Ditchley House instead whenever there was a full moon.

On 14 September, to highlight the plight of the people of Stepney in the East End, a communist local councillor organised fifty working-class people, including a group of what *Time* magazine called 'ill-clad children', to charge into the Savoy Hotel. With the help of sympathetic staff, the group quickly located and occupied the air raid shelter, making a statement that if it was good enough for the rich, it was good enough for the Stepney workers and their families. The next day, the press was full of stories about this audacious occupation of the Savoy Hotel shelter and the terrible conditions of the air raid shelters in Stepney.

After Black Saturday, German bombs began to fall all over London. A visitor to central London recorded the scenes:

Arrived at London at 9.30am. A huge hole at Waterloo made it impossible to get out the ordinary way. Went down towards Lambeth Bridge. Terrific damage in St. Thomas' Hospital. Thought of the nurses there.

A hole in the Archbishops Wall at Lambeth Palace. Walked up Millbank and passed the Houses of Parliament. All seemed well there. Whitehall looking shabby and many of the Government offices bombed out.

... Walked along the Mall. Some of the embassies bombed out and at Buckingham Palace a large band playing. Half the windows there patched up with cardboard. Walked through Green Park into Piccadilly. Great destruction in Piccadilly. Not as much destruction in Oxford St. as I had expected to see.

In New Oxford St. the destruction tremendous. Craters everywhere making the streets smelly.

How bravely the shops carry on. Went into St. Mary Woolnoth and heard an address from Professor Cromstead on 'What Christ means to me'. The lovely playing of 'He that shall endure to the end'.

Walked over London Bridge and Tower Bridge. Not much destruction in the docks. The Tower hit at one corner. Pudding Lane where the Great Fire broke out again in ruins. Shall we rebuild as worthily as they did? The Monument to the Great Fire standing there. Went into St. Paul's. The majestic old Cathedral with the round ... altar. Yet it seemed immensely ... and quiet.

Edward said it will be hard to picture a Christmas tree without and within.

Went into Gammages. A huge 500 lb bomb ... from the neighbourhood. Did a little shopping in Gammages.

Went on the Underground. The spaces marked for sleepers on the platform. A cruel smell and vile air. What sights. Remember them. The last thing I saw was an exhibition in Charing Cross of local prints. The lovely flowers. Ah! brave old city. But how much more can it stand?[19]

The widespread bombing inflicted the misery of homelessness on those bombed out of their homes. Nineteen days after the first attack, 25,000 people were homeless and being cared for in rest centres in the London region, with 14,000 of these being in the borough of the London County Council. The burden of helping the homeless fell on local councils, which were completely unprepared for the demands for food, shelter and clothing and the few rest centres that existed were quickly swamped by people. Unexploded bombs or even the threat of them were responsible for nearly a third of the homeless people and others had been forced to leave their homes when infrastructure such as gas and water and electricity services was damaged or destroyed. These persons were not eligible for help from air raid distress funds as they had not actually lost their homes and belongings. The rate at which unexploded bombs were reported often far exceeded the rate at which they were made safe by the Army's bomb disposal squads and by 27 November 1940, there were more than 3,000 unexploded bombs awaiting disposal in London.

The destruction and damage of houses, exacerbated by the effects of unexploded bombs, rapidly created a host of social problems. The most urgent issue in the early days of the raids was the poor condition of the rest centres themselves, which had to be resolved before the next problem of rehousing the homeless could be tackled.[20] The rest centres were usually located in schools, although all types of buildings were used. Proper meals were not provided and children and adults were forced to subsist on bread, margarine, potted meat and corned beef, jam, biscuits and tea, varied only by a serving of soup. There was no bedding apart from a few blankets and there were few beds or even chairs to accommodate the distressed people, who often arrived clad only in night clothes, neighbours' coats or rugs. Washing facilities were generally primitive and inadequate.

At one rest centre, an elementary school in Stepney, a Red Cross volunteer recorded the scene:

> At night the floor was crowded with people lying on blankets, mattresses and bundles of clothing. In the light of dimmed hurricane lamps, some 200 to 300 homeless people had the use of ten pails and coal scuttles as lavatories. By the middle of the night these containers ... overflow so that, as the night advances, urine and faeces spread in ever-increasing volume over the floor. The space is narrow so that whoever enters inevitably steps in the sewage and carries it on his shoes all over the building ... The containers are not emptied until 8 a.m. By dawn the stench ... but I leave this to your imagination. Seven basins were available for these people to wash in; no soap, no towels. Water was heated over coals, drinking water kept in zinc baths.[21]

Although Churchill and other commentators had warned in the 1930s of the potential civilian casualties from air raids, few preparations had been made by successive governments other than for the construction of air raid shelters. The council rest centres were only supposed to give temporary shelter and refreshments to the victims of bombs before they returned home. The advent of large numbers of homeless people requiring accommodation for weeks on end was unprecedented but the councils did what they could, dispensing blankets, corned beef sandwiches and endless cups of tea. Each night of air raids produced a new influx of people needing shelter and, as more parts of London were bombed, the homeless problem became widespread.

Before the war, the government had tried to estimate the number of homes that would be lost and figures varied considerably. Given that the number of houses destroyed would not be known until the war was over, a compensation scheme was introduced on 6 June 1940 which promised some compensation after the war based on the economic situation at the time, available funds and the total number of houses lost. In order to meet urgent cases of need, arrangements were made through the newly created National Assistance Board to make advance compensation payments to replace lost clothing and furniture for those who qualified:

> Advances in respect of furniture will be made where the total income of the claimant's household does not exceed £400 a year, and in respect of clothing where the total income of the claimant docs not exceed £250 a year if there are no dependants or £400 a year if there are dependants. An advance in respect of furniture will be made up to £50 or the amount of the damage, whichever is the less. An advance in respect of clothing will be made up to the amount of the damage or £10 where there are no dependants, £20 where one dependant, or £30 where more than one dependant, has also suffered damage.[22]

This scheme provided some relief for the homeless who qualified but many missed out and there was some swindling of the scheme as people who had lost their homes often had no means of identification, which was taken advantage of by some unscrupulous individuals.

A month after the Blitz began, in a speech to the House of Commons, Churchill claimed that people were saying, 'We can take it!' and that he had been surprised by the high morale of the people he met while visiting bomb-damaged areas in person.[23] Other people were not so convinced: some council social workers reported a deterioration in civilian morale and the emergence of a more desperate counter-slogan, 'This must stop at all costs!'[24] As the Blitz bombing rose to a crescendo in September and October, Churchill instigated the Night Air Defence Committee in October, which he chaired, to better co-ordinate the actions of the services and authorities.

Churchill visited the city of Bristol on a morale-boosting visit the day after a Good Friday raid of 11 April 1941 in which 180 were killed. School children were gathered up from the local schools and given flags and banners to wave.

Newsreels of the day showed cheerful, flag-waving crowds but his presence caused some resentment:

> There was such hostility from some of the women who lived in John Street where they'd lost friends and relatives that one of the women went and snatched things away ... She was snatching flags and when Churchill actually turned up, the women turned on him, became very hostile and started booing and shouting abuse at him.
>
> Not only were they very tired, not only were they fed up with the bombing but they were also very, very hungry ... People couldn't bottle it up any more and Churchill was the focal point. There was also a great deal of bad feeling against some of the officials. There were suggestions that there was a lot of black marketing going on. They were the epitome – they looked content. But look at us! We're down on our uppers! That's what came out at that demonstration.[25]

The hostile reception given to Churchill was also mentioned in the diaries of other civilians so the newsreel footage of cheering crowds on Churchill's visit to Bristol did not present the complete picture. Averell Harriman, who accompanied Churchill, was moved to make an anonymous donation to the City of Bristol, which was acknowledged by Clementine Churchill.[26]

Even Buckingham Palace and St Paul's Cathedral were hit. Firefighters became exhausted and women were drafted in to assist where they could to help with the co-ordination of brigades:

> Women were so used to broken nights with babies that they could cope with the nights of raids and the men simply couldn't stand it. They were dropping on their feet with tiredness but the women weren't.
>
> In the end women did everything – driving the ambulances, driving all cars, doing all the hose-winding up at the end and all the telephone work. The only thing they didn't do was actually fight the fires. Where it took three men, it would have taken at least five women to hold a fully laden hose. And so that was the only thing we didn't do. Every little fire station had three women allotted to them. The women would say to me: 'I'm sitting under the table and my last appliance has gone out. What am I to do? Will you send me another fire engine?' There were bombs raining down. They were terribly brave. I'd say: 'I just haven't got one.'
>
> I remember one night when I was on duty and the sky was so bright you could read a newspaper in the yard of Lambeth Headquarters. Little tiny

specks of molten fire were coming down. Churchill kept on ringing up the Chief Fire Officer saying: 'Whatever happens, you must save St Paul's! St Paul's must be saved!' There wasn't a single fire engine left anywhere to go and then the Almighty stepped in and changed the wind. I met Churchill afterwards and reminded him.[27]

As the RAF provided the only way to hit back at Germany, Churchill was concerned that the numbers of bomber aircraft in the raids be increased at a time when fighter planes needed to be built to continue to protect Britain:

On no account should the limited Bomber force be diverted from accurate bombing of military objectives reaching far into Germany. But is it not possible to organise a Second Line bomber Force which, especially in the dark of the moon, would discharge bombs from a considerable and safe height upon nearest large built-up areas of Germany which contain military targets in abundance? The Ruhr of course is obviously indicated. The object would be to find easy targets, short runs and safe conditions.[28]

At a War Cabinet meeting on 30 October, Churchill continued this line of thought, saying that whilst 'we should adhere to the rule that our objectives should be military targets, at the same time the civilian population around the target areas must be made to feel the weight of the war'.[29] He regarded this as a somewhat broader interpretation of the current policy and not as any fundamental change. No public announcement on the subject would be made.

The first four months of the Blitz in Britain resulted in 22,000 civilian deaths and 250,000 people being made homeless. Churchill spoke of the forbearance of the general public, 'the courage, the unconquerable grit and stamina of the English'. But they had no choice other than to spend a cold night shivering in air raid shelters fearful of a bomb landing nearby at any time.

The British public also had to bear the brunt of the war in terms of taxation and rationing. Rationing was extended in January 1941 to include pork and offals for 'poor people', the entire meat ration being reduced to 1s 6d a week, but extra cheese was provided.[30] Two months later, the scheme was extended to include preserves such as jam and marmalade and tinned meats and fish.[31]

Private industries and individuals were affected by the increases in direct and indirect taxes. A married man with two children earning £5,000 before the war saw his tax increase from £1,536 to £2,356. Businesses that increased their profit over pre-war levels were required to pay this increase in its entirety as tax.

There was no escape in the simple pleasures of life. The price of a pack of cigarettes increased by 50 per cent, as did the price of a pint of beer (and it was diluted). Spirits were increased in price by 25 per cent and a new purchase tax on clothes, hardware and furniture was introduced.[32]

The night-time air raids ended at the start of 1941 and from then on there were mainly daylight raids until the end of May, when the majority of the German air fleets were redeployed for the invasion of Russia. It was Hitler's decision to invade Russia that ended the purgatory of the Blitz. The decision by Churchill to bomb Berlin and the subsequent retaliation ordered by Hitler on London cost many British civilians their lives. The last raid on 1 May saw nearly 1,500 people killed but marked the end of the first Battle of London.[33]

Bombing Casualties in Britain 1940–41

Year	Dead	Seriously Injured (admitted to hospital)
1940	23,767	30,529
1941	19,918	21,165

A further 100,000 were slightly injured requiring first aid treatment and 20 per cent of these needed hospitalisation.[34]

The RAF continued its night-time raids on Germany during the Blitz but was hampered by a lack of heavy bombers and navigation problems. In a thirteen-month period to June 1941, the RAF dropped fewer than 30,000 tons of bombs compared with the Luftwaffe's more than 57,000 tons on Britain.[35] Despite a focus on German oil production facilities, the RAF was frequently switched to other targets such as the Channel ports, U-boat bases, towns and transportation hubs with dramatically less impact on German civilians.

The disposition of the French fleet continued to be a major concern of Churchill's, as was the newly installed Vichy government. Following Oran, an operation was planned against the Atlantic port of Dakar (French West Africa). De Gaulle, the unilaterally declared representative of Free France by Churchill, wanted to establish a Free French movement in the West African French colonies. Several colonies had already declared for de Gaulle – Chad Congo, Ubangi and distant New Caledonia. De Gaulle believed he would be their liberator and that the poorly defended colonies were sufficiently distant from France to more than likely declare their loyalty to Free France on his arrival. Churchill supported this venture in order to foment trouble in the colonies between the Free French and Vichy France and committed a naval task force to Dakar, running a further risk by denuding part of the home fleet when Britain was faced by invasion. The War Cabinet was consulted and the attack (Operation Menace) approved on 13 August. However, word of the operation had leaked to Vichy France, which sent a force of cruisers to reinforce Dakar that managed to evade the British ships sent to intercept them en route. The British Chiefs of Staff then proposed an alternative plan to the proposed direct approach by landing at Duala and entering Chad to take Dakar from the landward side. De Gaulle insisted on the original plan being kept as he expected to be welcomed with open arms. The British task force arrived off Dakar on 23 September 1940 but, unlike at Oran, this time the Vichy French were ready for the Royal Navy. The battleship *Richlieu* and the Dakar fortress guns opened fire on the British warships. The defenders refused to meet with de Gaulle, and when troops were landed at nearby Rufisque they had to be evacuated the same day. The entire expedition was abandoned and the British fleet withdrew twenty-four hours later.

5

GREEK DRAMA

Having survived and won the aerial Battle of Britain, the invasion threat to Britain was largely averted. Britain was still in the process of re-equipping and increasing the size of its armed forces as rapidly as possible. The strategic questions for Churchill were how to direct the war towards victory and what would Germany's next move be? Churchill had ordered the bombing of German cities by the RAF, which for the foreseeable future was the only way to carry the war to Germany. Hitler's attention had already turned back to the east and the *lebensraum* that Russia offered. At the OKW conference of 21 July, even before the Battle of Britain had commenced, Hitler had ordered planning to begin for the invasion of Russia.[1] Churchill had some knowledge of these plans from the decrypted Ultra signals of the Luftwaffe in particular, which he was regularly receiving. These indicated the transfer of many front-line units away from the English Channel. While not providing incontrovertible proof of German plans, they provided a good indication of the objective of the next German campaign.

However, it was the Italians that took the initiative and opened the next theatre of the war. Before the armistice with France was signed, Hitler and Mussolini met on 19 June and Mussolini's expectations of getting the spoils of war such as Tunisia in North Africa were dashed by Hitler's strategy of creating Vichy France. Having gained nothing from entering the war except concessions in East Africa and territory captured in France which included the city of Nice when the French colonies affirmed their allegiance to Vichy France and Pétain on 29 June, Mussolini ordered the invasion of Egypt in order to at least gain Egypt and the Suez Canal as a measure of compensation. Wavell's pre-emptive raids were no longer considered a sufficient deterrence.

After the invasion of Somaliland and several frontier skirmishes, on 13 September the Italians entered Egypt from Libya, beginning the North African Desert Campaign. Churchill had met with General Wavell on 8 August and had not been impressed by him, so much so that Churchill afterwards wrote a directive detailing precisely how Wavell should deploy his forces in the Middle East as though Churchill were the Commander-in-Chief himself. Another British evacuation of 3,000 men had taken place from Somaliland (East Africa) the previous month when 25,000 Italian troops had invaded the country; this had irked Churchill at the time but he later recognised that the evacuation was 'strategically convenient'.[2] Churchill was determined to resist the potential Italian threat to Britain's Middle East interests with whatever forces could be collected together. For Britain, the Middle East was a strategically important communications hub for the British Empire in the Far East via the Suez Canal. It was also a vital source of oil required by its economy and the armed forces, especially the Royal Navy following Churchill's decision in the First World War as First Lord of the Admiralty to change to oil-fired boilers for warships rather than coal. Churchill had enthusiastically supported the move towards powering Royal Navy ships with oil rather than coal as larger and faster ships could be built that were capable of being replenished at sea. However, this change could only be made if Britain had a secure supply of oil that was not threatened by hostile countries. Rather than buy oil from Royal Dutch Shell, Churchill was instrumental in the British government in 1914 taking a 51 per cent share in the Anglo-Persian Oil Company (APOC) to guarantee future supplies. Turkey controlled Mesopotamia (modern-day Iraq), where there were further oilfields as yet undiscovered; a concession for exploration was given to the Turkish Petroleum Company, which was 50 per cent owned by the APOC. With the break-up of the Turkish Ottoman Empire after the First World War, Britain acquired a mandate over Mesopotamia, where oil was eventually found in 1927. Even with Iraq's independence in 1933, the British still had direct interests in oil in both Persia and Iraq. Churchill and the British at this point in the war were therefore very sensitive about any threat to their oil supply from Germany.

In sending reinforcements to Egypt that included the Australian 6th Infantry Division from Singapore to replace the 4th Indian Division, which was redeployed to East Africa in December, Churchill gambled that the German invasion of Britain would be postponed or cancelled. The War Cabinet also approved the transfer of three tank regiments from Britain's weak Home Army to Egypt on 26 August. The convoy route through the Mediterranean was thought to be too risky and it was decided to send the convoy via South Africa, much to Churchill's displeasure as he believed the dangers in the Mediterranean were much exaggerated.[3]

In the ensuing desert campaign, conducted brilliantly by General Wavell, two Allied divisions including the 7th Armoured Division, routed twelve Italian and two Libyan divisions, and by February 1941 had forced them back across 500 miles of Libyan desert to El Agheila. An advance on Tripoli was considered, but, with the despatch of the 7th Australian Division and an Indian brigade from Wavell's meagre reserves to Syria, the Desert Army was not strong enough to continue the advance. Churchill paid particularly close attention to the North African campaign at this time because of its strategic importance and as it was the only place that British troops were in action.

In looking eastwards to Russia, Hitler needed to cement relationships with other countries bordering Russia and obtain access to a secure supply of oil. Rumania became the focus of Germany's attentions and was forced to cede vast tracts of land to its neighbours under both German and Russian pressure. In July 1940, Bessarabia and Northern Bukinova were ceded to Russia and the Ukraine. On 30 August, Northern Transylvania was lost to Hungary through German and Italian mediation. A month later, further territory was ceded, this time to Bulgaria. After these territorial losses, the power of King Carol was considerably weakened and eventually he was forced to abdicate in favour of his son. Subsequently, a fascist government under General Ion Antonescu came into being on 4 September. German troops moved into Rumania from 8 October, giving Germany access to the vital oilfields at Ploesti.

However, once again it would be the Italians that initiated another conflict – this time to widen the war on the European Continent. On 28 October, Italy invaded Greece from Albania, much to the displeasure of Hitler who was not informed of Italy's intentions. Mussolini had begun to resent being a junior partner in the alliance and had not been informed about the German entry into Rumania; the fact that other countries and not Italy were being given new territories by Germany for nothing continued to rankle considerably with Mussolini.

Greece had a large merchant navy fleet and in 1940 was courted by both Germany and Britain. In September, a trade agreement was signed with Germany. An alliance had been made with England in May 1939 after the occupation of Czechoslovakia that promised Greece aid in the event of being invaded. The Italians gambled that the Greeks would submit to the terms of an ultimatum and were not expecting armed resistance when they invaded. The Greek Army had not mobilised and the only defenders were a few border forces.

In response to an urgent appeal from the Greek government following the Italian invasion, at the Defence Committee meeting on 31 October the British decided to act. The despatch of a squadron of Blenheim bombers from the meagre forces in Egypt was approved and ordered to proceed to Eleusis Airport near Athens.[4] The RAF Commander in the Middle East (Air Chief Marshal Longmore) lamented in a telegram to Portal that it had become 'politically absolutely essential to send a token force to Greece at the expense of my forces here'.[5] On 1 November, a British battalion occupied Suda Bay in Crete to deny the island to the Axis and to build a refuelling base for the Royal Navy, while other troops were to occupy the island of Lemnos in the Northern Aegean. On 3 November, the first British troops and aircraft arrived in Greece.

Hitler stated on 31 October that any extension of the war in the Balkans was to be avoided, but on 12 November he ordered staff to prepare plans for the invasion of Greece in response to the arrival of British aircraft in Greece.[6]

The German Field Marshal Fedor von Bock, convalescing in hospital, wrote:

> The Führer called, sat half an hour at my bedside, and was very friendly and concerned. The overall situation was covered in detail. He is furious at Italy's escapade in Greece … The ultimate – and highly undesirable – outcome is that the Rumanian oil fields will be threatened by the British air force units from Salonika. This danger is so great that it may oblige us to take countermeasures.[7]

Hitler had only just contrived diplomatically to get access to the Rumanian Ploesti oilfields and now these were threatened by the arrival of British aircraft in Greece; the attack by Italy would also drive Greece further into the hands of the British.

Hitler wrote to Mussolini on 20 November 1940, his anger evident at the dictator's failure to keep the peace in the Balkans. Among other things, he stated:

> I wanted, above all, to ask you to postpone the operation until a more favourable season, in any case until after the presidential election in America. In any event, I wanted to ask you not to undertake this action without previously

carrying out a blitzkrieg operation on Crete. For this purpose I intended to make practical suggestions regarding the employment of a parachute and of an airborne division.[8]

By the end of November, however, the Greeks had managed to contain the Italian invasion and were able to go on the offensive, driving back the Italian troops. One woman wrote of these events, 'What a lovely spot of cheering news from the Mediterranean! Now perhaps we shall be getting a real move on. Who wants Italy as an ally anyway?'[9]

The lack of progress by the Italians prompted widespread derision towards them, such as this comment from a housewife in England:

November 26th 1940
    The Italians have been kept well on the run now and have been pretty well hustled out of Albania. Lovely! The old 1938 joke is coming true:
    Hitler to Chamberlain: 'I have Italy on my side this time.'
    Chamberlain to Hitler: 'Quite right too. We had them last time.'

Hitler's response to the arrival of British aircraft was Directive No. 20 (dated 13 December 1940) which outlined the future Greek campaign, Operation Marita, as a build-up of forces in Rumania before moving them across Bulgaria to occupy the northern coast of the Aegean and the rest of mainland Greece if necessary. Planning for Operation Marita went ahead in tandem with the extensive planning for Barbarossa, while simultaneously, diplomatic initiatives were in progress in order to achieve Hitler's goals without military action.

Britain ultimately decided to send three squadrons of Blenheims and two of Gloster Gladiator fighters, even though this reduced the aircraft available for Wavell in the Libyan campaign.[10] Hampered by a lack of suitable aerodromes and forbidden by the Greeks to deploy inland near Salonika so as not to antagonise the Germans, air bases had to be set up near Athens, which meant long flights to the Albanian front.

The RAF squadrons operated against Italian ports and supply lines, enjoying initial success until this was tempered by the deteriorating winter weather and the appearance of more numerous modern enemy fighters. All five RAF squadrons had arrived in Greece by the end of the year.

After twelve months of war, British orders being placed in the United States with the urgent need for Britain to rearm and re-equip its armed forces had caused the rapid reduction of Britain's gold reserves. In August, the Treasury warned that Britain, having also taken over France's orders in the United States, was in danger of exhausting its reserves altogether by the end of the year. Since January, Britain's gold reserves had declined from £525 million to £290 million, with many orders still being produced and unpaid for.[11] Churchill put off contacting the Americans until the result of the November presidential elections was known, with Roosevelt being returned for an unprecedented third term. On 8 December, Churchill finally sent a telegram informing Roosevelt of Britain's imminent bankruptcy: 'It is our British duty in the common interest, as also for our own survival, to hold the front and grapple with the Nazi power until the preparations of the United States are complete.'[12]

Roosevelt did not reply directly but the US Treasury demanded a payment that was due. A shipment of gold was organised to be loaded on to an American warship in South Africa, which was duly done on Christmas Day. Refreshed after a two-week holiday, Roosevelt had been considering Britain's problem and at a press conference on 16 December outlined his plans to lend or lease war material to certain countries. The Treasury Secretary, Henry Morgenthau, was charged by Roosevelt to draw up the legislation and get it through Congress. Britain was then forced by the Americans to sell some of its assets in the United States to Americans at knockdown prices in order to convince Congress of its financial plight. The Americans, particularly Morgenthau, believed the British were not stating their true worth and were 'crying poor'. Britain was in no position to refuse the American demands and Roosevelt and Morgenthau certainly took advantage of Britain's plight, using British orders and payments to kick-start American armament and heavy industrial manufacturing. In one of his fireside chat radio broadcasts to America, Roosevelt explained the legislation to the public: the United States would become the 'arsenal of democracy' to supply substantial aid packages to Britain, Greece and China that Roosevelt believed would ensure that Germany and Italy could not win the war. Access to this arsenal had not been free and Britain would finish the war with huge debts to America; the final post-war loan for retained Lend-Lease items was not repaid until 2006.

As the legislation was drawn up, Roosevelt sent Harry Hopkins, a close advisor, to report on British morale and the country's immediate requirements. Hopkins carried a message from Roosevelt to Churchill to the effect that the President was determined that they would win the war and would do whatever was required to see this achieved.[13] On meeting Hopkins on his arrival on 10 January, in the course of general conversation about the war, Churchill admitted that Greece was lost but would be reinforced anyway.[14] With the

Italians not yet defeated, this new commitment of forces would result in a dangerous weakening of the position in Egypt. Only the previous day, the Defence Committee had agreed to support Greece: 'It was of the first importance from the political point of view that we should do everything by hook or crook to send at once to Greece the fullest support within our power.'[15]

The Chiefs of Staff accordingly sent the following signal to all Commanders-in-Chief:

> His Majesty's Government have decided that it is essential to afford the Greeks the maximum possible assistance with the object of ensuring they resist German demands by force. The extent and effectiveness of our aid to Greece will be a determining factor in the attitude of Turkey and will influence the USA and Russia. This decision means that Greece must have priority over all operations in the Middle East once Tobruk is taken because help for the Greeks must, in the first instance at any rate, come almost entirely from you.[16]

British strategy in the Balkans had several objectives. Firstly, Britain wanted to create diplomatically a Balkan Front or bloc against Germany composed of Turkey, Greece, Yugoslavia and Bulgaria. Turkey, because of the size of its army, was considered the most important potential ally. Secondly, aid and troops would be given to Greece so that it could resist German advances as British interests in the Mediterranean and North Africa would be further threatened if Germany had access to the Greek ports and islands. The British Chiefs of Staff were also concerned about the possible German occupation of Turkey and the ability of Germany to thrust from there into the Middle East through Syria and Palestine.[17] Thirdly, Britain was particularly concerned about world public opinion should Britain fail to support Greece, the cradle of democracy, as it had pledged to do so in March 1939. Lastly, the public and material support of the United States was essential if Britain was to continue the war and emerge victorious; the Lend-Lease Bill was aimed squarely at ensuring Britain's survival.

These objectives can be seen in the various War Cabinet and Defence Committee meetings over the first tense three months of 1941. At a Defence Committee meeting in mid January, Churchill stated:

> We must take this course to show the world and our own people that we were helping Greece and to show Turkey that we stood by our friends.

We wanted Turkey to come into the war and hoped that Yugoslavia might join us. Russia might then be ready to move though fear would regulate their action …

… The reaction of US opinion had been extremely favourable and the President was thinking of aid to us in the largest terms. We did not need, at present, US troops, in fact, it would be a mistake to use shipping to transport them.[18]

January and February saw extensive diplomatic negotiations between the Balkan countries and Britain and Germany. Roosevelt even sent another personal emissary, Colonel Donovan again, to talk with the leaders of each country and report back to him. Donovan carried a message from Roosevelt that stressed America's commitment to the defeat of the Axis and that Britain was receiving the fullest moral and material support. Substantial aid under Lend-Lease was also promised to Greece.[19] Churchill duly sent a note of thanks to Donovan for his efforts.[20]

General Wavell was sent from the Middle East to liaise with the Greeks and the Greek President Metaxas during the period of 13–15 January but preliminary discussions about the stationing of more British troops in Greece revealed that the Greeks did not want them, primarily so as not to antagonise Germany. This meant that any troops sent in response to any German aggression would have to come from North Africa and would be unable to arrive in time to offer much support to Greece.[21] In order to meet any German attacks successfully, British troops needed to be already deployed in Greece.

On 8 February, the Lend-Lease Bill passed through the House of Representatives by 260 to 165 votes and Churchill could see light at the end of the tunnel. A measure of opposition that Roosevelt faced in getting the Bill through can be seen in the number of the bill: HR 1776, the year of America's independence from Britain. Churchill made a radio broadcast aimed at further influencing American public opinion the next day just as Hopkins was leaving England to report to Roosevelt:

Put your confidence in us. Give us your faith and your blessing, and under Providence all will be well. We shall not fail or falter; we shall not weaken or tire. Neither the sudden shock of battle nor the long-drawn trials of vigilance and exertion will wear us down. Give us the tools and we will finish the job.[22]

All previous British attempts aimed at getting Turkey into the war on Britain's side were then dashed by a telegram from the Turkish President refusing a British offer of stationing ten squadrons of aircraft there (aircraft that the British did not in any case possess).[23] The offer was rejected on the basis that, if accepted, the presence of British troops would be tantamount to a declaration of war on Germany.[24] Now it became essential that if British troops were going to be deployed anywhere in the Balkans, they should be to Greece. Wavell certainly did not have enough forces or equipment to spare to reinforce both Greece and Turkey.

A telegram was duly sent to General Wavell advising of the Turkish refusal and the need for Greece to accept British troops. The telegram noted in a summary of the general situation that the first condition was a 'very favourable [development] in supply of material from US'– a reference to the passage of the Lend-Lease Act that would benefit both Britain and Greece.[25] However, once again, the Axis took the initiative. German troops began to infiltrate Bulgaria on 11 February via Rumania and the growing presence of so many German troops in the region enabled further German diplomatic pressure to be put on Turkey and Greece. A few days later, Turkey and Bulgaria concluded a peace agreement.

President Metaxas suddenly died on 29 January 1940 and was replaced by General Papagos, with Alexandros Korizis as the new Prime Minister. In early February, a new Greek offensive began in Albania with RAF planes being used in the ground support role to boost the morale of Greek soldiers in the front line rather than concentrating on Italian lines of supply. In a last-ditch attempt to create a Balkan Front and convince Greece to accept British troops, the War Cabinet despatched Eden and John Dill, the Chief of the Imperial General Staff, to the region on 15 February. Churchill still believed that if Greece was attacked by Germany there was a chance Turkey could be convinced to come to Greece's aid. After a conference with Wavell in Cairo to determine exactly what forces were available for Greece without compromising the position in North Africa, Eden and Dill flew to Athens on 22 February for a meeting with Papagos and the Greek government. The Greeks had doubts about the numbers of British troops that could be sent and whether a sound defensive line could even be created but the British were able to convince the Greeks after ten hours of talks that the Germans could be stopped by their combined forces.

In the War Cabinet of 24 February, the despatch of British troops was again debated. With the defeat of the Italians in Libya, Wavell was more confident that the necessary troops could be found without endangering the position in Egypt. Churchill was in favour of the operation:

> He, himself, was in favour of going to the rescue of Greece, one of the results of which might be to bring in Turkey and Yugoslavia, and to force the Germans to bring more troops from Germany. The reaction of the United States would also be favourable.[26]

Churchill also reported that the normally downbeat Wavell approved of the operation, as did Eden and Dill as per their telegrams after the conference in Cairo. Churchill, perhaps wary of being responsible for another Norwegian fiasco, had sent Dill and Eden to the region in order to make the final decision, thus spreading the political risk of any adverse outcome. Eden was well aware of what Churchill wanted from one of his telegrams:

> Do not consider yourselves obligated to a Greek enterprise if in your hearts you feel it will only be another Norwegian fiasco. If no good plan can be made, please say so. But of course you know how valuable success would be.[27]

The Australian Prime Minister, Robert Menzies, was visiting London and was present at this meeting; he expressed reservations about the commitment of Dominion troops to a 'forlorn hope'. Churchill's response was that, 'The enterprise in Greece was an advance position which we could try to hold, without jeopardising our main position.'[28]

The United States was then used as an excuse: 'It was recalled that Colonel Donovan had stressed in a telegram to the President the importance of the formation of a Balkan front. If we now forsook Greece it would have a bad effect in the United States.'[29]

Subject to the approval by the Australian and New Zealand governments, which would be contributing the greater part of the forces destined for Greece, the War Cabinet that evening approved the despatch of troops. Menzies recorded in his diary that the entire Greek question was settled in forty-five minutes after Churchill announced he was in favour of the project and it would have only been ten minutes if Menzies had not raised some issues. Menzies wondered whether the Cabinet was composed of ministers of great clarity of mind and directness or who were yes-men to Churchill. Later in April Menzies wrote, 'Winston is a dictator; he cannot be overruled, and his colleagues fear him. The people have set him up as something little less than

God, and his power is therefore terrific.' While this comment ignores the fact that this issue had been discussed at many previous meetings, this vignette does give an outsider's insight into Churchill's conduct of the War Cabinet meetings to support those left to us by the likes of John Colville, a Private Secretary to Churchill, whose secret diary was initially critical of Churchill and the Cabinet:

> The PM does not help the Government machine to run smoothly and his inconsiderate treatment of the Service Departments would cause trouble were it not for the great personal loyalty of the Service Ministers to himself. He supplies drive and initiative but he often meddles ...

A New Zealand division and an Australian division from North Africa were to be sent to Greece immediately along with a British armoured brigade and support troops; further troops were designated as follow-up forces. Given that Commonwealth troops made up the bulk of the troops, code-named Lustre Force, the Australians pressed for an Anzac commander but were refused, command being given to General Wilson by Wavell.

Three days later, the Australian government gave a qualified approval to the operation, provided that evacuation plans be made before the operation started. The War Cabinet was still hoping that Turkey would come to Greece's assistance with its twenty-seven divisions in the Thrace region when the Germans invaded.[30] The Chiefs of Staff concluded, 'Finally, from a political point of view, failure to help this small nation putting up a gallant fight against one aggressor and willing to defy another would have grave effect on public opinion throughout the world and particularly in United States.'[31]

On the Home Front, the prospect of the war widening further by involving the Balkans was not well received by everyone:

> Feb 14th 1941
> With everybody fighting and killing each other, and sinking each other's ships, and crops not getting planted, and the labour shortage everywhere due to men being soldiers instead of growing soon – how long will there be famine over the world? Whole countrysides, it is said, are laying waste in China through the war there, and there is the wasted farm land in Europe. Men cannot fish in the plentifully stocked sea because of mines and U-boats – such senseless, useless waste. Food and beauty for all in this world, and yet soon none will have the first and care about the second – so wrong and twisted.[32]

German engineers began the construction of pontoon bridges across the River Danube in Bulgaria from 28 February and on 1 March Bulgaria signed the Tripartite agreement with Germany; German troops officially entered the country a day later. As Bulgaria was now a German ally and Turkey and Bulgaria had a peace agreement, it was unlikely that Germany was going to attack Turkey and Greece's position was now very exposed. In defiance, the Greek Prime Minister, Korizis, made a radio broadcast to America: 'We are indifferent to the threat and with the help of the great Allies and the sympathy of powerful friends across the sea, we will go on to victory.'[33]

Eden and Dill then returned to Athens for further talks and, after a long debate over several days, an agreement was finally signed with the Greeks on 4 March for the deployment of British troops.

It was suggested that Menzies get the views of the Australian commander in the Middle East, General Blamey, on the proposed Greek operation but a draft telegram was never sent. Wavell claimed he had the support of the Australian and New Zealand commanders but this was not the case. Menzies had met briefly with Wavell in Egypt on his way to England on 13 February and an outline of the operation was discussed. Blamey then met with Wavell on 18 February and was told that the plan had already been discussed with Menzies.[34]

As the Australian troops embarked on 5 March, the difficulties of the planned operation increased. Certain Greek Army units had not redeployed to the proposed defensive positions on the Aliakmon Line as previously agreed and the determination of Churchill to proceed with another venture (Operation Mandibles, the seizure of the Dodecanese Islands) meant there would be fewer British aircraft available for support in the event of a German attack. The Germans had also mined the Suez Canal, forcing its closure and thus preventing the passage of troopships needed for Greece, so that the initial troops for Greece had to be transported by warship from Egypt. There were also concerns that the arriving Anzac troops would not be able to reach their defensive positions on the Aliakmon Line before the Germans attacked and, to make matters worse, there were reports of German troops arriving in Libya in as yet unknown strength. The War Cabinet agreed to do nothing but wait for further information from Eden and Dill.

Blamey advised his Prime Minister, Menzies, in a letter on 5 March that it was the Australians and New Zealanders that were supplying all the infantry and that the British were only providing an armoured brigade and rear echelon troops. He further informed Menzies that he had grave doubts about the whole venture.

In the War Cabinet meeting in London next day, Menzies complained that he had recommended to the Australian War Cabinet that the operation proceed and now that the situation had worsened he was in a difficult position as it appeared that the whole operation was to take place solely on the basis of written commitments given by the British to the Greeks on 4 March, even though the risks had greatly increased: 'Although it might be true that our position vis-à-vis the United States would be prejudiced if we did not go to the help of Greece, it must be remembered that if we did so and were driven out, the effect on our prestige might be worse.'[35]

Menzies also described the written commitments as embarrassing on the part of Eden and Dill. A meeting was quickly arranged between Blamey, Dill and Wavell in Cairo on 6 March; Blamey later complained that his opinion was not sought, not only on this occasion but also at the previous meeting in February. The New Zealand commander, General Freyberg, also had the same complaint and said that he was merely presented with instructions during his meeting with Wavell.

Again, a decision was deferred until word was received back from Eden, whose telegram was discussed at the War Cabinet meeting on 7 March. Eden, Dill and Wavell, at a meeting the previous day in Cairo, were all in agreement that the operation should proceed; Blamey and Freyberg had also apparently expressed their willingness.[36] Despite the Chiefs of Staff having underestimated the time the Germans needed to reach the Aliakmon Line by one to four days, the decision to proceed was reaffirmed.[37] In recognition of Menzies' concerns at proceeding on the basis of very few facts and only a promise, *noblesse oblige*, Churchill requested an appreciation be prepared to support Menzies' position for the Australian War Council, which he would never receive. The Australian War Council had sent a telegram to Menzies only the previous day warning about the arrival of German troops in North Africa and the British must have had the same information.

British and Commonwealth troops began to land in Greece from 7 March. The Greeks, realising fully the seriousness of the situation, were in no doubt that if they allowed British fighting troops to enter their country, war with Germany was ultimately unavoidable. To their credit, however, they preferred to resist any invader rather than capitulate in the face of overwhelming force. Eden sent Churchill a telegram affirming his views on Greece as both he and the British Ambassador to Greece, Michael Palairet, had been concerned that the British were going to abandon the country:

Collapse of Greece without further effort on our part to save her by intervention on land, after the Libyan victories had, as all the world knows, made
forces available, would be the greatest calamity … No doubt our prestige
will suffer if we are ignominiously ejected but we should presumably escape
the ignominy and in any event to have fought and suffered in Greece would
be less damaging to us than to have left Greece to her fate.[38]

On 9 March, the Italian Army in Albania mounted a new offensive, making
the withdrawal of any Greek troops from that front very difficult and doubtful.
Considerably annoyed at not being consulted and doubtful about the whole
enterprise, Blamey then sent his own appreciation on 10 March to the Australian
War Council in Canberra, concluding, 'Military operation extremely hazardous
in view of the disparity between opposing forces in numbers and training.'[39]

On 11 March, the Lend-Lease Bill, having previously passed through the
Senate by sixty votes to thirty-one, was signed by Roosevelt, who immediately approved large shipments to Britain and Greece. Churchill cabled to
Roosevelt, 'Our blessings from the whole British Empire go out to you and
the American nation for this very present help in time of trouble.'[40]

In a letter to Winant, the new American Ambassador to Britain, on 8 March,
Churchill was more expressive: 'The news about the Bill is a draught of life.'[41]

To Hopkins, Churchill sent a telegram: 'Thank God for your news. The
strain is serious.'

When the details of the Lend-Lease legislation was announced that week
by the world's newspapers, many led with headlines trumpeting Roosevelt's
undeclared war on the Axis countries in Europe.

On 10 March, Churchill cabled Roosevelt with details of the British intentions in Greece but the President was already well aware of the situation as the
arrival of British troops in Athens had been widely reported in the newspapers.
With the German occupation of Bulgaria and Turkey's ambivalent but largely
neutral position, by 5 March the diplomatic pieces were beginning to fall into
place and only the question of Yugoslavia remained unresolved. Churchill
commented in a telegram to Eden, 'We have done our best to promote Balkan
combination against Germany.'[42]

The Germans continued with their preparations and mounted further
diplomatic efforts in Yugoslavia in an effort to make it sign the Tripartite
Pact. Churchill made a desperate appeal to the Yugoslavian government on
22 March but, under increasing pressure as German troops massed in Bulgaria,
on 25 March Prince Paul signed up to the pact, thereby neutralising Yugoslavia

diplomatically vis-à-vis Germany. Yugoslavian sovereignty was guaranteed by Germany, which did not even insist on the passage of its troops through the country. There was widespread internal condemnation of the pact, particularly from the Serbian community. Churchill telegraphed the British Ambassador in Belgrade urging him 'to do anything to reinforce the German trend of sub-jugation of countries and not forget any alternative action'.[43] From London, Churchill requested Leo Amery broadcast a provocative call for the Yugoslav people, already demonstrating against Germany, to resist 'the betrayal of your honour and independence' and prevent ratification of Yugoslavia's adherence to the Axis alliance. Two days later, a coup d'état was made by several Serbian Air Force officers, the pact renounced and the Army mobilised. The newly formed British Special Operations Executive (SOE) under Hugh Dalton played a major part in encouraging the coup. SOE had been working with the main Yugoslav political parties and dissident groups since mid 1940 to encour-age opposition to Germany and acts of sabotage. Churchill later requested an expression of appreciation be sent from the Defence Committee to Dr Dalton, as he was then known, for his activities in Yugoslavia.[44]

In a frank telegram to the acting Prime Minister of Australia, Churchill admitted that the situation a month ago had been bleak and been dictated by *noblesse oblige*, but the coup in Yugoslavia had dramatically improved the situation.[45] America immediately promised substantial aid to Yugoslavia under Lend-Lease provisions, despite having frozen $50 million of Yugoslav credits in America two days previously when the pact was signed. Germany insisted that the Tripartite Pact be honoured, and when this demand was rejected a furious Hitler ordered the invasion of Yugoslavia, code-named Operation Punishment, at the earliest opportunity. After a flurry of last-minute planning and movement of troops, on 6 April Germany simultaneously invaded both Yugoslavia and Greece.

6 April 1941

I wonder if we are so used to dreadful shocks that we are hardening. Today, when we heard news on the wireless of Germany declaring war on Yugoslavia and Greece, there was none of that sick shock we had when we heard of Holland and Belgium being overrun ... Soon it looks as if the whole world will be alight and the prophesised Armageddon upon us all.[46]

German units previously designated for the invasion of Russia had to be moved to Bulgaria to launch their attack into Yugoslavia. The Allied Lustre Force –

a total of 58,000 men – on reaching its positions on the Aliakmon Line found that defensive works by the Greeks had barely commenced. The events in Yugoslavia forced a British armoured regiment to quickly occupy defensive positions in the Vardar Valley on the border with Yugoslavia. The 3rd RTR had been re-equipped after Dunkirk with new A13 tanks when despatched to the Middle East but was forced to exchange them for obsolete A10s, fifty-one of fifty-two of which subsequently broke down in the campaign. Most of the Greek Army was fighting in Albania with only a dozen or so battalions on the Aliakmon Line. Three Greek divisions were defending forward of the Metaxas line near the Bulgarian border in Thrace as Greece did not want to abandon Thessaloniki.

The German forces of nine divisions including two Panzer divisions thrust into Greece from three different directions. The central thrust cut through Yugoslavia westwards before turning south at Dojran to outflank the Metaxas line. Invading southern Yugoslavia, the 9th Panzer Division and a motorised SS division first captured Skopje and then turned south, entering Greece through the Vardar Valley, thus getting behind the Aliakmon Line. With the Greek forces putting up little resistance as well and being continually harassed by German aircraft, which again operated with total air supremacy, the outnumbered Anzac forces had no option but to begin a fighting withdrawal south. Alternative positions at Mount Olympus could not be held and a retreat to Thermopylae began on 15 April. The RAF in Greece was augmented by one extra bomber and Hurricane squadrons but now had to cover Lustre Force while faced with overwhelming numbers of German and Italian fighters.

Yugoslavia capitulated on 15 April and the Greek President suggested that the British forces prepare to re-embark to 'save Greece from devastation'.[47] On 16 April, the decision to evacuate Lustre Force to Crete was made by the Defence Committee.[48] Rudimentary plans for such a possibility had been made at the start of the campaign by both British Army and naval commanders.[49] Meanwhile in North Africa, Rommel's forces had reached Tobruk and the situation there was becoming equally desperate. Somewhat surprisingly in view of the British commitment to Greece, Churchill, in a directive of 18 April, instructed the Middle East Commanders-in-Chief that if there was a clash of priorities between Greece and Libya, priority should be given to Libya rather than the evacuation from Greece.

Evacuations from Greece began on 24 April and continued for five days, the evacuation of 80 per cent of the original force being completed by 30 April. A total of 50,732 men by Royal Navy were embarked including Greeks,

Yugoslavs and some civilians. Some 7,000 men were left behind and more than 10,000 became prisoners. Nearly 900 men were killed, two-thirds being Anzacs, and 1,225 wounded, nearly all Anzacs.

	Killed	Wounded	Prisoners
British	146	87	6,480
RAF	110	45	28
Australian	320	494	2,030
New Zealand	291	599	1,614
Total[50]	**867**	**1,225**	**10,152**

The British corps and divisional commanders were ordered to leave early, so there were few senior officers to organise the beach parties and evacuation, resulting in chaos at some embarkation points. The majority of the evacuated troops were taken to Egypt but a large number went to the island of Crete.

Crete had been occupied since November 1940 by the 14th Infantry Brigade but no preparations had been made for its overall defence. With the arrival of 21,000 men evacuated from Greece with only what weapons they could carry, there was a total of 32,000 men on the island with an additional 10,000 Greek soldiers, but few artillery or anti-aircraft weapons. Wavell was instructed by Churchill to hold Crete at all costs. Wavell delegated command to a reluctant Freyberg, who immediately cabled the New Zealand government asking that the decision to defend the island be reviewed in light of the few aircraft available and the inability of the Royal Navy to prevent any landings. German paratroops began dropping on 20 May and the battle was over in ten days once the Germans captured the vital Maleme airfield and could fly in reinforcements. The German paratroops had no heavy weapons either but could rely on the Luftwaffe as aerial artillery. During the battle, the RAF was forced to withdraw its fighters from Crete, citing inadequate anti-aircraft protection, and from then on could only provide limited fighter support from Egypt. A second evacuation had to be mounted from 27 May and 18,000 men including 1,500 wounded were evacuated to Egypt.

In the Battle of Crete, another 1,742 men were killed, 1,737 wounded and 11,835 taken prisoner, not including naval losses.[51]

German casualties in Crete were also very heavy. There were more than 6,000 casualties amongst the paratroops, with up to 4,000 believed killed; the Germans would never again mount an airborne operation in the war and their parachute regiments would fight as ordinary infantry units.

The Balkan campaign proved to be a disaster for Britain and Churchill. British diplomacy failed to establish a Balkan Front and the very presence of British aircraft and support troops in November prompted the Germans to begin planning the occupation of Greece. The Germans had no territorial ambitions in the region and were merely seeking to secure their southern flank diplomatically while maintaining access to the Ploesti oilfields. The position of Turkey was ultimately mistaken by the British and attempts to lure it into the conflict with the offer of non-existent squadrons of aircraft failed. Yugoslavia was not so fortunate: the coup d'état supported by the British earned Hitler's wrath and the country was consequently invaded by Germany. Moreover, the entry of German troops into Yugoslavia gave them a back-door route into Greece behind the British line of defences. The British ejections from Greece and then Crete were yet further military humiliations with heavy casualties and the complete loss of all precious artillery and heavy equipment. This possibility had been previously countenanced by Churchill in the War Cabinet as early as 5 March: 'We are advised from many quarters that our ignominious ejection from Greece would do us more harm in Spain and Vichy than the fact that of submission of the Balkans which with our scanty forces alone we have never expected to prevent.'[52]

However, Spain was determined to remain neutral and Britain was almost at war with Vichy France so its stocks could not get any lower.

Given that the Greek military venture was always regarded as hazardous, it is clear that political objectives were the drivers of this venture. It has even been suggested that Lustre Force went to Greece as a political gesture and planned to conduct a skilled fighting withdrawal from day one. The loss of British prestige in the eyes of global public opinion surely tells against this. The most important reason why troops were committed to Greece was the United States. The Lend–Lease bill was going through Congress and it was vital that Britain be seen to be defending the rights of democratic countries worldwide if it was to receive the material support so desperately needed to continue the war when nearly bankrupt. Churchill commented during a Defence Committee discussion on how to release the bad news from Greece to the press: 'The Press must not lose sight of the fact that the Battle of the Atlantic and the attitude of United States of America were the two decisive factors of the war.'[53]

Therefore to ensure the passage of the Lend–Lease act, 2,609 soldiers died, a further 2,962 were wounded and 22,000 taken prisoner, many of them Australians and New Zealanders, whose countries had small populations that could not afford to sustain such losses. The despatch of troops to Greece also had dramatic repercussions in North Africa, where the desert army had been considerably weakened. The Australian War Cabinet 10,000 miles away had warned of the dangers of the arrival of German forces in Libya but this could not be acted upon as the decision had already been made to send troops to Greece and risk an attack from Libya. The Australian official war correspondent interviewed Blamey after the expedition and Blamey made these points:

> We went in with our eyes open and the 6th Division was thoroughly well equipped. The guarantees were between governments.
> We were told that the landing was tied up with the Lend-Lease Act in USA – if we didn't come to the aid of Greece, the Act would not be passed.[54]

Rommel, having been ordered by OKW not to start a major attack until another Panzer division had arrived in May, ignored this instruction and began his unofficial desert offensive on 24 March with the seizure of El Agheila and a week later the Mersa Brega position.[55] The 7th Armoured Division had been sent back to Egypt to refit and the few tanks of the 3rd Armoured Brigade were not able to counter-attack the Germans. In less than ten days, Rommel had broken through the British defences to the open desert and a week later, on 10 April, was attacking the isolated garrison of Tobruk. Wavell dared not send any more men to Greece, despite Britain's commitment to its ally.

Criticism of Churchill became commonplace. 'It is Norway all over again,' reflected Lord Hankey on 22 April. 'Just the same mistakes. The vital need for air forces overlooked. No one seems to have realised that there were not enough aerodromes in Southern Greece.'[56] It was Norway all over again, with the Germans enjoying complete dominance of the skies and the British lacking both fighter aircraft and anti-aircraft guns.

So loud was the discontent over Greece that, in an effort to stem the criticism, Eden tabled a no-confidence motion in his own government's conduct of the Greek campaign on 7 May 1941, after which the government received a vote of confidence of 477 ayes to 3 nos. After denying acting like a dictator and ignoring the advice of Chiefs of Staff or generals in the field, Churchill assumed responsibility for the situation: 'when all is said and done … I am the one whose head should be cut off if we do not win the war.'[57]

On 11 April, having returned to England, Eden gave a summary of the events in Greece to the War Cabinet. In concluding, he made a number of points:

(1) Hitler's plan in the early spring had been to over-run all the Balkans by peaceful methods. He had hoped to deal with Greece and Yugoslavia as he had dealt with Roumania and Bulgaria.

(2) Having secured bases in the Balkans, he meant to attack our positions in the Eastern Mediterranean, neutralising Turkey and intimidating Russia.

(3) This plan had, to some extent, been retarded and thrown out of gear by the Greek resistance and the Yugoslav coup d'état which would not have taken place but for the help which we had given to Greece.[58]

As events had unfolded, Eden and Churchill had at last realised what Germany's real strategy had been. Although wrong about the second point above, it was British actions following their own incorrect assessments of German intentions that had triggered the invasions of both Greece and Yugoslavia and precipitated the subsequent ejection of British troops from Greece and Crete. Therefore Britain and Churchill were directly responsible for the German invasions of Greece and Yugoslavia and their subsequent occupation, which also cost many British lives (mainly Dominion troops), the loss of more equipment and the reverse in North Africa. The only positive outcomes were that the Lend–Lease Bill was passed to ensure Britain's survival and that American beliefs that they would have to become involved in the war were hardened. German forces of occupation would also now have to be deployed in Greece and Yugoslavia, which would have given some satisfaction to Churchill. A completely unintended outcome of the Greek fiasco was that Hitler's invasion of Russia, Operation Barbarossa, was delayed by what would be a critical six weeks.

6

PLACENTIA AND ANGLO-AMERICAN WAR PLANS

As agreed by Churchill and Roosevelt, American and British officers met in Washington from 29 January to 27 March 1941 to begin planning the joint conduct of the war should the United States become embroiled in it. The preliminary plans finally developed, known as ABC-1 to the Americans, determined that the Atlantic and European theatres were the most important for action against Germany, the predominant member of the Axis. If and when Japan entered the war, a defensive stance would be taken in the Pacific, thereby creating the concept of 'Germany first' that would drive Allied strategy for the remainder of the war.[1] The plans also proposed the exchange of British and American military missions, which duly took place; the US Navy and Army personnel in London organised their staffs from May 1941 for continuous consultation with the British Chiefs of Staff so that if and when the United States entered the war, co-operation and action with the British would be smooth and immediate. To avoid unwarranted attention, the military personnel on both sides of the Atlantic wore civilian clothes. From these joint discussions and further talks in early 1941 evolved the preliminary agreements on how the war would be prosecuted. The main objectives of ABC-1 were:

(a) To determine the best methods by which the armed forces of the United States and British Commonwealth, with its present Allies, could defeat Germany and the Powers allied with her, should the United States be compelled to resort to war.

(b) To co-ordinate, on broad lines, plans for the employment of the forces of the Associated Powers.[2]

The evacuations from Greece forced Churchill and the British Chiefs of Staff to dramatically reassess Britain's military position. Britain still faced the threat of invasion and German success in North Africa was now imperilling Egypt itself and the Suez Canal. While a lifeline had been thrown to Britain in the form of Lend-Lease, it was apparent that the strength of Britain's depleted Army was not enough to defeat Germany and Italy, let alone an increasingly belligerent Japan. In reply to a heartening telegram of support from Roosevelt which implied that further withdrawals may be necessary before the war was won (i.e. from Egypt), Churchill directly appealed to Roosevelt for the United States to enter the war 'in order to counter the growing pessimism in Turkey, the Near East and in Spain'. Roosevelt had also expressed concern about Germany invading Tunis, Morocco and Algiers, to which Churchill's response was, 'You alone can forestall the Germans in Morocco.'[3]

Roosevelt avoided this plea in his reply a few days later. The CIGS Dill provided a gloomy memorandum of the military situation, warning that Britain was still threatened by invasion and therefore no more reinforcements, particularly armour, should be sent to the Middle East in order to preserve the defences of the United Kingdom:

> A successful invasion alone spells our final defeat. It is the United Kingdom therefore and not Egypt that is vital and the defence of the United Kingdom must take first place. Egypt is not even second in order of priority, for it has been an accepted principle in our strategy that in the last resort the security of Singapore comes before that of Egypt. Yet the defences of Singapore are still considerably below standard.[4]

Churchill had little time for this assessment by his most senior British Army officer after he had convened a Defence Committee meeting on 21 April which approved the shipment of an armoured brigade to Egypt by the Royal Navy through the hostile Mediterranean in an operation code-named Tiger. In his rebuttal of Dill's arguments, Churchill again expressed his view that the Japanese were unlikely to attack Singapore.

While Anglo-American plans were being formulated, Churchill used his position as head of the Defence Committee, which was also responsible for supply as well as operations, to organise the replacement of Britain's losses in weapons and aircraft. The equipment left behind at Dunkirk had been enough to fully equip at least eight infantry divisions. Churchill did not change the previously agreed fifty-five-division model for the Army but insisted that thirty-six divisions be ready by the end of May 1941 and the balance six months later, which was to include seven armoured divisions.[5] One of Churchill's first acts as Prime Minister had been to form on 17 May 1940 the Ministry of Aircraft Production to improve the production of new and existing aircraft. However, as there were existing programmes and schemes already in progress, it was difficult for the MAP to make much of an impact immediately. The differences between quantities demanded and those that could be manufactured resulted in increasing requirements for purchases from America to bridge the gap, which continued the depletion of Britain's gold reserves.

A General Priority Production direction had been issued on 14 June 1940 for items of the highest priority which included aircraft but surprisingly not tanks, which were forced to wait until 9 July 1941 after the Battle of Britain before being elevated to the status of the highest priority. The shortage of tanks was an immediate problem following the fall of France and production was forced to take precedence over the development of new models. Tank production also competed with aircraft production for machine tools, gauges, tools and skilled labour as well as taking steel plate from the Royal Navy destined for warships.[6] The A22 tank, which would become the Churchill, was slow coming into production just when a heavy model was needed for defending Britain from invasion.

Hess

On 11 May 1941, after the Greek debacle, Churchill received a surprising message that Rudolf Hess, Hitler's deputy, had arrived by parachute in Scotland. Hess had taken a plane from a base in Germany and flown to the UK the previous night before bailing out of his aircraft near Glasgow, intending to meet with the Duke of Hamilton, who had been identified by the Germans as apparently being opposed to Churchill. A letter written by Hess to the Duke had been previously intercepted by MI5 so it is possible that the flight was known about in advance by British Intelligence. Hess was taken into custody and later met with the Duke, who immediately went to see Churchill at his alternative weekend country residence at Ditchley House. To firmly identify Hess, a German-speaking Foreign Office official was quickly sent to Glasgow. Once this had been done, Hess was questioned extensively and it was revealed that he was on an unofficial peace mission to bring about the end to war in

Europe, provided there was a change of government in Britain. Whether this mission was undertaken with or without the knowledge of Hitler is not clear, but a clue was provided when Hitler reportedly did not fly into one of his characteristic rages on hearing of the news of the defection of his deputy, a man who had been by his side since the 1920s. The German military made a number of investigations but there was no real reaction from Hitler. It is clear now that this was a last-ditch attempt by Hitler to secure peace with Britain. The fact that Hitler was prepared to sacrifice his deputy to achieve this is indicative of the importance of the peace initiative, which was once again designed to secure diplomatically one front before launching another in the invasion of Russia. The OKW and Hitler did not want a potential threat from Britain in the west while Germany was conducting its campaign against Russia in the east. Hitler, however, publicly denied all knowledge of the flight and declared Hess a madman. The Foreign Office official's report from Glasgow went only to Churchill, Beaverbrook, Attlee and Eden and remains secret to this day. On 13 May in a speech to the House of Commons, Churchill claimed to be baffled by Hess' actions. This was a blatant lie as the minutes of a later War Cabinet meeting record Churchill as saying:

> Hess arrived, hot from Hitler's entourage, and came to do great service for Germany at great risk. He wanted to be conducted to the King to say that we had no backing here and to get a government of the Danish complexion installed … to give us a last chance to join the crusade against Russia.[7]

Taking a cue from Hitler, it was decided to treat Hess as a mental patient and, following an extensive debriefing, he was imprisoned with little access to the outside world; Hess would spend the rest of his life in prison until he committed suicide at the age of 93 in 1987.

US Convoys – Battle of the Atlantic

In order to resolve urgent military problems, it was Churchill's habit to set up committees in order to find a solution more rapidly and effectively, e.g., the Night Air Defence Committee during the Blitz. In response to the increasing British merchant shipping losses in the Atlantic bringing supplies from the United States, Churchill convened the Battle of Atlantic Committee on

19 March 1941 with himself as its head. Churchill immediately threw himself into the work required as if he could not delegate the tasks or trust anyone else to carry them out.

In early 1941, Canadian warships escorted merchant ships on the Iceland to the American continent leg of the voyage to assist the stretched resources of the Royal Navy. For the British, getting the US Navy to play a part in the Battle of the Atlantic was a major priority and the British found the Americans more than willing. On 18 April 1941, Admiral King extended the previously declared pan-American safety belt to include Greenland within the so-called Western Hemisphere and any belligerent vessels entering the zone would be regarded as having hostile intentions. The US Navy actively patrolled this zone but did not escort convoys or engage U-boats. Hitler had instructed that there should be no incidents with American ships before mid October, by which time the invasion of Russia would be completed. Prior to this, Hitler had chosen to overlook American aid to England rather than declare war on America.

Following the torpedoing of merchant ship SS *Robin Moor* in the South Atlantic on 21 May, Roosevelt made a speech on the 27th protesting the sinking of the vessel and declaring that an unlimited national emergency was confronting the country, singling out Hitler and Germany as a threat to the United States to which they would not yield. American naval patrols in the Atlantic would be 'extended' to defend the Western Hemisphere and Britain would be assisted with all possible aid. US warships began to report the positions of German U-boats they located to the British in an escalation of American involvement. That month, the British aircraft carrier HMS *Illustrious* arrived for repairs in America after being damaged by German aircraft in the Mediterranean. This had been sanctioned by Roosevelt even though it was in complete contravention of the Neutrality Act.

Roosevelt, in an effort to influence public opinion, also claimed that Latin America would be the next Balkans and that the US should not wait to be attacked. In early July, Roosevelt accepted a request from the Icelandic government (after heavy pressure had been exerted by Churchill) to take over the security of Iceland with American troops, thus freeing up nearly an entire British division that had been based there since 1940. The first US Marines began to arrive on 7 July and immediately began to construct a naval base with refuelling facilities and an airfield.

On 15 July, the Western Hemisphere definition was extended again by Admiral King to include Iceland, and to facilitate the occupation the US

Navy introduced Operations Plan Six on 19 July to escort all American and American-flagged vessels (plus those nationalities that wanted to join the convoys) to the country.[8]

On 25 July, the US announced a financial, trade and oil embargo against Japan after its occupation of Vichy French Indo-China. Japan, having no natural supplies of oil, imported all its requirements and on the imposition of the embargo only had six months stock of oil left. The countdown clock to war in the Pacific was now ticking; Japan could either go to war or comply with League of Nations and American requests to withdraw from China and Indo-China.

Syria

Under the terms of the armistice with Germany in June 1940, the French Army of the Levant (120,000 strong) was progressively demobilised to leave a force of about 35,000 colonial troops from Morocco, Senegal, Tunisia and Algeria backed by some Foreign Legionnaires. However, the British had fears that Syria might be used as a base for further Axis offensive operations in the Middle East and these concerns were reinforced by the arrival of an Italo-German mission in August 1940. Syria and Iraq then became the playgrounds of both German and British intelligence officers, each network seeking to shore up native support for their own regimes and foment trouble for their rivals. Churchill was keen to use de Gaulle's Free French forces for military action in Syria but this was resisted by Wavell. De Gaulle wanted a victory after his failure at Dakar but Wavell believed that the arrival of Free French forces would only stiffen and embitter the resolve of the Vichy Frenchmen. On 1 April 1941, German agents succeeded in initiating a coup d'état in Iraq by Rashid Ali and three other pro-German officers, forcing the regent to flee. After a brigade of Indian troops was landed at Basra, the coup was overturned within a month by British troops and the original government restored. German aircraft supported the Iraqi forces, using bases in Syria for refuelling and British aircraft attacked these in response. Even though the British had been ejected from Greece and were facing another battle for Crete, which was the main priority at the time and had to be held at all costs, Churchill insisted that Wavell forestall any German occupation of Syria with an expedition. In an effort to avoid any conflict, the Vichy French Commissioner in Syria asked the Italo-German mission to leave on 6 June, which it duly did. In view of the proposed expedition, Churchill thought it necessary to tell Roosevelt that Britain had no territorial ambitions on Syria.[9] Wavell protested that the expedition was a gamble with only a problematical chance of success, given the limited resources in his command.[10] As the Commander-in-Chief Middle East, Wavell had been ordered by Churchill to mount two offensives in opposite directions from Egypt when a part of his army had just been evacuated from Crete. Iraq was a sensitive area for the British and one in which Churchill had a vested interest because of its oilfields.

Churchill had also ordered that the offensive be resumed against Rommel as soon as possible. To replace lost tanks and aircraft, Churchill instructed that convoys were to be run directly to reinforce Wavell through the Mediterranean regardless. German and Italian aircraft dominated the skies, threatening the movement of Allied shipping and the Italian fleet was also at large. A large convoy, code-named Tiger, arrived successfully in Egypt on 12 May and delivered 238 tanks (including some new Crusader types) and sixty-four Hurricanes, one ship of the five loaded with tanks being lost on the voyage. In Operation Jaguar for the delivery of replacement aircraft to the island of Malta, four convoys were mounted in May and June in which 189 aircraft reached Malta from aircraft carriers, half of these flying on to Egypt.

Wavell's planned offensive, beginning with Operation Battleaxe, had the objectives of inflicting a defeat on Rommel, regaining lost territory and liberating the besieged garrison (largely Australian) at Tobruk. The Germans needed Tobruk as a deep water port to bring supplies close to the front line rather than overland from Tripoli. On 15 June, Operation Battleaxe commenced but after only three days the British were forced to withdraw to their starting positions and many of the new tanks were lost. The British Crusader tanks were new to their crews and found to be mechanically unreliable. Having gambled on the risky Tiger convoy getting through before the subsequent battle, which did not go as planned or expected, Churchill became even more unhappy with Wavell for what he saw as his over-cautious approach. As Wavell had presided over one too many losses, Churchill decided to relieve him on 21 June 1941, swapping Wavell with General Auchinleck in India.

As North Africa was the only theatre where the British were actually engaged in ground combat with the Germans, there was keen interest in the progress of the campaign from the British public:

My uncle Bert, a desert rat, was at the siege of Tobruk and one day my gran closed all the doors and windows of the house and banked up the kitchen range. The temperature rose alarmingly and we sat and suffered thinking of uncle Bert and his colleagues in the desert. Gran said that at least we could open the doors and escape the heat but poor Bert was stuck with it.[11]

In London, following the cessation of the first aerial Battle of London, the people of the city were learning to relax again in the warm summer sun:

July 5th 1941
A glorious day (in London) and the population looked much better than three months ago. In Hyde Park there is a central dump for rubble, etc – it's a young mountain with a road over it. I wonder how many houses have helped make it. Next to the mountain were bowlers playing hard! Hundreds were bathing in the Serpentine and allotments abound everywhere.[12]

Meanwhile in Syria, on 8 June a small force in four columns consisting of an Indian brigade plus an Australian division (less one brigade in Tobruk) and a Free French division entered Syria and Lebanon in Operation Exporter from Palestine and Iraq, from where British troops had put down the coup the previous month. De Gaulle was convinced that the Vichy French troops would not fight or would desert but this again proved to be far from correct. Seeking to salvage some pride after their defeat by Germany and regarding the Free French as traitors, the Vichy forces resisted strongly. Frenchman fought Frenchman in the rugged desert and mountains of Africa, many miles from France. Arab tribes were also offered independence by de Gaulle in an effort to encourage them to side with the Allies.

After an initial Allied advance, a determined Vichy French counter-attack slowed its progress. However, with more air reinforcements being available after the premature end to Operation Battleaxe in Libya and considerable British naval support along the coast, Damascus was captured on 21 June and the Vichy French forces were outflanked by motorised columns from Iraq which penetrated behind their defences. Damur in Lebanon was captured by the Australians on 9 July, thereby threatening Beirut, so a cessation to hostilities was requested on 11 July by the Vichy forces and an armistice duly signed on the 14th. The Free French and de Gaulle at last had some military and political success as they took over the administration of Syria and Lebanon. Wavell wrote afterwards in his report to the Secretary of State, 'We must be again considered fortunate in achieving our objective with forces which were really insufficient for their task. It was only skilful handling and determined fighting that brought about success.'[13]

This was the first successful British Army operation of the war that had been conceived and carried out at Churchill's direction and was once again against the French.

Russia

Stalin became Chairman of the Soviet of People's Commissars on 7 May 1941, which made him head of the Russian government. The British were well aware of German troop movements and the redeployment of Luftwaffe squadrons from France and the Balkans to Eastern Europe before June 1941 through the decrypts of intercepted German signals. At the beginning of June, Eden had warned the Soviet Ambassador to Britain, Ivan Maisky, about a possible invasion but he, along with Stalin, showed little reaction. The Russians seemingly took no steps to prepare for war, perhaps believing that the British warnings were false and that they were secure from German attack by the Russo-German non-aggression pact. However, the Russians did have defensive plans based on a three-echelon defence of infantry, armour and reserves. This plan was never implemented as units were not mobilised or deployed in time before the German attack and those positioned according to the plan did not co-ordinate their actions with each other. Following the purges within the Army in the mid 1930s, Stalin needed time to modernise, rebuild and reorganise his armies and their officers. [14]

On 15 June, Churchill gave Roosevelt the news about the potential invasion. [15] The rest of the world waited with the Russians seemingly oblivious to the threat. Churchill said the day before the invasion of Russia in an aside to his Private Secretary, 'If Hitler invaded Hell I would make at least a favourable reference to the Devil in the House of Commons.'[16]

The Germans had massed 141 divisions including nineteen armoured and fourteen motorised in three army groups on the Polish, Hungarian and Rumanian borders for Operation Barbarossa. [17] This total was approximately 75 per cent of the entire German Army. The total Russian European strength was estimated by the Germans as being 213 divisions while other later estimates were of 170 divisions. [18] This rapidly rose to 212 divisions by end of July following the rapid mobilisation of the Russians. [19] With Britain still unvanquished, according to Hitler, the invasion of Russia had a new strategic objective of removing Britain's last hope.[20] This was more than likely stated by Hitler in order to reduce senior OKW Army officers' concerns about Germany continuing to fight on two fronts after the failure of the Hess mission.

The invasion of the Soviet Union began on 22 June 1941 after a border incident was fabricated by the Germans. Few policymakers in Washington or London thought that the Soviets would be able to resist the Nazi onslaught for more than six weeks, while Hitler also believed the campaign would last no longer than this. The British government, with its main efforts focussed on dealing with the Germans in Europe, was also concerned that Japan might take advantage of the situation to seize British, French or Dutch territories in Southeast Asia.

On receiving news of the attack on Russia, Churchill and Eden discussed their relief that the German Army was now fighting another country and therefore Britain had by default another ally, albeit a communist one. Churchill had publicly warned of the consequences of the invasion in a radio broadcast on 22 June:

> Hitler is a monster of wickedness, insatiable in his lust for blood and plunder. Not content with having all Europe under his heel, or else terrorized into various forms of abject submission, he must now carry his work of butchery and desolation among the vast multitudes of Russia and of Asia. The terrible military machine, which we and the rest of the civilised world so foolishly, so supinely, so insensately allowed the Nazi gangsters to build up year by year from almost nothing cannot stand idle lest it rust or fall to pieces … So now this bloodthirsty guttersnipe must launch his mechanized armies upon new fields of slaughter, pillage and devastation.

Churchill was a sworn enemy of communism and was opposed to it almost as much as Hitler and the Nazis. However, in order to defeat Germany, Churchill was prepared to offer whatever assistance Britain could afford to Russia on the basis of any enemy of Germany being a friend of Britain. A key problem for Churchill and Roosevelt was determining whether Russia could resist the Germans and if not, how long could she hold out before capitulating? This issue had to be resolved before any commitments to sending any aid could be made. Churchill sent his first telegram to Stalin on 8 July, and on the 12th an Anglo-Soviet agreement was signed in Moscow declaring mutual assistance and that neither country could make a separate peace with Germany.

In America, Roosevelt once again had to grapple with negative public opinion on Russia. For most of capitalist America, the conflict between communism and the Nazis was one to be watched from afar. To Roosevelt and Churchill, however, aiding Russia meant progressing the defeat of Germany, provided the Russians could survive the initial Nazi assault. Additional problems for Roosevelt were that Russia was a great distance away via hazardous shipping routes and the immediate Russian requirements were unknown. When Russia had not capitulated in the first four weeks as some had predicted, Hopkins volunteered to fly to Moscow to meet with Stalin to provide an estimate of the situation at first hand.

With things going badly, Stalin made his first appeal for a Second Front in France on 19 July so as to relieve the pressure on the Red Army. Churchill sent the first of many apologetic telegrams, pointing out how strained British resources were after fighting for nearly two years and how strongly defended the coast of northern France was with forty German divisions in France.[21] However on 25 July, Churchill promised aid to Russia in the form of 200 Tomahawk fighter aircraft, boots and raw materials such as 20,000 tons of rubber.[22]

A list of requirements was received on 30 June from the Russian Foreign Minister, Molotov, but after an examination of British production it was found that there was little that could be sent to Stalin. Britain needed much of the equipment itself, such as fighter and bomber aircraft, while the Russians had also requested hitherto secret British radar sets and night fighters. On 12 August, Churchill wrote that the mission to Moscow should not start until late September, by when it would be known where the winter front lines would be located.[23]

It was not until 13 October that Roosevelt notified Stalin that the first shipments of tanks, aircraft and trucks had started to leave US ports the previous day bound for Russia.

Placentia Bay

In late July, a delegation of visiting American senior military officers expressed their concerns to Churchill and the Chiefs of Staff that British strategy in the Middle East was neglecting the all-important battle in the Atlantic on which Britain's survival depended. While these concerns were addressed in a meeting in Downing Street on 24 July, two days later Japanese actions in Indo-China and the American embargo radically altered the situation in the Far East. Hopkins, who was accompanying the military delegation, suggested a meeting with Roosevelt, which Churchill readily accepted. The two leaders met for the first time in the war from 9 to 12 August 1941 aboard their respective warships off the coast of Newfoundland at Placentia Bay, ironically at one of the bases given to the Americans by Churchill in exchange for the old destroyers. On first meeting, Churchill and Roosevelt were each silent for a minute until Churchill said, 'At long last, Mr President,' to which Roosevelt replied. 'Glad to have you aboard, Mr Churchill.' Churchill then gave Roosevelt an introductory letter from King George VI and made an official statement which, despite two attempts, a sound-film crew present failed to record.

The talks were preceded by a staged but moving Sunday service with British and American sailors sharing hymn sheets; the conference proper started on Monday, 11 August with talks at diplomatic, military and premier levels. Military officials made plans and confirmed strategy agreed at previous meetings of the various military missions earlier that year, most notably the latest version of the ABC-1 plans. One of the potential joint Anglo-American operations discussed was a landing in north-west Africa to prevent their occupation by Germany and to exploit rifts within the Vichy French colonies and the new government in France. Such a strategy would also put pressure on Rommel's army from the rear and resulted in the first plans for Operation Gymnast being developed. Harry Hopkins reported favourably on his recent visit to Moscow and Roosevelt immediately agreed to substantial war material for Russia under Lend-Lease, which would require the US to ramp up production further, and a mission to be sent to Moscow to determine actual Russian needs. The Americans agreed to a greater escort role in a new naval plan for the Atlantic and the US Navy would now be responsible for all escort duties for convoys of ships of all nationalities west of the 26-degree-west longitude, i.e. to and from Iceland and a mid-ocean meeting point. This meant that British warships would no longer have to operate from Canada at all. Most of the conference was taken up by the discussion and drafting of the Atlantic Charter, a broad joint statement of war aims and a blueprint for the post-war democratic world. The Charter's first draft of five points was prepared by Churchill himself, perhaps as a sweetener for Roosevelt but also to try to secure some commitment from Roosevelt on entering the war.[24] The final version of the Charter included eight 'common principles'. Both countries agreed not to seek territorial expansion; to seek the liberalisation of international trade; and to establish freedom of the seas and international labour, economic, and welfare standards. The third point of Churchill's draft made a statement to the effect that the United States and Great Britain were committed to supporting the restoration of self-government for all countries that had been occupied during the war and allowing all peoples to choose their own form of government. Churchill seemed to have disregarded or been oblivious to the threat of future self-determination for the colonies of the British Empire contained in this clause. The governments of Burma and India immediately fastened on to this clause when it was announced and demanded clarification from Britain, which subsequently claimed the Charter referred only to European countries.[25] The preservation of the British Empire was paramount to Churchill.

The sixth principle is notable for a phrase which was tantamount to a joint declaration of war by Britain and the United States on Germany: 'They hope to see established a peace after the final destruction of the Nazi tyranny ...'

In line with a slightly more bellicose approach to Japan, Roosevelt was also to deliver a strong warning to Japan after the meeting.[26]

In the midst of the talks, Roosevelt received word that the Selective Service Act amendment had been passed by one vote, an indication of how much US public opinion was still divided on the possibility of war and how much work Roosevelt still had to do before the United States could enter the war. If it had not passed, all conscripts previously called up a year ago would have been sent home, destroying America's rearmament programme.

The meeting ended on 12 August and Churchill was very happy with the progress made, apart from Roosevelt's reluctance to discuss the one subject Churchill wanted most, which was when the United States was going to enter the war. Churchill had been warned before the conference by Hopkins not to pursue this matter directly with Roosevelt.[27] The British military staff reported after meetings with their American counterparts that the US Army was unenthusiastic and not ready for war as it was still in the process of rebuilding and equipping. According to one observer, not a single American Army officer was keen to join the war with Britain.[28] General Marshall had pointedly made reference to the fact that supplies to the British (and now the Russians) under Lend-Lease were needed for the equipping of American forces; the three countries were effectively in competition with each other for Lend-Lease production. This was all in stark contrast to the US Navy, which was apparently keen to become involved. Churchill believed he had started to forge a personal relationship with Roosevelt, who was allegedly 'keen to come in': 'I am sure I have established warm and deep personal relations with our great friend.'[29]

Churchill then reported on the discussions with Roosevelt to the War Cabinet:

> If he was to put the issue of peace and war before Congress, they would
> debate it for three months. The President had said that they would wage war,
> but not declare it, and he would become more and more provocative. If the
> Germans did not like it they could attack American forces ... everything was
> to be done to force an 'incident'.[30]

Roosevelt may well have not have reciprocated Churchill's feelings. Given the
President's sensitivity to public opinion, he had requested that no reporters
be present. However, not only did Churchill disregard this but British reporters present were disguised as staff of the Ministry of Information. When this
was revealed by Hopkins, Roosevelt was annoyed and Churchill was immediately forced to confine the reporters to British ships. After claiming to have
been snubbed at their first meeting in the First World War, Roosevelt was
further put out when they finally met again when Churchill did not recall
their previous meeting. Roosevelt was astonished and a little put out at this
apparent gap in Churchill's famous phenomenal memory concerning their
initial introduction.[31] Discussions between the two did not come readily and
had to be facilitated by the likes of Hopkins. The two leaders were like fencers
or wrestlers circling each other, appraising each other and looking for points
of weakness while planning their moves:[32]

> It would be an exaggeration to say that Roosevelt and Churchill became
> chums at this conference or at any subsequent time. They established an easy
> intimacy, a joking informality and a moratorium on pomposity and cant and
> also a degree of frankness in intercourse which, if not quite complete, was
> remarkably close to it.[33]

At dinner on 10 August, Roosevelt indelicately raised the subject of free trade
and freedom for colonies, which was an anathema to Churchill but who managed to resist the bait.[34] Despite the fears about a clash of personalities, the
two blended quite well.[35] Churchill was at his most deferential and respectful
towards Roosevelt, not just respectful of his rank as head of state (Churchill
was after all only the King's Prime Minister) but because he needed to make
a good impression.

Roosevelt hoped the publicity after the meeting and the declaration of
the Atlantic Charter would further influence public opinion and help bring

the US into war. With the conference, the Atlantic Charter and the fact that Britain was purchasing supplies from America, which had been widely covered in the British and American press, it was demonstrated to Germany, Japan and Italy that America would be involved in the war sooner rather than later.

Britain desperately needed American supplies under Lend-Lease to be sent directly to the Middle East. Churchill had already authorised in August 1940 the creation of an Atlantic ferry service using RAF and Canadian pilots to fly purchased aircraft across the Atlantic at its narrowest point to Takoradi in the Gold Coast (modern Ghana), a British colony. Even with the enactment of Lend-Lease, the United States could not supply aircraft directly to Britain or West Africa in American commercial shipping as both were in a declared war zone and West Africa was a British colony. State Department lawyers looked for ways to circumvent the existing legislation and eventually the definition of the United Kingdom as the 'British Isles' was redefined to mean just that and not include overseas colonies. At Roosevelt's direction, Pan American Airways set up a new civilian company to ferry aircraft across the Atlantic to Takoradi and on to the Middle East.[36] After he returned from his meeting with Churchill at Placentia, Roosevelt announced on 19 August that the airline would soon begin ferrying war planes and transporting war supplies to Egypt by way of the Takoradi route. This was a violation of both American Neutrality Laws and international laws but there was little reaction in the American media to this announcement.

One housewife saw through the declarations of the Atlantic Charter: 'The British and US co-operation discussed by Roosevelt and Churchill on board HMS Prince of Wales is a declaration of war in all but the actual deed.'[37]

The incident so desired by Churchill was not long in coming. From 1 September, the US Navy plan was implemented for it to begin escort duties to and from Iceland or to meet British escort ships mid ocean. The US Navy, with the assistance of the Canadian Navy and some Free French vessels, was now escorting convoys almost two-thirds of the voyage across the Atlantic. With the increased involvement of American warships, the likelihood of an incident or clash with a German U-boat increased. On 4 September, a First World War vintage destroyer, the USS *Greer*, made and kept sonar contact with a U-boat for a number of hours. A British plane then attacked with depth charges and in response the U-boat fired a torpedo unsuccessfully at the *Greer*, which then counter-attacked with depth charges. The US Navy was now at war with Germany in everything but name and the aggrieved Americans could claim Germany had fired the first shot.[38] German U-boats were still under strict orders not to get involved in an incident with American ships.[39] In a radio broadcast a week later, Roosevelt announced a 'shoot-on-sight' policy, publicly articulating previously secret orders issued months prior wherein American ships and aircraft could fire on German or Italian naval forces should they be found within 100 miles of an American-escorted convoy or Iceland.

On 7 September 1941, Churchill ordered a dramatic increase in RAF bomber production to escalate the bombing offensive against Germany; 3,500 were to be provided over the next two years on top of existing programme targets.[40] So great was the increase that it could not possibly be met from British production alone and the balance would have to be provided by the United States. Despite this increase, Churchill had come around to a different view to that of twelve months earlier and did not believe that bombers could win the war alone, contrary to the opinions of Harris and other RAF officers. Churchill later minuted:

> It is the most potent method of impairing the enemy's morale we can use at the present time. If the United States enters the war, it would have to be supplemented in 1943 by simultaneous attacks by armoured forces in many of the conquered countries which were ripe for revolt. Even if all the towns in Germany were rendered largely uninhabitable, it does not follow that the military control would be weakened or even that war industry could not be carried on.[41]

In September, the possibility of Sweden entering the war against Germany arose and Churchill on the 24th of that month ordered plans to be drawn up for an expedition back to Norway to seize Trondheim and assist the Swedes. The initial report by the Chiefs of Staff on 2 October was not enthusiastic or detailed and Churchill immediately directed that Brooke, then Commander-in-Chief Home forces, be charged with its planning, having discussed Norway with him at Chequers on 12 September. The report from the Chiefs of Staff on what was code-named Operation Ajax was transformed later into the Norwegian landings frequently championed by Churchill for the next three years as Operation Jupiter. Brooke duly presented his plans a week later but had arrived at the same conclusion as the Chiefs of Staff that the operation was impracticable because of a lack of air support as in the previous year. Unhappy with Brooke's report, Churchill then had the Chiefs of Staff prepare an appreciation of Brooke's plan which, much to Churchill's chagrin, agreed with it.[42]

This attempt to circumvent the Chiefs of Staff was indicative of a growing poor relationship between Churchill and his main military advisors.

On 17 October, the destroyer USS *Kearney* left a westbound convoy it was escorting to assist a nearby eastbound convoy being attacked by U-boats. The *Kearney* dropped depth charges and hunted U-boats all night before being hit by a torpedo, which forced the destroyer back into port. In an effort to further galvanise public opinion, Roosevelt made another radio broadcast on 27 October, declaring that America had been attacked and it was necessary to use force to keep the shipping lanes open. Roosevelt also claimed to have a German map of South America showing it reorganised from fourteen countries into five 'vassal' states of Germany, including Panama and its strategically important canal.[43] The map had its desired effect on many American citizens but was in fact a fake drawn up by British Intelligence personnel operating in the United States.[44] Roosevelt also claimed to have a letter indicating that Germany would abolish all existing religions, in a further attempt to influence American public opinion.

Following a request from Churchill for shipping assistance made at their Placentia meeting, on 10 November the British 18th Division set out from Halifax in American vessels bound for the Middle East in a convoy escorted by US Navy warships. The voyage was without incident to the Cape of Good Hope, where British escorts took over; with the outbreak of war with Japan the division was subsequently diverted to Singapore.

Two weeks later, the destroyer USS *Reuben James* was sunk while escorting a convoy to Iceland in a battle with U-boats. On 13 November, legislation went through Congress amending the Neutrality Act further so that American merchant ships were permitted to be armed and to enter war zones. Merchant ships carrying American aid under Lend-Lease could now make the voyage all the way across the Atlantic. Roosevelt had indeed thrown a lifeline to the beleaguered Britain and American entry into the war was only a matter of time.

PEARL HARBOR AND US REARMAMENT

Roosevelt had been controlling the march of the United States to war with Japan as early as 1934 but its dramatic arrival would bring no salvation for Britain or Churchill. While the United States was still unprepared for war in December 1941, Roosevelt had already put into place rearmament programmes to increase the armed forces which had begun with the US Navy in 1934. Recognising Japanese aggression in the Pacific would require a large naval fleet to combat it, Roosevelt increased the budget for new warships first as the construction of these would take several years. This programme received a boost with Roosevelt's speech to Congress on 28 January 1938 for increased naval funding, which was approved. In the years 1934 to 1941, the US Navy constructed and commissioned five new aircraft carriers, two battleships, thirteen cruisers and more than seventy destroyers while the submarine fleet doubled, all as a result of Roosevelt's increased funding.

However, the other services did not receive additional funding until a conference on 14 November 1938 that Roosevelt held at the White House with his top military and civilian advisors following the Munich crisis in Europe.[1] Roosevelt asserted at that time that the United States must be prepared to defend the Western Hemisphere as a bulwark for the North American continent. 'It is his conviction that, more and more, Japan will depend on Germany and Italy and that, in order to contain the ambitions of these powers, England, France and America will be obliged to combine their efforts.'[2]

Following discussions in early 1938 with French officials who were trying to source modern fighter aircraft, Roosevelt became convinced of the importance of air power as a strategic weapon. However, following ambitious proposals by the US Army and Air Corps after the November conference, Roosevelt ultimately only approved a programme of 5,500 new aircraft while the regular Army received no additional funds. Two months later, Roosevelt expanded his definition of the Western Hemisphere to reach as far as the Rhine River and the German frontier in the Senate Military Committee of 19 January 1939.[3] This was received with incredulity by Congress and a public outcry ensued, forcing Roosevelt three days later at a press conference to declare that this statement was a lie and then retreat into silence.[4]

The US Army at the end of June 1939 was small with only 188,000 regular soldiers plus 199,000 part-timers in the National Guard, but 50,000 men of the regular Army were overseas protecting America's colonial interests in the Philippines, Panama, Alaska and Puerto Rico.[5] The US Army, like the British, was poorly equipped largely with First World War vintage rifles and artillery. Restrictions that had proscribed the maximum average size of the Army were, however, lifted by Congress in November 1939, which permitted a modest increase to 200,390 that excluded the Philippine Scouts.

With the outbreak of war in Europe in 1939, plans made by the US Army to increase the numbers of regular troops to 280,000 were almost endorsed by Roosevelt, who at the last minute approved only a further modest increase to 227,000 men. At that time, the American Army was only the seventeenth largest in the world. General Marshall, who also became Chief of Staff on 1 July 1939, commented later:

> … that was all the public would be ready to accept without undue excitement. He indicated that he would give us further increases up to the figures we proposed … Our people can proceed in their planning on the basis of an increase to 250,000 for the Regular establishment, and an increase of 126,000 for the National Guard – provided that no publicity is given.[6]

The US Joint Planning Board had regularly reviewed its assessments of the international situation as a part of its strategic studies as tension rose in the late 1930s. Its main plan in the event of war with Japan, War Plan Orange, was revised in early 1938 and the Board predicted that the main aggressor nations would be Germany, Italy and Japan. The most critical theatres were perceived as the Atlantic and the Caribbean and therefore the Pacific theatre was accorded a holding strategy only. As the Orange Plan took into account only one enemy nation, the plan was revised in 1939 to create five alternative strategic plans that assumed more than one enemy, hence the use of the code word 'Rainbow' for later plans. The first Rainbow plans assumed Britain and France would at least be able to hold Germany and Italy but with the defeat of France and the retreat of the British in May and June 1940, revisions became necessary and the Rainbow 4 plan was adopted. As Britain continued to resist Germany, Rainbow 5 became operational, the other plans being eventually cancelled. The development of the Rainbow Plans continued throughout 1940 and early 1941, and not being at war did not stop Anglo-American discussions from occurring even before the ABC-1 meetings of 1941. Roosevelt had in fact approved joint American and British naval discussions as early as January 1938 and further General Staff conferences had taken place over August and September in 1940.

With the outbreak of hostilities in Poland in 1939, a French delegation went to the United States with the objective of purchasing 1,000 fighters as quickly as possible. So great was the French need that France agreed to invest $10 million to double the production of engines, the production bottleneck at the time which was of great significance for the expansion of the American aircraft industry. Britain and France in late 1939 then decided on a joint approach to purchases from the United States, particularly as Roosevelt and Treasury Secretary Henry Morgenthau were keen to increase the output of aircraft to supply Britain and France. Roosevelt in February 1940 required a decision quickly as any delay would jeopardise the whole scheme, his administration having already made a great effort (in light of the existing Neutrality legislation) to meet Allied requirements. They were prepared to do more if asked to do so at once; otherwise the needs of the American armed forces would have to be given priority.[7]

At a British and French Supreme War Council meeting, the details of an Anglo-French team in the United States were discussed. A scheme was approved to buy from American aircraft manufacturers 8,000 engines and 4,700 airframes at a cost of $614 million (excluding an order for 4,000 engines already placed by France for aircraft to be built in France).[8] Such was the size and impact of the French and British orders that the official US Army Air Forces history later wrote, ' ... the initial expansion of the American aircraft industry in 1939–1940, and one which was of great benefit to the country, was paid for by Great Britain and France.'[9]

Morgenthau later claimed that this British and French investment speeded American production of war planes by a crucial twelve to eighteen months and believed such orders would help increase the capacity of US manufacturers. Morgenthau was later appointed by Roosevelt as the head of procurement and aircraft allocation on 22 January 1940 as the President apparently did not trust the War Department to deliver on time. This arrangement also allowed American aircraft to benefit from combat experience in Europe and incorporate improvements such as self-sealing fuel tanks, armour plating and bulletproof cockpit glass. In May 1940, Roosevelt asked Congress for 50,000 planes, which required US production to expand from 2,000 planes a year to more than 4,000 a month.[10]

For their part, France and Britain had publicly declared they expected at least a three-year war with Germany, but with the forced rearmament and orders placed on America, their reserves of gold quickly became depleted. Orders on American companies had to be paid for with US dollars, which had to be purchased, and consequently the foreign exchange rate kept going up, increasing the cost to the French and British, who would have also been less than happy to learn that US aircraft manufacturers were making more profit on export sales than sales to their own forces. Some of these discussions were taking place well before the Neutrality Act was amended on 4 November 1939, allowing an arms trade with belligerent nations such as Britain and France on a cash-and-carry basis once a presidential proclamation had been made, thus in effect ending the arms embargo, which was a key plank of the Neutrality Act.

On 17 June 1940, after an unexpected increase in supplemental appropriations by Congress, the Secretary of War directed the regular Army be increased to an enlisted strength to 280,000 by 31 August 1940. With further developments in Europe, other increases were planned up to an Army of 530,000 men but doubts were raised as to whether this could be furnished by volunteers alone. On 31 May 1940, the President requested legislative authority from the Congress to bring the National Guard into Federal service as it was required for use outside the United States, which was approved in August. The Army was in the process of increasing from a total strength of 264,118 on 30 June 1940 to 1,455,565 on 30 June 1941.[11]

By December 1941, the US Army had increased in size to 1,686,000 men including the Air Corps and the new Armoured Force. By including the National Guard for twelve months' service, there were now twenty-nine infantry divisions, five armoured divisions, five cavalry and sixty-four air groups, the Army having expanded considerably from a peacetime size of three regular infantry and one cavalry division. The Selective Service Act for conscription in peacetime was introduced on 16 September 1940, whereby all men aged 21 to 35 registered with local draft boards and were selected for twelve months' service by lottery. Nearly a year later, in 1941, when faced with the disintegration of the newly formed Army as the service of the initial draft of twelve months was nearly finished, Roosevelt got the length of service extended by Congress beyond twelve months by just one vote when meeting Churchill at Placentia. All these men required training and housing in camps, which was a challenge for the US Army in the winter of 1940–41.

Although never expressed publicly by Roosevelt, America, with its rearmament programmes for the US Navy, Army and Air Force, was clearly getting prepared for war with Japan long before Pearl Harbor. In this respect, Roosevelt, despite being the President of a still isolationist America, had demonstrated a better grasp of international politics in the Pacific than Churchill.

As a consequence of Roosevelt's rearmament programmes and the world war, the US economy boomed. By 1943, more than 8 million men had joined the forces in some capacity following the creation of millions of new jobs, finally putting an end to the massive unemployment of the 1930s.[12] Women also entered the workforce on an unprecedented scale to perform the work of the absent conscripted men. Roosevelt's New Deal programmes had begun to slow down in the late 1930s and the Second World War provided an enormous boost to employment and wages that the New Deal had not delivered.

Pearl Harbor

Following Roosevelt's strong message to Japan after the Placentia Bay meeting, further diplomatic negotiations began with Japan in Washington, although the intentions of the Japanese remained unclear. As the Germans thrust deeper into Russia towards Moscow, some observers thought that the Japanese would take advantage of the situation and attack Russia, despite the Russo-Japanese non-aggression pact of April 1941. Others believed that either America itself or British and Dutch interests in Southeast Asia were at risk.

Churchill had become increasingly unhappy and critical of the performance of his Chiefs of Staff, on one occasion remarking that the senior British commanders in the Middle East needed a court martial and a firing squad. On 17 November, Churchill finally replaced the CIGS Dill, known as 'Dilly-Dally' by Churchill; Brooke was offered the position, assuming the role on 1 December. Within two days Brooke was convinced that the Mediterranean theatre should be at the centre of British strategy for the conduct of the war by conquering North Africa, reopening the Mediterranean sea lanes and attacking Italy.[13]

Regarding the Far East, Britain and Churchill were extremely reluctant to get into a war with Japan without America. All the possible permutations of Japanese aggression on the British and Dutch and American colonies (BDA) were examined and plans for joint co-operation devised at a series of international staff conferences in Singapore, but no agreement was reached. From August, the Americans were committed to reinforcing the Philippines and did not want to send naval units to Singapore. The British also wanted to know what role the US Pacific fleet concentrated at Pearl Harbor would play in any future conflict with Japan. The British Defence Committee on 17 October examined a proposal from Eden to send warships to the Far East. The Royal Navy was already looking at sending some older and slower battleships and it was Churchill who invited the Admiralty to consider sending a modern fast warship as a greater deterrent.[14] Three days later it was decided, against the advice of the Admiralty, to send HMS *Prince of Wales* towards the region as both a deterrent and to assuage Australian concerns about the region; a highly visible stopover was made in Cape Town to publicise the voyage. The decision to send the *Prince of Wales* onwards to join the *Repulse* at Singapore is not recorded because the records of any discussion by the Defence Committee meeting have not survived, as Churchill requested in a minute next day that they not be circulated.[15] On 9 November, however, the Admiralty itself directed the *Prince of Wales* on to Singapore.

As war with Japan became more likely, Churchill was forced to rethink his previous position that Japan would not risk an attack on Singapore but there was little that could be done in the short term. As war neared, Churchill said that the Japanese would be fools if they joined the war, but 'Hong Kong will be a gone coon, I suppose, if they come in.'[16]

Churchill assured Roosevelt that Britain would declare war on Japan 'within the hour' if the United States was attacked. An attack on the Dutch would bring a British declaration of war and vice versa but as for the position of the United States, Roosevelt continued to hedge his bets by saying that the USA would only be heavily involved in the event of a Japanese attack on either. Churchill was at pains to wait for the reaction of the United States to any hostile action in order that Britain should not be seen to be dragging the United States into another British war again.[17]

After fruitless diplomatic talks with representatives of the new Tojo government and Roosevelt's rejection of a Japanese offer to withdraw its troops to the positions previously occupied in July, the United States was essentially on a war footing from 27 November. On 15 November, General Marshall had briefed journalists off the record about the United States being almost at war, and on the 27th Roosevelt requested that the War Department notify American forces throughout the Pacific of the breakdown of negotiations and the possibility of hostile action at any minute. The US Navy issued a more direct message, saying that the despatch was to be considered a war warning.[18] As war neared in the Pacific, Britain officially declared war on three other European countries on 5 December:

Dec 6th 1941
The Finns have rejected our note to them asking where they stand and no answer has been received from Hungary or Rumania. We are now officially at war with these three countries. How difficult the history of this war will be for the children of the future. Britain nearly went to Finland's aid early in 1940 when Russia attacked her – now we are allied to Russia and fighting Finland.[19]

In the first week of December, it was clear from the reports of observers and decrypted Japanese naval and diplomatic signals that Japanese forces were on the move and that Japan was going to commence hostilities. The question was where? A troop convoy was spotted in the Gulf of Siam but contact was then lost. The British code breakers at Bletchley (and thus Churchill) were reading a Japanese naval code, JN 25, which revealed that another Japanese naval task force had sailed on 26 November into the Pacific for an unknown destination that necessitated refuelling at sea.[20]

The Japanese government on 6 December sent a fourteen-part final diplomatic telegram to its embassy in Washington with later instructions to pass it on to the Americans at a specific time. The British intercepted this message and, being more streamlined in their deciphering process than the Americans, Churchill would have read a decrypt on the morning of 7 December. At the same time, the final JN25 coded attack orders were decrypted and Bletchley sent a copy to Churchill and to Washington; the only unknown but vital piece of information was the target itself.

Roosevelt knew that if Japan went to war with the United States, Germany and Italy would be compelled to declare war on America by virtue of the Axis Tripartite agreement, thereby entangling the US in the European conflict by the back door. Harold Ickes, Secretary of the Interior, had said in October 1941, 'For a long time I have believed that our best entrance into the war would be by way of Japan ... And, of course, if we go to war against Japan, it will inevitably lead us to war against Germany.'[21]

At a White House meeting on 25 November, Roosevelt brought up the subject of war with Japan:

> We were likely to be attacked, as soon as next Monday, for the Japanese are notorious for making an attack without warning and the question was how we should manoeuvre them in to the position of firing the first shot without allowing too much damage to our ourselves.[22]

Churchill certainly had knowledge that Japan was going to attack somewhere, as did Roosevelt. The question as to whether either leader knew that the target would be Pearl Harbor has led to many conspiracy theories post-war. The truth, if different to what is already understood, may never be known as a result of the subsequent cover-up to simply hide the incompetence of the US military. What is well documented are the British concerns about the build-up of Japanese troops in Indo-China, the threat to Singapore and the urgent reports of an invasion fleet sailing for the Kra Isthmus and Malaya the day before, which seemed to be the much anticipated Japanese attack.[23] With the United States' decision to reinforce the Philippines, by October thirty-five heavy B-17 bombers (the largest force yet assembled by the Americans in the war) had arrived as a deterrent to further Japanese aggression in the region. This deployment, however, ensured that the Philippines, adjacent to the future Japanese communication lines to Indo-China, Malaya and Burma, would be invaded by the Japanese to neutralise this force in much the same way the deployment of British aircraft to Greece precipitated a German invasion. The Philippines had no other natural resources of value to Japan and although the Japanese had developed plans for their invasion, originally the Japanese Army had proposed to bypass the islands altogether.[24]

While the British were reading some Japanese naval signals, not one signal appears to have been decrypted before the attack that confirmed Hawaii as the target, although one in particular listed the berths of the major warships of the Pacific fleet but its significance was not realised. The Americans, however, had other sources of information as to the possible location of the Japanese fleet, which was supposed to be observing strict radio silence. All intelligence gathered by listening posts, observers and radio direction finders was collated by the US Navy's Office of Naval Intelligence, the ONI. A Dutch naval attaché in Washington, Captain Ranneft, recorded details in his diary of two visits to the ONI in Washington. On 2 December, Ranneft inquired about the situation in the Pacific and was shown the position of a Japanese task force with two aircraft carriers proceeding eastwards, then located halfway between Japan and Hawaii. During the second visit on 6 December, Ranneft asked after the same task force and was shown a position on the map about 300–400 miles north-west of Pearl Harbor. Requesting more information, Ranneft was reportedly told that it was probably in connection with Japanese reports of possible action against America. It did not occur to Ranneft that Hawaii might not know of the proximity of the Japanese vessels because the ONI staff appeared to be well aware of the situation. Aircraft carriers are always escorted by major fleets and a Japanese fleet moving eastwards across the Pacific has only a few possible destinations.[25] In direct contradiction of Ranneft's account, the Chief of the ONI, Admiral Wilkinson, later testified to the Congressional Pearl Harbor hearings that a large part of the Japanese fleet had gone missing for three weeks before the attack and that early December reports of the Japanese fleet still being in its home waters were obviously incorrect. Ranneft's diary is perhaps the only independent evidence of American knowledge of Japanese inten-tions but even today this record is disputed by historians because it reports the Japanese carriers to the west when they were north of Hawaii. British records of the time were either destroyed on Churchill's instructions or remain closed to the public.

On the morning of Sunday, 7 December, the Secretary of the Navy (Frank Knox), Stimson and Hull met to consider the fourteen-part decrypted Japanese diplomatic message and concluded that an attack was imminent. This meeting also considered an ONI report dated the same day that again showed that much of the Japanese fleet had not sailed from Japan, when in reality it was only 300 miles from Hawaii.[26] At this point in time, most senior American officials (e.g. Stimson, Marshall, Knox) believed that if the Japanese struck America anywhere it would be in the Philippines and this is evident from their reaction to the news of the attack when it came. On receiving the first radio message about the air raid, Knox exclaimed, 'My God! This can't be true, this must mean the Philippines?'[27]

Churchill went to Chequers for the weekend and significantly invited American guests, Winant, the new Ambassador to Britain, and Avril Harriman, a personal advisor of Roosevelt's. All were anxious about the forthcoming Japanese attack for different reasons. Over dinner, Churchill was unusually subdued and seemed preoccupied. Later in the evening, he turned on the wireless to hear the nine o'clock BBC news but missed the main headline, which was about the Japanese attack on Pearl Harbor. Disappointed to have not heard anything, Churchill and his guests continued to listen expectantly to the wireless. This stage-managed tableau by Churchill was fortunately retrieved by a butler, who had apparently been listening to another wireless set elsewhere, and announced that the Japanese had attacked the United States.

Churchill was instantly galvanised into action, announcing that Britain would declare war on Japan forthwith. Winant restrained Churchill and together they telephoned Roosevelt to get more details, using the telephone installed in a cabinet under the stairs at Chequers. Roosevelt confirmed, 'It's quite true. They have attacked us at Pearl Harbor. We are all in the same boat now.'[28]

However, only Congress could declare war and it was not until next day that the House of Representatives voted 382 to 1 for war with Japan. Roosevelt telegraphed Churchill with this result and Britain immediately declared war on Japan. Roosevelt continued his nautical theme in a message to Churchill: 'Today all of us are in the same boat with you and the people of the Empire and it is a ship which will not and cannot be sunk.'[29]

While Britain and America were at war with Japan, there still remained the question of Germany, for America had not declared war on the country. All Roosevelt's manoeuvres of an undeclared war on Germany and Churchill's desperate wishes had not achieved the agreed outcome of war with 'Germany first'. Churchill's policy of dragging the United States into the European war appeared to have been unsuccessful.

That Sunday morning, Japanese bombers and torpedo bombers had tried to cripple the US Pacific fleet at its base in Hawaii, Pearl Harbor. All eight battleships at anchor were hit and four sank, along with three cruisers and three destroyers. However, two strategically important aircraft carriers of the Pacific fleet were not in port as they were delivering aircraft to Wake Island and Midway in preparation for war and so survived the attack. Two of the battleships that were sunk were later raised and repaired along with four of those damaged, so the surprise attack was not as decisive as the Japanese hoped; vital oil tanks and dry dock facilities were also undamaged. However, more than 2,400 American servicemen were killed and another 1,100 wounded. Given that the United States was on a war footing, debate continues to this day as to why Hawaii was caught so unprepared for a Japanese attack. The Hawaiian commanders, General Short and Admiral Kimmel, accepted early retirement as several subsequent major Congressional inquiries plus the Army and Navy's own investigations have been content to lay the blame at their door. However, in 1999 both Kimmel and Short were exonerated by the US Senate of the charges of dereliction of duty. In March 1942, Admiral Stark, the

Chief of US Navy Operations, became another casualty of that 'day of infamy' in December when he was replaced by Admiral King on the Joint Chiefs of Staff committee.

As well as attacking the American fleet at Pearl Harbor, the Japanese had also launched an invasion of Thailand and Malaya. On 10 December, while steaming to intercept a Japanese convoy reported off Malaya, the *Prince of Wales* and *Repulse* were caught without air cover and quickly sunk by Japanese aircraft. Britain's naval deterrent had failed completely and the Royal Navy had lost one of its most modern warships. Churchill's predictions regarding the ability of ships to defend themselves against aircraft were found to be completely wrong. At a sombre War Cabinet meeting that day as Churchill anxiously awaited a German declaration of war on the United States, he claimed that the ships had been placed in the right spot but their sinking coupled with the losses at Pearl Harbor had completely changed the balance of naval forces and the Japanese now had control of the Pacific. Churchill went on to say that the entry of the United States along with the good news from Russia and Libya had vastly improved the war situation for Britain and he had no anxiety about the eventual outcome of the war.[30]

Next day, Churchill finally received the expected news that Germany and Italy had declared war on the United States, to which Congress responded in kind. Churchill and Britain's survival was now assured as in the space of six months Britain had gained two powerful Allies in Russia and America in the war against Germany. The bulk of the formidable German Army was now locked in a struggle to the death in Russia while the industrial might and vast manpower resources of the United States were now available to Britain in its fight against Germany and Japan.

In April 1941, the Russians and Japanese had signed a non-aggression pact to reduce tension on the Siberian–Manchurian border and for each to be able to focus on other potential military operations. With the Japanese now committed to war against the Americans and British, the Russian divisions positioned in Siberia to meet a Japanese threat from Manchuria could be redeployed to the front with Germany. Following this transfer, in December the Russian Red Army launched a counter-attack near Moscow just as German reconnaissance units reached the outer suburbs of the city. Further attacks were completely disrupted, the capture of Moscow was averted and the Germans were forced on to the defensive. While Germany had gained a new ally in Japan for the war against Britain and America, the Russo-Japanese non-aggression pact had allowed Stalin to reinforce the Moscow area. Believing the campaign would only last a few weeks, the German Army had not been equipped for a winter campaign. The six-week delay to the start of Operation Barbarossa caused by the invasion of the Balkans would ultimately prove very costly to the Germans.

In North Africa, the third attempt to relieve Tobruk was more successful when Auchinleck's offensive (Operation Crusader) that had been renewed on 18 November forced its way through to Tobruk on 7 December, raising the German siege. In anticipation of the British desert army being able to carry on its advance into Libya and destroy the Italians altogether, Churchill fastened on to an American suggestion first mentioned at Placentia Bay to land troops in French Morocco to the west of Libya at the invitation of General Weygand, the local Vichy French commander, if he could be persuaded to desert Vichy France. This plan was code-named Operation Gymnast and its intention was to land 55,000 British troops and capture Libya in an attack from two directions, which might well force Italy out of the war.[31]

America's declaration of war on Germany and the relief of Tobruk could not have been better news for Churchill and was the culmination of all his dreams:

> We had won the war. England would live; Britain would live; the Commonwealth of Nations and the Empire would live. How long the war would last or in what fashion it would end no man could tell, nor did I at this moment care … being saturated and satiated with emotion and sensation, I went to bed and slept the sleep of the saved.[32]

Some differences in the previously agreed strategy ABC-1 had emerged between the British and the American Chiefs of Staff during the talks at Placentia Bay. Marshall was clearly concerned about British commitments to the Middle East as he saw this as furthering British colonialism as well as a drain on equipment and reinforcements needed in other theatres. In order to cement in place the strategy of the new Anglo-American alliance, Churchill and his Chiefs of Staff immediately travelled to the United States by battleship, arriving on 22 December. The voyage was spent by Churchill and his staff preparing appreciations of the current war situation for discussion with their American counterparts. Churchill prepared a detailed paper in four parts concerning the war in the Atlantic, the Pacific and possible operations in 1943.[33] After operations in the Mediterranean to clear the North African coast and impose a ring of blockades around Germany, an invasion of the Continent would be made in 1943. Uppermost in the minds of the British was the fear that American public opinion and the US armed forces themselves after the savage Japanese attack on Pearl Harbor would demand action in the Pacific. Churchill's notes were then combined with reports of the Joint Planners to produce a British blueprint for the conduct of the war, which was known as WW1 General Strategy. Despite this combined effort, Churchill still presented Roosevelt on 23 December with a copy of his own notes.

When the question of whether the Americans should be addressed as politely as before their entry into the war was raised, Churchill replied, 'Oh! That is the way we talked to her while we were wooing her, now that she is in the harem we talk to her quite differently!'[34]

To the surprise and pleasure of the British, there was no American resistance in Washington. At a meeting of all the Chiefs of Staff with Roosevelt and Churchill on 23 December, both General Marshall and Admiral Stark confirmed their commitment to the ABC-1 strategy of 'Germany first', believing that if Germany was defeated, Italy and Japan would quickly follow. This was confirmed in American revisions to the British WW-1 document produced on 24 December by the Chiefs of Staff; the final American document was known as ABC-4.[35] Even more positively, Roosevelt committed during talks with Churchill the same day to landings in North Africa or wherever American land forces could be the most helpful.

The British strategy as per a Chiefs of Staff paper for the defeat of Germany was based on four principles:

Blockade
Bombing
Subversive activities and propaganda
Giving all support possible to the Russians.[36]

This defensive strategy was consistent with the strategies discussed with the Americans in February 1941 and at the Placentia Bay meeting. The British armed forces were still too weak to take on the German Army in its entirety directly, although Russia was now doing this for the Allies. The threat of invasion of Britain had receded with the movement of German forces from Western Europe to Russia, but there was still a remote possibility Germany could try to invade in the spring of 1942; certainly this was a thought that Churchill liked to keep in the minds of the Americans. As part of this peripheral strategy of isolating Germany and maintaining a blockade of essential supplies, Churchill was also determined to occupy or invade the French North African colonies with or without an 'invitation' from Vichy France; this would create trouble between Germany and Vichy France and have the unspoken benefit of assisting British operations in North Africa by threatening to trap the Italians and Germans in an offensive from two different directions.[37] The US was also concerned about German troops from Spain occupying the region, closing the Mediterranean and then threatening Dakar and the South Atlantic.[38] Dakar was sensitive to the Americans as it dominated the shipping routes from Europe to South Africa, the Mediterranean and was near to the closest point in Africa to South America. An operation to land troops in north-west Africa was discussed several times but Marshall took a conservative approach, citing lack of small arms ammunition and a need to study it in more detail as a failure could not be afforded. The earliest date for such an operation was 25 May but the final decision on launching the landings was referred to the President and the Prime Minister.

The British Chiefs of Staff did not see any possibility of a large-scale land offensive or a return to the European continent in 1942.[39] The possibility of a 'sacrificial' landing in Western Europe in the event of an imminent Russian collapse was discussed by Churchill and Roosevelt during their informal talks while Churchill was staying at the White House.

The joint Anglo-American strategy agreed on for the south-west Pacific and Pacific areas against Japan was purely defensive as per the original ABC-1 plans to enable a build-up of forces to take place for future offensive operations. Britain would defend Singapore and Malaya while the United States would hold the Philippines and support Dutch Indonesia; Australia was to be a base for future operations in the Far East. The only sour note of the proceedings, a portent of future events, was the news of a British dispute with the Chinese over Lend-Lease supplies destined for China which had been impounded in Rangoon by the British for possible use in the defence of Burma. This prompted Roosevelt to remind Churchill that the Chinese were rather sensitive because the British had closed the Burma Road for three months in 1940 in response to Japanese threats and the British desire to avoid war with Japan. Wavell had also apparently rejected a Chinese offer to send troops to help defend Burma.[40]

For the strategic administration of the war, General Marshall proposed a similar structure to the British Chiefs of Staff for the Joint Chiefs of Staff, with a Combined Chiefs of Staff organisation to be set up and function in Washington when the two Chiefs of Staff did not meet in person. The Combined Chiefs of Staff would have its own planning section, jointly manned by British and American officers. These arrangements were not greeted enthusiastically by the new CIGS, Brooke, who had remained in London, as the British had largely ceded control of strategy to the Americans, who had only been in the war for several weeks: '… they [Portal and Pound] have sold the birthright for a plate of porridge.'[41]

Another important decision was the proposal of a unified command (ABDA) in the Pacific for American, British, Dutch and Australian forces which was accepted by all member countries, although this process took another two weeks. General Wavell would be the Supreme Commander but did not assume command until 14 January, during which time the Japanese had made considerable advances in Malaya and the Philippines. Under the terms of his directive, Wavell was not permitted to command any national forces to assuage American concerns about any British bias towards the defence of Singapore.

Reinforcements for the Far East were not discussed until a meeting on 11 January, when both Marshall and Stark urged that shipping be made available. After further study, shipping could be provided if there was a 30 per cent reduction in Lend-Lease shipments to Russia. This was accepted by Churchill and Roosevelt with the understanding that the American occupation of Northern Ireland and Iceland would be delayed and any operation in northwest Africa could not be launched for another three months. Churchill and the British Chiefs of Staff were in no position, however, to negotiate with their new ally. In conclusion, the Prime Minister made several comments, 'He agreed on the necessity for this movement to the Far East; that it will have a very bad effect if one Asiatic power runs wild over the Far East; that it is very urgent to have General Arnold's planes sink their bottoms.'[42]

While Churchill was meeting with Roosevelt, the Foreign Secretary, Eden, met with Stalin in Moscow to discuss mutual assistance in the war against Germany and the possible entry of Russia into war against Japan. The talks were inconclusive but it is interesting to note that even at this early into the war Stalin was greatly concerned with Russia's post-war frontiers and reparations from Germany. Stalin wanted any agreement with the Allies to permit the Russian occupation of the Baltic states and the Finnish port of Petsamo, something Eden obviously could not agree to without consulting Churchill and Roosevelt. Stalin claimed the war was the result of disputes over frontiers and was anxious to ensure that Russia benefited territorially post-war.[43]

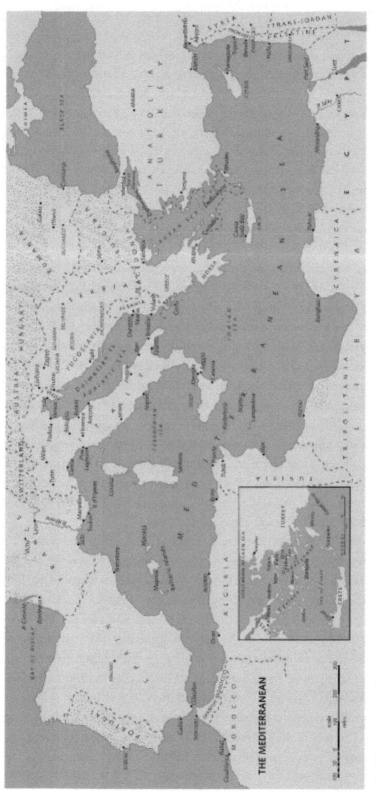

The Mediterranean Theatre.

In the three months following Pearl Harbor, all the British and American plans and assumptions were rendered largely redundant by Japanese successes in the Far East. The British colonies of Hong Kong and Singapore were captured, Malaya occupied and Burma and the Philippines invaded. The Dutch East Indies were also occupied. Churchill claimed that the loss of Singapore was one of the heaviest blows of the war but this is a little disingenuous. British policy in the Far East was based on sending a naval fleet to protect British colonies from any seaborne invasion but this policy was rendered redundant by the Atlantic and Mediterranean battles requiring all available warships and the Japanese overland advances from Indo-China that threatened Malaya. Hong Kong was regarded as indefensible by the British and was not to be reinforced. Following a report from the Joint Planners, the defence of Malaya had again been discussed by the Chiefs of Staff on 7 April 1941 and the taking up of positions in southern Thailand in the advent of a Japanese attack (Operation Matador) had been proposed in order to better defend Malaya. Churchill had written in a subsequent minute that it was improbable that the Far East would be attacked unless 'we are heavily beaten elsewhere'.[44] At a Defence Committee meeting in early April 1941, Churchill had stated that there were more pressing needs elsewhere than the completion of the defences in Malaya. A Joint Staff Planner wrote of Churchill's views on Singapore at this time, 'It is wrong to depend so much on one man who is so temperamental and so lacking in strategical knowledge and thinking in spite of all his other qualities.'[45]

Churchill would also have been conscious of his role in providing finance for the construction of the defences of Singapore when he was a parsimonious Chancellor of the Exchequer in the late 1920s.

The Japanese were also the beneficiaries of an intelligence windfall regarding Singapore. On 31 July 1940, the Chiefs of Staff had written a report that stated that without a naval fleet to send to the Far East, it would be difficult to prevent the loss of Malaya and Singapore if the Japanese attacked. This report, for some unaccountable reason, was sent by sea mail and the ship carrying it was captured by a German raider on 10 September; the mail was seized and transferred to the German embassy in Tokyo, which duly forwarded a copy of the report to Japanese naval authorities. The loss of the ship and these documents, although known to Churchill and the War Cabinet, was kept secret.[46]

Churchill, in a radio broadcast to the nation after the fall of Singapore, attempted to blame the American losses at Pearl Harbor for the successes of the Japanese forces. Again somewhat injudiciously, Churchill, in trying to put a positive spin on the defeat, must have made Roosevelt wince when he declared how important it was that America with its vast resources and power was now in the war as an ally: 'This is what I have dreamed of, aimed at, and worked for, and now it has come to pass.'

In blaming the Americans, Churchill refused to accept responsibility for a Malaya and Singapore campaign which had been conducted by just two Japanese divisions reinforced by a third for the final assault on Singapore. Privately, Churchill expressed a dreadful fear that the British soldiers were not as good fighters as their fathers were: 'We have so many men in Singapore, so many men – they should have done better.'[47]

Churchill decided not to hold a Royal Commission until the war was over but successive post-war governments including his own declined to instigate such an inquiry.

Lasting only ten weeks, the ABDA command under the unfortunate General Wavell officially ceased to exist from 23 February 1942. ABDA had been little more than an exercise in the rearranging of deckchairs on the *Titanic* but many thousands of British, Australian and Indian soldiers were taken prisoner. The previous day, General MacArthur was ordered by Roosevelt to leave the besieged Bataan peninsula in the Philippines and assume command of the South West Pacific Area (SWPA) from Australia after being invited (at Roosevelt's request) by the Australian government. The remnants of the American forces there held out until 6 May. In short, it was a disaster for the British Empire in Southeast Asia and the Japanese advance seemed unstoppable. Australia was clamouring for reinforcements and feared invasion, as did India, and Churchill was forced to consider how scarce troops could best be redeployed to prevent any further calamities.

The British forces in India had been weakened by the decision to send two Indian infantry divisions to the Middle East in 1941, which were used in Egypt and Iraq, leaving few troops to reinforce Burma or counter-attack the Japanese. As a consequence, Burma was overrun in a few months with British troops forced back across the border with India by the end of May 1942. Little had been done to reinforce Burma or strengthen its defences since the outbreak of the war in Europe. The British 18th Division, on its way to the Middle East, had been diverted firstly to Burma and then Malaya in anticipation of the Japanese attack and most of the division arrived just in time to fight in the fall of Singapore before being marched into captivity. A similar fate befell the Australian 8th Division.

On his return to England from America, an upbeat Churchill had briefed the War Cabinet on 17 January regarding his discussions with the Americans.

Britain had just got over the hump of the war, which would end in 1943 or 1945 at the latest, according to Churchill, and there was much to be pleased about; Roosevelt had declared that Great Britain was an essential fortress of the United Nations and would be aided as such, while the attitude of the Americans was much changed since Pearl Harbor. They were apparently keen on an operation in north-west Africa, which was not quite correct as while Roosevelt may have regarded such action favourably, Marshall had certainly not and had sent a memorandum to the President to this effect on 9 January. In it he warned of the risk of involving Spain and pointing out that ideally an invitation from Vichy French colonies needed to be received before any landings. The Americans were apparently full of resolve and vigour and would station troops in Northern Ireland to free up a British division deployed there. Churchill further stated that without the reinforcements sent to meet the threat in the Middle East (at his specific direction), according to the classic rules of war, 'We should not have got through but for Russia.'[48]

This was in recognition of the part that Russia had played in attracting the bulk of the German Army and the subsequent relieving of the pressure on Britain, which allowed reinforcements to be rushed to Egypt. However, as Churchill had acknowledged in his memoranda before the Washington talks, the entry of Japan had created new problems and Britain must expect more losses in the Far East before naval superiority over the Japanese was regained.

British and particularly American plans were reviewed from 28 February by General Dwight Eisenhower as the new head of US Army War Plans Division. He sought to establish priorities for future action, differentiating between what was regarded as essential and what was preferred, making the point that, 'The United Kingdom is not only our principal partner in this war; it offers the only point from which effective land and air operations against Germany may be attempted.'[49]

A shortage of shipping meant that operations could be pursued either in the Pacific or Atlantic but not simultaneously in the short term. A compromise strategy was to build up forces in both theatres as a prelude to offensive action but this would also be a more time-consuming process. After Eisenhower's review, American outline plans for the joint occupation of north-west Africa based on the British plans (Operation Super-Gymnast) were then shelved on 3 March as there was not sufficient shipping to reinforce the Pacific or England, Northern Ireland and Iceland plus transport Lend-Lease supplies to England and Russia. Coincidentally, Churchill, recognising that the movement of troops required shipping and that the necessary vessels could only come from the United States, requested the allocation of ships needed to reinforce the Far East in a telegram to Roosevelt on 4 March, lamenting that Gymnast would have to be postponed in consequence. Roosevelt 'agreed' to this on 7 March and in a second telegram two days later the President suggested that in order to simplify the global war, the areas of conflict should be divided up into three theatres of responsibility, i.e., the Pacific, the Middle East and Europe/Atlantic.

This was accepted by Churchill and so the US assumed responsibility for the Pacific and joint responsibility for Europe with Britain while North Africa would remain a British responsibility. Thus the first strategic action by Britain and the United States after Arcadia was to organise shipping to shore up the defences in the Pacific, in contravention of the 'Germany first' policy Churchill had laboured so long to set in place. However, this was not something the Americans were unhappy with as they had been forced to send three old battleships, an aircraft carrier (USS *Yorktown*) and nine destroyers back to the Pacific from the Atlantic to replace some of the losses at Pearl Harbor.

Britain could not afford more losses in the Far East and with India and Ceylon now threatened, Churchill was beset by criticism in Parliament, the newspapers and even from the Cabinet over the conduct of the war in the Pacific and the Middle East. His standing was not helped by the escape of the German warships *Scharnhorst* and *Prinz Eugen* from their bases in France back to Germany on 12 February though the English Channel, the moat of fortress Britain. An editorial in *The Times* newspaper stated, 'Vice Admiral Ciliax has succeeded where the *Duke of Medina Sidonia* failed ... Nothing more mortifying to the pride of sea-power has happened in home waters since the seventeenth century.'[50]

In the time-honoured ritual followed by most British Prime Ministers under personal pressure, Churchill duly addressed the criticism of himself by reshuffling his Cabinet. Churchill made a statement to the House of Commons on 17 February, promising an inquiry into the escape of the German warships, but refused to answer any questions on the fall of Singapore before walking out of the chamber. Several observers of Churchill at this time later recorded how angry and depressed he was by the turn of events.

Britain and Churchill badly needed some good news to lift their moods and this was provided by Mountbatten and his Combined Operations force, which had for some time been studying the problem of destroying the only dry dock in France (at St-Nazaire) capable of taking the German battleship *Tirpitz* in order to prevent the ship from being able to take refuge there after any sortie into the Atlantic. Mountbatten's team came up with an ambitious plan to ram an old destroyer packed with explosives into the gates of the dry dock and blow it up while commandos disabled the machinery that opened the gates. The destroyer would be escorted by sixteen lightly armed wooden motor launches with the necessary extra fuel drums stored on deck. The operation was approved on 25 February by the Chiefs of Staff and took place on the night of 28 March. The objective was achieved but with very high casualties; of the 611 men that took part in what became known as 'The Greatest Raid of All', more than 400 were killed or taken prisoner and fourteen motor launches were lost. To offset any negative publicity about the high casualties, eighty-nine decorations were awarded in total, including five Victoria Crosses, two of these posthumously.

The Channel episode had been particularly galling to Churchill as the ex-First Lord of the Admiralty and he decided to reinvigorate his Chiefs of Staff; Brooke was duly appointed chairman of the committee on 7 March in place of the ageing Admiral Pound, rather than the more senior Portal. Mountbatten would also attend in the future when Combined Operations matters were on the agenda.

Meanwhile in North Africa, after the initial advances and success of Operation Crusader, the British had been thrown back on the defensive once again by Rommel, largely because the Allied forces there had been reduced by the need to send reinforcements to support the new conflict with Japan.[51] This was a repeat of what had happened the previous year when British troops were sent to Greece, weakening the North African position. The Australian 6th and 7th Divisions already in the Middle East had been recalled to the Far East. Rommel had been reinforced and resupplied and his attack, which began on 21 January, was able to break through the extended British units, retaking Benghazi in late January. The British and Commonwealth units were peremptorily pushed back to the Gazala line just west of Tobruk in just two weeks. The importance of lines of supply was brought home to both the British and the Germans by the continued sinking of their supply ships in the Mediterranean and the significance of the island of Malta began to increase to both sides as a base of operations from which the supply lines to North Africa could be cut. Malta was effectively isolated by sea and was under increasing air attacks while the British could still not run regular supply convoys to the Far East through the Mediterranean because of the presence of the Italian fleet and strong German and Italian aircraft groups. Churchill cabled Auchinleck on 26 February with a request to hear of future plans regarding Malta and

North Africa and this telegram crossed with an appreciation from Auchinleck that anticipated a delay of four months before a new offensive against Rommel could begin. Churchill, under pressure because of the losses in the Far East and a no-confidence motion in Parliament, was furious with this proposed inactivity by Auchinleck and ordered him to return to England for consultations; to the astonishment of the Chiefs of Staff, Auchinleck refused to comply with Churchill's instruction, citing the urgent situation in Libya. Auchinleck was also critical of the performance of British tanks, which he claimed suffered from mechanical problems and were undergunned compared with the German tanks. An uneasy and tense situation between the two men remained for several months until May, during which time Auchinleck's position was supported by a deputation sent from England by Churchill to investigate the situation. Those sent included Stafford Cripps, General Nye (to examine problems with British armour) and Air Chief Marshal Tedder. An exasperated Churchill sent a sarcastic telegram to Auchinleck on 5 May regarding the proposed attack on 15 May:

> We feel the greatest help you could give to the whole war at this juncture would be to engage and defeat the enemy on your Western Front. All our directions upon this subject remain unaltered in their purpose and validity, and we trust you will find it possible to give full effect to them about the date you mentioned to the Lord Privy Seal.

Auchinleck replied next day, advising of another planned delay until 15 June. Churchill and the Chiefs of Staff were forced to resort to a direct order to Auchinleck to attack no later than June, absolving him of all responsibility should the attack fail and Egypt fall as a consequence.

Although the Blitz of the first Battle of London had ended almost a year earlier, the RAF Bomber Command offensive was continuing as a way of hitting back against Germany. In June and July 1941 a study had been made into the accuracy of RAF bombing and the results were a shock to the Air Ministry. Under the most favourable conditions, only one in three aircraft were bombing within 5 miles of their target, and at worst only one in fifteen aircraft were reaching their target over Germany on moonless nights. Churchill dashed off a minute to the Chief of Air Staff, 'This is a very serious paper and seems to require your most urgent attention. I await your proposals for action.'[52]

This document, known as the Butt report, stimulated considerable debate over its own accuracy, which in turn created wider debate over whether some of the resources allocated to Bomber Command should go to Coastal Command in its fight against the U-boats or even to the Navy or Army. Churchill made his position plain in a minute to John Anderson, a Cabinet minister, lamenting the production rates for heavy and medium bomber aircraft, which had a target of 4,000 as a first line strength by July 1943:'The latest forecasts show that of the remaining 16,500 only 11,000 will be got from our own factories. If we are to win the war, we cannot accept this position.'[53]

In November, the RAF had been forced to curtail its bombing missions after heavy losses to German night fighters. However, in February 1942 the debate was largely ended when Harris, an advocate of strategic bombing, was appointed Commander-in-Chief of Bomber Command. Churchill, however, continued to maintain it was not a war-winning strategy by itself:

> You need not argue the value of bombing Germany, because I have my own opinion about that, namely, that it is not decisive, but better than doing nothing, and indeed is a formidable method of injuring the enemy.[54]

The RAF's policy of high-level bombing had been criticised in some quarters, including by the Archbishop of Canterbury. A year later at a press conference with Roosevelt after the Trident talks in Washington, Churchill claimed the bomber offensive 'experiment' would continue but again stated that he did not believe that it would win the war alone.

The loss of Singapore meant that the British required a new naval base to protect waters off India and Burma and access to the Suez Canal. The island of Ceylon was to provide such a base and two brigades of Australian troops were sent there to bolster the island's defences. On 31 March, a strong Japanese naval force entered the Bay of Bengal with the intention of demonstrating the invincibility of the Japanese to India and destroying the newly formed British Eastern Fleet, thereby aiding Japan's campaign in Burma. There had been a great deal of political agitation for independence in India following the advances of the Japanese and the ejection of the British from Malaya and Singapore. India had sent troops to the Middle East and Malaya, and with the fall of Singapore 40,000 Indians were taken prisoner. These captives were then invited to join the pro-independence Indian National Army and fight for the Japanese; some 30,000 men consequently took up the offer and 7,000 later fought against the British in Burma and India.[55] Churchill sent Stafford Cripps to negotiate with Indian political leaders, but with both parties making intransigent demands, no agreement was able to be reached, much to Roosevelt's disappointment and Churchill's relief.

Forewarned by decrypts of Japanese messages, British ships fled Colombo but on 4 April HMS *Dorsetshire* and HMS *Cornwall* were attacked by aircraft from Japanese carriers and both sank within twenty minutes. The Americans were astonished that the British had still not learned the lesson of the ascendancy of air power over sea power following the loss of the *Prince of Wales* and *Repulse*. Uncertain of Japanese intentions and fearful of losing the last British naval base in the Far East, Churchill sent a telegram to Roosevelt, suggesting that there was an immediate opportunity for the Pacific fleet to intervene and compel the Japanese ships to return to the Pacific. Following further losses, including the aircraft carrier HMS *Hermes* on 9 April, the Royal Navy was forced to retire with its inferior slower ships all the way to the coast of East Africa. In desperation, Churchill again turned to Roosevelt, asking for urgent reinforcements and lamenting that, 'With so much of the weight of Japan thrown upon us we have more than we can bear.'[56]

Perhaps irked by Churchill's stance on India and already beset with his own problems of prioritising reinforcements for two theatres, Roosevelt declined Churchill's plea on 17 April but did offer to temporarily send some capital ships to England in order to release the equivalent British ships for duties in the Indian Ocean. Fortunately for the British, the Japanese fleet, having swept clear the Bay of Bengal of British ships, returned to the Pacific on 10 April for the next phase of its operations.

8

THE STRUGGLE FOR STRATEGY

The loss of Singapore and the retreat in Burma which had cut off the Burma Road supply route to the Chinese had convinced Roosevelt that the US would have to step in and take a greater role in determining the strategies for the war. Britain, although stretched to the limit of its resources, had gone from disaster after disaster in the first two years of war and almost could not be relied on as an ally. Out of this realisation, Hopkins and Roosevelt had put together the division of theatres of responsibility approved by Churchill in early March, with the Pacific to be an American responsibility and Europe a joint responsibility. Accordingly, the American planners were determined to take a more active role in the development of strategy and therefore not get involved in sideshows, a move that would likely be resisted by the British.

With the 'Germany first' strategy in mind but also having to contend with demands from the Pacific, especially from MacArthur, Eisenhower's study of 28 February recommended using Britain as a base to firstly step up the air offensive against Germany and then mount a landing in Europe later in order to assist Russia. Interestingly, British planners considering strategy at this time arrived at a similar conclusion:

> Our greatest contribution to a German defeat would be the creation of a major diversion in the West designed to upset German plans and divert German forces from the East. Lack of shipping precludes the strategy of such a diversion anywhere except across the Channel.[1]

This paper was referred for further studies by the British while in Washington over the next few weeks, the War Plans Department worked on other options. A common thread in all the studies was the shortage of shipping. Eisenhower prepared another memorandum on 25 March for Marshall, who made a presentation that day at the White House to Roosevelt, Stimson, Hopkins and the other Chiefs of Staff. Roosevelt sanctioned the development of more detailed invasion plans, which were drawn up two days later; Marshall and then Roosevelt approved the plans the same day, 1 April. As these plans had been prepared by the War Department outside the Combined Chiefs of Staff planning process, Roosevelt asked Hopkins and Marshall to go to Britain to discuss them with the British Chiefs of Staff, the Americans arriving on 8 April. Having taken the trouble to set up a Combined Chiefs of Staff organisation in Washington, the American plans were not submitted to the Combined Chiefs of Staff or their planners, almost as if the Americans did not want the British Chiefs of Staff to see them and have time to prepare objections before their arrival. In the interim, the British had also explored the possibility of an emergency landing in the Pas-de-Calais in a series of papers by the Joint Planning Staff. Even before Marshall arrived, on 6 April the British Chiefs of Staff had sent a telegram to their counterparts in America expressing their desire to help the Russians:'We consider the importance of helping Russia in 1942 is so great that the consideration of an offensive in 1943 should not prevent us from doing anything we can, however small, this summer.'[2]

The American plan brought to England by General Marshall (which came to be known as Marshall's Memorandum) was for a major landing on the Continent to afford the maximum possible support to Russia in April 1943. This landing (known as Operation Roundup) could not take place before April 1943 owing to a shortage of shipping and the time needed for the build-up of sufficient forces in the UK (under Operation Bolero).

This plan, which Marshall presented to the British Chiefs of Staff on 9 April, had one contentious feature which was a contingency for an emergency landing (Operation Sledgehammer) in force in 1942 if the Russians appeared close to collapse, or, in the event of a new scenario based on the Germans in Western Europe becoming critically weakened. Marshall described such an operation that year to assist the Russians as a 'sacrificial attack'. At a follow-up meeting on the morning of 14 April, the British Chiefs of Staff produced a paper in response which, while agreeing with the US long-term strategy, argued that the situation in the Pacific had to be stabilised first as the Japanese threatened India. If India was to fall, the Middle East would be at risk and Britain's ability to continue the war with Germany would be severely impaired unless substantial American naval forces or aircraft could be sent to the Indian Ocean or Britain to allow Royal Navy ships to be released to reinforce the area.[3] For Operation Sledgehammer, the Chiefs of Staff detailed three scenarios for the outcome of the Russo-German battle and only in the first scenario, which posited a Russian collapse, might the British 'be compelled' to make a supreme effort to draw off German forces from the Eastern Front. In the other two scenarios of Russia holding or even defeating Germany, no action was contemplated unless the Germans themselves were on the point of collapse.

There were enough caveats in this paper to set off alarm bells for Marshall, but these were ignored. Hopkins, although not a military person, was also swept along by the apparent British enthusiasm for Marshall's plan in his regular direct reports to Roosevelt. Marshall's Memorandum was then discussed again at an evening Defence Committee meeting with Marshall and Hopkins present; Brooke argued that if the Germans were successful in their Russian campaign, any landing on the Continent would in fact be more dangerous as the Germans would be able to divert more troops to France. The American view was that Operation Sledgehammer was needed precisely to prevent such a Russian collapse. Portal stated that any landing would involve heavy British aircraft losses and Mountbatten spoke of the shortage of essential resources, i.e., landing craft for such a landing.[4] In a response constituting a mild threat, Hopkins raised the question of American public opinion and its desire for action against Japan in the Pacific. The British finally accepted Marshall's plan in principle with a qualification about the Far East needing support. After the Defence Committee, for which no agreed minutes exist, Brooke recorded in his diary: 'A momentous meeting at which we accepted their proposals for offensive action in Europe in 1942 perhaps and in 1943 for certain.'[5]

As Churchill himself had proposed in December 1941 a major landing on the Continent in 1943, the only point of contention was Operation Sledgehammer that year. Churchill summed up the meeting in a somewhat anodyne fashion in a telegram to Roosevelt: 'Although it remained to work out the details of the plan, it was clear that there was complete unanimity on the framework. The two nations would march ahead together in a noble brotherhood of arms.'[6]

While paying lip service to Marshall by accepting his plans in general, the British had successfully avoided any firm commitment to the Americans and Russians for Operation Sledgehammer that year. They also secured continued American support for the Far East in the provision of shipping to transfer an

Australian division from the Middle East back to Australia, troops to Australia and New Zealand, heavy bombers for India and for the relief of British warships in the Atlantic, which could then be transferred to the Pacific. Once again, the principle of 'Germany first' had been put aside and initial American efforts would be in support of the Far East. The Americans had already arranged for General Stilwell, as the most senior American officer who spoke Chinese, to go to Burma to command three Chinese divisions that had entered northern Burma, and for the Tenth Air Force based in India to be strongly reinforced.

The British desperately needed American aid and troops to be based in England for a future major landing and so could not rigidly oppose Marshall's plan. At the same time, there was genuine doubt about the abilities of the Russians to withstand a second all-out German offensive. Furthermore, Churchill was not prepared to oversee another failed operation and evacuation from the Continent by the then somewhat demoralised British Army. There would be no action to assist the Russians, who would continue their life and death single-handed struggle with the bulk of the German Army. This attrition suited the British, who in the wider conflict were only thinking of their own survival unlike the more global-thinking Americans. Marshall's choice of the word 'sacrificial' in his memorandum was unfortunate as Britain was struggling to put new forces into the field after the considerable losses in the war so far, even though two of the proposed seven divisions of the proposed Operation Sledgehammer force would be American. Marshall and the British Chiefs of Staff both claimed they would continue to prepare plans for Operation Sledgehammer, Marshall making a pointed reference to this in a letter of thanks to Churchill after the London talks.[7]

The Americans appear to have left London on 17 April with the impression that Operation Sledgehammer would automatically proceed in view of the worsening situation in Russia. Churchill later said he saw this only as an option in the war against Germany and had other more pressing imperial defence concerns at that time in the Indian Ocean and in the Middle East. To take the fight to Germany, Churchill in fact preferred two other peripheral plans, Operation Gymnast in North Africa and Operation Jupiter, the occupation of northern Norway to assist Russia by providing air support from Norwegian air fields to help safeguard the passage of aid convoys to Russia. Perhaps fortunately, these were not discussed with the Americans.[8] There is no doubt that Marshall and indeed Roosevelt were deceived about Operation Sledgehammer by a Churchill anxious to secure American reinforcements under Operation Bolero for the larger operation Roundup in 1943. Brooke expressed his reservations but these were nullified by the sweeping statements of support made by Churchill to Marshall in the Defence Committee meeting of 14 April and telegrams to Roosevelt:

12th April
I must say that I thought the proposals for an interim operation in certain contingencies this year met the difficulties and uncertainties in an absolutely sound manner. If, as our experts believe, we can carry this whole plan through successfully, it will be one of the grand events in all the history of war.

17th April
Marshall explained that you had been reluctant to press for an enterprise that was fraught with such grave risks and dire consequences until you could make a substantial air contribution; but he left us in no doubt that if it were found necessary to act earlier, you, Mr President would earnestly wish to throw in every available scrap of human and material resources. We are proceeding with plans and preparations on that basis. Broadly speaking, our agreed programme is a crescendo of activity on the continent, starting with an ever increasing air offensive both by day and night and more frequent and larger scale raids in which United States troops will take part.[9]

These are Churchill's words and there can be no other interpretation of them – Operation Sledgehammer was on, provided the Americans opened the tap of resources for Britain. Post-war excuses that the Americans did not understand Churchill's manner of speaking are unfounded. Churchill, already under pressure from Roosevelt regarding the breakdown of talks for the self-government of India (the Atlantic Charter had come back to bite Churchill), told the Americans what they wanted to hear. Unfortunately the stage was now set for future recriminations and mistrust when the Americans finally realised the British position.

Once Marshall had left the country, the British Chiefs of Staff duly approved another paper for future Anglo-American operations on the Continent in 1942 and 1943 which had the objective of converting the United Kingdom into a base for future operations in Western Europe on which the British and Americans would descend in the spring of 1943. A bridgehead on the Continent in 1942 would only be attempted in the summer if a suitable opportunity occurred.[10] Bomber Command was also charged with inflicting the heaviest damage on the German aircraft industry. This report represented the true British position on strategy for 1942 at that time.

The Americans ultimately decided that they too did not have the resources to reinforce the Royal Navy in the Indian Ocean but did offer to place American warships under British command if the German battleship *Tirpitz* sallied out into the Atlantic.

To add to British problems, Marshal Pétain resigned as head of the Vichy government in France and was replaced by Pierre Laval, who was expected to take a more pro-German hard-line approach with the Allies. Admiral Darlan, who had been nominated as Pétain's successor, was forced to relinquish several Cabinet positions he held prior to Laval's appointment but remained C-in-C of the French armed forces. The Americans at last recalled their Ambassador to Vichy France (Admiral Leahy) in protest, having maintained diplomatic relations since the fall of France in mid 1940. The American diplomats believed that Laval was deeply unpopular in the French colonies of North Africa and there was a possibility they might rebel but at this stage Roosevelt urged there should be no discussion of any joint Anglo-American landings, now called Operation Super-Gymnast.[11]

The competing needs of the different theatres for American resources in May then precipitated a change in American strategic thinking. Not only was a build-up in the UK promised but the US had commitments for shipping to the Middle East, troops and aircraft for Australia and the Pacific, aid to Russia and to reinforcing China and India. MacArthur was clamouring for resources while Admiral King also strongly objected to aircraft being diverted to places such as Australia for MacArthur. Following a memorandum from Admiral King declaring that there were insufficient forces to hold the Pacific and that it needed to be made a short-term priority, Marshall wrote to Roosevelt on 6 May summarising the competing issues and of the need for the President to make a decision on whether Operation Bolero should be abandoned altogether. The importance of Russia to the war was emphasised: 'Russia must be sustained as an active, effective participant in the war. That issue will be decided this summer or fall.'[12]

Somewhat frustrated at the inability of his own Chiefs of Staff to reach a decision, Roosevelt conducted a review himself that day of possible actions, emphasising the contribution of the Russians:

It must be constantly reiterated that Russian armies are killing more Germans and destroying more Axis materiel then all the twenty-five United Nations put together. To help Russia, therefore, is the primary consideration.[13]

Roosevelt also made known his firm desire to see US troops in action in 1942 and referred to a Second Front which:

> ... might have to be created anyway, if Russia were to be seriously endangered, even if the operation on the part of the British and the Americans had to be called an operation of desperation.[14]

The Soviet Foreign Minister, Molotov, arrived in London on 20 May for talks with Eden and Churchill which culminated in the signing of the Anglo-Soviet agreement on 26 May. However, Molotov's primary mission was to plead for Allied operations to draw off at least forty German divisions from the hard-pressed Russian Front. Churchill reiterated all the arguments used in the debate over Operation Sledgehammer with the Americans the previous month and pointed out that Britain was already confronted by forty-four German and Italian divisions: eight in Norway, eleven in North Africa and twenty-five in France and Holland. Even at this stage of the war, Molotov admitted to Russia's intention of recognising the 1941 borders of Poland and not those that existed at the outbreak of war, which was in conflict with British guarantees made to Poland.[15] Churchill and the British government were prepared to meet the British schedules of aid under the Lend-Lease Second Protocol but were noncommittal about opening a Second Front, refusing to commit to any actions until Molotov returned from America. Molotov then went on to Washington, where he stayed from 29 May to 1 June, having been specifically invited by Roosevelt in a message to Stalin in April. Molotov received a much more favourable reception in talks with Roosevelt and Hopkins at the White House compared with that afforded by the British in London. On 30 May, Roosevelt briefed Marshall and King on the initial discussions with Molotov and the urgent Russian request for a Second Front as soon as possible that would be large enough to draw off the requested number of divisions. Marshall was asked whether the preparations for the Second Front were proceeding and he replied positively. The result of Molotov's visit was a draft joint Russo-American communiqué (issued both in Washington and London) which contained a strong commitment to open a Second Front in 1942: 'In the course of the conversations full understanding was reached with regard to the urgent tasks of creating a Second Front in Europe in 1942.'[16]

Armed with this document, Molotov sped back to London for further discussions with Churchill as arranged. Churchill, however, remained steadfast in his position of not committing to a Second Front in 1942 and later claimed the communiqué was intended only to deceive Germany. To underline the British stance and disarm any future argument or recriminations, Molotov was presented with an aide-memoire from Churchill to take back to Stalin on the issue of a Second Front which made no firm commitments for action in 1942 and specifically contained the phrase, 'We can therefore give no promise in this matter.'[17] By way of compensation, Churchill also offered to ship six RAF squadrons to Murmansk to help protect the Arctic convoys. While Churchill's aide-memoire was very specific, Molotov had largely achieved his mission and secured a public announcement by the government of America for a Second Front that year. However, if this was only to deceive the Germans, then the Russians too had been deceived.

Roosevelt had proposed a Second Front that year in his directive of 6 May, only five weeks after Marshall and King had visited London to hammer out an agreement on future strategy which provided for no Second Front and only a conditional landing in 1942. According to Roosevelt, the principal objective in the European theatre was to help Russia and he was convinced of the need for action in 1942 to start a Second Front in order to compel the withdrawal of German Air Force and Army units from Russia.[18] Molotov had confirmed Roosevelt's belief in the soundness of this strategy and, ever sensitive to public opinion, the President knew that the War Department had received letters from several American trade unions demanding a Second Front.[19] In May there had already been a major demonstration for a Second Front by 50,000 people in Trafalgar Square organised by the Communist Party and several more occurred during the year. Newspaper editorials in Britain, the United States and Australia all called for a Second Front in 1942 to aid Russia.

At the end of March, Churchill's scientific advisor Professor Lindemann had produced a memorandum on the bombing of Germany and proposed that German homes be targeted to break the spirit of the people by making a third of the population homeless. Lindemann believed this tactic of area bombing would overcome the deficiences of trying to precision bomb targets at night. After some scientific debate, this policy was adopted by the RAF. On 30 May, aided by new electronic navigational beams and four-engined heavy bombers, the RAF made the first 1,000 bomber raid on Cologne. In a formidable demonstration of power, more than 12,000 buildings were destroyed or damaged and 19,000 homes were destroyed or seriously damaged in the resulting fires. This was vindication of the beliefs of Lindemann and Harris and established the tactics for the rest of the war. The raid gave the Allies a small lift in their morale and was something the Americans were determined to copy once sufficient aircraft had arrived in the UK.[20] As part of Marshall's Memorandum in April and as agreed in the Washington talks following Pearl Harbor, an American heavy bomber force would be based in England to work alongside the RAF in taking the offensive to Germany. In the early summer of 1942, the first units of three bombardment groups of the designated VIII Bomber Command began to arrive and establish themselves on English airfields. It was USAAF practice to bomb during daylight and in training bombers had achieved a very high degree of accuracy, so it was agreed by the Allies that the US forces would bomb by day and the RAF would continue their missions at night. RAF bombing missions were usually carried out at night to avoid daylight interceptions by German fighter aircraft, but this had the drawback that targets were more difficult to identify and bomb accurately so the British had resorted to a policy of targeting entire urban and industrial areas in German towns and cities.

Mountbatten had arrived in Washington on 2 June at Roosevelt's request, officially to discuss the landing craft construction programme and Combined Operations training with his American counterparts. This visit was even offered by Roosevelt as evidence to Molotov and the Russians that planning for the Second Front was proceeding. Roosevelt had cabled Churchill on 6 June with the news of his change of thinking regarding a Second Front, promising to send further details but he never did. The Americans had also been unsettled by a telegram from Churchill on 28 May, which, while stating that all preparations were proceeding on the largest scale, said that 'Dickie' would explain the difficulties of launching a medium-scale operation in 1942; this telegram also mentioned possible operations in Norway and North Africa, which were seen by Roosevelt, Hopkins and Marshall as diversionary operations to the main cross-Channel landing.[21]

Roosevelt and Mountbatten met for dinner on 9 June and Mountbatten first outlined the difficulties of undertaking Operation Sledgehammer that year. Such was the gravity of these talks (with no one from the State Department present) that Mountbatten felt the need to send a letter recapitulating their main discussion points and from this the items discussed can be deduced. On learning of this change in the British position from what had been agreed and understood, Roosevelt pointedly asked Mountbatten to remind Churchill of his previous undertaking regarding an operation to take the pressure off the Russians. Mountbatten reaffirmed the latest British position that Operation Sledgehammer was not possible. Roosevelt then objected to American troops in the UK being used to defend Britain while British troops were being deployed in the Middle East, which the Americans regarded as a peripheral campaign. In line with a previous telegram from Churchill, Mountbatten then raised the question of the Americans mounting Operation Gymnast or even sending divisions to Egypt.[22]

The British knew that the deployment of American forces in the Middle East was not well regarded by General Marshall and therefore that left, as far as the British were concerned, north-west Africa and Operation Super-Gymnast as the only viable option for future action. Roosevelt's reaction to this change of British sentiment is not recorded but he had already raised the question of whether the transfer of American troops to Britain as part of Operation Bolero was even worthwhile. It is also likely that he threatened to make the Pacific theatre America's first priority. When Mountbatten returned to England and reported this conversation, Churchill was sufficiently alarmed to ask Roosevelt on 13 June for an immediate face-to-face meeting. The new CIGS, Alan Brooke, recorded in his diary that 'Churchill considered that Roosevelt was getting a little off the rails.'[23]

Churchill and his Chiefs of Staff had also reviewed the strategic situation in response to the telegram from Roosevelt on 6 June. The Chiefs had proposed a large-scale raid (Operation Imperator) by one division as a response to a *cri de coeur* from the Russians if and when the Germans looked like winning. Following a minute on 8 June from Churchill, the Chiefs of Staff committee decided once and for all that there would be no Operation Sledgehammer landing in 1942 unless the British were to create a permanent bridgehead in France.[24] In his minute examining future operations, Churchill also altered the scenarios in Marshall's Memorandum for the Allied conditional commitment to Operation Sledgehammer to two dependent conditions: firstly, in the event of a collapse in the morale of Germans and, secondly, that any landings would be permanent. Churchill knew that both were extremely unlikely in 1942.[25]

As the American build-up in Britain had been comparatively slow to this point, any troops mounting Operation Sledgehammer would have to be British. Roosevelt had apparently told Molotov that he would contemplate a sacrifice of 120,000 men if necessary to help the Russians and the British War Cabinet was distinctly unimpressed with this callous commitment by another country of British soldiers.[26]

There was now a major split between British and American proposed strategy which could only be resolved by the meeting of Roosevelt and Churchill. The British and Churchill would have to clear up the misunderstandings created regarding Operation Sledgehammer during Marshall's visit in April.

While Churchill and his party were en route, Roosevelt met with his Chiefs of Staff and asked them to reconsider the north-west African plan. Having only recently affirmed their strategic priorities in London in April along with Roosevelt's memorandum of 6 May, this request was very much to their frustration. Marshall had already prepared a paper opposing Operation Super-Gymnast on the basis of that the use of troops in north-west Africa would be incapable of decisive strategic results and divert resources from the build-up in the UK. This paper was used by Stimson in a further memorandum to Roosevelt on 19 June also opposing Super-Gymnast which was endorsed by Marshall and Eisenhower.[27]

On the arrival of the British, Churchill and Roosevelt began their discussions on 19 June in New York while the Combined Chiefs of Staff met separately in Washington, much to Marshall's dismay as Churchill would be able to bring to bear his personality and powers of persuasion on an apparently easily swayed Roosevelt. Although there are no records of the discussions, the two men undoubtedly covered all aspects of the war including future operations and Roosevelt would have told Churchill of his renewed interest in Super-Gymnast, the opposition to it from Marshall and his desire to see American troops in action in 1942.

Brooke opened the Combined Chiefs of staff meeting on 19 June by immediately stating that the Chiefs of Staff and Churchill were in Washington as a result of the talks between Mountbatten and the President, which is further evidence of how alarmed Churchill was at Mountbatten's report of his White House dinner. During the meeting the next day, both the British and American Chiefs of Staff agreed that future plans depended on the next few weeks of fighting in Russia and that Operation Super-Gymnast was unsound in view of the uncertain political situation in north-west Africa and the need to reduce supplies to existing theatres in order to stage such an operation. Marshall put forward the view that if the build-up in Britain (Bolero) was delayed by the mounting of Operation Super-Gymnast, then there could be no Operation Roundup at all in 1943.[28] A paper was duly written confirming their joint views for presentation to Roosevelt and Churchill.

However, Churchill was working in the opposite direction in his talks with Roosevelt and in a note handed to Roosevelt on 20 June he argued strongly against Operation Sledgehammer as being doomed to failure; he then added that in his view the Allies did not want British and American troops to be idle for 1942 and asked the question as to where they could be used, suggesting in the last line of the note that Operation Gymnast should be studied again.

Indeed, at this point Roosevelt and Churchill were diametrically opposed to their own respective Chiefs of Staff and the note was a canny move on the part of Churchill following the previous day's talks with the President to steer both Chiefs of Staff towards changing their position.

Roosevelt and Churchill then went by train to Washington, where they arrived on 21 June only for the conference to be overtaken by events in North Africa where an offensive by Rommel that had begun on 26 May had broken through the British lines and captured Tobruk on 21 June. Rommel had struck while the recently appointed General Auchinleck had prevaricated and the loss of Tobruk was a great shock to Churchill, who had already lost confidence in the general: 'Defeat is one thing, disgrace is another. I am ashamed. I cannot understand why Tobruk gave in. More than 30,000 of our men put their hands up. If they won't fight …'[29]

Roosevelt immediately offered reinforcements such as bomber and fighter groups and the US 2nd Armoured Division. When finding adequate shipping proved to be a problem, 300 medium tanks already allocated to the US 1st Armoured Division were offered instead along with 100 self-propelled guns, which Churchill gratefully accepted.

In a series of heated meetings at the White House the same day for which no records exist, Roosevelt and Churchill prevailed upon Marshall, Brooke and Hopkins to reverse their position and resume planning for Operation Gymnast. Stimson recorded in his diary, '… they had been having a good deal of a pow-wow and a rumpus up at the White House. He called Marshall up there and he and Harry Hopkins and Marshall and Churchill and Brooke have been having it out.'[30]

Roosevelt had been convinced by Churchill of the potential for operations in north-west Africa as Marshall had feared; this would also get Churchill off the hook for Sledgehammer as there would be few resources for such a cross-Channel operation after any landing in north-west Africa. After many hours of debate, an agreement was reached as recorded in a memorandum that day by Lord Ismay in which planning was to proceed for Bolero and Sledgehammer along with alternative operations in north-west Africa, Norway and even Spain to be ready as alternatives if the plans for Bolero and Sledgehammer did not offer a probable chance of success in 1942.[31] Marshall remained steadfastly opposed to Operation Gymnast and refuted many of the points in Churchill's note by pointing out that the Allies would not be idle if they mounted Operation Sledgehammer, which he believed was the best way of helping the Russians in 1942.[32]

In London, the fall of Tobruk had given further ammunition to Churchill's political enemies and on 25 June a motion of no confidence in his conduct of the war was proposed in the House of Commons. Egypt was once again threatened, German U-boats dominated the Atlantic Ocean and the situation in Russia remained critical. However, in the Pacific US naval forces had achieved a great victory at the Battle of Midway, sinking four Japanese aircraft carriers, which marked a turning point in that campaign being conducted solely by the Americans. The news from North Africa and of the no-confidence motion brought the Washington conference to an end prematurely. Marshall was very keen for Churchill to inspect the rapidly growing US Army and Churchill duly went to Camp Jackson in South Carolina on 24 June, where he watched a parachute drop and live firing exercises. Churchill was polite in his enthusiasm but remained sceptical that the inexperienced American troops could immediately compete with the Germans, saying that it took a minimum of two years to produce a trained soldier.[33]

In summary, no commitments to future strategy were made at the Washington conference, which only agreed to consider a number of alternatives, including Operation Sledgehammer, to which the Americans were now aware of the extent of British opposition. The likelihood of a Second Front to assist Russia had faded quickly. The tactics of Churchill and Brooke were finally admitted to after the war by a member of the Chiefs of Staffs secretariat:

> That Bolero should continue full blast until 1st September but we never seriously contemplated using these forces for a cross-Channel attack that year. Our idea was to get them onto our side of the Atlantic so that they would be committed for the war against Germany, and we hoped that if we had the forces in England we could persuade Roosevelt to use them in Africa ...[34]

Any ill feeling towards the British was tempered by the news from Egypt, about which the Americans were genuinely sympathetic. Roosevelt asked Marshall on 30 June what could be done immediately to support the British position in the Middle East but the general believed there was little practical assistance that could be offered in time as the next forty-eight hours would be critical.

Churchill and his staff returned to London on 27 June to prepare for the debate to more bad news in that his government had lost a by-election in Maldon, Essex. Mid 1942 marked the low point of the war for the British. The British Army in North Africa was retreating to Egypt and the Empire in the Far East was almost non-existent except for India and parts of Burma following the capture of Singapore, Malaya and Hong Kong by the Japanese. In the war at sea, the U-boat menace was increasing as the tonnage of shipping sunk each month was on the rise with the easy pickings off the American Eastern Seaboard. To make matters worse, a change of codes meant that the British had been temporarily prevented from decrypting signals to the U-boats from the German naval command. British convoys to take Lend-Lease materiel to Russia were losing more and more ships as the Germans deployed aircraft and U-boats against them, while warships including *Tirpitz* gathered in the Norwegian fjords. The Admiralty believed the convoys should be stopped unless the German threat from the air could be neutralised and Admiral King agreed. However, there was intense political pressure to continue the convoys from both Stalin and Roosevelt so Churchill ordered the next convoy, PQ 17, to sail; the operation would be justified if half the ships got through despite his misgivings. Even when presented with this pessimistic picture, the no-confidence motion was ultimately resoundingly defeated in the House of Commons by 475 votes to 25 on 2 July.

Acutely aware of the danger to the British positions in the Middle East, Churchill asked Roosevelt on 4 July to cable Stalin for permission to divert a shipment of forty Lend-Lease planes from the port of their arrival, Basra, to Cairo, to which Stalin agreed. Heavy bombers from the Tenth Air Force in India destined for use by the Chinese were also diverted to the Middle East to a howl of protest from Chiang Kai-Shek, who apparently accused Roosevelt of being insincere and posed in a subsequent letter a bitter rhetorical question as to whether the Allies were interested in maintaining the China in the war or whether China should sue for peace.

The British Chiefs of Staff decided to review all the arguments for and against Operation Sledgehammer in order for the War Cabinet to make a decision on it one way or another. Their report was examined at their meeting on 6 July with Churchill present; the Chiefs utilised Marshall's argument against Operation Sledgehammer, saying that it would jeopardise Bolero and subsequent operations in 1943 (Operation Roundup), just as Operation Gymnast would divert resources from Bolero: 'It was unanimously agreed that Operation Sledgehammer offered no chance of success and would merely ruin all prospects of Roundup in 1943.'[35]

This was confirmed by the War Cabinet next day and 8 July Churchill cabled Roosevelt with this final decision with a comment that the proposed landings in north-west Africa offered the best chance of relieving the Russian Front and included a sweetener of suggesting that Marshall should command the Roundup forces.[36] Churchill was also keen to mount Operation Jupiter in northern Norway but his enthusiasm for this operation was not shared by his own Chiefs of Staff, causing him to lament their lack of support and say that perhaps an advertisement should be placed in the newspaper for good ideas.[37]

Still opposed to Operation Gymnast, and galled by the British decision on Sledgehammer, Marshall wrote another memorandum to Roosevelt on 10 July which King countersigned, claiming that if Gymnast was undertaken there could not be a major cross-Channel operation in 1943 and therefore the United States should concentrate on the Pacific.[38] Roosevelt accordingly asked for copies of the plans for operations in the Pacific and Marshall had to admit that no detailed ones had been prepared. Now somewhat annoyed, on 14 July Roosevelt firmly rejected Marshall and King's memorandum as a red herring useful only for negotiating purposes. He resolved to send Marshall to London again in a last-ditch attempt to persuade the British to carry out Operation Sledgehammer, or at least achieve unanimity in purpose between the two Allies. Roosevelt also suggested that Marshall's memorandum be rewritten so as to make it not look like to future historians that the Americans were intending to abandon the British.[39]

The victory over the Japanese at Midway had restored the balance of naval power in the Pacific and the United States was ready to transition from defence to a limited offensive. Marshall and King's plans for the Pacific were, however, advanced enough for the first step against Japan to have been approved on 2 July by the Joint Chiefs of Staff. This was for a landing on the island of Guadalcanal at the southern end of the Solomon Islands with a target date of 1 August in order to contain the southward advances of the Japanese in the region. Despite the avowed strategy of 'Germany first', in the first six months of 1942 more than 228,000 American troops were sent to the Pacific theatre compared with only 74,000 to Europe for the war against Germany.[40]

Marshall and King, accompanied by Hopkins, left for Britain on 16 July after a stormy meeting at the White House regarding Pacific and European priorities the previous day, carrying explicit instructions from Roosevelt which included the statement, 'It is of the highest importance that US ground troops be brought into action against the enemy in 1942.'[41]

Dill, fast becoming a firm friend of Marshall's, sent a telegram to Churchill warning of the high feelings running in the White House and the likely attitude of Marshall and King on their arrival, both still convinced of their own beliefs. Marshall wanted a cross-Channel operation as soon as possible while King was not enthusiastic about Operation Gymnast and both were prepared to make the war against the Japanese their first priority if the British continued to prevaricate. A history book critical of Churchill's planning of the Dardanelles Expedition in the First World War and warning of the dangers of changing the decisive theatre once selected was being passed around by the US Chiefs of Staff to each other as required reading.[42]

Talks began on 19 July in London with Marshall still clearly wanting to take the fight to Germany immediately or make Japan the first priority; he was supported in this by Eisenhower and other senior American officers in England. A new German offensive in the south towards Stalingrad and the Caucasus was causing major problems for the Russians and the Americans believed that the survival of Russia was still in the balance so the need for Sledgehammer was greater than ever.

Churchill opened his own discussions with the American delegation on 20 July by stating that since the British had been unable to make a satisfactory plan for Operation Sledgehammer they were prepared to listen to any American plan with an open mind. Using a plan prepared by Eisenhower's staff in order to overcome likely British objections, Marshall countered by trying to convince the British to agree to an operation to establish a permanent landing in the Cotentin Peninsula. Argument continued for several days without any resolution and Marshall and his team were unable to come up with a credible alternative plan.[43] Marshall remained steadfastly opposed to anything other than a landing on the Continent, fearing that American forces would never disentangle themselves from the Mediterranean once committed; Hopkins reported on the progress of the talks each day to Roosevelt.

Finally, on 22 July, Churchill proposed to Marshall that he send a telegram to Roosevelt advising that they could not reach an agreement on Operation Sledgehammer. This came after Churchill and the Chiefs of Staff had canvassed the War Cabinet and again heard the unanimous British opposition to mounting Sledgehammer. Churchill had effectively called the Americans' bluff of threatening to divert resources to the Pacific and he already knew Roosevelt's preferred strategy and desire to see US troops in action somewhere.

Marshall was forced to send Roosevelt a telegram that night informing him of the lack of agreement and in response an unsurprised Roosevelt promptly cabled Marshall that night, instructing him to develop a plan for using American troops offensively anywhere in Africa or even Norway as long as it was as soon as possible.[44] Two days later, Marshall finally signalled that an agreement had been reached and there would be no Operation Sledgehammer in 1942. A joint memorandum was then prepared by Marshall, King and the British Chiefs of Staff for the War Cabinet. Preparations for Operation Roundup, the major landing on the Continent in 1943, would continue and a landing on the north-west coast of Africa would be made by December 1942 only if a Russian collapse looked inevitable or made Roundup impractical in 1943. The memorandum also recognised that if operations in north-west Africa went ahead, Operation Roundup would in all probability be impracticable for successful execution in 1943. There was sting in the tail of the memorandum; as there was no definite operation in 1942, Marshall stated that fifteen groups of aircraft including five groups of heavy and medium bombers previously designated for Britain were to be redeployed to the Pacific theatre.[45]

When Roosevelt was informed of the agreement reached in London, he promptly instructed that landings should be made in north-west Africa by 30 October, which ignored the fact that this was only agreed as an alternative operation in the event of a Russian collapse. Marshall and King, however, did not believe a decision regarding Africa had been reached in London and far from being satisfied with the outcome of their meetings with the British, informed Roosevelt on their return to Washington that if Roundup did not take place in 1943, the US was committed to a strategy in 1943 of '... a defensive, encircling line of action with respect to Germany except for air operations (which are to be intensified as much as possible) and for the blockade'.[46]

Marshall and King tried to point out at a Combined Chiefs of Staff meeting on 30 July that no decision had been reached and a decision for Africa (now renamed Operation Torch) meant no Roundup in 1943 but Roosevelt would have none of it, announcing the same day that the north-west African landings would take place as soon as possible.[47] Roosevelt had ignored the advice of his Chiefs of Staff and made this key military decision himself primarily based on his political requirement to get US troops fighting Germans anywhere in 1942, preferably before the 5 November Congressional mid-term elections. The quickest way to do this was to undertake Operation Torch against French north-west Africa. Other factors in Roosevelt's thinking were that the operation would provide an easy victory against a few Frenchmen more than likely to switch allegiance from Vichy France to the Allies. Disappointed by the opposition from King and Marshall, Roosevelt had reorganised the Joint Chiefs of Staff on 28 July by bringing in Admiral Leahy, the retired previous Ambassador to Vichy France, as the President's Chief of Staff to whom Marshall, King and Arnold would report. Admiral Leahy, who had been proposed for the position as Chief of Staff by Marshall, had provided Roosevelt with expert intelligence on the French colonies and their likely reaction to any landing. As this would be a largely American operation, this also avoided the political and military complications of sending American forces to Egypt or having British forces under American command. American troops would finally enter the Second World War not directly against Germany but in north-west Africa against the French as this was politically expedient for Roosevelt; assistance to Russia was only a secondary consideration. Churchill was pleased with the decision for north-west Africa, as he stated in a prescient minute of 23 July which foresaw the possibility of the flanking attack that was Gymnast becoming the main attack northwards into Europe or even combining it with a landing on the Continent in the summer of 1943.[48] Moreover, a failed Operation Sledgehammer and another evacuation that year from France would have made it much more difficult for Churchill to stay in office.

In private, many Americans were far from happy with the British stance. Stimson claimed that the British were fatigued and defeatist, having gone back on their promises, and were ignoring the help being offered by its vigorous ally.[49] Winant was also strongly in favour of a Second Front and expressed his unhappiness to Eden. At this point the American Chiefs of Staff, the Russians and de Gaulle's Free French were all strongly in favour of Operation Sledgehammer and only the British remained firmly opposed. The US Army, much to Marshall's chagrin, would fight its first action of the war against the French in an African sideshow.

Churchill had won his Battle of strategy with the US Joint Chiefs of Staff – a battle that would have major consequences for the prosecution of the rest of the war. Aware of Roosevelt's political sensitivities, Churchill had outmanoeuvred Marshall by exploiting the differences between the US Chiefs of Staff and their Commander-in-Chief. Eisenhower thought that the decision of, 'July 22, 1942, could well go down as the "blackest day in history", particularly if Russia is defeated in the big Boche drive now so alarmingly under way'.[50]

The Americans therefore became involved in the Mediterranean at the insistence of Roosevelt and not Churchill. The decision to make the landings in north-west Africa also had the effect of slowing the build-up of American forces such as bomber aircraft and infantry in England under Operation Bolero, although this was denied by Churchill and Roosevelt. They ordered preparations for Roundup to continue at full speed simultaneously but there were simply no other resources available for Gymnast at the time. A British Joint Planning Staff paper in July written during Marshall and Hopkins' visit that studied the possible effect of Operation Gymnast on Bolero/Roundup, concluded that Roundup could not be mounted until twelve months after Gymnast, as Marshall had foreseen.[51]

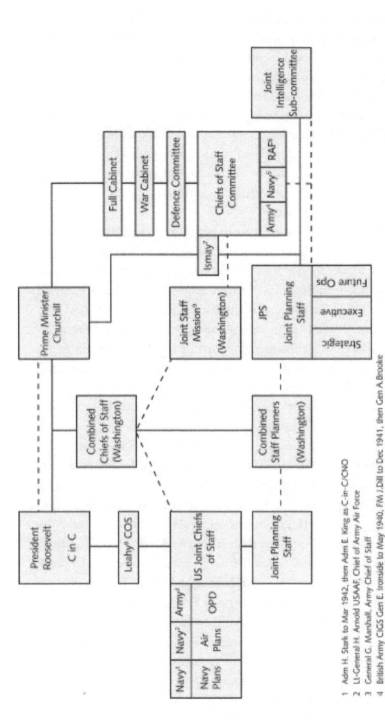

1 Adm H. Stark to Mar 1942, then Adm E. King as C-in-C/CNO
2 Lt-General H. Arnold USAAF, Chief of Army Air Force
3 General G. Marshall, Army Chief of Staff
4 British Army CIGS Gen E. Ironside to May 1940, FM J.Dill to Dec 1941, then Gen A.Brooke
5 Adm of Fleet D. Pound to October 1943, then Adm A. Cunningham
6 Air Chief Marshal C. Newall to Oct 1940, ACM C. Portal
7 Maj Gen H. Ismay (+ War Cabinet Secretariat) to Minister of Defence (Churchill)
8 Adm W. Leahy from July 1942, COS to C-in-C (Roosevelt)
9 Joint Staff Mission (COS representatives in Combined Chiefs of Staff meetings in Washington)

British Chiefs of Staff Committee was chaired by C. Newall (Chief of the Air Staff) to October 1940; D. Pound (Admiral of the Fleet) to March 1942;
and A. Brooke (Chief of the Imperial General Staff) for remainder of the war.

The combined Anglo–American organisation in mid 1942 for determining strategy in the Second World War.

Churchill and Stalin in Moscow

After heavy losses were suffered by the latest aid convoy to Russia, PQ 17, the Defence Committee suspended further attempts on 13 July.[52] Twenty-three ships of thirty-six had been lost to U-boats and aircraft, many more than was acceptable even to Churchill. After receiving reports that the *Tirpitz* had sailed, the decision was made to order the convoy to scatter. In his history of the Second World War, Churchill claimed he had no knowledge of this decision but the minutes of the War Cabinet of 1 August show that this was discussed that morning. Six RAF squadrons promised to Stalin by Churchill were to have been sent in the next convoy to set up a base of operations at Murmansk to provide air cover for the convoys and this news – coming after the diversion of the Lend-Lease planes at Basra and the fact that the British had not promised to mount a large operation in France that year as per the aide-memoire given to Molotov after his recent visit to London – angered Stalin. The German summer offensive had begun on 28 June with the intention of driving south to the Caucasus region with its oilfields and the Soviet forces were retreating in some disorder. Churchill duly received a frosty response to these developments from an understandably disappointed and hard-pressed Stalin on 23 July: 'In view of the situation on the Soviet–German front, I state most emphatically that the Soviet Government cannot tolerate the second front in Europe being postponed till 1943.'[53]

Stalin also declared that the arguments for postponing the convoys were 'untenable'. This telegram was not replied to by Churchill on the advice of Eden in the War Cabinet.[54] Stalin's message was delivered in person by Maisky, who also made several other complaints in his discussion with Churchill about British inaction, including the small numbers of recent heavy bomber attacks on Germany and raids on France, both of which had provided welcome boosts to Russian morale. Churchill assured Maisky that a raid would be launched in the near future. The War Cabinet was also concerned about the effects on public morale after the decision to not launch a Second Front that year, despite the continued deterioration in the Russian military position.

To help resolve their differences of opinion and inform Stalin of the decisions recently reached with the Americans regarding Operation Torch, Churchill, to his credit, at the end of July suggested a meeting between the two leaders. Once again Churchill hoped to influence an important diplomatic relationship with the force of his personality. In travelling to Moscow, the champion of capitalism would come face to face with the leader of its arch enemy, communism.

En route to Moscow, Churchill stopped in Cairo and made several changes to the Middle East command after inspecting part of the Eighth Army. In view of the importance of the region that included Syria, Palestine and Iraq, the Middle East theatre was split into North Africa and the Middle East and Auchinleck was relieved of his command to be replaced by General Harold Alexander. Auchinleck was offered command of the new Middle East region but he regarded Churchill's plans as unworkable and turned down the offer, spending a year on the reserve list before being appointed Commander-in-Chief of the Indian Army. General Gott was given command of the Eighth Army but before he could take up his position he was killed when the transport plane taking him to Cairo was shot down, so Montgomery was quickly appointed as his replacement.

Regarding Moscow, Churchill saw that he had a difficult and 'raw' task ahead of him and at the last minute asked Roosevelt if Harriman could accompany him as he had seen Stalin in Moscow in September 1941 as part of the mission to determine Russia's Lend-Lease requirements.[55] Eden, in a note to the Secretary of State, warned of the difficulties of having nothing positive to offer Stalin but the hope of something in the future – 'jam tomorrow'.[56] In Churchill's party were also Brooke, Tedder and Wavell but their plane was delayed by mechanical trouble so they missed the first meeting with Stalin and therefore it was fortunate that Harriman was accompanying the Prime Minister. The detailed minutes and notes of the meetings with Stalin afford considerable insight into the substance and tone of the discussions.

Already notified of the British and American decisions to not proceed with Sledgehammer, Stalin quietly listened to Churchill's list of reasons as to why an attack could not be launched. Churchill stated that the shortage of landing craft meant they could only land six divisions, which would not be enough to cause the diversion of German troops from the Russian Front. Then he gave a number of other reasons, including the inability to provide constant air cover and the need to preserve men and continue their training for the big landings planned for 1943. When Churchill related the details of the proposed Operation Torch landings with twelve American and five British divisions, Stalin's interest was piqued as it was anticipated that the Germans would have to reinforce their position in North Africa at the expense of the Russian Front.[57] Churchill held up the possibility of an Allied air force group operating from Persia into southern Russia when Rommel was defeated. A large raid was also mentioned for August, which could only be a planned operation against Dieppe, and with that the first meeting finished.

If Churchill was afraid that the Russians might seek a separate peace with Germany, the Moscow meetings did nothing to allay those fears. Any thoughts that the worst part of Churchill's mission was over were dispelled next day when Stalin handed Churchill a letter outlining his disappointment with the Allies failure to keep their promises and launch a Second Front.

The Soviet Army at this time was again under severe pressure. After the major counter-attack that halted the German drive on Moscow in December 1941, further Russian attempts to drive the Germans back in early 1942 were unsuccessful and resulted in the setback at Kharkov in May when a German counter-attack had cut off the Russian pincers trying to capture the city. Moscow was still in Russian hands but in the north Leningrad was besieged and Sebastopol in the Crimea to the south had fallen. On 28 June, the Germans began a new offensive, Case Blue, this time to the south and aimed at the oilfields of the Caucasus Mountains. Maikop was taken but its oilfields were set on fire and the German push towards Grozny continued. The 1st Panzer Army, leading the charge to Grozny, was then recalled to assist General Paulus' 6th Army in its drive towards Stalingrad. The Soviet Army in 1942 consisted of more than 200 divisions and ranged against them were a similar number of German and Axis divisions. The German Army had nearly the same number of divisions in 1942 as they did at the start of Operation Barbarossa in 1941 but many were not at full strength after the ravages of the first winter in Russia. Their number had been bolstered by twenty-five divisions of reinforcements of Hungarian and Rumanian troops which were not of the same strength or quality as the Germans. The June German offensive used ninety divisions, which were faced by eighty-one rifle divisions, thirty-eight rifle brigades, twelve cavalry divisions and sixty-two tank brigades opposite Army Group South with another seventeen rifle divisions, three rifle brigades, three cavalry divisions and three tank brigades in the Caucasus region itself.

The mood of the second meeting worsened after the presentation of the letter as Stalin accused the Royal Navy of fleeing during the attacks on the PQ 17 convoy and the British of being afraid to fight the Germans. Stalin also complained of a lack of aid from both the British and American governments and promises for a Second Front being broken. As the argument continued, Churchill expressed his disappointment that Stalin did not believe his statements and distrusted his motives. Churchill later replied to Stalin's letter in writing, denying that a Second Front had been promised. At a state banquet that night, Stalin continued with disparaging remarks about the British refusal to fight, this time in connection with Singapore.

The two leaders met for a final time on 15 August at the Kremlin and Stalin invited Churchill to his private apartment for dinner, although it was nearly midnight. No official records of the conversation were made but relations between the two men apparently improved after many toasts to each other. Anecdotes were told and questions about past events in the lives of each leader were asked and answered. Stalin asked a question about the size of the British Army and Churchill's reply of fifty-five divisions in the Middle East, India and Britain revealed its much smaller size compared with that of the Soviet Union. This information plus the revelation that Operation Torch would only utilise twelve divisions helped Stalin understand that the British and American armies were much smaller than the Red Army. Therefore there would be no Second Front or significant military assistance from Britain or the US apart from material aid and Russia would continue to bear the brunt of the fighting. Churchill mentioned again a serious cross-Channel raid for August.[58] Churchill believed he had 'established a personal relationship which would be helpful'.[59] On his return to England, Churchill expressed similar sentiments to the War Cabinet: 'He thought that he had established relations with Premier Stalin which would facilitate co-operation between our two countries, and he had formed the highest opinion of Premier Stalin's sagacity.'[60]

Brooke, who had witnessed some but not all of the talks and was not so sure that the meetings had gone that well, recorded:

> The two leaders, Churchill and Stalin are poles apart as human beings, and I cannot see a friendship between them such as exists between Roosevelt and Winston. Stalin is a realist if there ever was one, facts only count with him – plans, hypotheses, future possibilities mean little to him, but he is ready to face facts even when unpleasant. Winston, on the other hand, never seems anxious to face an unpleasantness until forced to do so. He appealed to sentiments in Stalin which I think do not exist there.[61]

Dieppe

On 19 August, men of the 2nd Canadian Infantry Division and three British commando units supported by a regiment of the latest Churchill tanks mounted a large-scale offensive raid on the port of Dieppe. This was part of the British strategy of trying to pin German forces in France and keeping them on the alert for an invasion. The Royal Navy was not prepared to risk large warships so close to France because of German air superiority so a small preliminary naval bombardment was carried out by the five destroyers escorting the fleet. Support would be provided by the RAF, which also hoped to lure the Luftwaffe into a major air battle. Possibly alerted by a small naval skirmish offshore when the convoy ran into some German trawlers, the shingle beaches chosen for the landing were well covered by German machine guns and many soldiers were killed trying to reach the cover of a low sea wall after their landing craft beached. The tanks struggled to manoeuvre on the shingle but twelve made it off the beach to make a sortie into the town until their passage was blocked by anti-tank obstacles whereupon they returned to the beach, only to be knocked out. The first wave of the assault was for the most part pinned down on the beach with heavy casualties, forcing the second wave to be cancelled and an evacuation of the survivors ordered. Churchill had dubbed this a 'butcher and bolt' operation, but it was the Canadians who were butchered.

Mountbatten had become the Chief of Combined Operations on 18 March 1942 and was a regular attendee at Chiefs of Staff meetings when Combined Operations were on the agenda. A favourite protégé of Churchill, Mountbatten was a comparatively junior officer who had been rapidly promoted by him and was not well regarded by the other Chiefs of Staff. Combined Operations were responsible for large-scale raids on the Continent as recommended by the Chiefs of Staff on 8 May as an alternative strategy to Operation Sledgehammer in order to assist Russia in the summer of 1942.[62] Even at this time, there was recognition by the Chiefs of Staff that the allocation of landing craft for raids would mean that none would be available for Operation Sledgehammer.

A Target Committee in April began to look at suitable objectives on the French coast and Dieppe was considered. Plans to raid Dieppe were devised in what became known as Operation Rutter and were approved on 6 June, with the War Cabinet informed on 11 June.[63] Intensive training by the 2nd Canadian Division was conducted on the Isle of Wight, but as Mountbatten did not witness any of the exercises as he was away in Washington, the operation was postponed to the beginning of July until after another training exercise on 22–23 June.

On his return from Washington, Churchill held a meeting on 30 June with Mountbatten and Brooke regarding Operation Rutter and Dieppe. Brooke was of the view that an operation of this kind was absolutely indispensable as a preliminary to a full-scale operation in order to gain valuable experience.[64]

Bad weather forecast and a German bombing raid on the ships assembled for the operation then forced the further postponement of Operation Rutter on 6 July. Mountbatten advised the operation would be undertaken at some future date as he was keen to keep his assault force together which was accepted by the Chiefs of Staff.[65] However, the force dispersed back to its bases the next day and reports of the training even appeared in British and Canadian newspapers later in the week.[66]

The senior officers at the Combined Operations HQ were disappointed by the decision to cancel the operation in view of two other previously cancelled missions until Captain Hughes-Hallett had the idea of launching the raid virtually as planned in the belief that even if the Germans had learnt about the plans for Operation Rutter, they would not be expecting a raid in the same place provided security was maintained.[67] On 9 July, the Chiefs of Staff invited Mountbatten to plan another operation as a substitute for Operation Sledgehammer and, as there was little time to prepare another operation from scratch, Mountbatten adopted Hughes-Hallet's suggestion of remounting the raid on Dieppe.

At the Chiefs of Staff meeting on 20 July, an unnamed operation was approved in principle with Hughes-Hallet as its commander.[68] This meeting was notable for being 'troublesome' with 'Mountbatten again assuming wild powers unto himself'.[69] Next day, the Chiefs of Staff debated this problem and resolved to rein in Mountbatten by requiring him to submit a procedure and an outline plan for future operations, this procedure being approved at their meeting on 27 July.

In the interim, two planning meetings had been held with the still-enthusiastic Canadian forces detailed for the operation but there had been several unpleasant exchanges of telegrams between Churchill and Stalin. Although he had just won his battle with the Americans to cancel Operation Sledgehammer, Churchill had promised an operation to Maisky and was under pressure from the press to open a Second Front. If he was going to avoid doing so, he desperately needed to be seen to be doing something else to help the Russians. No records exist due to the desire for secrecy surrounding the Dieppe Raid, but it is likely that Churchill asked Mountbatten to conduct the operation at this time. On 25 July, Mountbatten called the senior Canadian officers and told them that the Prime Minister and the 'War Committee of the Cabinet' had approved Operation Jubilee.[70]

Planning for the Dieppe operation resumed under the guise of Operation Jubilee. The revised plans would include aspects of the cancelled Operation

Imperator to lure the Luftwaffe into an air battle. For Churchill, it was a win–win scenario. If the raid was successful, it would help boost Russian morale and force the Germans across the Channel to be more vigilant; if things went badly, the British would have demonstrated the difficulties of making a landing on an enemy-held coast to both the Americans and the Russians and help justify the British refusal to mount Operation Sledgehammer.

The final plans for Operation Jubilee were approved by the Chiefs of Staff on 12 August, although they are not mentioned by that name.[71] Is it a coincidence that this was the same day as Churchill's first meeting with Stalin in Moscow when the Prime Minister again stated that a large raid would be made that month? Mountbatten had unusually asked the Cabinet secretaries to see all telegrams from Churchill while he was in Moscow but no direct communication appears to have passed between them. At the meeting with Stalin, Churchill said that he was prepared to lose 10,000 men in this operation, which was no more than a reconnaissance.[72]

On 15 September 1942, the Canadian government announced in *The Times* newspaper that the total Canadian casualties from this 'reconnaissance' operation amounted to 3,350 dead, wounded and missing out of an embarkation force of 4,912.[73] This was later confirmed as 907 killed, 586 wounded and 1,946 taken prisoner.

The high casualties of the operation caused a certain amount of disquiet, particularly among the Canadians. The 2nd Canadian Infantry division had been in England since early 1940 itching for a fight and had received a very bloody nose in its first operation. Churchill requested in a minute to Ismay on 21 December 1942 a report on the planning and approval process that Operation Jubilee had undergone. Ismay responded by sending a copy of Mountbatten's own report and tried to put the blame on Montgomery as being ultimately responsible. As Montgomery had no involvement with the final raid after Operation Rutter was cancelled and had already been posted to the Eighth Army, this was very misleading. Ismay's own memoirs make no reference to Dieppe at all. However, Churchill knew of the operation as he mentioned it in a telegram from Cairo four days before the raid and Mountbatten would never have launched the operation without his approval.[74]

The day after the raid, Mountbatten briefed the War Cabinet and there were no concerns recorded about its authorisation apart from a guarded comment from Portal to the effect that the operation had not been mounted with the sole intention of luring the German Luftwaffe into an air battle. Mountbatten claimed in a simplistic deduction that one of the lessons learnt was that opposed landings should not be made in the vicinity of heavily defended strategically important areas such as ports.[75]

Although the Dieppe Raid continues to be surrounded by controversy because of the actual plans for the operations and the casualties, it is clear that it was ordered by Churchill for largely political reasons to make some gesture towards helping the Russians. The official Combined Operations headquarters report on the raid is circumspect on the reasons for it and the approval process.[76] Hughes–Hallett after the war claimed that assistance to the Russians was only a secondary objective. However, the Canadians themselves had no doubts about why the operation went ahead. In a lecture given by a senior 1st Canadian Corps officer after the raid, the 'background of high policy' was the need to test the German defences and force men and material to be committed to the defences, the importance of which 'increased as German operations against the Russia gained momentum'.[77] Once again, large numbers of Dominion troops were casualties in a British operation, this time from Canada. Churchill himself stated in Parliament in September before the casualty list and more details had emerged, 'I personally regarded the Dieppe Assault, to which I gave my sanction, as an indispensable preliminary to any full-scale operations.'[78]

A week after the raid, the Commander-in Chief of OB West, von Rundstedt, ordered the construction of 15,000 permanent coastal fortifications that winter to strengthen the Atlantic Wall of the planned German fortress of Europe, Festung Europa, as ordered by Hitler in his Directive 40 of March 1942 following his original orders in December 1941.

9

TORCH AND CASABLANCA

As Operation Torch was to be largely an American operation, the original directive for it went to the Commander-in-Chief of Allied Expeditionary Forces, the newly promoted General Eisenhower, on 13 August. Eisenhower had been in England since 25 June as the commander of all US operations in Europe. Having worked on all the war plans since February, he was familiar with the evolving US strategy and was best placed to represent America in planning joint operations with the British. The main objective of Operation Torch was the elimination of all German forces in north-west Africa and the capture of Tunis in Tunisia. Once achieved, the operation would also considerably assist the British in their struggle in North Africa and the capture of Libya.

The detailed plans for Operation Torch were to be devised by the Americans and approved by the British; the British would supply shipping, naval escorts and the follow-up forces. Churchill returned from a visit of Cairo after a tour of Montgomery's battle positions to further difficulties in dealing with the Americans, who now wanted to change the scale of Operation Torch and land outside the Mediterranean on the Atlantic coast only. The American planners in Washington were initially concerned about sending shipping and troop convoys through the Straits of Gibraltar into the Mediterranean, given the possibility of Spain entering the war and assuming control of Gibraltar. If the Luftwaffe occupied Spanish airfields then this would pose a significant threat to the naval task forces, even if Spain did not enter the war directly.[1]

The British Chiefs of Staff on 22 August received a revised outline plan from Eisenhower which proposed simultaneous assaults on Oran, Algiers and Bone in Algeria with an overland advance to Casablanca.[2] In a covering letter

Eisenhower wrote that he believed the proposed landing force was inadequate and that an additional landing needed to be made at Casablanca on the Atlantic coast, even though this was hundreds of miles from Tunis.[3] Eisenhower commented, 'Chance of success depends more on political attitudes and reactions in Northern Africa rather than military actions.'

In their own appreciation, the British Chiefs of Staff came to a similar conclusion, noting the overland advance to Casablanca was in the opposite direction to Tunis: 'To sum up – the success of this plan depends on the early collapse of French resistance or the ability of the Royal Navy and the RAF operation to prevent the passage of Axis forces, particularly sea-borne forces, to Tunisia.'[4]

An urgent meeting was sought by the Chiefs of Staff with Eisenhower to clarify his intentions and to raise their own objections. The Allies expected a campaign against weak Vichy French forces and the British view was that landings should be made as far east as close to Tunis as possible to both reduce the distance to the city and conclude its capture quickly before the Germans could send any significant reinforcements to the region.

The US Joint Chiefs of Staff then modified the plan in a telegram on 25 August from the Joint Staff Mission which, after acknowledging the comments from the British Chiefs of Staff on the revised outline plan, modified the plan to landings at Casablanca and Oran only, claiming there were no more Army units available for other landings.[5] A firm date for the commencement of the operation had still not been provided. Eisenhower was not consulted about this change of plan and had been working with the British to make plans to land as far east as possible at Algiers, Oran, Philippeville and Bone. With the US Chiefs of Staff unable to agree to the landings proposed by the British, Churchill and Roosevelt once again became involved again in an exchange of telegrams to resolve the impasse.

Among the key problems emerging at this time were those of the perceptions and the attitudes the British and Americans had towards each other. The British, having been fighting the war for nearly three years, believed they knew more about strategy and fighting the Germans than the Americans did. The Americans, on the other hand, saw that those three years had brought little success for the British and only a string of defeats and evacuations. Even while the Torch planning was in progress, an American observer in the Middle East had cabled in July from Cairo after the staff there had begun evacuations in the face of Rommel's latest offensive that threatened Egypt: 'Rommel's success due more ineptness British generalship than his superiority in equipment.'[6]

According to Dill, the Americans, particularly Roosevelt, were very concerned that their first operation should not be a failure.[7]

On 26 August, Churchill sent a long telegram to Roosevelt. Churchill somewhat patronisingly pointed out the need for a firm start date to end the 'hemming and hawing', and the need for the appearance of overwhelming strength against a weak, divided opposition. Churchill suggested that he and Roosevelt rather than the generals and planners should worry about the political risks such as Spain coming into the war. Despite having categorically rejected Operation Sledgehammer, Churchill referred to the potential threat of an operation in the Pas-de-Calais in October which would keep the Germans busy so that they would not have the spare forces to overrun Vichy France.[8] This was a contradiction of what Churchill had said to Stalin in Moscow regarding the German occupation of Vichy France: '[Torch] would probably result in the German seizure of unoccupied France, but he did not care whether they threw Pétain into the sea or not.'

The new plan was discussed at the British Chiefs of Staff meeting on 26 August and, while understanding the American concerns, they thought that the best option was still to land at Algiers, Oran and Casablanca simultaneously and were somewhat dismayed by the revised plan. The Americans were still concerned about their lines of supply through the Mediterranean being disrupted either from Spain or by Vichy forces operating from Casablanca.[9] A further meeting, this time with Churchill, was held the next day and it was decided that both Churchill and the Chiefs of Staff would telegraph their comments to their respective counterparts.

Churchill's telegram to Roosevelt on 27 August pressed for Algiers and Oran with landings at Casablanca later and referred to the likelihood of high surf conditions on the Atlantic coast which might prevent a landing at Casablanca. Churchill also reminded Roosevelt of the promises given to Stalin: 'If Torch collapses or is cut down as is now proposed, I should feel my position painfully affected.'[10]

Eisenhower, Churchill and the Chiefs of Staff met at Chequers on 29 August to consider the American response, which was to the effect that if there was no Casablanca landing there would be no Operation Torch at all. As a concession, the British offered to cancel the easternmost Philippeville and Bone landings.[11]

Roosevelt's considered reply to Churchill's telegrams then arrived on 30 August. Pointing out the likely French hostility to any British-led landings, Roosevelt suggested making the assaults exclusively American but remained firm about the need for a Casablanca landing as 'a single line of communication through the Straits is far too hazardous in the light of our limited joint resources'. Roosevelt also claimed there was not enough 'cover' and shipping to do more than two landings, Casablanca and Oran, at the same time. Drafts of this telegram reveal the American fear of failure and its likely effects on world opinion, Allied and Axis alike.[12]

At the British Chiefs of Staff meeting the next day, Churchill professed that Roosevelt might well be right about the potential French reaction and pointed out that if the Americans led the operation, then the British could not be blamed if anything went wrong.[13] In his reply to Roosevelt, Churchill deferred to American leadership of the operation but pushed again for Algiers to be included, warning of lamentable results in the Mediterranean if the Germans reinforced Tunis first as a consequence of not landing at Algiers. Another compromise was suggested by Churchill, one that had been proposed by the Chiefs of Staff, that the assault forces be distributed more evenly from the Casablanca operation to other landings.[14]

A day later, Roosevelt offered the three landings provided the British organise the necessary extra shipping and pointedly reminded Churchill of the agreement between them for the US to handle the French in North Africa while Britain was to look after Spain.[15] This was acknowledged by Churchill twenty-four hours later when he suggested that the scale of the assault at Casablanca be reduced to reinforce the other landings as per the Chiefs of Staff proposal.[16] This was accepted by Roosevelt on 4 September, and so after a week of haggling the important details of the operation were finally settled.[17] Wary of making direct criticism of the planning process to Roosevelt, Churchill had written a letter to Hopkins, which he ultimately did not send when the President's telegram of confirmation arrived on 4 September.[18]

In North Africa, at the Battle of Alam Halfa beginning on the night of 30 August, Rommel's eastward advance was finally halted after a three-day battle and the two sides settled down to prepare for the coming British offensive, the delay giving the Germans more time to prepare their defences. Through their code-breaking activities, the British were reading most of the German signals from North Africa and knew almost daily the exact status of Rommel's forces and fuel situation. Also revealed were details of German and Italian supply convoys which the RAF and the Royal Navy intercepted with considerable success, causing Rommel's supply situation to worsen.

On 2 September the convoys to Russia were resumed as promised by Churchill when PQ 18 sailed, this time with an aircraft carrier to provide extra air support. The plans for Operation Torch were finalised that month but much to Churchill's disappointment (and no doubt Roosevelt's in view of the impending elections) the start date was delayed until 8 November. To fill the vacuum while awaiting the start of Operation Torch and Montgomery's offensive in North Africa, Churchill pushed the Chiefs of Staff to continue the planning of Operation Jupiter in Norway to enable air cover to be provided for future Russian convoys.[19]

An important staff conference with Eisenhower and the Chiefs of Staff was held on 21 September by Churchill at Chequers which resulted in a number of uncomfortable realisations that the Prime Minister discussed with the War Cabinet. These concerns were outlined in a telegram to Roosevelt in which Churchill claimed that, despite his 'persisting anxiety for Russia', a slow build-up of American troops in England due to a shortage of shipping caused by the needs of the imminent Operation Torch meant that the major landing of 1943, Operation Roundup, was 'regarded as definitely off'. Furthermore, losses to convoy PQ 18 (thirteen of forty merchant ships were sunk) and the unavailability of escort ships because of the requirements of troop convoys for Operation Torch meant that the sailing of the next convoy, PQ 19, would be postponed with no likelihood of resumption until January 1943.[20] At Churchill's request, Stalin had agreed to deploy more aircraft to help provide air cover for PQ 18 and successive convoys. Therefore at the very time when the German forces were entering Stalingrad itself, Stalin was once more to be given the news of no further material help from the Allies after having provided the additional aircraft support requested. More seriously, the prospects for Operation Roundup in 1943 were now extremely bleak, exactly as Marshall and King had foreseen.

To make matters worse, at the end of September, Churchill reported to Stalin that the 154 Airacobra aircraft in PQ 19 that had been deemed urgent for Operation Torch had been unloaded for American rather than Russian use.[21] Churchill finally informed Stalin of the suspension of Arctic convoys in a telegram on 8 October 1942, blaming the shortage of shipping caused by Operation Torch, only four days after Stalin had sent word of a deterioration of fighting around Stalingrad and requested more aircraft in a telegram on 5 October. Stalin was not advised of the postponement of the Second Front for 1943 but was asked to plan an operation to assist Operation Jupiter. Churchill offered to locate some heavy bombers near the Russian southern front when they were available after the Egyptian campaign to help the battle in the Caucasus. Arrangements were made by the British and Americans for thirteen merchant ships to sail independently from Iceland later in the month but Stalin chose to make no further comment, merely acknowledging Churchill's message. Only five ships survived the perilous voyage, three being forced to turn back and the remainder were sunk.[22] Stalin and the Russians were becoming increasingly suspicious of Churchill following these telegrams – suspicions that had been inflamed by the Hess episode and the diversion of three Russian-bound American Lend-Lease cargo ships from Iceland to Britain.[23] Any kudos Churchill had earned in his visit to Moscow was rapidly being lost.

In the anxiously awaited mid-term Congressional elections a few days before Operation Torch, Roosevelt's Democrats narrowly retained their majority, losing nine seats in the Senate and forty-five in the House of Representatives, the win being the smallest majority yet of Roosevelt's presidency.

Operation Torch, 8 November 1942

The British offensive in the Middle East began on the night of 23 October at El Alamein and after a three-day set-piece battle, the Eighth Army under Montgomery had broken through most of the German defences but were unable to exploit the breaches. This prompted a rethink by Montgomery, who realigned his thrusts northwards and this time he met with more success, the Australian 9th Division reaching the coast and cutting off much of Rommel's left wing. After ten days of being attacked and counter-attacking, the German forces were severely weakened and as British armoured units smashed through their lines, they were forced to give ground. This victory forced Rommel's Afrika Korps to begin a long retreat westwards and was the first major British success of the war against the Germans as well as an auspicious omen for the rest of the campaign in North Africa.

The changes in command had given Montgomery more time to build up his forces (time denied Auchinleck) and from intelligence decrypts he knew that Rommel was short of fuel and tanks and that the British had assembled a numerically superior force. These factors plus the deployment of 6-pounder anti-tank guns and the RAF having achieved aerial dominance before the battle meant the Allies had gained a comprehensive superiority over the Germans. In addition to these tactical advantages, the Allies were about to make a major landing directly behind the Axis forces. After El Alamein, the Axis threat to Egypt and the Suez Canal was finally eliminated and a complete victory in North Africa was seemingly assured.

In north-west Africa, the Allies landed at dawn on 8 November from three task forces, the easternmost at Algiers, the central task force at Oran and the westernmost at Casablanca. At Algiers, where a friendly reaction was expected, French batteries engaged two British destroyers trying to enter the harbour to land shore parties with the objectives of seizing the port facilities before they could be destroyed. One destroyer was sunk, the other landed its men before being forced to withdraw and the shore parties were eventually forced to surrender.

Landings to the west of Algiers were more successful, if a little chaotic, but quickly got behind schedule. In the city itself, pro-Allied French resistance members had occupied overnight all the key buildings except for the police HQ in expectation of the arrival of American troops. However, no Americans had arrived by 7 a.m. and the resistance began to lose control to the regular Vichy French authorities. In an apparent coincidence, Admiral Darlan was in Algiers and began negotiations with the local French commanders. Darlan ordered the commander defending Casablanca, General Nogues, to stop fighting but he refused. The Americans wanted to install General Giraud as the Commander of French forces in North Africa and there followed forty-eight hours of intrigue between Darlan, the local commanders, the American Ambassador to Algeria, General Clark and Marshal Pétain in Vichy France. Giraud's authority was not recognised in North Africa by the French colonial authority's forces, which complicated matters, and when Darlan finally ordered a ceasefire next morning, this was immediately countermanded by Pétain; at midnight Hitler settled the issue by ordering the occupation of the rest of Vichy France, which was rapidly achieved in two days with no attempt being made to seize the French fleet at Toulon. Churchill commented in a telegram to Stalin that:

> The German invasion of Vichy France which was foreseen by us and also by you in our conversations is all to the good. The poison of the paralysing influence of Vichy on the French nation will decline and the whole people will soon learn to hate the Germans as much as they are hated in the occupied zone.[24]

At Casablanca, the assault forces commanded by General Patton landed at three places north and south of the city, the furthest south being Safi, 140 miles away. At Safi, shore parties were landed by two destroyers in the harbour and the unloading of M4 Sherman tanks commenced soon after this was secured.

The two northern landings at Fedala and Mehdia were successful despite the loss of many landing boats and a slow advance on Casablanca began next day, hampered by sporadic French resistance and difficulties in getting equipment off the beaches. Fortunately, news of the ceasefire arrived and the local commander ordered a ceasefire. In Casablanca itself, shore batteries and the immobile battleship *Jean Bart* duelled with the American fleet standing offshore until the ceasefire came into effect. The landings at Casablanca were the most heavily opposed of the three ports due to the resistance by forces under General Nogues' control, while the assault at Algiers, which was only added to the landings at the insistence of the British, faced the least resistance. The Western task force under Patton composed of two infantry divisions and the 2nd Armoured Division plus two tank battalions played little further part in the campaign and remained in Morocco once Casablanca was captured.

At Oran, the experienced US 1st Infantry Division was landed either side of the port with the 1st Armoured division in support. An attempt to land in the port itself by troops from two cutters was strongly opposed by the French and stopped with heavy losses. Quickly forming up, the flank forces pushed inland to capture airfields and then swing round to take Oran from the landward side. Progress was slow against determined French resistance, but on the third day two columns of tanks entered Oran unopposed as news of the ceasefire filtered through and the defenders lay down their arms. The American GIs first combat in the European war with Germany was against Frenchmen and the three days of fighting cost them 1,254 men killed, wounded or missing.[25] French casualties were considerably higher.

The German commander of the Mediterranean theatre, Kesselring, acted quickly to reinforce Tunisia by immediately negotiating with the Vichy French to use two airfields near Tunis when news of the Allied landings was received. Approval was given on 9 November and a day later the first German aircraft and ground troops arrived while aircraft operating from Italy and Sicily began to bomb British and American troops. The reaction of the Vichy French forces had been completely misjudged by the Allies as French troops had resisted the British and Americans and the Germans were quickly given permission to reinforce Tunisia.

Reusing available shipping, the British 78th Division was landed at Bougie, east of Algiers, on 11 November and rapidly advanced eastwards to cross the Tunisian border on 15 November. The small port of Bone was also seized on 12 November along with an airfield which was captured by American paratroops just minutes ahead of the arrival of German transport planes, which were forced to return to base. Thus despite the Allied debate about landing too far east which was conceded by the British, within four days of the commencement of Operation Torch, the British had captured Bone, less than 200 miles from Tunis.

A race to build up troops in north-west Africa then began after the occupation of Vichy France by the Germans. The 10th Panzer and the 344th Infantry Divisions were ordered to Tunisia, along with two more Italian divisions plus many smaller units of paratroops, reconnaissance troops and a company of the new Tiger I tanks from the 501st Heavy Tank Battalion. By the end of November, 1,847 enlisted men, 159 tanks and armoured cars, 127 guns, 1,097 vehicles, and 12,549 tons of supplies, comprising twenty-eight shiploads, had been brought over.[26] The Germans moved quickly to block the exits from the mountainous territory in west Tunisia on to the coastal plain, while the British and Americans tried to push eastwards as quickly as possible.

The German Army units sent to Tunisia were all either new or had been based in France, thus Operation Torch did not force the diversion of any German Army units from the Russian Front. However, the Allied landings and the collapse of the Afrika Korps in Egypt after the Battle of El Alamein did result in more than three bomber Gruppen (100 bombers) and one fighter Gruppen (forty fighters) being redeployed to Tunisia from Sicily and Sardinia, and these were followed by others from Russia and even Norway. Several hundred transport aircraft were also sent to Africa as a result of the naval blockade of the supply routes across the Mediterranean from Italy. Many of these aircraft came from Luftflotte 4, which was supporting Army Group South in Russia, thereby reducing the available air support for the German troops trapped at Stalingrad.[27]

On 13 November, Darlan and Clark negotiated the switch of Vichy French forces to fight alongside the Allies. This was inevitably opposed by de Gaulle in London amid public concern that the Allies were dealing with a traitor but the agreement was allowed to stand. Churchill described the dealings with Darlan as being politically expedient. One objective of Torch had been achieved after a week of landing and all that remained was to eliminate the German forces and capture Tunis. However, American and British attempts to drive eastwards were repulsed by the Germans and by 2 December, as the weather worsened, the Allies were forced to concede that they would have to withdraw to resupply and build up their forces.[28] Despite a British division having entered Tunisia on 15 November, it was soon blocked by a small improvised German battle group and was not strong enough to make further progress eastwards.

As the British advance on Tunis was halted by the rapid German build-up and counter-attacks coupled with bad weather, so the American advance also came to a halt. The CCB of the 1st Armoured Division suffered severe losses both in battle and when its heavy vehicles including tanks became bogged and had to be abandoned. The planning for Operation Torch had given little consideration for the campaign after the initial landings and the Allied forces, even with the addition of the French divisions, were inadequate to capture the rapidly reinforced Tunis. The French forces that had switched allegiance were poorly equipped and did not possess any tanks, artillery or anti-tank weapons. The bulk of the fighting had fallen on the British First Army commanded by General Anderson and the US units in 2nd Corps commanded by General Fredenhall. Operation Torch had put ashore a large enough force to defeat the Vichy French but not the Germans, whose rapid arrival, reinforcement and effectiveness was not anticipated by the Combined Chiefs of Staff.

Meanwhile, Rommel had begun to retreat from a position in Libya and Tobruk was liberated on 13 November. A Wembley dentist recorded his reaction:

> It seems as if a miracle has happened. The great Rommel has suddenly become a complete failure; the undefeatable Germans, artists in attack, masters in defence, have suddenly become a mob of panic stricken, utterly demoralised soldiers running away so fast our forces are having difficulty in keeping up with him. Egypt is ours once again and Libya, it seems, will soon be ours too.[29]

Now threatened from two directions, Rommel on 24 November requested at a meeting with Hitler that all the German forces be withdrawn from North Africa, but this was refused with a vague promise to improve the supply situation. German reinforcements continued to pour into Tunisia and by January 1943 there were more than 100,000 Axis soldiers in the country in the newly created Fifth Panzer Army. What might Rommel have achieved if he had been given these extra units during his advance eastwards earlier that year? Hitler was apparently merely reinforcing defeat by insisting that Rommel hold his ground as more troops were despatched to Tunisia. However, this was part of a deliberate strategy decided at a conference on 17 November to keep the Allies occupied in North Africa for as long as possible as Operation Torch had demonstrated to the Germans that the British and the Americans had the offensive capability and shipping to make further landings in the Mediterranean in the future.[30] Under pressure at Stalingrad, Hitler needed more time to defeat Russia and could not afford a retreat in any theatre at the end of 1942. Moreover, Hitler was determined to prove his senior Army generals wrong in their assessments of both Russia and North Africa.

That autumn, British planners had been studying the options for 1943. A major concern to them was that although they had convinced the Americans in July to launch Operation Torch, this had been achieved at the cost of agreeing to a strategy that would make the successful execution of Operation Roundup in 1943 unlikely and was essentially a defensive, encircling strategy for the European theatre. However, this was entirely in accordance with the grand strategy for the defeat of Germany as envisaged by the British. Any satisfaction that Churchill and Brooke might have enjoyed from this victory over future strategy was soon dispelled by the arrival of telegrams from the Joint Staff Mission in Washington that informed them of a change in American thinking and that plans were being made to send more and more resources to the Pacific. It began to appear that Marshall had concluded from the July meetings that 'Germany first' had been abandoned by the British because of the defensive strategy agreed. This was greeted with horror by the Chiefs of Staff, who considered the switch to the Pacific a violation of this strategic principle that had been agreed in 1941. Even before the Operation Torch landings had begun, Churchill was thinking about future plans, calling the American intention of having twenty-seven divisions in Britain for Roundup in 1943 as 'moonshine' in a policy on the future conduct of the war drafted on 22 October.[31] This paper was then finessed by the Chiefs of Staff before a version that reviewed the evolution of strategy to date and advocated a return to the Continent in late 1943 was sent to the War Cabinet. Churchill also pointed out the possibilities that would be created by the clearing of North Africa such as an attack on the soft underbelly of the Axis through Sicily, southern Italy, Sardinia or even the Balkans. To Churchill, future operations depended on the outcome of Operation Torch.[32]

To help turn around American thinking, the Joint Planning Staff were also asked to prepare an appreciation of the need to defeat Germany first rather than Japan. After two attempts, the planners came up with a document that met with the approval of the Chiefs of Staff and had an emphasis on a heavy bomber offensive against Germany. Regarding an assault on the Continent in 1943, the paper was blunt: 'Despite the fact that a large scale invasion of Europe would do more than anything to help Russia, we are forced to the conclusion that we have no option but to undermine Germany's military power by the destruction of the German military and economic machine before we attempt invasion.'[33]

This paper largely determined the British position that was taken to the Casablanca conference in January 1943 but was not well received by Churchill, who was elated by the victory at El Alamein, Britain's first over German ground troops in the war, and the success of Operation Torch. Churchill took a completely different view of the paper, calling it negative and a product of 'safety first':

> Is it really proposed that the Russians will be content with our lying down like this while Hitler has a third crack at them? However alarming the prospect may seem, we must make an attempt to get on the mainland and fight in the line against the enemy in 1943.[34]

Therefore in November, Churchill appeared to be leaning towards Operation Roundup in 1943, much to Brooke's dismay. Roosevelt, for his part, appeared to be undecided about future strategy and suggested on 9 November that a survey should be made of future options once the southern Mediterranean shore was cleared. All options were proposed and considered, including landings in Sardinia, Sicily, Greece, other Balkan countries, Italy and even an attack on Germany from Turkey, provided Turkish support could be gained.[35]

A paper war then broke out between Churchill and the Chiefs of Staff, who went to great lengths to try to prove why Operation Roundup could not take place in 1943. In the course of the debate, Churchill pointed out that the Allies had undertaken to assemble twenty-one British and twenty-seven American divisions in England by 1 April 1943 ready for operations on the Continent yet the Mediterranean campaign employed only thirteen divisions, leaving a shortfall of thirty-five divisions. The American build-up in England was actually considerably slower than planned because of the demands of Operation Torch, a shortage of shipping and the diversion of troops to the Pacific. Nevertheless, Churchill stubbornly maintained that he was committed to Roundup in August 1943, apparently concerned about the reaction of Russia to reduced operations in 1943.[36]

Following a November letter from the Americans apparently scaling back Lend-Lease shipments, the worst British fears about the diversion of resources to the Pacific seemed to have been realised. Churchill cabled Roosevelt on 24 November to ask if the Americans had abandoned Roundup as the amount of Lend-Lease supplies allocated to the UK had apparently been halved. If this was the case, Churchill called it 'a most grievous decision' as Operation Torch was no substitute for Roundup and asked for another meeting as soon as possible.[37] Roosevelt cleared up the error next day but took the opportunity of reinforcing the notion of striking across the Channel in 1943 or 1944 as the conditions permitted.

Largely in response to Roosevelt's telegram of 9 November, Churchill wrote another paper on future Mediterranean strategy dated 25 November, focusing on Sicily or Sardinia and the need to bring Turkey into the war as an ally against Germany.[38] The idea to make Turkey an ally completely ignored the events of the First World War when Britain had refused an alliance with Turkey and Churchill, in early August 1914, had ordered two Turkish battleships being built in England to be impounded for use by the Royal Navy before Turkey had even entered the war, thus driving the country into the arms of Germany. Britain and France had then overseen a secret dismemberment of the Ottoman Empire at the end of the war under the Sykes Picot agreement of 1916. Churchill, too, was the architect of the Dardanelles campaign but seemed to think that the Turks would forget all this recent history and his part in it.

On 28 November, Churchill received a telegram from Stalin in response to the decision to resume the convoys to Russia from 22 December in which the Soviet leader reminded Churchill of his promise of Roundup in the spring of 1943, saying that, 'He hoped the Prime Minister had not changed his mind with regard to his promise, given in Moscow, to establish a Second Front in Europe in the spring of 1943.'

On 19 November, the Russians had launched their counter-attack on the German Sixth Army besieging Stalingrad and three days later had surrounded the city, trapping the Germans against the River Volga; the German besiegers had become themselves besieged.

On Admiral Darlan's orders, the French fleet in Toulon and the other ports of southern France were scuttled on 27 November to prevent the warships falling into German hands; Darlan had kept his promise to Churchill made in June 1940 after all.

With the Allied landings in Morocco, Algeria and Tunisia, the war was engulfing more and more countries and it seemed like it would never end to some civilians:

29th November 1942

I listened to Churchill with a shadow on my heart. It's bad enough to think privately all that he said without hearing it on the wireless – to see the long, hard and bitter road, to feel the shadows deepen rather than lighten, to envy the ones that think Germany will collapse in the spring, to have in mind

always the slave labour, the resources of rich Europe, to remember Goebbels'
words that whoever starved, it would not be Germany. I thought of all the
boys and men out East. How long will it be before they come home?[39]

At the Chiefs of Staff meeting on 30 November, Churchill asked that an
operation in August or September of next year be considered again in
light of the successes of Torch and the Russian offensive around Stalingrad.
Demanding attacks on Sicily and Sardinia, Churchill was now apparently
in favour of a landing in France. Opposition from Brooke finally forced
Churchill to confess that he had led the Russians to believe that Roundup
would be undertaken in 1943. Furthermore, as this had been done in the
presence of Harriman, as Churchill later admitted in a paper on 3 December,
then Roosevelt would have the same understanding.[40] The reaction of the
Chiefs of Staff to this bombshell is not recorded but Brooke was quick to
declaim that he had not heard the Prime Minister say anything of the sort
in his presence:

> He then stopped and stared at me for a few seconds during which I think
> he remembered that if any promise was made it during that last evening
> when he went to say goodbye to Stalin, and when I was not there! He said
> no more.[41]

This admission by Churchill of his promise to Stalin explained his renewed
interest in Operation Roundup. In the subsequent discussion over the next
few days, the Chiefs of Staff maintained their opposition to Roundup in 1943
but agreed to let the Joint Planning Staff examine the available divisions and
shipping for all possibilities.

In the same paper of 3 December, Churchill tried to recover the situation,
writing that the previous assumptions about German strength had changed
with their losses in Russia and the need for the German Army to have occupation forces in the Balkans, Italy, North Africa and the south of France, which
reduced the number of divisions standing along the English Channel. Allied
strategy therefore needed to be reviewed and Operation Roundup launched if
possible when conditions permitted in 1943 in order to honour the promises
made to Stalin before he complained of the limited number of British and
American divisions actually fighting.[42]

Despite Marshall having said that the mounting of Operation Torch would
be at the expense of Bolero and Roundup in 1943, which was later confirmed

at the staff conference in September with Eisenhower, Churchill, now that his promise to Stalin was common knowledge, was of the view that Roundup should be launched later in the year, around August. The details of Churchill's note of 3 December were cleverly forwarded by Churchill to Marshall (via Dill), who was naturally enthusiastic about any renewed attempt to launch Roundup as previously agreed once the shores of North Africa were cleared.[43]

Given his huge faux pas in Moscow, Churchill was obliged to brief the War Cabinet on 30 November when he read out Stalin's telegram and said that the changed situation made it all the more important for the British and Americans to start a Second Front in Europe in 1943 as the current activities in the Mediterranean, important though they were, could only be regarded as an inadequate contribution compared with the efforts that Russia was making.[44]

In early December, Roosevelt suggested to Churchill an Allied conference to determine strategy in 1943 and to try to ensure a cross-Channel invasion in mid 1943.[45] Churchill was enthusiastic about the idea: 'At present we have no plan for 1943 which is on scale or up to the level of events.'[46]

A firm invitation was subsequently extended by Roosevelt to Churchill on 21 December to meet in Casablanca next month.

Perhaps not surprisingly, the Joint Staff Planners in their next report on strategy agreed with the Chiefs of Staff. As the Bolero build-up had been slower than expected, as already commented on by Churchill, it was thought that the Allies had only enough resources for either operations in the Mediterranean or on the Continent but not both. In order to accelerate any build-up in the UK to a maximum of twenty-five divisions, only six of which could be organised as assault divisions, the Allies would have to forego the bomber offensive and all future amphibious operations in the Mediterranean and Burma. The British Ambassador to Russia, Sir Clarke Kerr, was in London at the time and advised the Chiefs of Staff on 15 December of Stalin's expectations of a Second Front in 1943 and likely sour reaction if there was none as the Soviet leader regarded North Africa as a sideshow. After a final round with Churchill on 16 December, the Chiefs of Staff won the day; the main British strategy proposed and approved was to knock Italy out of the war by pursuing vigorous action in the Mediterranean, the clincher being that their proposed strategy would bring the Russians 'more certain and possibly even greater relief' than a cross-Channel operation. The elimination of Italy from the war would require Germany to replace the thirty or more Italian divisions in the Balkans and Italy, some of which would have to come from the Russian Front, thereby bringing some relief to Russia.[47] The decision against Operation Roundup was based on an assumption that it would take until the summer of 1943 to assemble twenty-five divisions for the assault, which would mean a period of inactivity following the end of the North African campaign expected soon. In any case, for Roundup in 1943, 'the expedition was likely to be inadequate for the scale of resistance expected at the time of the assault' and a possible re-entry in August or September was only possible 'should conditions hold out a good prospect of success'. An adherence to 'Germany first' was also requested. A paper outlining this strategy was sent to the US Joint Chiefs of Staff over the New Year period as the preferred British strategy for 1943.[48]

Thus the British went to Casablanca for the conference with their American allies having already determined their position that the only option for 1943 was to continue operations in the Mediterranean – a position which Churchill was forced to reluctantly accept because he knew it would bring potential trouble with both Stalin and Roosevelt.

The Americans were naturally still keen to continue Bolero, launch Operation Roundup and go on the defensive after Torch; Churchill's telegram to Marshall seemed to have confirmed that the British were thinking along similar lines. At a meeting at the White House on 10 December between Roosevelt and his Chiefs of Staff to discuss post-Torch strategy, Roosevelt was anxious to continue the build-up in both North Africa and England while leaving options open for the future. Marshall's view of the commitment to North Africa was unchanged:

> He stated that he was particularly opposed to 'dabbling' in the Mediterranean in a wasteful logistical way and that, before any new operation was under-taken in that area, he wanted to make sure that the attrition which would certainly result could be justified by the objectives to be attained.[49]

Confirmation of the American preferred strategy was received by the British on 25 December. As the paramount immediate objective was to assure the survival of Russia, the American strategy was to go on the defensive in North Africa while developing air bases there to bomb Italy and Germany before launching Operation Roundup sometime in 1943.[50] Dill had reported to Churchill from Washington on the attitude of Marshall so Churchill was well aware of the enormity of the difficulties to come in getting the Americans to commit to further operations in the Mediterranean in 1943.[51]

While the British were anxious to get an affirmation of 'Germany first', the numbers of American troops shipped to Europe and Africa had increased dramatically while the number of troops in the Pacific had also continued increasing, so that by the end of 1942 there were approximately the same numbers of troops in both theatres. There were 346,000 troops (nine divisions and nineteen Air Force groups) in the Pacific and 347,000 men (eight divisions and forty-five Air Force groups) in Britain and north-west Africa.[52]

A renewed attempt to attack towards Tunis during 22–24 December by the Allies was unsuccessful, being largely thwarted by heavy rain. Eisenhower predicted that there would have to be a period of building up the Allied forces prior to the next offensive, which would not be for two months, admitting to the Combined Chiefs of Staff on 26 December that the reinforcement race with the Germans had been lost.

On Christmas Eve, Admiral Darlan was assassinated by an allegedly disaffected Frenchman but he had very few friends amongst the British, French, Americans or even the Germans. Giraud was appointed by Eisenhower as his successor, which stimulated a new rivalry between de Gaulle and Giraud as to who was to be the future leader of the Free French forces, Giraud holding a much higher rank in the French Army than de Gaulle. Churchill initially hoped they would work together and unite the Free French forces against Germany.

Eisenhower commented on the operations in North Africa to date:

> 7 Dec: I think the best way to describe our operations to date is that they have violated every recognized principle of war, are in conflict with all operational and logistic methods laid down in textbooks, and will be condemned in their entirety by all Leavenworth and War College classes for the next twenty-five years.[53]

Eisenhower was quite correct in his summary as, once ashore, the British and American forces were not strong enough to rapidly reach their objectives in Tunisia. This allowed weaker German forces to block Allied advances and the bad weather did the rest, giving time for further Axis reinforcements to arrive.

Beveridge Report

Following a survey of existing social benefit and insurance schemes in 1941, Lord Beveridge released his report in November 1942. The three main recommendations were for child benefits to be paid until the ages of 15 (or 16 if still at school), a national free medical system and a recognition that it was the responsibility of governments to avoid mass unemployment in the workforce post-war.[54] The report was universally acclaimed and heralded the start of a better social security system and the National Health Service in Britain. So enthusiastically was the report received by the press that Churchill was moved to write a note to the Cabinet warning, 'A dangerous optimism is growing up about the conditions of it will be possible to establish here after the war.'

The additional benefits to be introduced were to follow the establishment of a national minimum level of subsistence, below which no one would be allowed to fall. Housewives in England were enthusiastic:

> His scheme will appeal more even to women than to men for it is they who bear the real burden of unemployment, sickness, child bearing and rearing – and the ones who, up to now, have come off worst.[55]
>
> His plan 'treats man and wife as a team.' It was announced last week that Sir William Beveridge ... is soon marrying his secretary.[56]

Churchill was concerned about making promises to the people that could not be kept because of inflation and a war-ravaged economy that would not be able to afford the new scheme. A month later, Churchill had decided that as the conditions at the end of war were unknown, the legislation would be prepared but not enacted until after the people had a chance to vote on it.[57]

The New Year saw a gloomy British Chiefs of Staff paper on the fact that there was not enough assault shipping and landing craft to launch more than one large-scale amphibious operation at a time, be it Operation Anakim (Burma), Sicily or Operation Jupiter. The report also stated there would be insufficient landing craft by August 1943 to mount a cross-Channel operation of more than six brigades.[58]

The stalemate on the ground in Tunisia now began to overshadow strategic plans being made for the immediate future after the conclusion to the African campaign, which was supposed to have been over by Christmas. In response to another pessimistic report from Eisenhower on the lack of progress, the British Chiefs of Staff despatched a telegram to their US counterparts warning of the dangers of losing the initiative to the Germans, who were bringing in reinforcements faster than the Allies, if offensive operations were delayed for two months.[59] At the subsequent Casablanca conference, Eisenhower would claim that the forces that landed in North Africa were not equipped for offensive operations but only for capturing ports.[60] Eisenhower later also made the valid point that no one had foreseen the political intrigues surrounding the French, which took up a great deal of his time.

Casablanca

Against this background of once again differing views on the best strategy to win the war and preconceived positions, the British and Americans met at Casablanca from 15 January 1943. It had been intended that the conference take place at the conclusion of the fighting in Tunisia but the latest reports from Eisenhower indicated that would continue for several months. Stalin declined to attend the meeting and therefore the nation most heavily involved with fighting Germany was not present. A message that the German forces at Stalingrad were being liquidated was received on 5 January, so Stalin's presence and indeed contribution to the war effort was very much felt at the conference.

The Pacific theatre had seen American victories at Coral Sea, Midway and Guadalcanal while the campaign in Papua New Guinea was about to be concluded, eliminating the perceived threat to Australia of a Japanese invasion. The Japanese were believed to be going on the defensive and digging in to consolidate their vast territorial gains. Dill met briefly with the British Chiefs of Staff the day before the first Combined Chiefs of Staff meeting on 14 January and again warned of the likely differences with the Americans. Despite a meeting between Roosevelt and his Joint Chiefs of Staff at the White House on 7 January to determine a united approach, no agreement was reached other than to not make an immediate decision and to examine whether two large forces could be built up for operations in 1943, one in Britain and the other in North Africa. Marshall remained opposed to future operations in the Mediterranean. Thus while the British Chiefs were well prepared and united behind Churchill, there was no such unity among the Americans. Roosevelt's personal opinion, as revealed to the Canadian Prime Minister Mackenzie King during their meetings in early December 1942, was that the Dieppe Raid had demonstrated how dangerous any cross-Channel operation would be and he would prefer to continue in the Mediterranean, which could easily be supplied.[61]

Over the eight days of the conference, Roosevelt and Churchill met officially three times, at the start and end of the proceedings with a progress meeting on 18 January. The Combined Chiefs of Staff met once or twice a day to thrash out a joint strategy for the conduct of the war and then met separately with their respective leaders to summarise the daily discussions and take instructions.

While Brooke battled with Marshall in the Combined Chiefs of Staff meetings over the Mediterranean strategy versus Roundup, Churchill worked on Roosevelt regarding future plans. The two met in the evening of 14 January for private talks and then dinner. Next morning before the first plenary session, Roosevelt met with the Joint Chiefs of Staff to hear about the progress of discussions with the British and during the meeting Marshall's resolve for a European landing appeared to be wavering. General Mark Clark had spoken to Marshall of the need for further training before any future amphibious assault and it is possible that Roosevelt made his preference known, though this is not recorded in the minutes.[62]

The first plenary session was with Roosevelt, Churchill and the Combined Chiefs of Staff. Marshall maintained that what were needed were a major cross-Channel operation in 1943 as soon as possible and the end to further operations in the Mediterranean, while Admiral King was anxious to see the division of resources between the Pacific and the European theatres revised to at least 30:70 respectively. As Admiral King claimed that the existing ratio was 85:15, this would mean a substantial increase in resources for the Pacific. As the numbers of men committed to each theatre were already approximately equal, King was merely being provocative in making his position known. The British countered by asking King to define exactly what his requirements were for specific operations before the balance could be committed to Europe. As the movements and allocation of landing craft and assault shipping was the responsibility of the US Navy and King was its chief as well as being responsible for the Pacific theatre, the British had to be respectful in their dealings with him. The Americans believed the British were indifferent to the Pacific theatre while the British, in turn, were at pains to commit to joining the war against Japan once Germany was defeated. There was much debate about the 'Germany first' policy concerning the defensive policy being adopted for the war against Germany as opposed to the offensive policy in the Pacific. By 17 January, however, Churchill was confident that Roosevelt was 'strongly in favour of the Mediterranean being given prime place' and notified the War Cabinet accordingly.[63]

In an attempt to steal the headlines, the Germans conducted a very heavy air raid on London on the night of 17–18 January in which fifty-four people were killed, ten of them by anti-aircraft shells falling back to the ground.[64]

In time for the second plenary progress meeting on the 18 January, the views of the Combined Chiefs of Staff on the broad future strategy had started to align, despite their differences, as the Joint Chiefs of Staff now knew Roosevelt's preference. A draft paper was approved which provided the basis for detailed planning over the next four days. The Mediterranean strategy was adopted and confirmed, the main objective being to increase the pressure on Italy by occupying Sicily utilising the troops and assault shipping that were already close at hand. The British and Americans did not want to have their troops idle for any length of time once the North African campaign finished and thereby recriminations from Russia about the lack of a Second Front and the fact that the country was fighting Germany alone would hopefully be forestalled. The elimination of Italy would clear the sea lanes through the Mediterranean to the Suez Canal and thus the Far East while forcing Germany to provide divisions to replace the Italian divisions in Italy and the Balkans, some of which would have to come from the Russian Front. The next operation would be against Sicily with landings to commence during a favourable moon in July. It was clearly understood by the Combined Chiefs of Staff that this meant no Roundup until 1944 as it was discussed in a prior meeting on 16 January at which Brooke said, 'We should definitely count on re-entering the Continent in 1944 on a large scale.'[65]

Roosevelt was also informed by Admiral King of the British 'lack of enthusiasm' for Roundup, which would be unlikely before April 1944, at a Joint Chiefs of Staff meeting the same day. There was sufficient shipping to mount a cross-Channel operation or to invade Italy but not undertake both simultaneously.

At the second plenary meeting with Roosevelt and Churchill, Marshall remained opposed to the Mediterranean strategy and emphasised that it would be difficult, if not impossible, to undertake Roundup in 1943 once the Allies were committed to Sicily and that the US Chiefs of Staff had only agreed to Operation Husky, the invasion of Sicily, in order to knock Italy out of the war and free up 225 transport ships for operations in the Pacific and Burma.[66] This was understood by all at the conference. Lip service was paid to Sledgehammer, for which Churchill said preparations should continue in order to exploit a crack in morale and that everything should be done to make the operation possible that summer. The unconditional surrender of Germany and Japan was discussed, with Churchill saying that he would like to release a press statement to this effect after the conference but needed to clear it with the War Cabinet, which duly approved it on 20 January, adding Italy to the document. The occupation of Sardinia was canvassed as another option: this was favoured by

Mountbatten and Harriman as it could be conducted earlier in 1943 than any landings in Sicily or mainland Italy.

In the interim, de Gaulle had been invited to Casablanca to meet with General Giraud. After a great deal of prevarication, de Gaulle finally arrived and met reluctantly with Giraud. Eden was also invited to become involved, although he too was reluctant after having been not involved by Churchill for all the discussions on France and North Africa.

At the final conference session on 23 January, the plans for 1943 were presented and discussed. In Burma, the British were to undertake three operations to both liberate the country and assist the flow of aid to China. The importance of China to the US had been stated by Admiral King in a Combined Chiefs of Staff meeting to the effect that China had the geographical position and manpower resources which if provided with arms and equipment like Russia would enable it to fight as a major ally. It was Roosevelt's fervent belief that if Chinese manpower could be harnessed in the same way as the Russians did to resist Germany, then China would be able to make a considerable contribution to the defeat of Japan.

The first Burmese operation, Operation Cannibal, to recapture Akyab in the Arakan Peninsula and set up airfields for future operations, was already in progress. The second offensive, Operation Ravenous, was to establish a bridgehead over the Chindwin River in order to threaten Mandalay before the third assault, Operation Anakim was to land amphibious troops by 15 November 1943 (after the monsoon season) to retake Rangoon and complete the liberation of Burma. Approval for Operation Anakim had been mainly due to the efforts of Marshall, who again faced opposition from the British demanding the 'Germany first' policy be adhered to.

Operation Husky was agreed on with a target date of no later than a suitable moon in July 1943, the availability of armoured landing craft (the Americans had none) and trained landing craft crews being the limiting factors. Eisenhower was instructed to prepare a report within three weeks on the feasibility of conducting the operation earlier in June. Turkey was to be encouraged to enter the war on the Allied side. A British and American Combined Bomber Offensive was to be conducted from the United Kingdom with the objectives of the 'progressive destruction and dislocation of the German military, industrial and economic system and the undermining the morale of the German people to the point where their capacity for armed resistance is fatally weakened'.[67] U-boat construction facilities were deemed the most important target followed by, in order of priority, aircraft factories, transportation networks and oil facilities.

The build-up in Britain, Bolero, was anticipated to be slower than expected with no more than four additional US divisions expected by 15 August 1943. As all armoured landing craft would be allocated for Sicily, according to Mountbatten, that left none in England for a cross-Channel operation, for which the British could only muster two brigade groups for any assault and one as a follow-up without added American support.[68] An operation to seize a bridgehead on the Cotentin Peninsula in August was planned but was couched in the same previous conditions, requiring a collapse in German morale and adequate resources being available to mount the operation.[69] A Second Front across the English Channel was certainly not going to happen in 1943 as promised to Stalin and, worse, the Sicily landings would utilise all available naval vessels necessitating the suspension again of aid convoys to Russia. A telegram prepared for Stalin on the decision made at Casablanca from Roosevelt and Churchill after the conference mentioned neither of these points.[70] This joint message from the Allied leaders would inevitably further displease and disillusion Stalin, who was expecting to be sent details of the promised Second Front on the Continent.

By adopting the Mediterranean strategy to knock Italy out of the war, the British Chiefs of Staff got their way with surprisingly little argument from their American counterparts who, once aware of Roosevelt's preference, did not want to go against their President. Churchill's position regarding his promise to Stalin was also retrieved to some extent; now he could justify his position of pursuing operations in the Mediterranean to the exclusion of a Second Front on the Continent as being not only his decision but that of the Combined Chiefs of Staff and Roosevelt. The rationale for an operation against Sicily was in order to provide immediate relief to Russia but this decision in itself excluded the possibility of any Second Front in 1943, which was what Stalin and Russia urgently wanted and had been promised. Marshall, determined to launch Roundup in 1943, had again been outmanoeuvred by Churchill and had not been supported by his own President. Given Churchill's apparent preference for Roundup in 1943 passed on through Dill in December, Marshall was no doubt surprised by the British position at Casablanca for exploiting the Mediterranean further. One of the American strategic planners, Lt Colonel Wedemeyer, wrote in a report afterwards on Casablanca, '… we lost our shirts and … are now committed to a subterranean umbilicus operation in mid-summer … we came, we listened and we were conquered.'[71]

The British, for their part, were extremely pleased by the outcome of the conference, one planner writing of the final report to Roosevelt and Churchill,

'If before the conference he had to write down what he hoped its decisions would be, he could never have written anything so sweeping, comprehensive and favourable to British ideas …'[72]

On 24 January, the conference ended with a press conference. Churchill, after a breakfast with wine because he was wary of the possibly contaminated local milk, sat with Roosevelt in front of the waiting press correspondents. A reluctant handshake was orchestrated for the cameras between de Gaulle and Giraud, to the amusement of Roosevelt and Churchill. A joint communiqué had been issued by the Allies which did not mention unconditional surrender but Roosevelt, talking from prepared notes, declared to the world that Britain and America would see the war through to the total defeat or unconditional surrender of Germany. Churchill claimed to be very surprised by this public announcement – but as it was discussed on 18 January and in telegrams to the War Cabinet during the conference, he should not have been.[73]

SICILY

Following the Casablanca conference, Churchill flew to Turkey to meet with the Turkish Prime Minister as he was determined to bring the Turks with their large army into the war on the Allied side. However, the Turks were now as concerned about the Russians as they were about the Germans and the talks were ultimately inconclusive; Turkey was determined to remain neutral in spite of Churchill's effort to court it.

Stalin had already asked Roosevelt on 13 January as to why there had been a slowdown in north-west Africa and this was followed by another cable on 30 January requesting details of the proposed Second Front for 1943 after receiving the joint message from Roosevelt and Churchill regarding the Casablanca deliberations. Churchill finally replied on 9 February with an outline of the plans for Sicily and mentioned the planned August cross-Channel operation, but again provided many potential reasons for its delay or cancellation:

> We are also pushing preparations to the limit of our resources for a cross-Channel operation in August, in which both British and United States would participate. Here again, shipping and assault-landing craft will be limiting factors. If the operation is delayed by the weather or other reasons, it will be prepared with stronger forces for September. The timing of this attack must, of course, be dependent upon the condition of German defensive possibilities across the Channel at that time.[1]

In his reply on 16 February, Stalin claimed that the slowdown of military operations culminating in the likely April conclusion to the North African campaign rather than February had enabled the Germans to send twenty-seven more divisions to the Eastern Front and thus Operation Torch had failed to bring any relief to the Russians at all. Stalin went on to demand that the Second Front be opened earlier than the planned August or September that year. Churchill was then laid low with a bout of pneumonia following a chilled flight back from the Casablanca conference and it was left to Roosevelt to reply on 22 February, reaffirming a commitment to the European Continent when the North African campaign was over and shipping permitted. It was another week before Churchill himself could reply in a long telegram that admitted to a slow build-up of troops in the UK, stating again that this was due to the shortage of shipping. Stalin's mistrust of Churchill was mounting, as evidenced in his telegram of 15 March:

> I must give a most emphatic warning, in the interest of our common cause, of the grave danger with which further delay in opening a second front in France is fraught. For this reason the vagueness of your statements about the contemplated Anglo-American offensive across the Channel causes apprehension which I cannot conceal from you.[2]

Stalin also claimed to both Roosevelt and Churchill that by this time there were now thirty-six extra German divisions fighting in Russia.

While the Allies had been held up in the west of Tunisia by the bad weather and the need to build up their forces, Montgomery's Eighth Army had been steadily advancing on the heels of the retreating Afrika Korps through Libya. With the British capture of the undefended Tripoli on 27 January 1943 and increased air attacks on the Italian mainland, the morale of the Italians in North Africa and the Commando Supremo in Rome began to plummet. Rommel's army continued its withdrawal until it reached the Mareth Line in Tunisia at the end of January, where the line of defensive positions originally built by the French were frantically improved by the Germans.

On 11 February, Eisenhower sent his response to the Combined Chiefs of Staff direction to examine whether Operation Husky could be launched in June provided the fighting in Tunisia was over by 30 April. According to Eisenhower, 'owing to lack of time for training and preparation, a June assault was unlikely to succeed'.[3] For Churchill, this telegram was unduly pessimistic and the delay unwarranted as the Eighth Army was approaching from the east and soon the Germans in Tunisia would be under attack from two directions. Churchill had actually been urging for ways to be found to advance the date of the Sicily operation, not delay it. Accordingly, Churchill had written to Eisenhower and Hopkins and later asked the British Chiefs of Staff on 19 February to examine the possibility of using only British troops in the invasion.[4] Churchill was greatly concerned that once the fighting ended in north-west Africa, British and American soldiers should not be idle for any lengthy period and committed to a new theatre as quickly as possible so that Russians would not be only ones actively fighting Germans. Churchill declared in a minute to the Chiefs of Staff, 'We shall become a laughing stock if, during the spring and early summer, no British and American soldiers are firing at any German or Italian soldiers.'[5]

Evidently, the promise to Stalin regarding a Second Front was very much in Churchill's mind. Added impetus to the planned landings in Sicily came from anti-fascist groups in Italy that had contacted Churchill, who was anxious to enlist their support in knocking Italy out of the war.[6] Churchill's bluff to use only British troops worked well as the next day the Combined Chiefs of Staff ordered Eisenhower to carry out the operation in June as directed. In his reply to Churchill, Eisenhower pointed out that the Eighth Army needed to resupply before attacking the Mareth Line and could not commence its attack until mid March. The Germans then completely pre-empted Allied plans and build-up by attacking the Americans in what became the Battle of Kasserine Pass, breaking through their lines. The pause of the Eighth Army before the Mareth Line had given the opportunity for the Germans to switch elements of one of Rommel's Panzer divisions to the west. The German intention was to split the Allied forces in west Tunisia and threaten the rear of the British Corps, compelling it to withdraw to Algeria. The situation in Tunisia was restored when Allied reinforcements were rushed to seal off the gap in the front line and the German offensive was called off on 22 February, as revealed to Churchill by decrypts. This was fortunate for the Americans, who had been given 'a bloody nose to knock some of the cockiness out of us', according to one senior officer.

A directive from the Combined Chiefs of Staff to the British Chiefs of Staff for the planning team developing the plans for the cross-Channel attack was finally approved on 5 March 1943 and more detailed planning could commence.

The aggressive tone of Stalin's telegrams to the Allies was strengthened by the success of the Red Army at Stalingrad and in pushing back the Germans from Rostov and Kharkov; Russia had demonstrated for the second year that it could withstand German attacks. As Allied aid flowed in and Russian industry modernised and stepped up its production of war material, Russia was well on the way to not only defeating the German invaders but becoming a great world power in its own right. American relations with Russia were not helped by the American Ambassador in Moscow being quoted on 8 March as saying that Russia was concealing from ordinary Russians the amount of Lend-Lease aid being received and creating the impression that the country was fighting unaided.

General Alexander was appointed overall commander of the ground forces in Tunisia, forming the newly created 18th Army Group, after the German offensive at Kasserine and on 27 February he told Churchill that 'final victory in North Africa was not around the corner'.[7] On 6 March, the German Panzer battalions which had been moved again to concentrate near the Mareth Line launched a surprise attack on the assembling Eighth Army at Medinine, which was defeated largely by British anti-tank guns positioned to take advantage of an Ultra decryption of Rommel's battle plans. Montgomery's successful offensive to break the Mareth Line began on 20 March and Dominion troops entered Gabes on 29 March. The Allies began to exert pressure from two directions on the Germans and Italians, whose supply lines across the Mediterranean were being severely disrupted by Allied naval and air forces.

The news of the successful fighting in Tunisia was well received in Britain, which along with Churchill's speeches engendered a more optimistic outlook. On 21 March, Churchill made a radio broadcast to the nation and gave a brief overview of the war before presenting a vision of the post-war world with a four-year plan for Britain's future which would encompass social reforms such as those envisaged in the Beveridge Report. One civilian commented:

> I'm just reading a bit of Churchill's speech where he says that directly we've licked the Huns, anything in the way of heat will be turned on the Japanese but partial demobilisation will undoubtedly take place.[8]

On 24 March, Churchill cabled Roosevelt with a warning that, according to a Chiefs of Staff study, there was insufficient shipping to implement in full the decisions taken at Casablanca. There was a shortage of vessels for the proposed Sicilian landings and there was little prospect of even being able to carry out Operation Anakim, let alone continue Bolero, unless a great deal more shipping was provided for the Indian and European theatres.[9] At this point in time, Churchill was still concerned about the potential major diversion of resources to the Pacific by the Americans and the shortage of food and raw materials for Britain. This message was reinforced by Eden in person on a visit to Washington and on 30 March Roosevelt agreed to increase the shipping to the UK, even if it was at the expense of Operation Anakim in Burma.[10] On the same day, Churchill (after consultation with Roosevelt) informed Stalin of the decision to suspend all further PQ convoys until September because of the German naval strength concentrated at Narvik that threatened the convoys and the shortage of shipping needed for Husky. The German warships *Tirpitz*, *Scharnhorst*, *Lutzow*, a cruiser and eight destroyers were all based in Norwegian fjords at that time. Stalin was no doubt deeply unimpressed but confined his reaction to a statement about how the catastrophic cuts could not fail to affect the position of the Soviet troops.

Churchill sent a telegram to Roosevelt on 5 April with a copy of a minute sent to the British Chiefs of Staff about possible future operations post-Operation Husky if Operation Anakim was cancelled and suggested the occupation of the Italian mainland, as well as asking for American ideas. The Battle of the Atlantic was nearing its climax, Allied shipping losses were heavy but the number of U-boats lost by the Germans was mounting. Extended aircraft cover, improvements in ship- and aircraft-borne radar and better underwater detection equipment all contributed to turning the tide in favour of the Allies. In November 1942, in response to the numbers of ships being sunk, Churchill had set up the Anti-U-boat Committee, which he chaired to try to better co-ordinate Allied action. The American contribution of large numbers of escort vessels and aircraft eventually served to overwhelm the U-boats, which were reduced to operating in a small area of the Atlantic that Allied aircraft could not yet cover. For the war against Japan, Churchill took a simplistic view and stated that it was his belief that the best way to defeat Japan was to strike at the Japanese homeland rather than the individual tentacles gripping the rest of Southeast Asia, illustrating this with a nursery rhyme from which apparently much could be learnt: 'Lady Bird, Lady Bird, fly away home, your house is burning, your children are gone.' According to Churchill, such attacks would have greater effects than attacking the outposts alone.[11]

Meanwhile the first British offensive in Burma, Operation Cannibal to capture Akyab, had ground to a halt at the end of March without achieving its objective but with acrimony between Generals Slim and Irwin. The average British or Indian soldier was not properly trained for fighting or living in the jungle (unlike the Japanese) and this deficiency was one of the prime causes of the defeats in Malaya, Singapore and Burma. British Army units were trained and equipped as if they were fighting a war in the open desert. The jungle was classified as impenetrable, which of course it was to motor vehicles for transport and supplies, whereas to the Japanese infantry the jungle offered concealment and a means of making surprise attacks. British attacks along the roads on narrow fronts were easily blocked by the Japanese; wen the roles had been reversed in early 1942, the Japanese soldiers had taken to the jungle to outflank or bypass British roadblocks. These repeated defeats helped foster a belief in the invincibility of the Japanese and greatly affected British morale.[12] Churchill was less than impressed, as he commented to the Chiefs of Staff:

> This campaign goes from bad to worse and we are being completely out-fought and outmanoeuvred by the Japanese. Luckily, the small scale of operations and the attraction of other events have prevented public opinion from being directed on this lamentable scene. We cannot however count on a continuance of this.[13]

This disparaging comment was very uncharitable of Churchill. Many Indian divisions and even British units had been transferred from India to meet the requirements of the Middle East and Syrian/Iraq theatres and there were insufficient men to mount a large-scale operation against the occupying Japanese forces – a reality that was compounded by the unrectified problems of training and morale. Nevertheless, such was the Chiefs of Staff's disappointment with the Arakan campaign that the three Commanders-in-Chief including Wavell were summoned back to London on 9 April for further planning talks. Wavell had prepared a plan for future operations including Operation Anakim, which was rejected by the Joint Planners and the Chiefs of Staff at their meeting on 15 April; the Joint Planners recommended the cancellation of Operation Anakim altogether as the movement of the shipping required for it would mean no further operations in the Mediterranean. The Chiefs of Staff approved the recommendations subject to further discussions with Wavell on his arrival.[14] A later report recommended an alternative strategy of expanding the air route to China with additional long-range penetration group operations designed to protect the airlift to the country as a preferable alternative to fighting overland in northern Burma. The proposed changes were taken by Churchill to the Defence Committee and the War Cabinet:

> It could not be said that the conquest of Burma was an essential step in the defeat of Japan, though the Americans were in favour of the attempt. Nor would the occupation of Northern Burma mean the immediate resumption of traffic on the Burma Road; a year would be required for its restoration.

Everything pointed to an alternative line of action, and this the Chiefs of Staff would study with the Commanders-in-Chief.[15]

The planning for Operation Husky by Eisenhower continued, although shipping for the scale of the assault planned remained a problem and the starting date had not yet been fixed. The appearance of two German divisions on the island of Sicily together with other planning difficulties also caused Eisenhower to have second thoughts, much to Churchill's disquiet. At the Chiefs of Staff meeting on 13 April, another draft paper concluded once more that if priority to Husky was given as recommended, there would be insufficient landing craft for any cross-Channel operation in 1943 to assist the Russians as landing craft were being assembled in the Mediterranean and not Britain. Churchill claimed this sacrifice had not been made clear when the decision for Husky was taken at Casablanca, which was not true as the potential problem had been flagged in his own Chief of Staff's paper produced over the New Year period and discussed at the conference. There would be no Operation Roundup that year, and if the landing craft were relocated as planned for Operation Husky there would be no opportunities for alternative operations either.[16] In a subsequent minute, Churchill wrote of his decision not to tell Stalin of this development. There was also the problem of idle American troops that were starting to arrive in the UK; they were requesting training facilities for amphibious operations that would now not take place that year. Churchill contemplated whether the Bolero build-up should in fact be slowed down because of the waste of money and labour but then expressed his view that the build-up should continue for operations in 1944.[17] A few days later, Churchill confirmed in a minute to the Chiefs of Staff that there would be no Operation Roundup in 1943 owing to a lack of landing craft and American troops in England and that the planning team should be given other priorities.[18] Operation Roundup, which had been the major objective of Anglo-American strategy in 1942, was finally revealed for the illusion it was. However, the Americans had realised this was a consequence of the decisions taken at Casablanca. Another cable from the US Joint Chiefs of Staffs provided their understanding and clarification of the decisions taken at the conference and indicated a possible change of American thinking in that more resources were required for the Pacific theatre 'to maintain and extend unremitting pressure against Japan'. The build-up in Britain, Operation Bolero, was last on their list of priorities.[19] As this was contrary to the strategy agreed at Casablanca, this alarmed the British and later cables over the next fortnight provided more evidence that the Americans were pursuing a different strategy. At Casablanca it was agreed that the Americans would send 80,000 more troops to England in the first quarter of 1943 but only 15,000 had arrived. While a shortage of shipping was a problem globally, it was clear to the British that large numbers of troops were being sent to the Pacific.[20]

A planning conference with Eisenhower, Alexander and Montgomery in late March determined that a June date for Husky was impracticable and the operation should be postponed to 10 July, which met with Churchill's begrudging approval as it was a delay of only two weeks. Marshall then proposed on 16 April at a Combined Chiefs of Staff meeting that Husky be launched before the Tunisian campaign had been concluded, an idea which was eagerly seized upon by Churchill but the British Chiefs of Staff thought impractical.[21] Such an operation would surprise the Axis forces in Sicily and hasten an end to the fighting in Tunisia. This was Marshall's last attempt to end the Mediterranean campaign quickly in order for the build-up in Britain to be accelerated for any chance of a landing in France in late 1943; Eisenhower came to the same conclusion as the British Chiefs of Staff.

The British Pacific and Indian Commanders-in-Chief (Wavell and others) had been invited to Washington on their way back to India to discuss strategy in the Far East and operations to assist China. Churchill was anxious to see that there should be no deviation from the 'Germany first' policy and suggested he and Brooke should also attend to offer his commanders 'political support'. Accordingly, Churchill telegraphed Roosevelt on 29 April to propose a meeting to settle operations post-Husky and Anakim together but the British had already virtually decided that Operation Anakim was dead. Knowing that Hopkins was a close confidante of Roosevelt, Churchill used him as a back channel to the President and wrote a more explanatory telegram to him about the outstanding issues in the knowledge it would be discussed with Roosevelt, who subsequently agreed to the conference.

On 4 May, Churchill left for the Washington conference, which was code-named Trident. En route, the North African campaign ended with the British and Americans victorious; on 7 May US troops entered Bizerte and the British arrived in Tunis. German resistance ended completely on 13 May and a total of 275,000 prisoners were taken. The North African theatre was a long way from Germany but the Allied victory assured the continuation of communications to the British Empire in the Far East via the Suez Canal and that the Middle Eastern oilfields remained in British hands. The campaign had lasted four months longer than planned and although it saw no German Army units transferred to Tunisia from Russia, the numbers of transport aircraft redeployed significantly affected the ability of the Luftwaffe to resupply the trapped soldiers at Stalingrad. Bomber aircraft such as the venerable Heinkel III had to be used for this task and suffered heavy losses. As at Stalingrad, when Hitler refused to allow his trapped Army to withdraw, in North Africa Hitler overruled his staff and insisted on reinforcements being sent to prolong the fighting; three German divisions including two Panzer divisions were subsequently destroyed in the campaign. General Warlimont of the OKW went as far to describe after the war the Tunisian campaign as being the most decisive campaign for it established a 'springboard for a thrust into the groin of Fortress Europe, the naturally weak and practically unprepared south flank'.[22] This was the soft underbelly of Europe as envisioned by Churchill when meeting Stalin in 1942 and this quote to some extent vindicates the British leader's peripheral strategy that was adopted to defeat Germany. As the conclusion of the African campaign took five months longer than planned, the invasion of Europe could not happen in 1943 and was effectively postponed to 1944; Operation Torch arguably extended the war by a year. Despite victory in North Africa, the threat still remained to the British in the Mediterranean from Italy and her large navy and air force. One immediate consequence of the Operation Torch landings on 8 November 1942 had been to compel the Germans to occupy the whole of France, adding some 400 miles of Mediterranean coastline to be defended to that of northern France, requiring another German Army of occupation to be found.

Trident conference

Churchill, as on the previous trip to America, used the voyage to prepare papers on strategy which included an overview of the situation in the Far East, stating that the unsatisfactory course of the Burma campaign in 1942 could not be repeated in 1943–44.[23] At preliminary British Chiefs of Staff meetings on board the *Queen Mary* liner, the conclusion of the discussion over the previous weeks was confirmed, i.e. that Operation Anakim could not be mounted largely because the diversion of shipping to Burma would limit operations in the Mediterranean, the difficult jungle terrain and the monsoon season, which would limit the amount of time for operations. The failure to capture Akyab in Operation Cannibal as an advanced base for further action also reduced the scope for future operations.[24] The offensive to secure northern

Burma (Operation Ravenous) had not been undertaken either, although this was cancelled when the Chinese refused to participate, much to the relief of the British. It was recognised that the Americans would, however, demand an alternative to Anakim. Churchill was very opposed to any operations in the jungles of northern Burma and had his own ideas about suitable amphibious operations on other islands or the tip of Sumatra (Operation Culverin) but it was agreed to recommend only an increased airlift. In a minute, Churchill demonstrated the fear and respect the British had for the Japanese jungle fighting abilities:'Going into swampy jungles to fight the Japanese is like going into the water to fight a shark. It is better to entice him into a trap or catch him on a hook and then demolish him with axes after hauling him on to dry land.'[25]

With respect to post-Husky operations, the Chiefs of Staff proposed that after Sicily the invasion of Italy should be undertaken to knock that country out of the war.[26] Churchill went so far as to write that the operations after Sicily in Italy should have priority over Bolero, the build-up in the UK, paradoxically in order to improve the chances of the success of a future Roundup.[27] Several aide-memoires were prepared by British planners on the Mediterranean, the Far East and the defence of Australia to ensure that all members of the delegation were on the same page for the coming discussions with the Americans.

The Americans endeavoured to be better prepared for this round of talks. They would take the initiative by providing the agenda and their own pre-conference papers instead of always considering British papers. The various American strategic planning committees had been busy in the last two weeks of April examining future strategic options for the defeat of Germany. The Casablanca decisions were reviewed and other operations considered including the capture of Sardinia and landings on mainland Italy, on which the Americans were not keen. While recognising the merits of continued pressure in the Mediterranean, it was thought that the Combined Bomber Offensive against Germany together with landings in France were the best way to defeat Germany. If the British wanted to pursue operations against mainland Italy, they would have to do so alone. Aware of a divergence of opinion amongst his own staff, Roosevelt called a meeting at the White House on 8 May determined to present an agreed, united strategy to the British when they arrived. The preferred American strategy was now for an assault on France as soon as possible, as recorded by Admiral Leahy:

It was determined that the principal objective of the American Government would be to pin down the British to a cross-Channel invasion of Europe at the earliest practicable date and to make full preparations for such an operation by the spring of 1944.[28]

The Washington Trident meetings took place between 12 and 25 May at a time when the war situation had changed markedly for the British. The North African campaign had been concluded, Britain had not been invaded and now had powerful Allies in Russia and America. The Germans had been defeated at Stalingrad while the Japanese, having suffered reverses at Midway, Guadalcanal and Papua New Guinea, were now on the defensive. The prospects of the Allies winning the war were a lot brighter than any time before, but once again Stalin was not present at the meeting of the major Allies. However, there were still fundamental differences of strategy between the British and the Americans. Given the British preference for operations in the Mediterranean and apparent opposition to any form of a cross-Channel landing, the Americans believed the British had to be made to commit to landings in France. The British for their part were worried about the diversion of American resources to the Pacific.

At the first meeting with Roosevelt on 12 May, Churchill outlined the rewards of achieving the greatest prize of knocking Italy out of the war – the removal of the threat of the Italian fleet, the possible involvement of Turkey, a reduction in the pressure on Russia by compelling the Germans to reinforce their unreliable Italian ally and the employment of two armies that would be idle if a cross-Channel operation was not undertaken until 1944. Roosevelt responded by saying that it had not been decided whether Italy could be knocked out by an air offensive alone or would require its occupation but emphasised that a cross-Channel operation had to be undertaken in the spring of 1944.

With the issues spelled out by the two leaders, the respective Chiefs of Staff locked horns over the Mediterranean strategy, which the Americans saw as diverting resources from both Operation Bolero and the Pacific campaign. Operation Roundup was the preferred American strategy and further Mediterranean operations would, in their view, jeopardise the concentration of forces in England and as a result the cross-Channel assault in 1944. The British view was that landings in Italy would draw off German units from France, thus assisting any cross-Channel operation, and argued such an operation was the best way to assist Russia rather than having two armies idle for the next six months. Considerable debate took place regarding which Mediterranean operations could be undertaken with the resources already available. The arguments continued for several days and it was agreed that each nation should produce a further paper to summarise their arguments. The subsequent papers reiterated each of the protagonist's position but with sharper language from the Americans, who believed:

> The elimination of Italy is not a prerequisite for the creation of condi-
> tions favourable for Roundup; that the elimination of Italy may possibly
> be brought about without need of further amphibious operations in the
> Mediterranean, by a successful Husky and an intensified bomber offensive
> against Italy.[29]

This coming summer was seen as being decisive for Russia and in reality the British and American armies were incapable of taking any action to influence German operations against their ally. The Americans warned of more and more of the resources that were required for Bolero and the Far East being sucked in to the 'vacuum' of the Mediterranean. The British paper merely reaffirmed a commitment to France in 1944 but stated that to forego further operations in Italy would be to adopt a defensive attitude, surrender the initiative to the Germans and permit the enemy's defences in France and the Low Countries to be strengthened. At the Combined Chiefs of Staff meeting on 18 May to consider the two papers, discussions began to get heated. Marshall pointed out that the operations in North Africa had been delayed by a relatively small force and that a German decision to defend Italy might 'make any intended operations extremely difficult and time consuming'. A little later the room was cleared of everyone except the Chiefs of Staff themselves and the talks continued behind closed doors without any minutes being taken. This session produced a draft joint paper, which was discussed again behind closed doors later in the day. Brooke recorded his frustration of that day: 'The Americans are now taking the attitude that we led them down the garden path taking them to North Africa! Then at Casablanca we again misled them by inducing them to attack Sicily!! And now they are not going to be led astray again.'[30]

The final decisions were approved next morning and outlined in a terse paper. A date was set for the cross-Channel operation of 1 May 1944 and seven veteran divisions were to leave the Mediterranean by 1 November to take part, making a total of twenty-nine divisions to be assembled in Britain for the assault. The remaining units already in the Mediterranean were to be used in operations subject to the approval of the Combined Chiefs of Staff with the objectives of eliminating Italy from the war and pinning down the maxi-mum number of enemy forces.[31] The closed sessions allowed differences to be aired and decisions to be arrived at as required by Churchill and Roosevelt; Roosevelt in particular was anxious for a firm date for the cross-Channel operation in view of the presidential elections of 1944.

The question of strategy in Burma proved to be just as contentious for the Chiefs of Staff. The British had failed to capture Akyab and the planned limited offensive from northern Burma had not started at all when the Chinese troops did not advance. The Americans were eager to boost aid supplies to China by reopening the Burma Road from India and expanding the air route over the Himalayas, while the British were reluctant to mount any serious operation in Burma before Germany had been defeated, believing that aid to China could be sustained by an increased airlift alone. Operation Anakim was seen as physically impossible by the British. This time there was dissension in the ranks of the Americans themselves as Stilwell wanted to force the Burma Road open by land operations in northern Burma while General Chennault, commander of the Chinese Air Force, believed an increased airlift and air offensive was the best way to help the Chinese.

At the second plenary meeting on 14 May, Roosevelt listened to the arguments of Stilwell and Chennault as well as hearing from Wavell on the difficulties of operations in Burma. Roosevelt then cut across the debate and suggested that the objectives should be to maintain 7,000 tons of supplies a month by air to the Chinese as well as reopen the Burma Road and it was up to the military advisors to advise the best ways of achieving this. Marshall gloomily summed up the unfulfilled plans to date, reminding everyone that Operation Ravenous had been the first plan but Wavell had objected to it as being unsound for supply reasons, Brooke had objected because of the insecurity of the southern flank and Chiang Kai-Shek had objected because it was not coupled with naval action. Having then agreed on Operation Anakim, this was now considered impracticable as well.[32] The objectives set by Roosevelt were then examined by the Combined Chiefs of Staff planners, who produced two papers, one for the airlift and the other for the overland operations. The British Chiefs of Staff thought the airlift was too optimistic but agreed to support it. The operation to reopen the Burma Road relied on the support of thirteen Chinese divisions with six British divisions but Wavell believed the Chinese would not advance again and the British would sacrifice many men to achieve nothing. The Combined Chiefs of Staff met on 20 May to discuss the proposals and as with the Mediterranean theatre, no agreement could be reached and a subsequent meeting that day was held behind closed doors. The resulting draft paper provided for an intensified airlift combined with vigorous and aggressive land operations by the British and Chinese to recapture Imphal and Ledo in order to secure the air route to China in preparation for reopening the Burma Road. Amphibious operations against Ramree Island and Akyab in the Arakan were also to be undertaken. The British attempt to go slow in the Burma theatre and rely on the airlift to sustain the Chinese had failed. Despite the Burmese theatre being a largely British operation, they were unable to refuse the demands of the Americans, who were solely concerned with keeping China in the war.

The Combined Chiefs of Staff decisions on Italy and Burma were approved by Roosevelt and Churchill at the last plenary meeting. Regarding Burma, the final report had an important condition that no further American troops were to be committed to that theatre. Directives were prepared for both Eisenhower regarding future operations in Italy and COSSAC (Chief of Staff for future Supreme Allied Commander) for the proposed cross-Channel attack in 1944. Plans for an emergency landing in France in 1943 were to be maintained in the event that a suitable opportunity occurred.

Other decisions at Trident were less controversial but ultimately of far greater importance. The Americans and the British had agreed to work jointly on the development of the atomic bomb following meetings in Washington in June 1942. The British, however, had been hampered by a lack of resources and the US had thrown itself so enthusiastically into the project that it had made rapid progress, but had stopped sharing information with its ally. Churchill discussed the project, known as Tube Alloys, with Roosevelt in private and it was agreed to resume sharing information. At this point, the destructive force of such a bomb was theoretical and it was not known that it could work in practice. As a result of other discussions regarding the proposed heavy bomber offensive on Germany, the Casablanca directive was modified at Trident to make German fighter production facilities targets of the highest immediate importance as the reduction in enemy fighter strength was seen as an important prerequisite for the success of the Combined Bomber Offensive in bombing industrial and military targets in Germany. The bombing campaign would be conducted in four phases involving more and more aircraft in each and six raids a month would be conducted by American daylight bombers in addition to RAF missions at night. A directive for the offensive, now called Operation Pointblank, was duly given to the US VIII Bomber Command and the RAF Bomber Command by the Combined Chiefs of Staff on 10 June 1943. The build-up of American heavy bombers in England had been temporarily slowed by the diversion of some planes to North Africa.

The decision to occupy the Portuguese Azores as a base for anti-U-boat operations in order to close the Atlantic gap in the Allied air cover was also taken.[33] The seizure of the islands was to be a British responsibility and when the War Cabinet met to discuss Churchill's telegram outlining the Combined Chiefs of Staff plan, there was an outburst of protest from all members except for one. Arguments were put forward to the effect that the Battle of the Atlantic was all but won and while Britain's situation might have warranted it in 1940, this was not the case now. Such an occupation, if not achieved peacefully, would be akin to the actions of Nazi Germany and would certainly be in violation of Churchill and Roosevelt's own Atlantic Charter. The War Cabinet resolved that a diplomatic approach to Portugal should be made first and the whole matter should be deferred until Churchill's return.[34]

For Churchill, Trident had been successful but costly. At the price of hav ing to commit to a cross-Channel operation in May 1944, operations were to be continued in the Mediterranean. The only sour outcome had been the decision for major operations to be launched in Burma. However, it was now the monsoon season and no offensive action could be taken until November at the earliest. Instead of going back to India, Wavell was recalled to London for further discussions, when he was again relieved of his command, his successor again being Auchinleck.

As post-Husky operations were of extreme importance to Churchill and as no decision had been reached, Churchill proposed to fly immediately to Africa to meet Eisenhower accompanied by Marshall. No doubt Churchill relished the opportunity of bringing all his arguments and powers of persuasion to bear on Eisenhower. Churchill was, '… determined to obtain before leaving Africa the decision to invade Italy should Sicily be taken'.[35]

At this point, the continuation of the Mediterranean strategy had two possible options, one to capture Sardinia as favoured by the Americans and the other mainland Italy as proposed by Churchill 'with all its possibilities'. On meeting with Eisenhower in Algiers on 29 May, Marshall and Churchill found that the general, after listening to the British arguments, was ready to invade Italy immediately if the landings in Sicily were successful and rapidly concluded. Brooke had spoken with Eisenhower before the meeting and had pointed out the futility of landing a few divisions on the French Continent when the bulk of the German Army was fighting in Russia and therefore the aim should be to assist their ally sooner rather than later by forcing German troops to be diverted to Italy. Afterwards, Eisenhower stated that he saw no point in diverting forces from Sicily to assemble in Britain as they were merely 'a drop in the bucket', taking his cue from Brooke. Churchill said that it was still necessary to have a large force in the UK ready for cross-Channel operations in case the Germans should be ready to crack. He iterated the apparent desire of the British to cross the Channel and invade Europe.[36]

Prior to their second meeting, Churchill wrote a memorandum in support of knocking Italy out of the war and sent it to all parties. At the subsequent meeting, Churchill became very passionate about the need for landing on the Italian mainland, likening the alternatives between Sardinia and Italy to the difference between a mere convenience and a glorious campaign. He 'passionately wanted to see Italy out of the war and Rome in our possession', and was prepared to send an extra eight divisions from the Middle East to be put under Eisenhower's command to make this happen.[37] This was the first mention of Rome as an objective by anyone. Marshall queried how many extra service and AA troops would be needed for the landings on the Italian mainland and was told 63,000, at which point Marshall remarked that this quantity of men requiring extra shipping had not been discussed before. In reply Churchill stated:

> It would be hard for him to ask the British people to cut their rations again but he would gladly do so rather throw away a campaign which had possibilities of great success. He could not endure to see a great army idle when they might be engaged in eliminating Italy from the war. Parliament and the people would become impatient if the army were not active, and he was willing to take almost desperate steps in order to prevent such a calamity.[38]

What the people of Britain would have thought of Churchill's offer to cut their rations again can only be imagined. In 1943, there were shortages of most common foods especially fresh meat and fish; the arrival of American spam at least provided a substitute for meat when available. One woman wrote:

> Everything was scrupulously rationed and we ate some strange things to supplement our diet.
>
> Tea tablets were used to make the tea look stronger; babies' dried milk or 'National' milk was added if it could be obtained; and saccharine was used as a sweetener. Some even resorted to using honey or jam. What a concoction – but we drank it. Bread was heavy and a dull grey colour, but it, too, was rationed – so we ate it.
>
> Sweets were devised from a mixture of dried milk and peppermint essence with a little sugar or icing sugar if available. Grated carrots replaced fruit in a

Christmas or birthday cake while a substitute almond paste was made from ground rice or semolina mixed with a little icing sugar and almond essence. Dried egg powder was used as a raising agent, and this same dried egg could be reconstituted and fried, yielding a dull, yellow, rubbery-like apology for the light and fluffy real thing – but there was nothing else, so we ate it.

Bean pies and lentil rissoles provided protein to eke out our meagre meat ration, and the horse-meat shop, which previously had sold its products only for dogs, now bore a notice on some of its joints occasionally, 'Fit for Human Consumption'. This horse-meat was not rationed, but it did have to be queued for and sure enough eventually it appeared on our table. It had to be cooked for a long time and even then it was still tough. Nevertheless, it did not get thrown out.[39]

The problem for the Allies, and Churchill in particular, was that at this point in time American or British Army units had not been engaged in fighting Germany or Italy since mid May. While the RAF continued its nightly raids and the Royal Navy fought the Battle of the Atlantic, the British Army was not involved in any major offensives, not even in the Far East as it was the monsoon season. Therefore no pressure was being applied anywhere to cause the diversion of German units from the Russian Front to relieve the Soviet Army. Stalin would rightly not be pleased by this, especially as aid convoys had been suspended due to the shipping being required for Operation Husky. Once again, the Red Army was bearing the brunt of the war in its Battle of attrition with the Germans without any support from Britain and America.

Marshall, however, still wanted to wait to see how Husky fared before committing to any future plans, while Eisenhower reminded those present that his plans had to be approved by Combined Chiefs of Staff anyway.[40] Churchill declared his satisfaction at the agreement reached, despite no decisions being taken and Marshall's reluctance to commit to anything in the immediate future. All were agreed that it was best to put Italy out of the war and capture Rome as soon as possible.[41] Once Churchill had departed, Eisenhower set up two planning teams to consider operations against Sardinia or mainland Italy after Operation Husky. The Allies effectively would invade Sicily without having agreed any future operations in the Mediterranean.

A new threat to Anglo-American relations with Russia emerged on 13 April when the Germans announced the discovery of thousands of bodies of Polish officers in the Katyn Forest near Smolensk, allegedly murdered by the Russians. The claim was initially dismissed by the Allies as false and an attempt by the Germans to blame the Russians for their own crime. However, the Germans invited a delegation of international forensic scientists to visit the site, who verified the claim. Protests by the Polish government in London to the Russians were then used as an excuse by Stalin on 25 April to break off diplomatic relations with the Poles, thus ending any further Russian discussions with Poland about its frontiers after the war. A British diplomat to the Polish government, Sir Owen O'Malley, then wrote his own report examining both German and Russian claims and concluded that the Russian version of events was untrue.[42] Churchill, concerned about the greater strategic picture, refused to challenge the Russians directly and played down the massacre, writing to Eden that, 'There is no use in morbidly prowling around the three year old graves at Smolensk.'[43] A copy of O'Malley's report was forwarded to Roosevelt in August, but there was no response.

On the 3 June, de Gaulle and Giraud finally embraced in Algiers to set up a French Committee of National Liberation with each as co-president. It was hoped by Churchill and Roosevelt that this would see an end to the quarrels amongst the French generals.

News of the postponement of the Second Front to 1944 was not well received by Stalin when it was delivered on 4 June in a telegram from Roosevelt which was actually drafted by Marshall. In a strongly worded telegram to Roosevelt on 11 June, Stalin spoke of the negative impression that the decision, reached without him, for the postponement of landings from 1942 to the spring of 1944, would create in the Soviet Union. Roosevelt had warned Stalin only the previous month that the summer would bring a renewed German offensive, which Stalin was already expecting, so the news of the postponement could not have come at a worse time for Russia. Churchill was not addressed in Stalin's telegram but this slight was no doubt indicative of Stalin's understanding of the relationship and comparative standings of Roosevelt to Churchill and the sizes of their respective armed forces. The British Army was only a quarter the size of the Red Army and even the Americans would have more divisions than the British when they completed their mobilisation.

Nevertheless, Churchill replied on 13 June setting out the reasons for the delay, using the same arguments as previously. Stalin duly responded to Churchill on 24 June with further accusations, iterating each broken promise and his view that, as the war situation had improved for Britain and the US, the many difficulties of a cross-Channel operation had actually been lessened:

I must tell you that the point here is not just the disappointment of the Soviet Government, but the preservation of its confidence in its Allies, a confidence which is being subjected to severe stress. One should not forget that it is a question of saving millions of lives in the occupied areas of Western Europe and Russia and of reducing the enormous sacrifices of the Soviet armies, compared with which the sacrifices of the Anglo-American armies are insignificant.

Roosevelt, without informing Churchill, had on 5 May suggested an informal meeting with Stalin in Alaska as he believed that as the relationship between Churchill and Stalin had deteriorated to such an extent that the Soviet leader might prefer to deal with him. Roosevelt sent a letter to Stalin by means of a special envoy in which he expressed this desire to meet. Churchill was considerably put out when he found out about this from Harriman and sent an indignant telegram to Roosevelt on 25 June. Roosevelt denied that he had even made the suggestion but pointed out the benefits of just such a low-key meeting. The President further suggested he meet with Churchill at Quebec after any meeting with Stalin at the end of August.[44] To his Ambassador in Moscow, Churchill suggested that this was possibly the end of his personal correspondence with Stalin.

On 15 June, the CIGS, Brooke, was (much to his joy) offered by Churchill the position of Supreme Commander for the eventual cross-Channel operation, now to be in 1944. This offer was later repeated on 7 July by Churchill in the garden of No. 10 Downing Street.

On 5 July, the Germans finally launched their major offensive in Russia for 1943, Operation Citadel, with the objective of encircling the huge numbers of Soviet troops in a salient that bulged into the German lines. This would be the third crack at the Russians by the Germans, as Churchill had cautioned would happen. The attack was repeatedly delayed to allow for the new German Tiger and Panther tanks to be assembled in quantity, which allowed the Russians, warned by intelligence decrypts sent by the British, plenty of time to build formidable lines of anti-tank defences. Nevertheless, the German advance made some progress but the meeting of their two armoured pincers to complete a planned encirclement was prevented by the largest tank Battle of the war at Kursk, from which the Russians emerged victorious.

Operation Husky, Sicily Landings

The landings in Sicily would be made by two armies, Patton's Seventh Army of three divisions in the assault wave on the left flank in the Gulf of Gela and the British Eighth Army on the right flank of four divisions. This amphibious assault by seven divisions was greater even than that of Normandy in 1944 and was the largest of the entire war. The role of the Americans was to push inland and protect the flank of the British advance along the east coast to Messina, the division of responsibility reflecting the British General Alexander's scepticism (and indeed Churchill's) regarding the capabilities of the Americans after the Kasserine Pass debacle.[45] Landings on a total front of 100 miles were to be supported by American paratroops dropped behind the beaches to seize the high ground overlooking the beaches and vital road junctions; British glider troops would also land simultaneously near Syracuse. The US planners of Operation Husky were also concerned about moonlight on the proposed date of the operation; the airborne assault aircraft needed it to navigate by while the Navy was concerned about the possibility of air attacks at night – Eisenhower settled in favour of the Air Force argument.[46]

The island was defended by between 200,000 and 300,000 Italian troops of dubious quality organised in six coastal divisions and four regular infantry divisions. The two German units present were the 15th Panzergrenadier Division and the newly formed Hermann Göring Panzer Division, which was not fully equipped and was understrength. The 15th Panzergrenadier Division was moved to the western end of the island to oppose any landings there so the only German unit in the vicinity of the proposed landings was the Panzer division. The defenders recognised that they had no chance of defending the island if the Allies became established ashore and therefore their tactics were based on defeating any landings immediately on the beaches.

The Allied landings preceded by paratroop drops began without a naval bombardment on 10 July 1943 to little opposition. High winds severely disrupted and scattered the units of the airborne assault, resulting in only small forces being able to attack their objectives. Limited counter-attacks on the Americans by Italian tanks and infantry were beaten off once ashore but one attack by German tanks and engineers all but destroyed an infantry battalion of the 45th Division. Although the landings were disrupted by heavy seas, by the end of the first day the Seventh Army occupied a bridgehead 50 miles long and had penetrated inland up to 4 miles. The British landings were equally successful and Syracuse was occupied with little difficulty.

Another more determined counter-attack was made by the Axis troops next day in an attempt to reach the beaches. German tanks reached Gela and other attacks got to within 2,000 yards of the beaches, disrupting the movement ashore of supplies and follow-up forces. Artillery and naval gun fire were instrumental in defeating these attacks as scheduled armoured forces had been unable to land due to the attacks in progress. The Americans suffered 2,300 casualties in a single day but managed to cling to their beachhead. Patton then decided to reinforce the threatened position near Gela that night with 2,000 paratroops from his reserves. As the planes carrying these men arrived over the American fleet offshore, they were mistaken for German aircraft in the moonlight and were fired on. The debate over moonlight for operations had an unfortunate, unforeseen consequence – of 144 transport planes, twenty-three were shot down, thirty-seven damaged and 229 men were killed, wounded or missing.[47]

With the news of the landings in Sicily, Hitler ordered the Operation Citadel offensive in Russia to be halted and the 1st SS Panzer Division was transferred to Italy, leaving its tanks and equipment behind. This was the first German unit diverted from Russia as a result of any British and American actions in the Mediterranean theatre in the war to that point.

The Americans were able to resume their advance inland over the next few days while the British drove up the east coast, encountering increased resistance from the Germans in the form of the 1st Parachute Division redeployed from France. So great was the resistance that Alexander approved a request from Montgomery to change the inter-army boundary line so that the British could use an inland road (Highway 124) that had previously been allocated to the Americans in order to advance northwards around the opposition they were facing. There was confusion as British troops occupied Vizzini in front of the advancing Americans. The situation was finally clarified in a telegram at midnight on 13 July from Alexander to Patton confirming that Montgomery now had exclusive use of the highway. This meant that the US 45th Division, which had been making progress against the Hermann Göring Division, would have to disengage and move westwards around and behind the US 1st Division, allowing the Germans some respite. Although the Americans had no specific orders from General Alexander other than occupying a line westwards from Vizzini once ashore, they were disappointed at what they regarded as a slight to the abilities of their forces.

Montgomery began a new offensive on 13 July to take Catania by using paratroops to seize a bridge south of the town. Again the transport aircraft were subjected to both friendly and enemy anti-aircraft fire and were widely scattered. Of 1,900 men in the British parachute brigade, only 200 men with three small anti-tank guns reached the bridge.[48]

Relegated to a support role, Patton looked towards the Sicilian capital of Palermo as a significant objective in his area of control. However, before Palermo could be taken, a port on the south coast, Porto Empedocle, had to be captured with minimal forces along with Agrigento, as directed by Alexander so as not to imperil the Seventh Army's primary mission of protecting the British left flank. These two towns were captured on 16 July but Patton had already the day before issued instructions for the reorganisation of his Seventh Army in order to prepare for an operation to capture Palermo. Alexander issued a new directive on 16 July for the British to attack Messina from two directions around Mount Etna. Patton presented his own plan to Alexander on the 17th, to which Alexander reluctantly agreed; Patton was determined to capture Palermo and claim some prestige for the Americans, issuing new orders on 18 July for a 'reconnaissance' by three divisions towards Palermo and to drive northwards to the coast with the remainder of his forces to split Sicily into two halves. On 19 July, Hitler ordered another division, the 29th Panzergrenadier Division, to Sicily despite having admitted at a conference two days earlier that the island could not be held and that a withdrawal would have to be made.[49] Hitler was once again apparently reinforcing defeat but he was actually keeping entire British and American armies at arm's length from Germany with minimal forces.

Meanwhile, Montgomery and the British were making no progress and he realised that he did not have enough troops to attack Messina from both the south and the landward side of Etna, deciding on 21 July to bring in reinforcements in the form of the 78th Division from North Africa.

The American bombing of Rome on 19 July while Mussolini was having a fruitless meeting with Hitler caused considerable panic among the Italian High Command and set in motion a plot against the Italian leader. On 25 July, Mussolini was arrested and his government overthrown by senior officers on the orders of the Italian King, the Italians being more than weary of the financial cost and loss of life in the war. Ordinary Britons saw cause for jubilation too:

> With Mussolini overthrown and the end of Fascism in Italy, we can look forward to enormous developments in the war. Italians are celebrating the fall of the fascist system and anti-fascist riots are occurring in many places.

Mr Churchill has announced that if Italy does not surrender, total war will continue against her.[50]

Although the Allies were taken by surprise by the downfall of Mussolini, there was no immediate declaration by the new Italian government of the cessation of hostilities and the Allies continued their battle to occupy Sicily. Having agreed on a policy of unconditional surrender of all Axis forces only six months previously at Casablanca, the British and Americans then disagreed over issuing an immediate demand for such a declaration and found themselves in a vacuum as to how to proceed. Eisenhower proposed a radio broadcast of simple terms be made to the Italians, while Roosevelt was not keen to impose harsh conditions on them. On 26 July, Churchill also sent a detailed proposed list of conditions on the Italians for the Americans to consider utilising. The British Chiefs of Staff had approved a draft instrument of surrender in June which had been forwarded to the Americans by Eden a week earlier.[51] A debate then ensued for several days as to which surrender document could be used by whom and what terms would be offered. Eisenhower sent his suggested surrender terms to the US Joint Chiefs of Staff on 29 July and eventually on the 30th the British War Cabinet accepted a slightly amended version.[52] The sudden involvement by Eisenhower in the politics of surrender was interesting in view of his complaints about the political manoeuvring in North Africa following Operation Torch. Roosevelt, however, ultimately rejected the British surrender document as being unsuitable.

Against little Italian resistance, Palermo had been captured on 22 July by Patton's forces. Two days previously, on the 20th, Alexander had ordered Patton to send reconnaissance patrols eastwards along the northern coast. Montgomery's progress had once more bogged down at Catania and it had become clear that the Eighth Army was not strong enough to invest Messina from two directions. On the 23rd, Alexander ordered Patton with all available units eastwards towards Messina. The steep mountainous terrain of the northeastern corner of Sicily includes the volcano Mount Etna and provided many easily defendable positions. The Germans planned to defend a line around Etna from Catania to San Fratello on the northern side of Sicily while the bulk of their troops were evacuated from Sicily altogether. The subsequent American advance was extremely slow and costly in hot weather against the Germans, who made skilful use of the terrain and fortified houses in towns such as Troina and San Fratello in their resistance.

The news of the Allied advances in Sicily was well received in an increasingly war-weary Britain:

> I suppose the Italians will cave in some time soon, and that shouldn't help
> Germany much, but the end seems still rather far off. The Russians are amazing ... Hitler must feel pretty low as they keep on and on attacking and
> never seem to run out of men and material.[53]

In an effort to overcome the German defences on the northern coast, the Americans planned small amphibious landings ('end-runs') in order to bypass the German positions. The first amphibious landing of a reinforced battalion on 8 August to bypass defences at San Fratello achieved surprise but failed to cut off most of the Germans from the newly arrived 29th Panzergrenadier Division which had already withdrawn, but did succeed in taking thousands of Italian prisoners. The Germans then conducted a planned withdrawal along the entire front line and withdrew in an orderly fashion towards Messina, commencing a full-scale evacuation to mainland Italy on 11 August.

The slow pace of the British and American ground forces meant that only the Allied air forces and navies could disrupt the German evacuation; the Germans accordingly concentrated all their anti-aircraft guns around Messina. Patton, who was now desperate to beat Montgomery into Messina, on 10 August ordered a further amphibious landing for the next day at Brolo, behind the new German forward positions. The same force that was used at San Fratello landed successfully and for a few hours prevented the withdrawal of German troops but vigorous German counter-attacks and the destruction of most of the artillery landed ashore in a raid by American planes soon compelled the force to relinquish its blocking position on the coastal road and take to the hills. A link-up with advancing American units was made in the early hours of next morning but again the bulk of the 29th Panzergrenadier Division managed to withdraw and escape. On 11 August, Patton ordered a further landing at Bivio Salica using a whole Regimental Combat Team supported by a parachute battalion to be dropped inland to capture the bridge at Barcellona. However, elements of the 3rd Division reached Barcellona before the airborne mission could even begin and the operation was cancelled, although the amphibious landing was to go ahead at a different location, Spadafora, 10 miles further east. General Bradley, the commander of the 2nd Corps, protested that the ground troops were advancing quickly against only light resistance and would outpace the amphibious force. The Americans advancing on the coastal road reached Spadafora early on 16 August while the amphibious landings took place that same morning on to the originally planned beaches at Bivio Salica, now behind the American front line so as not to risk further casualties from friendly fire. That day, the bulk of the German evacuation from Sicily to the mainland was completed.

American troops finally entered Messina on 17 August, only hours after the final German troops had left. Patton had won his race to the city but the Allies had missed the opportunity to either trap all the German Army units on Sicily or intercept the flotilla of boats transporting them to mainland Italy, where they were able to regroup for further battles. While the Straits of Messina were strongly defended by German anti-aircraft guns, Allied warships made little attempt to interfere with the evacuation. The fact that three and a half German divisions in good terrain for defence were able to successfully fight a rearguard action against two Allied armies of twelve divisions and numerous tank brigades for thirty-eight days was largely overlooked by Churchill, Eisenhower and Alexander, but not Marshall.

The Germans managed to evacuate from Sicily 39,569 men, of which 4,444 were wounded, plus 9,605 vehicles, 94 guns, 47 tanks, 1,100 tons of ammunition, 970 tons of fuel and 15,700 tons of miscellaneous equipment and supplies.[54] American casualties in Operation Husky were 2,237 men killed and 6,544 wounded or captured; British casualties amounted to 12,843 men, which included 2,721 men killed.

Franklin D. Roosevelt at the Quebec conference. *Left to right, seated*: Mackenzie King, Roosevelt, Winston Churchill; *standing*: General H.H. Arnold, Sir Charles Portal of Great Britain, General Sir Alan Brooke, Sir John Dill, Admiral E.J. King, General George C. Marshall, Sir Dudley Pound, Admiral William Leahy. (09-1875M FDR Museum/Library)

Franklin D. Roosevelt, Joseph Stalin and Winston Churchill (left foreground) in session at Yalta. (48-22 3659(55) FDR Museum/Library)

Winston Churchill at the 1943 Quadrant conference in Quebec. (48-22 3868(532) FDR Museum/ Library)

Roosevelt and Churchill with the Combined Chiefs of Staff during the Casablanca conference. *Left to right, seated*: Lt General Henry Arnold, Admiral Ernest King, Churchill, Roosevelt, General Alan Brooke, Admiral Dudley Pound, General George Marshall; *standing*: Brigadier Ian Jacob, Lt General Hastings Ismay, Vice Admiral Mountbatten, Brigadier General John R. Deane, Field Marshal John Dill, Air Chief Marshal Charles Portal and Harry Hopkins. (66-210 FDR Museum/Library)

Winston Churchill, a very unwell-looking Franklin D. Roosevelt and Joseph Stalin at the Yalta conference. (48-223659(69) FDR Museum/Library)

Franklin D. Roosevelt with Henri Giraud, Charles de Gaulle and Winston Churchill on the lawn of the Anfa Hotel, Casablanca. The moment of the awkward handshake, Roosevelt and Churchill can barely conceal their mirth. (61-465(22) FDR Museum/Library)

Planning Operation Husky in Eisenhower's villa in Algiers, June 1943. *Left to right, seated*:
Anthony Eden (Foreign Secretary), Field Marshal Alan Brooke (Chief of the Imperial General
Staff), Churchill, General George C. Marshall (US Army Chief of Staff), General Dwight
Eisenhower (Supreme Commander North Africa); *standing*: Air Marshal Arthur Tedder,
Admiral Andrew Cunningham, General Alexander and General Bernard Montgomery.
(BHC 003026)

The three architects of the victory at El Alamein together in Egypt in August 1942. *Left to right*: General Sir Harold Alexander (C-in-C Middle East); Churchill; Lt General Sir Bernard Montgomery (Commander Eighth Army). (BHC 000063)

Normandy, 12 June 1944. American and Navy chiefs pay their first visit to French soil to see the progress of the battles on the beachhead. In the group are General Dwight D. Eisenhower (Supreme Allied Commander, Allied Expeditionary Force), General George C. Marshall (Chief of Staff US Army), Admiral Ernest King (US Navy) and General Henry H. Arnold (Commanding General US Air Force). (BHC 000494)

A burning building in Sheffield which was bombed in December 1941. (BHC 030003)

Children from London's East End, who have been made homeless by the random bombs of the Blitz, outside the wreckage of what was their home, in September 1940. (BHC 030007)

A London railway station in 1940 with troops arriving while children who are being evacuated from London leave for the reception area. (BHC 030011)

Basic foodstuffs were directly rationed by an allowance of ration book coupons. This tray shows the weekly ration of sugar, tea, margarine, 'national butter', lard, eggs, bacon and cheese as issued to an adult in Britain during 1942. (BHC 030030)

An improvised air raid shelter under the arches of a railway bridge somewhere in south-east London in November 1940, showing people sleeping on wooden benches, tables or on mattresses. (BHC 030042)

An Anderson air raid shelter remains intact amidst the debris after a land mine fell a few yards away. The three people who had been inside the shelter were not hurt. The effects of air raids in this area of London can be clearly seen behind the shelter. (BHC 030052)

Aldwych Underground station in 1940. Overcrowding has forced some people to sleep on the tracks once the evening train services finished. (BHC 030059)

Churchill visiting Bradford in December 1942. He is giving his famous 'V for Victory' salute and was apparently unaware of the more lewd meaning of the palm inwards gesture until later in the war. (© IWM H_025966)

II

ITALY AND QUEBEC

Eisenhower had not yet made up his mind as to which was the better future option, to land in Sardinia or on the Italian mainland, and sent an outline of his plans for each to the Combined Chiefs of Staff on 30 June, copied to the British. Churchill thought Eisenhower unduly pessimistic and commented to the British Chiefs of Staff that the general was torturing himself, getting 'sicklied over with the pale cast of thought'. Churchill continued:

> We cannot allow the Americans to prevent our powerful armies from having full employment. Eisenhower now seems to be wriggling away to Brimstone. We must stiffen them up and allow no weakness. I trust the Chiefs of Staff will once again prevent through the Combined Chiefs of Staff this weak shuffling away from the issue by the American generals.[1]

Eisenhower had to get approval for all operations from the Combined Chiefs of Staff and was merely following procedure. Churchill also maintained the pressure on Alexander, working alongside Eisenhower: 'You know my hope that you will put your right paw on the mainland as soon as possible. Rome is the bulls-eye.'[2]

In a minute of 13 July, Churchill had proposed an amphibious assault at the 'knee' of Italy, near Naples, to cut off all the German and Italian forces in the 'foot' of Italy once airfields became operational in Sicily. This was another typical product of Churchill's thinking to outflank the Axis defenders: 'Why should we crawl up the leg like a harvest bug from the ankle upwards? Let us rather strike at the knee … '[3]

Marshall and Eisenhower came round to the view that mainland Italy should be invaded as soon as possible but the latter was reluctant to land troops further north than the foot of Italy. Marshall, on 16 July, asked the Combined Chiefs of Staff to consider landings (code-named Operation Avalanche) near Naples to facilitate an overland advance to capture Rome in order to quickly eliminate Italy from the war. This they did, immediately asking Eisenhower for his plans which he outlined two days later and were subsequently approved. Marshall's request was enthusiastically seen by Churchill as American endorsement of his Mediterranean strategy. That month the US Secretary of War, Henry Stimson, was in Britain notionally to visit United States forces but ended up having several meetings with Churchill. The Second Front in France was discussed but Churchill was clearly in favour of continuing the Mediterranean campaign and marching on Rome to knock Italy out of the war. The approval by the Combined Chiefs of Staff for the Naples landings at Salerno was discussed and Stimson informed Churchill that the operation had been approved by the Americans merely to bring a rapid end to the Italian campaign. A fierce debate ensued and Churchill admitted that he was not enthusiastic about the 1944 cross-Channel invasion, Overlord, but would go through with it as agreed, despite fearing the Channel would be filled with the corpses of Allied soldiers. Stimson duly reported to Marshall and Roosevelt this conversation with Churchill, the attitude of the British to the cross-Channel assault and the beliefs of many American officers that the British wanted the Italian campaign to supplant Overlord.[4]

Later that month, Churchill became concerned that the slow build-up in Britain would still be insufficient for a landing in France and so the best option for the Allies was his Norwegian venture, Operation Jupiter. The Overlord Plan called for twenty-seven divisions for France, which Churchill did not think were enough to guarantee the success of the landings because of 'the extraordinary fighting efficiency of the German Army'. Churchill advocated that the right strategy for 1944 was:

A)   Maximum post-'Husky' certainly to the Po, with an option to attack westwards in the south of France or north-eastwards towards Vienna, and meanwhile to secure the expulsion of the enemy from the Balkans and Greece.

B)   'Jupiter' prepared under the cover of 'Overlord.'[5]

Churchill clearly was not optimistic or enthusiastic about Operation Overlord and was expecting far greater outcomes from the Mediterranean strategy other than the elimination of Italy from the war. Marshall, too, was in favour of a landing at Naples but Eisenhower was against the idea, citing a lack of air cover for the naval task force. Spitfires from North Africa did not have the range, leaving only American P-38s and carrier-borne aircraft to support any landing near Naples. A Joint Planning Staff paper on the proposed landing near Naples concluded that the best area for any landings was north of Naples but should not be attempted unless the Luftwaffe was significantly weakened in the next few weeks.[6] Such landings would have the primary objective of helping to knock Italy out of the war and a secondary objective of trapping the German forces in the 'heel' and 'toe' of Italy should they decide to reinforce that area.

Even though the United States was still wavering in commitment to another amphibious landing in Italy, the British realised that such a further Mediterranean operation would require changes and retentions of shipping in the Mediterranean at the expense of any operations in Burma and across the Channel. Brooke admitted in his diary that this would not be greeted with great joy by the Americans.[7] This was self-evident as it was exactly what the Americans had feared at Trident when they had objected to the Mediterranean operations as being diversionary and having a potential impact on the cross–Channel plans.

The Combined Chiefs of Staff finally approved the development of plans by Eisenhower to invade mainland Italy on 20 July. The same day, the British Chiefs of Staff demanded immediate bold action and, anticipating that Eisenhower would approve the draft plans for another amphibious landing on the west coast of Italy, issued a 'stand-still' order to the Commander-in-Chief in the Mediterranean for all shipping, landing craft and warships that might be needed for the operation. A similar telegram was sent a day later to the US Chiefs of Staff, requesting that they do the same. The US Chiefs of Staff were aghast at this recommendation from the British. Operations and their allocated resources that had been agreed at Trident were now being imperilled by the British proposal and stand–still order for their own shipping. A strongly worded American telegram on 26 July pointed out that the US Chiefs of Staff had not agreed to operations requiring extra men and material, and that they were concerned by the slowdown in preparations for operations in Burma against Akyab and Ramree which were required to be executed as agreed without any postponement due to the stand-still order.[8] A firm directive was then issued to Eisenhower the same day by the Combined Chiefs of Staff to plan for a landing at Naples on the understanding that no additional troops or shipping would be provided; the operation would have to be carried out with forces already in the theatre.

The Joint Chiefs of Staff believed Eisenhower already had sufficient shipping resources for any follow-up operation after Sicily which in all practicality meant that only four divisions could be used in another amphibious assault. The rapid success of the landings in Sicily meant that the seven divisions that were required to be transferred back to UK in time for Overlord as decided at Trident would still be available for a few more months and hence further operations were possible. The divergent British and American views of how strategy should be prosecuted after Sicily and particularly the unilateral British 'stand-still' order led to plans for yet another Churchill–Roosevelt conference, this one code-named Quadrant, which would take place in Quebec. Following Roosevelt's suggestion on 14 July of a staff conference, Churchill promptly accepted two days later; an invitation was extended to Stalin, who did not reply for three weeks, being heavily involved in directing the Russian response to Operation Citadel, the latest German offensive. The dramatic news of Mussolini's arrest gave added importance to the next conference as Italian morale was generally believed to be very poor. The British refused to cancel their 'stand-still' order, saying that it would be discussed at the coming conference.

Quadrant, 19–23 August 1943

Before the Quadrant conference, General Marshall and his staff were convinced of the need for a showdown with the British, who they believed were unenthusiastic about any cross-Channel landing in 1944. In July 1942, Marshall had strongly opposed any Mediterranean campaign and was forced to postpone any plans for a cross-Channel operation while accepting Operation Torch at Roosevelt's direction, largely for political reasons. Since then the Mediterranean strategy had dominated Allied plans and operations and the Operation Roundup had become unpracticable in 1943.

A key strategic decision needed to be made regarding the seven divisions then in the Mediterranean that were due back in Britain by 1 November to begin training for the cross-Channel invasion, now called Operation Overlord. Russia had proved that it could resist Germany and was no longer in danger of collapse as it was in 1941 and 1942, although it was currently battling the latest

German summer offensive. Russia's survival meant that Overlord would no longer be the single major blow that would be decisive in knocking Germany out of the war but one of a number of blows delivered by the Allies from different directions. The choice was whether to make Overlord the main attack as planned, which would reduce the Italian theatre to a subsidiary operation, or to continue to employ resources in an invasion of the Italian mainland, which would have the benefit of tying down German troops in Italy and might lead to future options to attack Germany's soft underbelly. Marshall strongly believed in the benefits of Overlord and was determined that the Allies should adhere to the strategy agreed at Trident. The British, on the other hand, were committed to knocking out Italy from the war and now wanted the additional prestige of capturing Rome. The seven divisions slated for withdrawal were seen by the British as indispensable for any advance northwards through Italy. There were thirty Italian divisions in the Balkans and five in the south of France and following the surrender of Italy, Germany would have to replace these with its own equivalent divisions which would have to come from France or the Russian Front, thereby providing immediate assistance to the Russians and increasing the chances of success of a future Overlord.[9]

At a series of meetings between Roosevelt and the Joint Chiefs of Staff before the conference, Marshall strived to establish a united American position. Roosevelt, while being strongly in favour of Overlord, wanted to do more in Italy and proposed sending seven fresh divisions to the country to replace those to be withdrawn for the cross-Channel invasion. Marshall and Stimson argued that seven new divisions would be better employed in Overlord, for which the British were believed to have little appetite.[10] Stimson, who had just returned from his meetings with Churchill and the Chiefs of Staff in London, reported that the Prime Minister was certainly concerned about potential heavy losses in a cross-Channel attack and continued to favour a peripheral strategy of using landings in Norway and the Balkans to force the further dispersal of German forces. The American decision-making process was helped by a telegram from Eisenhower indicating that there were adequate troops in the Mediterranean for his future plans and many reports of low Italian morale, especially in the Balkans. It was essential to appoint an American commander as quickly as possible for Overlord in order to ensure it became a reality, according to Stimson. This view was shared by Roosevelt and his preference was for Marshall to command the assault. The US Chiefs of Staff believed that the British were not keeping firmly enough to the considered decisions of Trident and were tending too readily to postpone or cancel agreed operations. The importance of knocking Italy out of war was understood by the Americans, but they were not prepared to see Operation Bullfrog (an attack on Akyab in Burma), the Pacific or Operation Overlord suffer as a consequence of any further new commitments in the Mediterranean.[11]

Churchill and his Chiefs of Staff used the voyage to Halifax, Nova Scotia, to go over the plans for the future conduct of the war and to be briefed on aspects of Operation Overlord and the campaign in Burma. The tide of war had turned in the Battle of the Atlantic; since reaching a climax in April, U-boat sinkings had increased dramatically while merchant ship losses had declined sharply.

As Allied strategy was dependent on the availability of shipping and landing craft, the British 'stand-still' order to vessels under their control had angered the Americans and was seen as more evidence of future British intentions in Italy. Landing ships required for operations in Burma had been retained in the Mediterranean on the instructions of the British Chiefs of Staff, who could see no good reason for carrying out the proposed Operation Bullfrog before February or March of 1944.[12] The British were also frustrated at their failure in previous discussions to convince the Americans of what they saw as the undesirability and impracticability of operations in Burma.[13] Churchill was given an overview of the plans for Overlord and noted that three conditions had been imposed by COSSAC in order for it to have a reasonable chance of success. The first was a reduction in the strength of the Luftwaffe fighter force, the second was that the Germans should only have twelve or fewer full strength divisions in France and the third was that the Germans should not be capable of transferring more than fifteen divisions from the Russian Front.[14] Therefore Russia was expected to assist with Overlord by pinning down German troops in the east which was contrary to all Allied plans to that date and would not have impressed Stalin.

In order to head off any accusations from the Americans of wanting diversionary Mediterranean operations, Brooke and the British Chiefs of Staff decided to avoid any mention of the Balkans, Vienna or southern France as possible operations after the liberation of Rome and would claim that a line Milan–Turin was the only objective in Italy in order to assist future operations in France.[15]

Before their arrival, Dill at the Joint Staff Mission in Washington sent a telegram warning of the possible difficulties ahead in the talks with the Americans, who were adopting a contentious attitude to British strategy. Operations such as Bullfrog, Overlord and the Pacific theatre were apparently sacrosanct to the

Americans, who thought that the British did not mean business in Burma and never had meant business, despite being responsible for that theatre. Dill further warned that the position of the US Chiefs of Staff was that the British must do their bit in Burma while tempering their ambitions in the Mediterranean or greater priority would be accorded to the Pacific.[16] Therefore the conference would begin with both nations already somewhat exasperated with each other.

From Halifax, Churchill's party took a train to Hyde Park in New York to meet separately with Roosevelt, while the British and American Chiefs of Staff began their discussions in Quebec on 14 August. The talks between Roosevelt and Churchill were straightforward. In view of the lack of progress in Burma, Churchill proposed to reorganise the Far East Command by splitting it into two separate commands, one for India and one for operations in Burma, to be known as the Southeast Asia Command (SEAC). The commanders for both Southeast Asia Command and the European theatres were then agreed, with Mountbatten to become the Supreme Commander in Southeast Asia and Marshall to command the European operations.

British participation in the atomic bomb project, Tube Alloys, was confirmed with research and development to be done in America with Britain as a full partner.

However, the discussions of the Combined Chiefs of Staff did not go smoothly and quickly descended into rancorous exchanges as the tension and mistrust that had been building since Trident came into the open. At the first session on 14 August, two meetings were held to discuss the progress of the war in Europe and in the Far East. For the meeting next day, the US Chiefs of Staff produced a paper which stimulated much discussion about future operations in Italy and how they would affect Overlord.[17] While Brooke argued that Italian operations would help make Overlord a success, Marshall was adamant that priority had to be given to Overlord and said that if the British had their way there would be no more than a corps of US troops in England, and so the whole war should be reoriented towards Japan. The result was the US Chiefs of Staff amended the paper and delivered it to the British Chiefs of Staff next day in the middle of their morning meeting with Churchill; an introduction had been added that insisted that a decision had to be made as to which was the main effort in the European theatre – Italy or Overlord. The introduction concluded:

> The United States Chiefs of Staff believe that the acceptance of this decision must be without conditions and without mental reservations. They accept

the fact that a grave emergency will always call for appropriate action to meet it. However, long range decisions for the conduct of the war must not be dominated by possible eventualities.[18]

In this amendment, American suspicions of British diversionary operations and the failure to adhere to previously agreed strategic decisions can clearly be seen. The British were outraged by what they saw as an unacceptable proposal and hurriedly drafted their own amendments. The minutes of the meeting are curiously brief and the reaction of Churchill was not recorded. The ensuing Combined Chiefs of Staff meeting was held behind closed doors, but Brooke later recorded in his diary:

> Our talk was pretty frank – I opened by telling them that the root of the matter was that we were not trusting one another. They doubted our real intentions to put our full hearts into the cross-Channel operation next spring, and we had not full confidence that they would not in future insist on our carrying out previous agreements irrespective of changed strategic conditions.[19]

The Anglo-American strategic debate had been distilled to an argument over whether agreed plans should be adhered to or whether flexibility should be permitted if circumstances changed. It took another closed session the next day before the British were able to convince the Americans of the wisdom of pursuing operations in Italy with available forces which came at the cost of reaffirming a commitment to Overlord and its build-up. Despite the debate in progress in Quebec, on 16 August, Eisenhower, encouraged by the quick end to the Sicilian campaign, made the final decision to launch Avalanche on 9 September, subject to the approval of the Combined Chiefs of Staff.[20] The next day, the fighting in Sicily finished. The British 'stand-still' order for their shipping was duly revoked on 19 August.

Brooke received the devastating news on 15 August that in a meeting with Churchill, Roosevelt had pressed for the appointment of Marshall as the Supreme Commander for Operation Overlord and Churchill had acquiesced with apparently little thought of the promise he had made to Brooke, claiming that command would naturally go to the nation that provided the most resources. The American contribution to the war was now so great that the United States was now the dominant partner in the Alliance, a fact of life that Churchill (and Brooke) were increasingly forced to accept. Nevertheless,

Brooke was extremely disappointed both at the decision and Churchill's insouciance; the relationship between the two men was never the same again. On 16 August, Churchill had received confirmation that the Italians were seeking peace and would even change their allegiance from Germany to the Allies. Despite these overtures, Churchill, no doubt fired up by the American attitude, then prepared his own paper on future war policy and stressed the importance of capturing ports in Italy as this would free up landing craft for Overlord and the Indian theatre. The occupation of Italy no further north than a line from Leghorn to Ancona was contemplated because of the widening of the River Po basin north of this line and the extra resources this longer front line would require. Regarding the Far East, Churchill was fixated on landings to occupy the tip of Sumatra but found himself at odds even with his own Chiefs of Staff.[21]

The question of strategy in the Far East proved fortunately to be not as contentious as that of the European theatre. A plan by the US Chiefs of Staff for operations in the Pacific and the Far East was considered on 17 August which iterated the British commitments to the limited advances agreed at Trident, namely a northern advance to be made by Chinese troops from Yunnan and Ledo in conjunction with British forces from Imphal, the objective being to clear the Japanese from northern Burma and allow the completion of the Ledo Road to link up with the Burma Road. The amphibious and overland Operation Bullfrog against Akyab was also to take place as a prelude to liberating Rangoon next year.

In July, Auchinleck, the Commander-in-Chief in India, had informed the Chiefs of Staff of a delay in Operation Bullfrog until 1 January 1944 at the earliest while requesting additional landing craft and shipping and a reduced scope of operations for northern Burma up to the limit of all-weather roads. This was not well received by Churchill when the plans were discussed at a Defence Committee meeting:

> It was most disappointing to find that as a result of his examination of the problem, General Auchinleck had found it necessary to limit his operations in this way and, at the same time, ask for additional forces. When reporting our plans at the next Combined conference we should be criticised by the Americans for our lack of enterprise and drive.[22]

Churchill's solution was to launch Operation Culverin against the tip of Sumatra as an alternative but Brooke saw no particular extra benefits to be gained from such an operation. Extensive monsoon rains in India then caused heavy flooding in Calcutta and disrupted the only railway to the front line in northern Burma; consequently Auchinleck recommended that all operations be postponed or abandoned. Nevertheless, in order to demonstrate British enthusiasm for operations in Burma, Churchill had brought along to the conference Brigadier Orde Wingate, who had led a jungle raid behind Japanese lines in February 1943. Wingate addressed the conference to explain how long-range penetration groups in the jungle could be successfully supplied from the air, although a third of his men on the first operation had failed to return.[23] Later Mountbatten presided over a demonstration of the strength of synthetic ice that could be used to build floating airfields code-named Habbakuks (as envisaged by Churchill) by firing a revolver into blocks of ice, from which a ricochet nearly hit the assembled Chiefs of Staff. An officer outside the room was heard to say, 'My God! They've now started shooting!'[24]

On 19 August, after five days of deliberations the Combined Chiefs of Staff presented their conclusions in the form of a progress report to Churchill and Roosevelt. Churchill continued to press for an operation against Sumatra in a public contradiction of his own Chiefs of Staff and pointed out the preconditions that had to be met for a successful Overlord. This report was then amended to include points raised at this meeting and a final version was discussed and approved at a second meeting with Roosevelt and Churchill on 23 August.

Despite the tensions between the British and the Americans, the decisions reached in Quebec largely reinforced those of previous conferences, especially Trident, which was exactly what the Americans wanted.

The Combined Bomber Offensive (Operation Pointblank) would be built up in order to disrupt and reduce Germany's military production as a prerequisite to Operation Overlord. The change of target priorities to making the destruction of German aircraft production the highest priority made in June was agreed and it was noted that German fighter production had already increased by more than 20 per cent over the last twelve months. Of the 1,068 aircraft proposed during the Trident conference for the VIII Bomber Command, only 816 aircraft had arrived at bases in England, 105 having been diverted to North Africa.

Regarding future amphibious assaults, Operation Overlord for 1944 was to have the overriding priority with all other operations subservient to it in terms of the allocation of resources. Only if Overlord was impossible for any reason would other plans such as Operation Jupiter be considered. Operations to eliminate Italy from the war and capture Rome in order to establish air bases for the bombing of southern Germany were to be conducted but only with forces already available, while the seven veteran divisions would leave Italy for Overlord as planned.[25] Although negotiations were proceeding for Italy's surrender, landings on the mainland and the amphibious landing near Naples, Operation Avalanche, were confirmed for early September. At the behest of Churchill, a new objective of establishing airfields in the Rome area or further north had been approved.

The Azores in the mid Atlantic were to be occupied on 8 October regardless of the reaction of the Portuguese to provide an air base for operations against U-boats. Diplomatic talks between Britain and Portugal had been successful but their progress had been frustratingly slow for the Allies. Regarding the Far East, the Americans were not enthusiastic about occupying the tip of Sumatra and the two staffs were unable to reach agreement on all the necessary decisions for operations against Japan. However, Operation Bullfrog against Akyab was postponed until the spring of 1944, as was any advance in northern Burma. It was agreed that the British would present their strategy in the next few weeks once Churchill and his Chiefs of Staff had settled their differences of opinion on preferred strategy, whilst the American Pacific offensive would continue with 'island-hopping' operations such as the occupation of the Gilbert and Marshall Islands. The Allied joint strategy against Japan would be decided at a future conference. Agreement was reached on a draft of a 'Four Power declaration' for the post-war world involving Britain, America, Russia and China.

Most importantly for future Anglo-American plans, this conference saw from the US Chiefs of Staff the emergence of a plan to land re-equipped French forces in the south of France as a diversion for Overlord.[26] Churchill, however, doubted the abilities of the French forces to carry out this operation which nevertheless became part of the final agreed strategy.

The US Chiefs of Staff instructed Eisenhower to declare Rome an open city and to refrain from further bombing raids on it. Churchill announced the appointment of Mountbatten as Supreme Commander Southeast Asia command; General Stilwell was notionally to be Mountbatten's deputy but was in charge of all US forces in the China, Burma and India theatres, responsible for opening the Burma Road and continued liaison with the Chinese.

Quadrant may have not taken any major new decisions except for the south of France diversion but at least it did much to clear the air between the Allies. The major achievement from the British point of view was the American commitment to Operation Avalanche and the invasion of mainland Italy, although no new resources would be committed to the Mediterranean theatre. Again, from a desire to not have two armies inactive for any length of time preparing for Overlord, the Mediterranean campaign was allowed to continue; it was also too late in the season to transfer large forces to England for a cross-Channel assault that year, so the invasion of Italy went ahead by default to eliminate Italy from the war and pin down German divisions, thereby potentially providing assistance to the Russians and weakening the German forces in northern France. The Americans had at least succeeded in keeping Operation Overlord as the major undertaking for 1944. Marshall's approval of the plans for the Avalanche landings was sent to Eisenhower in a telegram from Roosevelt and Churchill on 2 September.[27]

Meanwhile in England, American troops had continued to arrive under Operation Bolero and with the repeated postponement of the invasion of the Continent until 1944, many found themselves with little to do. In the southwest of England, where the Americans were mostly billeted, their increasing presence began to be felt:

> Soon the towns and streets were full of American soldiers chewing gum, they were all so well dressed that they looked like officers. I didn't feel very happy about this. Our boys had been in the thick of it for years and their uniforms were nowhere near as smart, nor did they receive as much pay. It didn't seem fair that these soldiers were taking over our city. On the other hand I'd heard they were very friendly and generous giving children sweets and chewing gum and some girls received pairs of the new nylon stockings.
>
> The real differences however became apparent when these Yanks, as everyone affectionately called them, invaded the Dance Halls and Ballrooms. No Waltzes and Quicksteps for them, it all became Jitterbug and Jive. Being physically fighting fit young men their dancing took on the form of an athletic performance. Their partners changed as well and girls that had shyly taken the floor for a Foxtrot were now being thrown in the air and slung between legs. Instead of looking at smart young men and pretty dresses, we now watched Tarzan and the swirl of legs, stocking tops, suspenders and knickers.
>
> These Yanks, being away from their wives, sweethearts and families, had quite a lot of spare cash and it became their habit to walk close behind any girl they fancied jingling the cash in their pockets. Lots of us young women, starved of luxuries, fell for this, coupled with the sweet talk, and

soon became the proud possessors of the fine nylon stockings, make-up and extra food for the family, then later, not a few became the mothers of bonny bouncing babies.[28]

Stalin was invited to Alaska on 18 August by Roosevelt, having turned down Churchill's invitation of 19 June to a meeting at Scapa Flow. This invitation, too, was rebuffed. After the extreme disappointment of the news of no Second Front, Stalin became increasingly difficult in his correspondence with Churchill. On 9 August, Stalin said he was unable to leave Russia but would like a meeting of responsible representatives. Stalin then complained on 22 August that he was not being informed of all details of negotiations with Italy:

> To date it has been like this: the U.S.A. and Britain reach agreement between themselves while the U.S.S.R. is informed of the agreement between the two powers as a third party looking passively on. I must say that this situation cannot be tolerated any longer.[29]

This message angered both Roosevelt and Churchill, who had tried to keep Stalin informed and had extended invitations to meet several times. Stalin suggested the setting up of a political–military commission in Sicily to discuss the surrender terms for Italy and any other German ally that might want to settle for peace. Stalin's displeasure and frustration was also expressed in his dismissal of his own Ambassadors to the Allies. In the United States, Litvinov was replaced by Andrei Gromyko during the Quadrant talks, whilst the previous month (28 July) the Soviet news agency had announced that in London, Maisky would be replaced by the relatively junior Feodor Gousev. The two outgoing Ambassadors were believed by Stalin to be too cosmopolitan and favoured the West in diplomatic discussions.

On the same day Italy finally signed the surrender documents in secret, 3 September 1943, the British began landings across the Straits of Messina on the Italian mainland as part of Operation Baytown. In a hastily organised expedition (the appropriately named Operation Slapstick) as a result of negotiations for the Italian surrender, the British 1st Airborne division was also transported by sea to Taranto, where it arrived on 9 September. No transport planes were available as all of them had by then been allocated to the American forces for Operation Avalanche at Salerno. Despite the surrender of Italy being the stated objective of the Allies at both Casablanca and Trident, the landings still went ahead, largely because Churchill had added Rome and its nearby airfields as objectives to facilitate an Allied bomber offensive against southern Germany. The surrender did, however, deliver Italian shipping and the Italian Navy into Allied hands, thus finally eliminating the threat to British shipping in the Mediterranean and opening up the sea lanes to Malta, Egypt and the Suez Canal.

Both the Baytown and Slapstick operations were successful as they were largely unopposed; the Germans had withdrawn from the region northwards in expectation of an amphibious landing further north. In the two weeks following the arrest of Mussolini, the Germans had quietly reinforced Italy with nine extra divisions including two Panzer divisions. Believing that the Germans would occupy Rome as soon as the armistice was announced, the Italians tried to repudiate it. On 8 September, despite the pleas of the Italians, an irritated Eisenhower broadcast the news of the armistice which the Italians were forced to confirm an hour later. That night, as a part of a planned response to the well-telegraphed Italian political machinations of the previous six weeks following the overthrow of Mussolini, German troops immediately occupied Rome. The 16th Panzer Division was ordered south towards Salerno to defend the coast after German reconnaissance planes had spotted concentrations of Allied shipping. In the space of twenty-four hours, Italy went from being an ally of Germany to being occupied by Germany. Planned American paratroop drops to capture Italian airfields near Rome as part of Operation Avalanche were inadvertently thwarted by these German moves and had to be cancelled at the last minute which, in view of subsequent events, was fortunate for the 82nd Airborne Division.

On 9 September, Churchill reminded Roosevelt of the need to withdraw troops in time for Overlord and emphasised that there was no real need to advance into the plains of northern Italy unless the Germans withdrew.[30]

At Salerno, the landings on 9 September were designed to capture the port of Naples in order to deliver a further blow to Italian morale and potentially trap any German units in the south of Italy, as envisioned by Churchill. The Allies chose to land 30 miles south of Naples in the bay at Salerno where there was a narrow coastal plain surrounded by mountains and steep hills. Control of the passes through the mountains away from the coast would be a vital objective of the joint Anglo-American assault force as they were the only routes inland. The landings were not preceded by a naval or air bombardment, although a diversionary naval bombardment was made on beaches in the estuary of the River Volturno near Naples. Air support was principally from one aircraft carrier and four auxiliary carriers. At the northern end of the bay, charged with securing the passes, were the British 46th and 56th Divisions, and to the south the American 36th Division would make the landings. Not only was the 16th Panzer Division now defending Salerno but there were two more Panzer divisions and two infantry divisions not far away. The German tanks immediately mounted strong counter-attacks which were beaten off, and by the end of the day the Allies were well established ashore and up to 3 miles inland, although a 10-mile gap remained between the two forces.

The delays in the negotiations and signing of the Italian armistice had allowed the Germans to reinforce Italy so that when the landings began at Salerno they were met by German troops, not demoralised Italians. No attempt was made by Eisenhower to bring forward the date of the landings in response to the peace feelers from the Italians (as early as 5 August via an emissary in Tangier) in order to exploit the situation. The date for Salerno was set on 16 August by Eisenhower before serious negotiations began, even though he was well aware of the Italian initiatives; Eisenhower had even been rebuked by Churchill for his involvement in a peace negotiations telegram to Hopkins that stated that 'generals do the fighting and the politicians the talking'.[31]

German reinforcements arrived at a greater rate than Allied follow-up troops and the situation remained in the balance for the next two days, with only small further advances inland. On 12 September, the strongly reinforced Germans attacked the American left flank held by the follow-up 45th Division, which had just arrived ashore. Without strong air cover, the Fifth Army was dependent on naval gunfire and limited aerial support, and the beachhead was nearly split by the Germans. Instead of cutting off the Germans in the south of Italy, the beachhead was forced to fight for its very survival. However, after some initial gains, the Germans were in the end unable to break through to the sea and after two days of heavy fighting, the American and British lines held. More Allied reinforcements landed and the Fifth Army began to try to fight its way across the mountains before breaking out to Naples. The Eighth Army arrived from the south on 16 September to link up with the landings and the Germans began to withdraw to defensive positions further north. On 1 October, the British entered a severely bomb damaged Naples and a day later the Americans occupied the city and began reconstruction of the harbour facilities. From being an operation to reduce Italian morale even further and cut off German troops in the toe of Italy, the Allied troops landing at Salerno were nearly repelled by the Germans.. The Italians had already surrendered and their country had been occupied by the Germans, so the Axis defenders at Salerno were German and not Italian. If Eisenhower had delayed the surrender announcement, the Salerno landing might not have been so strongly opposed. As in Sicily, the steep hills around Salerno had been difficult to advance through as they greatly favoured the newly arrived German defenders.

Marshall was critical of Eisenhower's planning process for Avalanche: '... it would seem that you give the enemy too much time to prepare and eventually find yourself up against a very stiff resistance.'[32]

Eisenhower quickly rebutted this criticism, pointing out that a large-scale operation had to be mounted in order not to be driven back into the sea and this took time to prepare. Shipping and landing craft also had to be transferred from the earlier Baytown landings to take part in the Salerno landings, which took time. With the capture of Naples, the Germans withdrew to their winter defensive positions on the Volturno Line. Roosevelt cabled Stalin with this news and predicted that British and American armies would be in Rome in a few weeks.

ITALIAN CIRCUS

After the Quadrant conference, Churchill returned from Quebec to Washington with Roosevelt on 1 September and stayed at the White House for the next ten days. The British naval Chief of Staff, Admiral Pound, was forced to resign after being unable to recover sufficiently from a previous stroke he had concealed. Following the formal surrender of Italy, Churchill became obsessed with the possibility of easily capturing lightly garrisoned Italian islands in the Dodecanese, which would provide valuable air bases to support attacks on Germany from the Balkans and help to convince Turkey to enter the war. A previous idea of Churchill's to capture these islands (Operation Mandibles) had been cancelled because of the developments in Greece in 1941. As far back as 27 July, only days after Mussolini's arrest, Churchill was thinking of the capture of Rhodes as part of his plans to bring Turkey into the war:

> I suppose that the Planners are all keyed up with plans for taking over Rhodes on the assumption that the Italians will ask for an armistice. What is the composition of the garrison at Rhodes, German and Italian? We ought to get there as quite quickly if it's humanly possible, as I need this place as part of the diplomatic approach to Turkey.[1]

Following the successful landings on mainland Italy, Churchill wrote another memorandum on future strategy, which was discussed on 9 September when he met with Roosevelt and US Chiefs of Staff. The paper proposed that once Naples and Rome were secured and the main German defensive line reached, then the Allies should consider sending troops into the Balkans and the recapture of Sardinia, Corsica and Rhodes.[2] Marshall and the other Chiefs of Staff met beforehand to consider this memorandum and took the opportunity to again try to create a united front against what they saw as the continuation of Churchill's peripheral campaign in the Mediterranean. Whilst agreeing that the Italian campaign should go on the defensive when the German fortified positions in the north of Italy were reached, Marshall and the US Chiefs of Staff were adamant that nothing should detract from the preparations for Overlord and if the British wanted to mount operations in the Eastern Mediterranean then they would have to use their own resources from the Middle East.

On 10 September, however, the Combined Chiefs of Staff stated they were in agreement with the general concept of future operations in Italy, which included the capture of the Dodecanese and the larger islands of Sardinia and Corsica. Churchill refused to relinquish the opportunity of liberating the Dodecanese Islands without a shot being fired if the Italian garrisons could be induced to surrender.[3] With the American refusal to support any action against the islands, although approved at the Quebec conference, Britain would have to find its own resources. General Wilson was told by Churchill in a telegram of 9 September, 'This is a time to play high. Improvise and dare.'[4] The British Chiefs of Staff had already approved on 3 August orders for the Commanders-in-Chief in the Mediterranean to prepare to take advantage to the best of their abilities of any favourable opportunities in the Dodecanese. Operations to take Rhodes (Operations Accolade and Handcuff) were duly considered by the Middle East Command with what limited resources it had.

However, Operation Accolade to capture Rhodes had to be cancelled and its allocated shipping was dispersed only a week before the Italian general surrender on 3 September. On the 8th, the Italian garrison on Kastellorizo surrendered to a small British force. An approach was also made next day to the Italian commander of the forces on Rhodes to surrender but this was prevented by a German force of 7,500 men on the island, which promptly attacked the 40,000-strong Italian garrison and forced its capitulation. With Rhodes now controlled by the Germans, the British turned their attentions to the islands of Kos, Leros and Samos, which were duly occupied during the period 10–17 September by small detachments from the 234th Brigade from Malta. Kos had an airfield from which two squadrons of Spitfires could begin to operate. Churchill still desired that Rhodes be captured and on 25 September asked Eisenhower for more troops for this purpose.

On the Italian mainland, the Germans had withdrawn to defensive positions on the Volturno Line while winter defensive positions on the Gustav

Line around Cassino were prepared. The two British and American armies slowly advanced northwards, having to break through a series of defensive lines and positions constructed by the Germans in terrain ideal for defence. General Alexander on 23 September estimated that Rome would be liberated at the end of October.[5] Foggia, an essential air base for continuing the aerial bombing campaign against Germany from the south, was captured on 25 September. However, it took until 11 October before the Eighth Army pushed the Germans back sufficiently to ensure the Foggia airfields were out of range of German artillery and could be used by the Allies. Marshall reported its capture to Roosevelt as one of the objectives of the Italian campaign (to establish air bases to launch raids on targets in southern Germany) having been achieved; Marshall was hoping that the end to the fighting in Italy was in sight but on 17 October Alexander informed Brooke that progress had slowed considerably because of tenacious German defence and Rome would not be taken as predicted. Alexander concluded that another amphibious landing would more than likely be required to break the developing stalemate.[6] The Bernhard Line, the last line of German defences before the Gustav Line, was reached by the Allies in early November. From initial success and rapid progress, the slowing Allied advance caused the morale of some British civilians to fall again:

> By September 16th it was obvious that all was not going well for us in Italy. We felt so confident when the Italians surrendered that at least the major part of the country would open its arms and let our troops flood in ... When it collapsed, the Germans disarmed the Italians and sent their own picked troops to guard the coastline. Perhaps if the Italians had not given in so soon and we went on advancing in Italy against Italian defenders we would have been more successful.[7]

Eisenhower, Alexander and Churchill had all underestimated the severity of the Italian terrain and its suitability for defence. From a distance the rounded hilltops of the Apennine Mountains do not look very high or formidable. Closer up, it can be seen that the hillsides rise very steeply from a narrow coastal plain to meet at the peaks in sharp arêtes to form ridgelines rather than a flat top. These ridges traverse the Italian boot laterally from one sea to another, forming interlocking vertebrae for the spine that is the Apennines running the length of southern and central Italy. These limestone or sandstone ridges and hilltops provided ideal observation posts and defensive positions for the resolute German defenders. For the Allies, the ridges seemed to stretch endlessly before them, barring their northward advance; as soon as one ridge was captured, another lay behind it across a narrow valley. The mountainous terrain prevented the British and Americans from exploiting their superiority in tanks and artillery while the worsening weather decreased the amount of available air support. The narrow coastal plains provide the only flat lines of communication and even then the ridges in places come right down to the shoreline such as at Terracina. In winter, the coastal plains are traversed by rivers swollen with heavy rain, making crossings or the construction of bridges very difficult. On maps, the Apennines do not look like a major obstacle and this was the mistake Churchill made in making Italy the route of the thrust into the soft underbelly of Germany. This strategy was followed despite the difficulties experienced in the hills of Sicily, the southernmost part of the Apennine chain, only weeks earlier.

Eisenhower had achieved the elimination of Italy from the war as directed at Quadrant and his secondary objective in the country was to cause as many German divisions as possible to be retained there. To divert any Allied units from this task at this juncture could have disastrous consequences in the event of a major German counter-attack. Intelligence appreciations by the British in both August and September stated that the Germans were likely to abandon Rome and defend a line from Pisa to Rimini, and perhaps this was the origin of Churchill's belief that Rome would be quickly captured.[8,9] This was not to eventuate as, following a suggestion from Kesselring, in early October Hitler ordered that the positions south of Rome be held; the Allies would have to fight their way to the eternal city. The terrain at Cassino where the Italian peninsula was its narrowest was admirably suited for defence; if the entire British and American ground forces in Europe could be tied up in a difficult campaign in the Italian peninsula then this suited the Germans while the bitter life and death struggle of attrition continued on the Russian Front. This was similar logic that saw the Germans despatch reinforcements to North Africa in order to keep the campaign there going.

Despite reverses in other theatres, the Germans reacted strongly to the British seizure of the Dodecanese Islands and further aircraft were deployed to the Aegean region. Hitler and the OKW feared that the Allies would launch an offensive towards Germany through Greece and Yugoslavia, thereby avoiding having to cross the Alps. Foggia was regarded as the gateway to the Balkans from which further Allied amphibious landings could be made into either Istria or Yugoslavia. A less likely route was through the Dodecanese Islands and therefore a demonstration of strength was needed by the Germans to keep Turkey at least neutral. By late September, the Germans completed the redeployment of their available divisions to meet these threats. Further reinforcements were brought into Italy so that there were eighteen divisions to halt any Allied advance northwards.[10] In Yugoslavia and the rest of the Balkans there were also at least another eighteen divisions, eight regiments and twenty-two security battalions in anticipation of a landing and to combat the active Serbian Cetniks and Croat Partisans. While the Allies had achieved their objective of tying down large numbers of German troops, there were so many that Eisenhower and Alexander were faced with the problem of being outnumbered in the event of a German counter-attack. At that point in time, the Allied Armies were being held by only six German divisions at the Volturno Line.

On 3 October, a German amphibious force landed on Kos, supported by paratroops which captured the airfield. The British force of 1,500 men and 3,500 Italians was quickly routed and took to the hills; the capture of the island was completed next day and the Germans took 1,388 prisoners. With the loss of Kos, the British also lost all the air protection for the other islands. Churchill was not pleased and in a minute of 4 October lamented the loss and demanded both an investigation into the quick capitulation as well as action to retake the island.[11] On the 7th, Churchill made an appeal to Roosevelt over Eisenhower's head for resources for the capture of Rhodes. After several weeks of debate, the US Joint Chiefs of Staff had decided to leave any decision about diverting resources to the Eastern Mediterranean from Italy to Eisenhower's discretion and the general, as well as Marshall, was opposed to any such diversion of men from the build-up in Italy. Roosevelt communicated this bluntly to Churchill on 8 October, emphasising that Overlord should not be prejudiced in any way. Not to be denied, Churchill sent a request for a meeting with Marshall and Eisenhower to Roosevelt on 8 October, having told Brooke of his intentions the previous day of making a quick trip to Tunis to attend a scheduled planning conference. Churchill was anxious that there be further discussions before the Americans completely ruled out the use of landing craft allocated to Operation Overlord. It should be noted that only Churchill and his Middle East commanders were in favour of this Eastern Mediterranean strategy, all the British and American Chiefs of Staff including Eisenhower were against it. Churchill remained fixated on the islands to the point of being unreasonable.

Brooke wrote in his diary on 7 October:

This is all to decide whether we should try and take Rhodes which he has set his heart on. He is in a very dangerous condition, most unbalanced and God knows how we shall finish this war if this goes on.

And the next day:

I am slowly becoming convinced that in his old age Winston is becoming less and less well balanced! I can control him no more. He has worked himself up into a frenzy of excitement about the Rhodes attack, has magnified its importance so that he can no longer see anything else and has his heart set on capturing this one island even at the expense of endangering his relations with the President and with the Americans, and also the whole future of the Italian campaign. He refuses to listen to any arguments or see any dangers.[12]

A firm telegram from Roosevelt drafted by Marshall ended any further debate, but still Churchill urged that the Dodecanese at least be considered at the conference in Tunis. Rhodes was duly discussed but no forces could be spared as the Germans had sent strong Army and Luftwaffe reinforcements to Italy from Russia and France after the Italian surrender. The Luftwaffe had established aerial dominance over Italy and the Aegean, which was severely hampering any Allied operations. These German troop movements and intelligence decrypts had revealed to Eisenhower that a line of German defences would be created south of Rome on the Gustav Line, which settled the matter once and for all as the Allies now faced a harder battle to reach Rome. This decision was very disappointing to Churchill: 'I will not waste words in explaining how painful this decision is to me.'[13]

Churchill and Wilson now had to face the prospects of the Germans massing to retake all the islands, which were only weakly held by not much more than a battalion of troops on each. A fundamental problem was that air cover could only be provided by long-range aircraft from the Middle East or Cyprus. The first German attempts to seize Leros suffered a setback when a convoy of troops to Kos was intercepted by the Royal Navy with heavy losses of men and craft. A new flotilla of landing craft was assembled and in the interim Leros was subjected to heavy air attack. Leros was reinforced with two more battalions just before German operations to invade the island began on 12 November with landings at two different places supported by another parachute drop. Within four days, the Germans were successful and 3,200 British soldiers and 5,300 Italians were captured. The British were subsequently forced to abandon the other islands and the Italian garrisons were left to their fate. This was another major defeat for the British but was the last successful German operation of the war, facilitated by the air superiority of the Luftwaffe as in the first two years of the war. It was a serious reverse for Churchill and the British public was shocked. The Prime Minister, who was on his way to the Middle East for the Tehran conference, advised Eden to not answer any questions on the Dodecanese Islands in detail in Parliament.[14] Samos was evacuated on 20 November and even Kastellorizo had to be given up again on the 28th.

A memorandum by Churchill on 20 November revealed his anger at the loss of the islands, claiming it was the first German success since El Alamein. Churchill bemoaned the fact that the Americans had refused to support any operations in the Eastern Mediterranean when Eisenhower had all the resources and that the shadow of Operation Overlord was denuding British forces in Mediterranean.[15] However, Churchill had asked for the diversion of Allied forces at a critical point in the Italian campaign which he had promulgated and was now threatened by strong German reinforcements. Marshall and Eisenhower had stood their ground, fearing another British diversionary operation, and Churchill had gambled by sending only weak detachments of men with little air support to the islands when the Americans refused to help. Therefore Churchill, having failed to heed the lessons of Greece and Crete, threw the dice and lost.

Stalin was at last prepared to admit that the Italian landings had stopped the arrival of new German divisions in Russia, an indication that its reserves in Europe were almost depleted. On 8 September, Stalin finally agreed to a meeting in Iran at Tehran and a secondary meeting for Allied Foreign ministers at Moscow to discuss the emerging post-war political situation. The German summer offensive had been defeated and Stalin could afford to leave Russia for a few days. There was no end to Churchill's difficulties with a frosty Stalin, however; on 1 October a telegram from Churchill regarding the resumption of aid convoys from 12 November was answered two weeks later by Stalin, who declared that the aid convoys were 'an obligation'. Churchill was so incensed by this that Stalin's telegram was returned 'unread' to the new Ambassador, Gousev.

On 10 October, Churchill proposed a meeting with Roosevelt in Cairo before going on to see Stalin but the President declined, saying he preferred to meet with Stalin first and that a Combined Chiefs of Staff meeting should be held afterwards. A little shocked at this, Churchill reiterated his request on 20 October, pointing out that it would be ninety days since Quebec, during which much had changed and another meeting was required to determine post-Overlord strategy; Roosevelt this time agreed to meet.

The South African General Smuts, a confidant of Churchill's, was in favour of continuing in the Mediterranean while Churchill's fears of high casualties in the proposed cross-Channel operation remained. Despite the fact that the British and the Americans had committed to Overlord for 1944, Churchill still wanted other operations to be considered. The Dodecanese Islands and an advance through the Balkans were still very much in the minds of Churchill and Brooke, as recorded by a junior officer on 17 October:

CIGS feels very strongly we should exploit the openings in the Med and extend the range of our offensive operations to the Aegean and Balkans. The Germans are sitting on a volcano in the Balkans ... the PM has come around to this point of view too, and has just said he would like to tackle the Americans about it.[16]

At a staff conference on 19 October, Churchill and the Chiefs of Staff once again discussed their reluctant commitment to Overlord by waging war on the basis of 'lawyers' contracts' and how Overlord was detracting from operations in Italy. Churchill, still smarting from the American refusal to help in the Dodecanese, complained about the agreed Allied strategy:

It was unsound to miss present opportunities for the sake of an operation which could not take place for seven months, and which might, in fact, have to be postponed to an even later date. He felt that by tying ourselves to undertake Operation Overlord there was a serious risk that we should undertake two operations, each employing approximately equal forces and neither being strong enough for the purpose for which it was required. We would thus give the enemy an opportunity of concentrating and defeating our forces in detail.[17]

Churchill was concerned that compromises to Allied plans would result in the falling between two stools, as he later expressed in a telegram to Roosevelt. There were again major strategic differences between the British and the Americans, the British (i.e. Churchill and Brooke) were firmly of the view that the Mediterranean strategy was the only correct one to be implemented and offered the best possibility of seriously weakening Germany before any cross-Channel assault. The British viewed Operation Overlord as merely one of a series of blows against a collapsing Germany rather than the main blow itself, which was the American view. At the same meeting, Churchill spoke of his fears of Overlord failing and resulting in another Dunkirk. The Joint Planning Staff were requested to produce a paper comparing the proposed Normandy landings with the possibilities of the Italian campaign as Churchill claimed he was ready to talk to the Americans again about the 'wrong' Allied strategy. An American diversion of the bulk of their resources to the Pacific was even acceptable, provided they left behind the forces already in Britain.[18]

The British adherence to the Mediterranean strategy was confirmed in a briefing paper to the planning staff next day when Brooke asked them to study how aid and British troops could be used in the Balkans and what operations could be undertaken in the Dardanelles with a view to linking up with the Russians.[19]

With the British now firmly of the opinion that Allied strategy was wrong, Churchill believed that an urgent review of strategy with the Americans was needed again and when Roosevelt agreed to an Anglo-American conference before meeting Stalin, Churchill provided an incentive for the meetings by stating in a telegram three days later that:

> Our present plans for 1944 seem open to very grave defects ... It is arguable that neither the forces building up in Italy nor those available for a May Overlord are strong enough for the tasks set them.[20]

This telegram duly worried Marshall and Roosevelt as intended and Marshall drafted a strong reply that was never sent, Roosevelt merely agreeing to meet beforehand on 20 November in Cairo. To Marshall on 24 October, Churchill lamented the transfer of the best British divisions to England but said he was eager to hear the news of the American's appointment to command the cross-Channel operation. From being excited about the prospects of capturing the Dodecanese Islands and wanting resources to be diverted from Italy, Churchill now wanted units to be retained in Italy.

Brooke, in his diary of 25 October, also complained about the consequences of adhering to Marshall's strategy:

> Our operations are coming to a standstill and that owing to a lack of resources, we shall not only come to a standstill but also find ourselves in a very dangerous position unless the Russians go from one success to another. Our build-up is much slower than the German and far slower than I had

expected. We shall have an almighty row with the Americans who have put us in this position with their insistence to abandon the Mediterranean oper-ations for the very problematical cross–Channel operations.[21]

It is notable that Brooke and Churchill at this point in the war were blaming the Americans for the setbacks in Italy, rather than arguably faulty strategy, German resistance or the Italian terrain. Following a telegram from Alexander about the German build-up in Italy, by 26 October Churchill and the Chiefs of Staff were convinced that the best Allied strategy was to maintain the offen-sive in the Mediterranean and ensure Rome was liberated. The problem was that the deadline for transferring troops to England for Overlord was nearing and the relocation of landing craft had already begun, which had the potential of both delaying the build-up in Italy and causing a stalemate by limiting future operations. Churchill put this view to the Combined Chiefs of Staff and asked that Eisenhower and Alexander be backed to the fullest extent, quoting Alexander's report and claiming that a total of twenty-four German divisions identified in Italy were faced by only eleven Allied divisions following the slower than expected Allied build-up.[22]

Churchill in a telegram the same day to the Secretary of State revealed the true depths of his feelings regarding the Italian campaign and Overlord:

I will not allow, while I am responsible, the great and fruitful campaign in Italy which has already drawn heavy German reserves into action to be cast away and end in a frightful disaster, for the sake of OVERLORD in May.[23]

At this point in October, as Italy had been knocked out of the war and a large number of German divisions were engaged in the country, the only outstand-ing goal was the liberation of Rome. Churchill, in his telegram, had spoken of the 'fruitful' campaign and clearly expected further developments or exploita-tions from it. Brooke fumed at the strategic limitations of the Americans to his diary:

We should have been in a position to force the Dardanelles by the capture of Crete and Rhodes, we should have the whole Balkans ablaze by now and the war might have been finished by 1943!! Instead to satisfy American short-sightedness we have been led into agreeing to the withdrawal of our forces form the Mediterranean for a nebulous 2nd Front and have emasculated our offensive strategy. It is heartbreaking![24]

Eden, who was meeting with Stalin at the time in Moscow, was primed by Churchill to explain the situation in Italy and the possible delay in launching Overlord to the Soviet leader, who apparently took the news very well. Eisenhower emphasised in early November that a conclusion to the Italian campaign might be delayed until early 1944 if an appropriate defensive line in Italy could be reached if there were no more landing craft for further amphibious operations to bypass the German lines of defence.[25]

Churchill was to join Roosevelt in Cairo on 20 November for preliminary talks and to meet Chiang Kai-Shek before they would both travel on to meet Stalin in Tehran on 28 November. The British delegation left England on the 12th by battleship, the same day the Germans attacked the island of Leros, which fell five days later, much to Churchill's disappointment: 'I was grieved that the small requests I had made for strategic purposes almost as high as those already achieved should have been so obdurately resisted and rejected.'[26]

On 5 November, the British Chiefs of Staff, with the agreement of their US counterparts, permitted Eisenhower to retain sixty landing craft in Italy for future operations until 15 December as Overlord would not be greatly affected by this delay in their transfer to England.[27] The US also sent two divisions as urgently requested by Eisenhower to partially make up for the loss of the seven transferred to England for Overlord. These transfers were to be concluded before 1 January 1944. In the front line, ignoring garrison troops and transfers, on 1 November the British and Americans would have twelve British, five American and three native French divisions, a total of twenty divisions – not the eleven claimed by Churchill earlier.

At the Quebec conference, Churchill had agreed that the European Supreme Commander should be an American in view of the number of troops and resources the Americans were contributing to the war. The American view was that a Supreme Commander was required for all operations against Germany whereas the British did not want a Supreme Commander but a unified command for each theatre. Thus Churchill was opposed to the concept of a Supreme Commander as he was determined to have a free hand in the Mediterranean and not be subject to any American control.[28] Roosevelt professed to be keen for Marshall to take up the post for the cross-Channel operations as he was the logical candidate but when news of his appointment finally got into the newspapers in Washington, there was a considerable backlash against the President for sending his most experienced Chief of Staff out of the country and he was forced to reconsider his choice of commander.

The Combined Bomber Offensive of the RAF by night and the VIII Bomber Command by day continued against targets deeper and deeper in Germany. However, after the daylight raid on the Schweinfurt ball bearing factory on 23 October, the losses to the unescorted American B-17s and B-24s were so great that further unescorted long-range daylight raids had to be suspended. Sixty-two bombers were shot down out of 228 that took part in the raid and of the ones that returned to England, 138 were damaged. October also saw the arrival in England of the first units of the US Ninth Air Force, which would add to the offensive power of the heavy bomber force.

On 1 November, Churchill brought to the War Cabinet's attention the fact that Britain had exhausted its manpower and that any future increase to the armed forces would be at the expense of labour for industry. British manpower was now fully mobilised and was in fact beginning to decline, so the need to defeat Germany quickly was more important than ever.[29] In America, the US Army had not achieved its planned quota of ninety divisions by this time and it was decided by Roosevelt to put a ceiling on the Army of ninety divisions or 7.7 million men. This meant that an extra fifteen divisions planned for 1944 would not now be formed.

Sextant/Eureka conference

The Sextant meetings would be the first time in the war that the three leaders of the three major Allied powers would meet face to face. Russia had resisted the German invasion and offensives for more than two years and there was no longer a danger of the country capitulating. Stalin was still anxious for a Second Front to be launched but had learnt to be wary of promises from Roosevelt and particularly Churchill. The Allies' thoughts were turning to victory and the post-war world. For the Americans, the Sextant meetings were all about ensuring that the British remained committed to Overlord, and they were ready for yet another showdown. Taking a leaf from Churchill's book, Roosevelt met twice with his Joint Chiefs of Staff and Hopkins on board the battleship USS *Iowa* on the way to Malta to determine their positions before the coming conferences. At their meeting on 15 November, the President approved the Joint Chiefs of Staff rejection of future operations in the Balkans or the Eastern Mediterranean. During discussion on the future Italian government, Roosevelt referred to the British as being 'monarchist minded', while

Hopkins said that Churchill was up to his old tactics and wanted to go back to the old system. Roosevelt also said it was his preference to hold talks with the Chinese separately from the British.[30] Four days later, at a second meeting, the issue of the appointment of a Supreme Allied Commander for all of Europe was discussed. The minutes of the meeting make it clear in a discussion of the disproportionate commitments of the US Army and Air Forces that the Americans strongly believed that the choice of commander and his responsibilities should be as per their recommendations. The Americans were assuming the mantle of the larger partner in the Anglo-American alliance and expected to get their own way more and more on the direction of the war. The Balkans were again discussed and Marshall reiterated his strong point of view that if the British wanted to ditch Overlord in favour of operations in the Balkans, then the Americans should pull out of Europe and switch their resources to the Pacific. As Churchill had already expressed his doubts about Overlord, once more the stage was set for a head on-collision between the respective Chiefs of Staff and their commanders. The Americans were also concerned about the attitude of the Soviets, who did not seem to appreciate the efforts made to ship Lend-Lease material to them and were reluctant to exchange military information of any kind. The government-controlled Soviet press had kept up critical editorials on the lack of a Second Front and the Russian diplomatic Ambassadors to both London and Washington had been changed by Stalin. Some concerns about the emerging strength of the Red Army had been reflected in a discussion General Marshall had with Roosevelt in the early spring of 1943 over the possible post-war chaos in Europe if the Western and Soviet drives against Germany did not keep pace with each other. Marshall later wrote in a memorandum:

> I also gave him as my personal opinion the fear that if we were involved at the last in Western France and the Russian Army was approaching German soil, there would be a most unfortunate diplomatic situation immediately involved, with the possibility of a chaotic condition quickly following.[31]

At the Quebec conference, Hopkins apparently had a document entitled 'Russia's Position' from an unknown military source which warned of Russia's dominant position in post-war Europe with Germany crushed and no other country able to oppose it. According to the document, the United States must give every assistance and do all it could to remain on friendly terms with Russia if the Soviets were to enter the war against Japan in the Pacific.[32]

Therefore, despite their concerns about the future of Europe, the Americans would bend over backwards to maintain a good relationship with Stalin at the Tehran conference and until Japan was defeated. This thinking would underpin American relations with Russia for the rest of the war.

At the Foreign Ministers' conference in Moscow, 19–30 October 1943, the British and American decisions at Trident and Quadrant for a Second Front and Operation Overlord in the spring of 1944 were reaffirmed to the Soviet delegation. The Soviets claimed at this time that two German divisions had been moved to Russia because of a lack of pressure from the Allies in Italy.[33]

There were still issues in the China, Burma and India theatre that remained to be resolved. Churchill was completely wedded to the 'Germany first' policy as an excuse for inaction at the expense of the Far East. The United States had supported China for many years and was committed to sending supplies to the country by means of an airlift and by completing the Burma Road. Churchill did not see the same value in China as an ally that the Americans did. At the same time, because of the difficulties of fighting in the jungle with disease and sickness responsible for more casualties than actual fighting, Churchill continued to be very reluctant to commit any more troops to the region once the Japanese threat to India had receded. The most important objectives to Churchill were the restoration of British prestige in the region by defeating Japan and the reoccupation of Hong Kong and Singapore. But the defeat of Germany had to come first.

At the first two meetings with Roosevelt in Cairo, which Chiang Kai-Shek attended, the focus of discussions was China and Burma and no decisions regarding the European theatre were taken. Chiang Kai-Shek arrived earlier than expected and there was little time for the British and Americans to meet before the conference proper. The planned offensive in the Far East, Operation Anakim, as decided at Casablanca, had not taken place and had been postponed several times by the British because of a lack of resources. By late 1943, the Americans had concluded that their Pacific forces would more than likely reach the eastern coast of China before either the British or Chinese forces could come in from the landward side.

At the first plenary meeting on 23 November, Roosevelt did not achieve his desire to meet the Chinese alone and Churchill was present at the meeting with Chiang Kai-Shek. Mountbatten was also present and outlined his plans for a land offensive in northern Burma (Operation Tarzan) and an advance into the Arakan Peninsula again, plans which had not yet even been approved by the British Chiefs of Staff. Chiang Kai-Shek was not enthusiastic and

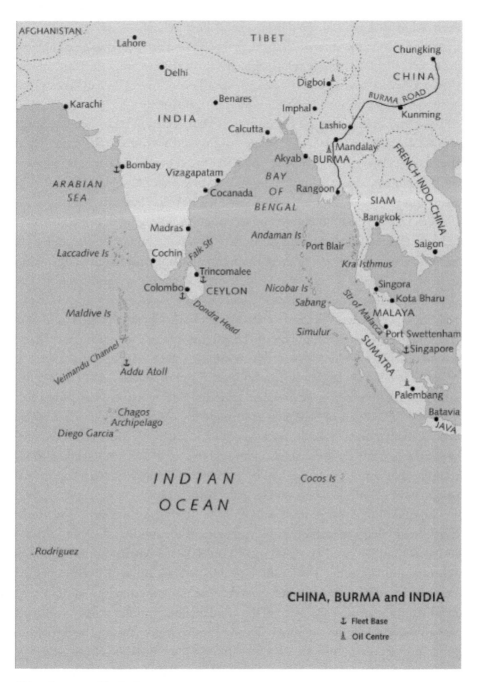

China, Burma and India theatre.

demanded that a naval operation take place simultaneously with the land operation. Churchill immediately disagreed as the naval fleet's task would be to ensure no further Japanese reinforcements arrived in the region. The Chinese then asked that any decision be deferred until other meetings had taken place; they too wanted to meet with the Americans separately.

The tensions between the British and the Americans quickly flared up at the second Combined Chiefs of Staff meeting which took place the same day as the first plenary meeting. Brooke and King had a heated debate – as recorded by Stilwell, who was present for the talks with Chiang Kai-Shek, 'Brooke got nasty and King got good and sore. Brooke an arrogant bastard.'[34]

At the Combined Chiefs of Staff meeting the following day with Chinese generals in attendance, the Chinese again demanded simultaneous operations in Burma. Marshall bluntly told them that Chinese troops must assist in operations to open the Burma Road as the Chinese had specifically requested the road be opened in order to receive American supplies.[35] At a private meeting with Chiang Kai-Shek later, Roosevelt promised the Chinese that an amphibious landing in the Andaman Islands in the Bay of Bengal (known as Operation Buccaneer) would take place within the next few months. As all of these operations were to be undertaken with largely British troops, Churchill was less than enthusiastic. This promise emerged in a Combined Chiefs of Staff meeting on 26 November when the US Chiefs of Staff pressed strongly for Operation Buccaneer which was suddenly non-negotiable. Buccaneer would use the landing craft Churchill wanted to employ in Culverin (a landing on the tip of Sumatra), whilst Brooke thought they should be transferred back to the Mediterranean to bring the full resources of the Allies to bear on Germany through Italy.

The question of future strategy in the Mediterranean was discussed by the Combined Chiefs of Staff on 25 November and the British Chiefs of Staff had revealed they favoured an operation in the Eastern Mediterranean through Rhodes and the other Dodecanese islands to link up with Russia via the Dardanelles and help bring Turkey into the war.[36] As expected by the Americans, nearly thirty years after the fiasco of the Dardanelles campaign in 1915, Churchill was considering another operation in the region. A paper prepared by the British Joint Planners on the Turkish entry into the war was edited and copies presented afterwards to the meeting, which was held in a closed session so no minutes survive to record the American reaction.[37] The debate resumed next day and once more the Mediterranean issues were discussed behind closed doors. Brooke himself wrote afterwards in his diary, 'It was not long before Marshall and I had the father and mother of a row!'[38]

The provision of shipping resources for the proposed operations Buccaneer and Overlord proved to be the subject most difficult to reconcile, with the Americans insisting on Operation Buccaneer in view of the promise to Chiang Kai-Shek. Brooke pointed out that the shortage of landing craft would mean that if operations were undertaken to capture Rome and Rhodes followed by Operation Buccaneer, then Overlord would have to be delayed. This not surprisingly was hotly disputed by the Americans, as were the possible movements of landing craft back from the planned Operation Buccaneer to the Aegean for use in the Mediterranean. At the end of the day, the Americans were surprisingly (in view of their pre-conference positions) in tentative agreement with the British, provided Buccaneer or Overlord were not significantly delayed in any way. The question of landing craft for the Mediterranean was resolved at a subsequent meeting when Eisenhower's request to retain the sixty-eight LSTs allocated for Overlord longer until 15 January was approved. A postponement of Overlord until 1 June 1944 was discussed with a simultaneous landing to take place in the south of France, code-named Anvil, which further complicated the shipping position.[39]

On reaching Tehran, Churchill hoped to see Roosevelt before the first meeting of the Big Three but Roosevelt contrived to meet Stalin first, alone. The Americans were housed in the Soviet diplomatic quarters because of an alleged assassination plot against Roosevelt and their villas were almost certainly fitted with listening devices. The Russians had already complained again that the developing stalemate in Italy had led to the redeployment of German divisions to Russia.

At the first plenary session on 28 November, Stalin promised to enter the war against Japan when Germany was defeated, much to the surprise of the British and Americans. This was exactly as Churchill had hoped in a message to MacArthur in July.[40] Stalin, however, saw the Mediterranean as a diversion as he did the Balkans, Yugoslavia, the liberation of Rome and Turkish involvement, and therefore he strongly advocated the landings in France for May 1944. In fact the American and Russian views of future strategy in Europe were remarkably similar and the British were fortunate that no other meetings were scheduled to discuss the Mediterranean while in Tehran. Stalin also pressed for a commander to be named, fearing the British and American failure to do this so far was further evidence of their unwillingness to mount Operation Overlord. As a consequence of this, Stalin asked a direct question of Churchill: 'Did the Prime Minister and the British Staffs really believe in Overlord?'[41]

Churchill replied in the affirmative with the by now customary 'provided stated conditions were met'. Aware of the disbelieving mood of the Americans and Russians, Churchill was forced to reiterate his commitment to the decisive Operation Overlord while continuing to argue for other operations to be considered. His opinion was that the best way to help Overlord and Russia was for Turkey to be encouraged to enter the war and that the Mediterranean armies should not be idle for six months before Overlord. Churchill even refused to give an undertaking that Overlord would not be delayed. It was left to Stalin to repeatedly bring the discussion back to Overlord. For post-war Europe, Roosevelt outlined a plan to divide Germany into five autonomous regions after the war. Reparations from Finland would be expected by Russia.[42]

Over dinner on 29 November at the Soviet embassy, Stalin adopted a derogatory attitude towards the British and particularly Churchill. According to an American account of the occasion:

> The most notable feature of the dinner was the attitude of Marshal Stalin towards the Prime Minister. Marshal Stalin lost no opportunity to get in a dig at Mr Churchill. Almost every remark that he addressed to the Prime Minister contained some sharp edge, although the Marshal's manner was entirely friendly. He apparently desired to put and keep the Prime Minister on the defensive. At one occasion he told the Prime Minister that just because Russians are simple people, it was a mistake to believe that they are blind and could not see what was before their eyes.[43]

As the evening wore on, Stalin continued his baiting of Churchill. When it came to the subject of post-war Germany, Stalin, having previous alluded on several occasions to Churchill having affections for Germany and wanting a soft peace, declared that at least 50,000 German officers of the High Command Staff must be physically liquidated. Roosevelt, in an effort to defuse the suddenly tense situation, quipped that only 49,000 officers should be killed. Churchill, aware of the reports of the Katyn massacre, knew what the Russians were capable of and could contain himself no more. Taking great umbrage at this potential act of dishonour and infamy, he stormed out of the room. He was pursued by Stalin and Molotov, who entreated him to return, saying it had all been a joke.

There were three official meetings between the Big Three but equally important conversations were held in more informal meetings in the compound's villas and during meals at the Soviet embassy. Discussions were also held regarding post-war frontiers, a subject that Russia was very much interested in. The question of Poland was first considered with Russia insisting that it would retain the Polish territory recently occupied in 1939 which approximately corresponded to the old Curzon Line. Churchill suggested the Poles be compensated with parts of East Prussia and that Britain would therefore recommend the deal to the Poles as the best they would get.

The Russian promise to enter the war against Japan following the defeat of Germany was regarded as enormously beneficial by the British as it in theory offered established Russian airfields as bases to mount bombing missions against Japan, and therefore there was not the same urgency to undertake any further land-based operations from Burma to support China. Thus China's potential role in defeating Japan and importance as an ally would be drastically reduced by the Russian entry into the Pacific War.

The year 1943 had seen the beginning of ever increasing large-scale bombing operations against areas of German military production and particularly against aircraft building facilities. The RAF had dropped 40,000 tons of bombs in the third quarter of 1943 compared with 15,000 in the first; the figures for the VIII Bomber Command were 15,879 tons and 2,688 tons respectively until unescorted daylight operations were suspended after the Schweinfurt raid.[44] In response to the increased air raids, the Germans had relocated many of their fighter forces from the Eastern Front so that by the end of the year more than 68 per cent of fighters were concentrated in the west. The Allied bombing had slowed the rate of increase of the production of planes but their numbers were still increasing. The end of July had seen combined British and American air raids over successive days on the city of Hamburg, resulting in a firestorm in which 40,000 people died. The morale of German civilians had plummeted and larger evacuations from city centres began. Thousands of houses were damaged and therefore uninhabitable with many millions of people homeless – many Germans were experiencing the Blitz for themselves.

The last meeting of the three leaders on 30 November considered a final report of the progress to date. The main resolutions regarding the conduct of the war by the Big Three at their first meeting of the war were the confirmation of Overlord for May 1944 supported by a landing in the south of France (Anvil) with the largest possible force that the available landing craft permitted. Overlord was to have total priority over all other operations. Partisans in the Balkans were holding down twenty-one German divisions and Churchill, after lamenting the lack of support for them, succeeded in getting a directive for more aid to be sent and to try to bring Turkey into the war. The timing of Operation Overlord had already slipped to 1 June, according to Brooke, because of the extension of time for the use of LSTs in Italy.[45] Regarding future strategy in the Pacific against Japan where the British were not involved, it was relatively straightforward for the Combined Chiefs of Staff to determine their next actions; it was agreed that the main effort against Japan should be concentrated in the Pacific along two lines of advance, with other operations in the north Pacific, China, and Southeast Asia theatres all to be assigned subsidiary roles.

Stalin, before leaving Tehran on 1 December, agreed to launch a major Russian offensive in the summer of 1944 to coincide with the Overlord landings. This was another major commitment for the Allies as Germany would then be threatened by major blows from two different directions (and possibly a third if the Mediterranean developed its true potential as envisaged by the British). A very important private meeting between Stalin and Roosevelt took place in the afternoon on 1 December regarding Poland. After acknowledging the importance of 6 or 7 million Polish voters in the forthcoming presidential elections, Roosevelt stated that he was in favour of the new frontiers for Poland as proposed by the Russians but would make no further public comment for fear of alienating the Polish vote. Roosevelt asked that Stalin make a public declaration about future elections to which Stalin vaguely assented, saying that there would be plenty of opportunities for the Poles to express their will.[46] Thus in a few brief minutes the fate of Poland was sealed by Roosevelt and Stalin without the involvement or knowledge of Churchill, despite the previous discussions between the three leaders.

Roosevelt and Churchill returned to Cairo for further talks as the question of future operations in the Far East was still unresolved. It was pointed out by Admiral Cunningham that if absolute priority was to be given to Operations Overlord and Anvil in 1944 there would not be adequate naval warships to undertake a third amphibious landing anywhere. With the renewed commitment to Operation Overlord by the Combined Chiefs of Staff, Churchill claimed to no longer attach as much importance to Rhodes as previously in view of the proposed Operation Anvil against the south of France. With the Russian promise to enter the war against Japan, the 'operations in the Southeast Asia Command had lost a good deal of their value' and Brooke again suggested that it might be necessary to withdraw resources from the proposed Operation Buccaneer in order to bolster Overlord and the Mediterranean.[47] Roosevelt firmly disagreed with this, saying that the Allies had a moral obligation to do something for China. Complicating matters was that the southern France landing had only just been agreed; detailed planning in terms of numbers of troops and landing craft had not been completed and were therefore unknown.

At a meeting next day, the Far East question was still unresolved and continuing to simplify the issue from the British point of view was the Russian promise to enter the war. Particularly troubling to Churchill were a series of telegrams from Mountbatten and his planning staff claiming that 50,000 men were needed for Operation Buccaneer against an estimated 5,000 Japanese, which was viewed with disbelief.[48] Churchill was upset and in a bad temper, remarking in one meeting with Roosevelt, '... That he was disturbed by the growth in the forces required for operation Buccaneer. If a superiority of 10 to 1 was required, this in fact made the conduct of the war impossible.'[49]

These messages and a Joint Planning Staff paper recommending the cancellation of both Operations Tarzan and Buccaneer due to the proposed Russian entry into the war against Japan were considered at the Chiefs of Staff meeting on 4 December and approved. The Americans were not convinced either about the potential of Operation Buccaneer and believed that the Chinese would not want it if there was no associated amphibious and naval operation, but Roosevelt was insistent that it proceed. At the plenary meeting on 4 December, Roosevelt also expressed amazement at Mountbatten's estimate and suggested that he be told to make do with what resources he already had. Marshall warned of a build-up of Japanese forces in Burma following the well-publicised appointment of Mountbatten and stated that if the British and the Americans could not come up with any plans then the enemy would take the initiative. Since Mountbatten's appointment, another Japanese division had been transferred to Burma and another was on its way, to make a total of six divisions in the country.

The plenary meeting the next day produced no resolution and Roosevelt conferred with his Chiefs of Staff. Marshall and King were both opposed to any postponement of Operation Buccaneer as this was tantamount to a reverse and would be a broken commitment to China. However, Roosevelt convinced them all except King of the need to delay Operation Buccaneer until after the next monsoon and to press ahead only with the preparations for the land-based Operation Tarzan, or an increase in the airlift if that was preferred by the Chinese after they had digested the news of the postponement of the operations. Marshall was perhaps reluctant to oppose Roosevelt at this juncture and allowed himself to be talked around while only Admiral King remained steadfastly opposed to any change.[50] Roosevelt sent a message to Churchill with his decision: '"Buccaneer" is off.'[51]

In summary, any landing craft and other resources needed for Operation Anvil and the defeat of Germany would be redirected from Southeast Asia to the Mediterranean. On being informed of this decision, Mountbatten signalled that there were no other alternatives to Operation Buccaneer with the limited forces in his command and that Operation Tarzan would collapse if Buccaneer did not go ahead.[52] This was all very much to Churchill's satisfaction and at this point the British were happy for the Mediterranean and Operation Anvil, the proposed landing in the south of France, to be given priority over Burma.

In agreeing to this, Roosevelt had reneged on his own promise to Chiang Kai-Shek, made ten days previously, and once again he had made a decision against the advice of his Chiefs of Staff. While Churchill had been annoyed by Mountbatten's estimate, ultimately it tipped the scales against Operation Buccaneer. Churchill and the British Chiefs of Staff had won the battle to retain landing craft in the Mediterranean at the cost of having to recommit to Overlord. The British gains came at the expense of China as the Far East theatre had lost the most in terms of promised then cancelled operations. Churchill, now that the Japanese threat to India had been halted, was not disappointed by this either: 'The British Chiefs of Staff, like myself, recoiled from the idea of a strenuous and wasteful campaign in North Burma for the sake of building a road to China of doubtful value.'[53]

For China, this was a landmark decision which marked a downturn in US–China relations. China's importance as an ally in the fight against Japan had been replaced by an increasing reliance on Russia.

Roosevelt sent a telegram to China on 5 December with the bad news regarding Operation Buccaneer and gave Chiang Kai-Shek the option of delaying Operation Tarzan. The prospect of war with Germany being ended in the summer of 1944 was offered as the reason.[54] The final report for Sextant was then rewritten to include the cancellation of Buccaneer with the resources allocated for it to be distributed between Anvil and Overlord. The Chinese replied that they understood Roosevelt's actions but expressed disappointment, especially after an initial Tehran communiqué had dispelled their pre-conference concerns about British and American commitments to the Far East and China being left to face a common enemy as best it could. In order to boost the morale of the Chinese, Chiang Kai-Shek requested a billion-dollar gold loan to strengthen the economy.[55] With this brazen attempt to get money and the failure to support operations to open the Burma Road, Roosevelt's opinion of the Chinese fell considerably and he took a much firmer line in future communications. Operation Tarzan was, of course, eventually post-poned once again. On 6 December the Combined Chiefs of Staff had agreed to make the Pacific theatre, rather than MacArthur's SWPA, the main effort of the war against Japan and approved the development of further plans on this basis. Next day, the British Chiefs of Staff instructed Mountbatten to return a large proportion of his amphibious craft back to Europe. The Combined Staff Planners duly completed their latest 'Overall Plan for the Defeat of Japan' on 23 December and a copy was sent to London.

In a series of meetings over three days in Cairo with the Turkish President, Churchill was unable to convince him to enter the war but did manage to get permission for British aircraft to use some Turkish airfields for possible opera-tions against Rhodes.

Now that the basic strategy was decided, the Americans were more com-fortable in settling the command issues. On 6 December, Roosevelt confirmed Eisenhower as Supreme Allied Commander in place of Marshall, who was greatly needed in Washington. This was against the advice of Hopkins, Stimson and Churchill and even Roosevelt's own inclination. There had been many requests from both military and political circles for Marshall not to go overseas and he himself wrote of Roosevelt's decision: 'As I recall, the President stated in completing our conversation, "I feel I could not sleep at night with you out of the country."'[56]

General Wilson was duly appointed Supreme Commander of the Allied Forces in the Mediterranean to replace Eisenhower from 8 January 1944, which was the unified command sought by the British at Sextant and allowed them to assume direct control of the Mediterranean theatre. The position of Supreme Commander for a theatre was acceptable to the British provided it was a Briton. Churchill, on 14 December, had proposed to the War Cabinet that either Montgomery or Alexander should lead the assault in Overlord. The Cabinet had responded:

> The general opinion of Ministers was in favour of General Montgomery, both on merits and from the point of view of its reception by public opin-ion. Some Ministers, however, favoured General Alexander having regard, not merely to his achievements, but also to the capacity which he has shown to work smoothly with the Americans.[57]

The final decision regarding Montgomery was left to Churchill, who decided in his favour.

The confirmation by the British of the dates for Operation Overlord at Sextant finally ended American doubts about the commitment of their ally, despite the previous promises at Trident and Quadrant to undertake the operation. This permitted the transfer of troops and equipment to Britain to continue at the same rapid rate since the Trident talks of May. By the end of 1943, there were finally more American divisions in the European theatre than the Pacific, there being seventeen in Europe and thirteen in the Pacific. American Army planners, no doubt with Marshall's concurrence, had taken the unofficial view that as long as US divisions were being committed to diversionary operations in the Mediterranean, then divisions would continue to be sent to the Pacific to maintain the pressure on the Japanese in response to the demands of MacArthur and Nimitz.[58] The lack of a British commitment to Overlord meant that the American deployment of troops to the Pacific had occurred at a faster rate than planned and it was only in October 1943 that the number of divisions in Europe exceeded those in the Pacific for the first time.[59]

In Britain, as the inexorable build-up of American troops and war material gathered pace, the south-west of England became congested with soldiers. There was always tension between black and white GIs and over Christmas that year this erupted into violence:

> It was only a few days from Christmas Day and the town was literally crawl-ing with Yanks. My Father, who had been working at The Observer Corps HQ in Union Place, was on his way home to Hendra after finishing at 10.00pm. As he approached Francis Street, he could see a lot of US soldiers fighting outside the Globe Public House. He estimated the were 40 to 50 coloured and white soldiers involved who were using broken bottles, glasses and knives on each other in the road. Several bodies were lying about in the road covered with blood. Trucks arrived filled with Military Police, who were dressed in white helmets, belts and gaiters. They quickly waded into the melee, swinging their staves, and knocked to the ground many of the US troops. Other MPs picked up the unconscious ones and threw them bodily into the backs of waiting lorries. Army ambulances took away the badly injured. Father said the MPs rid the street of troops and debris in a matter of fifteen minutes, and after they had cleaned up and gone off into the night, no one would have even suspected anything so violent had occurred.

As soon as the General commanding the area learned of the incident, he ordered the segregation of black and white troops during off duty time and that they only be allowed out on alternate evenings – blacks on one night, white the next night. He also warned they would be confined to camp for the duration if any similar incidents occurred. He also apologised to the public for the behaviour of his troops and as a gesture of goodwill authorized a New Year's children's variety show at the US army PX. A whole week's worth of army issued rations of candy, chocolate, tinned fruit and doughnuts was given out after the show to the children of Truro.[60]

Exhausted by the latest round of meetings and further meetings in Cairo to implement the decisions of Sextant, Churchill on the return journey to England became ill with pneumonia on 11 December and was bedridden for the next thirteen days at Eisenhower's villa in Carthage. Nevertheless, he received visitors and kept up with his correspondence. As Churchill convalesced throughout December, he began to take a closer interest in the Italian campaign and a future amphibious landing.

In London, the Chiefs of Staff considered the Far East and the Sextant determinations regarding the Pacific theatre at their meeting on 20 December. The Pacific region was to come first over Mountbatten's Southeast Asia and it was proposed that British Far East forces would be moved into MacArthur's South West Pacific area, thereby ensuring that Southeast Asia became a subsidiary theatre. It was noted by the Chiefs of Staff that Churchill was apparently unaware of the latest developments in Pacific strategy and had still been strongly in favour of Culverin as late as November.[61] These preparations for the war ahead against Japan were summarised by a paper just before the end of the year. As the Pacific theatre now had priority, operations in Burma were restricted to those operations to open the land communications with China along the Burma Road and to secure and improve the air route to China.[62] The Chiefs of Staff were then shocked to later learn that Mountbatten had told Chiang Kai-Shek of his plans for a small amphibious landing (Operation Pigstick) with his remaining amphibious craft; at this time the planning for Anzio was in full swing and landing craft were an issue as they were in short supply. This proposal had been made by Mountbatten without the approval of the Combined Chiefs of Staff, much to the embarrassment of the British Chiefs of Staff who were engaged in a heated exchange of telegrams with Churchill over the availability of landing craft. Churchill had a Royal Navy officer with him providing planning information that differed to that being put forward by the Chiefs of Staff. In an effort to ease the situation, the Chiefs of Staff ordered three more LSTs be sent from India, thereby almost completely reducing Mountbatten's amphibious capability. Perhaps realising his faux pas, Mountbatten then contrived to have Operation Pigstick cancelled. However, Churchill was not pleased with the despatch of the three LSTs as this would be regarded by the Americans as further evidence of British procrastination in Burma, as it surely was.[63]

From January 1944 until the end of the war, Churchill continued to pursue the Polish problem, organising many meetings in an effort to find a solution to the question of post-war Polish frontiers but refusing to accept a new, alternative Russian-installed government in place of the Polish government-in-exile in London. It was not until a visit to Moscow in late 1944 that Churchill learnt of Roosevelt's bargain with Stalin.

Anzio

With the Combined Chiefs of Staff approval for Eisenhower to retain sixty-eight LSTs in the Mediterranean until 15 December on 8 November, Eisenhower accordingly asked Alexander to plan for another amphibious landing near Rome. On the same day, Eisenhower requested an extension of the retention of the LSTs for another month and Alexander promptly ordered the Fifth Army to begin the planning process for the landing. Thus even before the Sextant conference, the Combined Chiefs of Staff had provided extra resources for use in continuing the Mediterranean strategy and then at Sextant permitted the LSTs to be retained for another month.

Alexander's plan was for part of the US Fifth Army to land at Anzio, 30 miles south of Rome, and advance to the Alban Hills 20 miles inland, which were the last remaining suitable defensive positions for the Germans before the capital. The landings would disrupt the German defences along the Gustav Line and permit the rest of the Fifth Army in Italy to thrust from Cassino to Frosinone. General Clark of the Fifth Army had a slightly different conception of the plan, which was that the landings would be a subsidiary operation to assist the main army in advancing from Cassino to Frosinone and then on to the Alban Hills. This misconception was not addressed and Clark doubted the success of the plan, which was to land a maximum of two divisions at Anzio. As the Fifth Army was already stalled at Cassino and as there was no chance that it could advance quickly enough to link up with the proposed landings,

Clark recommended on 18 December with Alexander's agreement that the plan, Operation Shingle, be cancelled. This meant that the capture of Rome would not take place in 1943 as envisaged by Churchill and would be delayed until sometime in 1944.

Brooke made a visit to the Italian front from Cairo and on his return on 19 December discussed with Churchill in Carthage the apparent stagnation of the Italian campaign and the fact that the valuable landing craft had not been utilised for anything other than supply duties. The rugged Italian terrain had made an impression on Brooke when he tried to describe it two months later: 'He says that the terrain defies description. It is like the North-West Frontier; a single destroyed culvert can hold up an army for a day.'[64]

This was the very terrain that Churchill and Brooke had decided to advance through as the foundation of their Mediterranean strategy and this admission by the CIGS is particularly damning of the Chiefs of Staffs' understanding of the conditions in Italy about which any Allied soldier fighting in the country could have told him, as no doubt Wilson and Alexander tried. Churchill, however, immediately sent a telegram to the Chiefs of Staff committee demanding a report and action, describing the stagnation of the Italian campaign as becoming scandalous.[65] Brooke then flew back to England where he and the Chiefs of Staff did not play much further part in the Anzio planning process other than trying to assemble the necessary landing craft.

Three days later, the Chiefs of Staff reply to Churchill proposed a two division landing to outflank the German defences on the Gustav Line by retaining for an extra three weeks the landing craft due to be returned to the UK for Operation Overlord. Eisenhower had been planning for an assault with one division only because of the limited availability of landing craft and was already thinking ahead to Operation Anvil, which would also require landing craft. Churchill, convalescing after his illness, threw himself enthusiastically into planning the landing and was now convinced that the operation would break the stalemate in Italy and allow the opportunities of the Italian campaign to be realised: 'We must have the big Rome amphibious operation … In no case can we sacrifice Rome for the Riviera. We must have both.'[66]

The proposed landing was then discussed by Churchill and five Commanders-in-Chief including Eisenhower, Wilson, Alexander and Tedder over Christmas and it was agreed that it could be launched with a minimum of two divisions provided the LSTs were retained. In order to ensure Wilson had enough landing craft, on 25 December Churchill cabled Roosevelt with the request to keep fifty-six LSTs in the Mediterranean until 5 February with a landing at Anzio on or about 20 January. Churchill reluctantly acknowledged that other amphibious operations such as planned against Rhodes (Operation Hercules) and in Burma (Operation Pigstick) would have to be shelved.[67]

On 27 December, Roosevelt approved the retention of landing craft on the strict understanding Overlord was not to be delayed further. Twelve landing craft were to be sent from the Mediterranean as planned and another fifteen arriving from Southeast Asia were to be sent straight on to England, which would leave enough for an assault by two divisions at Anzio. However, there would not be enough shipping to maintain supplies for more than a two-division landing.

Clark was informed in late December that Operation Shingle was back on and that plans had to be revised. The expected return of the LSTs to England by 3 February at the latest still presented a problem as the Anzio force could only be resupplied and built up for eight days after the landing on 22 January. In view of the ongoing supply problems for any landing because of the limited availability of landing craft, there were some who thought that Shingle would still be cancelled. However, after two planning conferences with Churchill on 7 and 8 January, Operation Shingle got the green light on the basis of twenty-four extra LSTs that had been demanded by Clark being made available for resupply until the success of the operation was assured, i.e. after four weeks. Churchill said British prestige would suffer immeasurably if it failed to make a success of the Italian campaign, which was only half finished, and 'It was unthinkable that we should admit to failure in the Mediterranean.'[68]

The planned landing was a risky venture, which the Allies acknowledged in their planning, but Eisenhower deemed the risk worth taking. The Allied armies to the south would have only eight days to break through the Gustav Line and link up with the beachhead before an evacuation with a total loss of equipment would have to be considered.[69] The Anzio force of two reinforced divisions was expected to cut off the retreat of the nine German divisions in the Gustav Line (more when the Fifth Army attacks started and German reserves were moved south from Rome) and the Germans were thought to be capable of assembling only a maximum of three divisions for any counter-attack against Anzio.

The Germans were anticipated by the British to react in one of three ways to the Anzio landings; they could try to destroy the beachhead, be destroyed themselves or retreat from the Gustav Line; the possibility of another stalemate was not considered.

Clark then planned to get the rest of the Fifth Army as close to Anzio as possible before the landings began by means of an offensive to gain the entrance to the Liri Valley, which would provide the quickest route of advance to Anzio. The proposed attack by the Fifth Army plus two divisions from Eighth Army would attempt to break the Gustav Line in the Liri Valley and force the Germans to commit all reserves to the area. The Anzio landings a few days later would then, in theory, cause some German forces to be transferred away from the Gustav Line, thus facilitating a larger breakthrough by the Fifth Army. However, the final plans saw the Anzio landings instead of being a subsidiary operation as originally planned become a large operation in its own right to menace the German rear and seize the Alban Hills.[70] Instead of 24,000 men as originally planned, now nearly 110,000 men would be landed, supported by armour and artillery units, and these were still expected to cut off all the German divisions to the south on the Gustav Line.

The US VI Corps, commanded by General Lucas, consisting of the US 3rd Division, the 1st Division (British) supported by armour from the 46th RTR and the 751st Tank Battalion plus US parachute regiments, was to make the assault. Lucas was very apprehensive about the operation as the Germans were bound to react vigorously following the landings, which if not eliminated would imperil their forces on the Gustav Line as the Allies intended. Only two German divisions had been identified as available reserves near Rome but Lucas was still not convinced: 'This whole affair had a strong odour of Gallipoli and apparently the same amateur was still on the coach's bench.'[71]

To gain entry into the Liri Valley, Fifth Army had to first cross the Rapido and Garigliano rivers in an offensive due to start on 17 January. The CCB from the US 1st Armoured Division was to exploit northwards along the Liri Valley once a gap in the German line had been made. Clark was still not convinced of the feasibility of the operation and in order to ensure that VI Corps was not destroyed, sent word to Lucas that an advance to the Alban Hills was only to be conducted if the beachhead and port of Anzio were not threatened. Clark considered that the Anzio force was still too small to both hold the beachhead and advance inland. To underline this thinking, the proposed drop zones of the parachute regiment were changed from points halfway to the Alban Hills to the Anzio beaches themselves.[72] A practice landing at Naples by the Anzio assault force provided an ill omen when forty-three DUKWs were sunk and nineteen 105mm artillery howitzers lost.

The Anzio landings on 22 January were largely unopposed by the Germans, who were completely taken by surprise. The day was warm and sunny and many soldiers commented that it was difficult to believe there was a war on as they splashed ashore. The British 1st Division landed to the north of Anzio with only minor difficulties and by the afternoon was 2 miles inland with the port of Anzio cleared and working to receive the rest of VI Corps supplies. The American 3rd Division was 3 miles inland by mid morning and dug in to await the inevitable counter-attack, as did the British.

The German reserves in Rome had been drawn off as planned to reinforce the Gustav Line following the British attack across the Garigliano, which had secured a bridgehead. The American 36th Division had been unsuccessful and badly mauled in an earlier attempt to cross the Rapido. The German Commander in Italy, Kesselring, was forced to bring a motley array of units from Italy, France, Germany and the Balkans to rope off the Anzio beachhead and the assembly of these units would take time. Fortunately, the Allied Anzio force did not appear to be moving inland and Kesselring immediately ordered elements of the Hermann Göring Panzer Division to block the roads to the Alban Hills. Two days later, the Anzio force had still not moved as the German reinforcements began to arrive in the area. By 28 January, the Hermann Göring Panzer Division was fully assembled and with a Panzergrenadier and an infantry division was ready to attack on 2 February. At this time it was evident that the Anzio landings were not going well as the beachhead had not expanded very far and the Fifth Army was not even close to linking up with it from the south.

Lucas was anxious to maximise the build-up of troops in the beachhead before trying to break out and the US 1st Armoured Division (less its CCB) plus the 45th Division were on the way by sea, but Clark became concerned by the lack of aggression being shown by Lucas, as was Alexander. It was not until 30 January that Lucas began to move out of the beachhead. The British 1st Division attacked and captured Campoleone but the tanks of the 1st Armoured Division, with orders to exploit any gap created and head for Rome, got bogged in flooded low-lying ground. In the south, American Rangers spearheading the 3rd Division efforts to take Cisterna were caught in a German ambush and suffered heavy casualties. The attack had fizzled out by 1 February and Clark and Alexander directed Lucas to prepare for the counter-attack by the ever-increasing forces being assembled by the Germans. The German counter-attacks finally began on the night of 3–4 February with the elements of two divisions attacking the British at Campoleone and a powerful corps of the elements of five divisions attacking from Cisterna. A total of eight additional German divisions had been moved into Italy from France, Greece and Yugoslavia.

The VI Corps lines held despite fierce fighting but Lucas decided to withdraw his forces to shorten the front line; construction of a last line of defences was begun which was located along the positions occupied at the end of the first day of the landings. Savage fighting continued for the next two weeks, the Allies supported by heavy artillery, naval gunfire and aircraft, but the Germans in a series of counter-attacks were unable to break through the lines to the sea. Additional Allied reinforcements were poured into the beachhead to ensure its survival, including the 56th Division plus various parachute regiments.

Having returned to England on 18 January, Churchill became increasingly dismayed by the situation, which was rapidly becoming a stalemate, and began to agitate for a change of command. Churchill sent a telegram to this effect to Alexander on 10 February, while the question was raised by Dill of Marshall in Washington. Lucas was eventually relieved on 22 February and replaced by General Truscott of the 3rd Division. Referring to the Anzio landing, Churchill apparently said at the end of February, 'We hoped to land a wildcat that would tear out the bowels of the Boche. Instead we have a vast whale with its tail flopping about in the water!'[73]

Meanwhile, attempts by the Fifth Army to break the Gustav Line at Cassino were also unsuccessful and costly. The incessant rain and cold Italian winter affected all soldiers and operations, making the deployment of tanks off roads difficult if not impossible for both sides. The American II Corps was withdrawn, exhausted from its battles near Cassino and replaced by a New Zealand Corps. General Freyberg demanded that the monastery of Monte Cassino be bombed as it was 'a military necessity'. The subsequent attack by the New Zealand Corps once the monastery had been destroyed on 15 February was also unsuccessful.

A renewed German attack on the Anzio beachhead on 29 February was again defeated by overwhelming Allied artillery and close air support. The Germans failed to concentrate their attacking forces against one sector of the Anzio lines in order to achieve a breakthrough and Anzio slid towards a stalemate similar to that the Fifth Army found itself in and around Cassino. On 15 March, the Allies bombed the town of Cassino itself and reduced many of the stone houses to rubble, which the German defenders then used as cover. All attacks by the New Zealand Corps were repelled and the rubble also restricted the use of any tanks to support the attacks. Churchill sent a telegram in frustration to Alexander:

> I wish you would explain to me why this passage by Cassino, monastery, hill,
> etc, all on a front of two or three miles, is the only place which you must

keep butting at. About five or six divisions have been worn out going into these jaws.[74]

Anyone who has visited Monte Cassino would instantly understand how the monastery dominates the terrain around it, something not appreciated by Churchill. Exhausted by their unsuccessful struggle to break through the German positions, the British and Americans remained in their positions at Anzio and Cassino for the rest of March and April until May. The bold plan to outflank the Gustav Line and liberate Rome had failed and the Anzio beachhead now became a liability requiring precious shipping to maintain. Further attacks at Cassino were hampered by the transfer of more troops to Anzio from Fifth Army, fatigue and bad weather. The Anzio beachhead was heavily shelled by the Germans when there was not a shortage of ammunition and quickly came to resemble a network of trenches from the First World War. By May, there were six divisions within the beachhead but the supply of these units did not become as much a problem as anticipated.

During the four months of the Anzio Campaign, VI Corps suffered more than 29,200 combat casualties (4,400 killed, 18,000 wounded with a further 6,800 men taken prisoner or missing) and 37,000 non-combat casualties from illness and disease. Two-thirds of these losses occurred in the period from the initial landings to the end of the German counteroffensive on 4 March.[75]

The Anzio force was never big enough to achieve its objective of seizing the Alban Hills and holding off at least nine retreating German divisions if they were compelled to withdraw from the Gustav Line. The Fifth Army and Eighth Armies were unable to break through as planned in the face of the determined German resistance at Cassino and the Anzio landings became another Salerno where, rather than providing a threat to the rear of the Germans, the survival of the Anzio beachhead itself was threatened once the Germans assembled a far larger force to attack it than the Allies thought possible. The bold gamble by Churchill had not paid off and the Mediterranean strategy remained stalled in Italy. Churchill later admitted, 'Anzio was my worst moment in the war. I had most to do with it. I didn't want two Suvla Bays in one lifetime.'[76]

This fear was not reflected later in Churchill's written history, which merely commented that the Allies had pinned down nearly twenty good German divisions, some of which could have been transferred to France.

13

OVERLORD AND BURMA

In 1942, the Japanese had occupied most of Burma and chased the British and Indian troops out of the country back into India. The Japanese invasion had the primary objective of stopping American aid and supplies coming via Rangoon and moving inland by road into China. India was temporarily threatened but the onset of the monsoon rains from May to December hampered any further Japanese advance, allowing the British valuable time to regroup although they also had to deal with an active and growing anti-British independence movement in India and a serious famine in Bengal.

Following Pearl Harbor, American strategy was to continue to supply aid to China in order to keep it fighting in the war against Japan as well as to implement future plans to set up air bases in the country for long-range bombers to target Japan. Roosevelt hoped that the Chinese population could be mobilised against Japan in the same way the Russians had done against Germany. With the Japanese occupation of parts of the Chinese coast, Formosa and the Philippines, aid to China could no longer be sent by sea and the only possible supply route was overland by the Burma Road. A complication for the Americans was that, as per the theatre agreement of 1942, Burma was the responsibility of the British.

In northern Burma, a force commanded by the American General Stilwell of two Chinese divisions that had retreated into Burma plus additional American engineers had been charged with constructing a new link to the Burma Road from Ledo towards Myitkyina since December 1942. In October 1943, this force was supplemented by a regiment of American troops that became known as Merrill's Marauders. While Stilwell's force toiled to build what would become known as Stilwell's Road, the British 15th Corps had pushed down the coast from 21 December 1942 in an advance towards Akyab as part of the Arakan campaign. Some units of the 15th Corps were temporarily surrounded by the Japanese but supplies were dropped from the air and the advance was able to continue towards Chittagong and Akyab. The 15th Corps was eventually resoundingly defeated by the Japanese in April 1943 and forced to withdraw almost back to India after heavy losses and a dramatic fall in morale. The first Chindits brigade under Wingate had begun its mission on 8 February 1943 to penetrate behind Japanese lines and demonstrated that British soldiers could fight in the jungle by achieving their mission of cutting the Burma railway (but only for two weeks). About a third of the force, 800 men, failed to return and many that did come back suffered from disease and malnutrition, only 600 being fit for active service. The raid had been an expensive failure according to General Slim, commander of the 15th Corps.[1] However, the exploits of Wingate were heralded by Churchill as an example of what British troops could do in the jungle. Churchill ordered Wingate to accompany the British delegation to meet Roosevelt at the Quebec conference in August 1943 to show that the British were doing something in Burma and that these raids could be used successfully in jungle fighting. In March, two more brigades were dropped behind Japanese lines near Indaw. These forces required a substantial number of transport planes to drop supplies to them, which brought the British into a conflict of policy with the Americans over the use of aircraft that were being used to supply China. Wavell had paid the price for the unsuccessful Arakan campaign and was replaced by Churchill as the Commander-in-Chief India on 20 June 1943; command passed once again to Auchinleck. However Auchinleck's tenure was to be brief for, at the Quadrant conference in August 1943, a directive was made to create a new Southeast Asia Command for operations outside India, i.e. Burma, China and Malaya, along the lines of the Middle East Command, and Mountbatten was chosen by Churchill to be the Supreme Commander of this new Command.

Wavell was far from happy with this change and in thinly veiled criticism of Churchill recorded afterwards in his despatch to the War Office:

> During the operations recorded in this despatch I received neither encouragement nor help nor understanding of the difficulties, only criticism for the failure of a bold attempt to engage the enemy with inadequate resources, in hazardous circumstances. That my plans were not unsound is, I think, shown by the fact that the plans adopted by the South-East Asia Command for the

winter 1943–44 have been practically the same as those I laid down for the previous winter; and that the Long Range Penetration Groups which were initiated by Major-General Wingate under my direction have been adopted and extended as a result of the experience I originated.[2]

Churchill declared in a minute of October that Mountbatten's recent appointment and reorganisation of the Command including training for the troops would provide suitable excuses for inactivity over the next three or four months.[3] The monsoon was about to end and considerable flooding had already caused operations to be postponed; December was normally the first month after the monsoon in which offensive operations could be conducted.

The basic strategic choices for the British and Americans had been between a naval-based, island-hopping strategy utilising twin drives through the Pacific (one via New Guinea and the Dutch East Indies perhaps via the Philippines, the other via central Pacific islands) towards Japan or an eastwards drive from British forces already in India. The plan approved by the Combined Chiefs of Staff at Sextant put the main weight of effort in the Pacific, with the new Southeast Asia Command relegated to a subsidiary theatre with limited amphibious operations and offensives only possible with what resources were already available to keep the supplies to China moving.[4]

Admiral King had also implied that as US naval strength was twice that of the Japanese, British naval help would not be required in the Pacific. With the adoption of the Pacific strategy and the promised entry of Russia from the north once Germany was defeated, this gave the Allies a firm strategy to defeat Japan. Following the cancellation of Operation Buccaneer after the Sextant conference, Chiang Kai-Shek refused permission for Chinese divisions to advance from the Yunnan province to help open the Burma Road. The Chinese leader regarded the amphibious operation to seize Akyab (Operation Pigstick) as an inadequate replacement for operations against Rangoon and so this too was cancelled and the landing craft ordered to return to Europe. This left the Southeast Asia Command without any planned operations for the coming year and a relative sideshow to other theatres. In *The Second World War*, Churchill claims that later he did not agree with the Pacific policy agreed at Tehran as he did not have the opportunity to fully consider it at the time.[5] When discussed at the Defence Committee meeting of 19 January 1944, the War Cabinet and Churchill declared their disagreement with the plan accepted only in principle by the Combined Chiefs of Staff and the British Chiefs of Staff. Churchill even claimed to the Defence Committee that he had not even heard of the proposed operations before. These statements by Churchill are simply untrue; the Prime Minister met with the Chiefs of Staff or Brooke most days of the conference and given his propensity for reading all papers and minutes it is beyond belief that he was not aware of the evolving strategy for the war against the Japanese, particularly given the debate over Operation Buccaneer. The minutes of the final plenary session at Sextant, when the final report was read through paragraph by paragraph, show that Churchill raised some objections to other matters but none regarding strategy in the Far East. The final report referred to the strategy paper CCS 417 for the war against Japan, in which it was proposed to make the Pacific the major effort. After initialling the report, Churchill had gone on to proclaim:

> ... the report a masterly survey of the whole military scene. He gave it as his opinion that when military historians came to adjudge the decisions of the Sextant conference, they would find them fully in accordance with the classic articles of war.[6]

The acceptance or not by the Americans of a British fleet for the main operations in the Pacific against Japan was then the catalyst for a major disagreement between Churchill and his Chiefs of Staff over the strategy to be followed in the Far East to defeat Japan. Churchill was in favour of sending all or part of a British fleet from the Indian Ocean to the Pacific in 1944 but that would preclude the Army and Air Force in the Far East and Southeast Asia from any major operations and he did not want to see them standing idle for any length of time. Churchill was not convinced the strategy decided on at Tehran would be successful and he was adamant that Operation Culverin, the seizure of the tip of Sumatra, was still the best option for beginning an advance towards Japan in late 1944 rather than waiting for the American Pacific route.[7] Operation Culverin was Churchill's pet project, which he had compared to the strategic importance of Gallipoli in the First World War.[8] Churchill was particularly anxious to regain the lost parts of the British Empire and restore British prestige with the liberation of Burma, Malaya, Singapore and Hong Kong, in which Operation Culverin would be the first step.

The Chiefs of Staff, however, believed that the strategy of making Mountbatten's SEAC a subsidiary theatre to contain as many Japanese units as possible while giving priority to the Pacific was the correct strategy, which set them on a collision course with Churchill.

As Mountbatten had only arrived in Southeast Asia in early October 1943 and his headquarters did not become operational until mid November, Churchill decided to wait for a delegation of officers from his new command to arrive and present their future plans. The officers arrived in mid February and presented a plan to the War Cabinet and Chiefs of Staff for using the forces in Burma to carry out a series of amphibious landings in Sumatra (Operation Culverin) and then Malaya before making other landings north-eastwards along the Chinese coast. Mountbatten's plan abandoned the attempt to force a land route through to China while bolstering the air route over the Himalayas in order to bring an immediate increase in tonnage airlifted. However, any such plan that appeared to reduce the efforts to get supplies through to the Chinese would inevitably be regarded poorly by the Americans and on 17 February, the US Chiefs of Staff expressed their concerns about the failure of the British to issue Mountbatten with a clear-cut directive and their understanding that his plan proposed action against Sumatra rather than assisting in the securing of northern Burma. The Americans urged that the Combined Chiefs of Staff order the capture of Myitkyina as soon as possible.[9] In his reply, Mountbatten denied that forces had been allocated to Operation Culverin and stated that all available forces were in fact heavily committed. Further, Mountbatten believed that Myitkyina could not be captured before the monsoon arrived because of a Japanese build-up in that area. Before his planners had travelled to England, Mountbatten had held a conference on 31 January with his senior commanders including General Stilwell to discuss this strategy; all were in agreement except Stilwell, who strongly opposed any relaxation of efforts in north Burma and disputed the British estimate of the time needed to construct the Ledo Road.

Stilwell's views were shared by the Joint Chiefs of Staff and Roosevelt repeated their opinion in a telegram to Churchill on 25 February: '... more being gained by an all-out drive into Upper Burma so we can build up our air strength in China and ensure the essential support for our westward advance to the Formosa–China–Luzon area.'

Roosevelt was anxious that Myitkyina be captured by Stilwell's force, which would require support from a planned British advance from Imphal, and also expressed his grave concerns at what was seen as a recent British tendency to favour plans for Sumatra and Malaya rather than surmounting obstacles in Burma.[10] Churchill, in his reply, attempted to allay Roosevelt's fears but pointed out that the British did not believe the Burma Road could be reopened before 1947. The Americans were set on the strategy determined at

Tehran to make the Pacific a priority but a decision had yet to be made as to who should make the main effort there, MacArthur or Nimitz.

Mountbatten's delegation went on to Washington in March to meet with the Joint Chiefs of Staff, where they found themselves in competition with a delegation already there, without his knowledge, from his own deputy in the Far East, Stilwell, with his own plans that included offensives in northern Burma. This difference of proposed strategy in Burma caused some embarrassment to both the British and Americans when the story was leaked to *Time* magazine. The Americans remained steadfast in their belief that China had to be supported by forcing through the construction of the Burma Road and an increased airlift over the Himalayas; consequently the Combined Chiefs of Staff did not approve Mountbatten's plans.

While the British and Americans debated strategy and postponed operations, the Japanese had been building up their forces and making their own plans for an offensive to drive the British out of Burma and threaten India once again. This was precisely as Marshall had feared and had mentioned in Cairo. On 8 March 1944, the main Japanese attack on the central Burmese front began with eight divisions and after initial success, crossed the frontier into India and laid siege to the British and Indian forces at Kohima and Imphal. The provision of supplies by air immediately became the critical factor to the survival of the surrounded men at Kohima and Imphal, as it was to all Allied forces fighting in the jungles of Burma. This was in stark contrast to the supply system for Japanese soldiers, who were forced to a great extent to live off the land.

Since the departure of Mountbatten's party for Washington, the Chiefs of Staff had reviewed their plan of Culverin and were still not in favour of it.[11] At this point in time the Allies already had two American campaigns in the Pacific for the defeat of Japan and Brooke did not feel that Culverin offered any additional benefits other than tying down Japanese forces and its resources would be better employed supporting the Pacific. From 25 February, a series of fractious staff conferences and meetings took place between the Chiefs of Staff, planners, the Defence Committee and Churchill following the news of the arrival of a Japanese fleet in Singapore. While the Japanese fleet remained there and its intentions were unknown, clearly any operation against Sumatra was out of the question. Churchill subsequently also decried the British strategy agreed in Cairo of sending a fleet to eastern Australia which would operate on the coat-tails of the US fleets in the Pacific where the British would be overshadowed by the successes of the Americans. At these heated meetings the Chiefs of Staff were accused by Churchill of overestimating the forces needed for Culverin to make it impossible to mount and of preferring to fight the Japanese in the Pacific. Using an unfortunate analogy, according to Churchill the tip of Sumatra would be another Anzio bridgehead.[12] In a memorandum of 29 February, Churchill threatened to go to the War Cabinet to get a decision on the two alternatives of mounting an operation against Sumatra or sending a fleet to the Pacific followed by four divisions of infantry to be initially based in Sydney once the war against Germany finished.[13] The Chiefs of Staff responded with both a written paper defending their Far East strategy, which was duly submitted on 1 March, and their own memorandum on the 8th. The memorandum gave Churchill further bad news about Operation Culverin as it in theory could not be mounted until six months after the defeat of Germany and therefore the forces in Burma would more than likely be idle as a consequence of this.[14] General Ismay warned Churchill that there was an irreconcilable cleavage between Churchill and his ministers on the one hand and the Chiefs of Staff on the other, and the latter might even resign, which would be 'catastrophic at the present juncture'.[15] Ismay urged another meeting be held as soon as possible, which took place on 8 March with the War Cabinet and Chiefs of Staff to review the entire future strategy for the Far East. While the continued presence of Japanese ships in Singapore completely ruled out Operation Culverin, Churchill believed that successive smaller amphibious operations and naval actions could well encourage the Japanese fleet to remain there, thereby greatly assisting the Americans in the Pacific. The essential issue, according to Churchill, was whether the centre of gravity for future British operations should be in the Bay of Bengal or the Pacific via SWPA and Australia. Churchill was eager that operations to liberate Malaya and Singapore should be undertaken as soon as possible and believed that going via SWPA was the long way round.[16] However, this meeting did not resolve the issues as Churchill did not want to take any decision that might limit future operations. There had effectively been no agreed firm British plan for Burma since May 1943, despite Mountbatten's appointment and the creation of the Southeast Asia Command.

Churchill then decided to satisfy himself whether a British fleet was needed by the Americans anywhere in the Pacific and duly exchanged telegrams with Roosevelt on 13 March; Roosevelt's reply made it clear to Churchill that the Americans had no need of a British fleet until mid 1945, therefore making British naval resources available for operations in the Bay of Bengal.

Operation Culverin having been denied, Churchill then discovered another island, Simalur in the Indian Ocean, which would lend itself to a British amphibious landing. This was much to Brooke's annoyance, as his diary of 17 March shows:

> I began to wonder whether I was in Alice in Wonderland or whether I was really fit for the lunatic asylum … I am honestly getting very doubtful about his balance of mind and it just gives me the cold shivers. I don't know where we are or where we are going as regards our strategy and I just cannot get him to face the true facts![17]

In response to the negative feedback from all the Chiefs of Staff regarding Simalur, Churchill firmly laid down in a minute of 20 March addressed personally to each Chief of Staff his directives for future strategy, which would have its centre of gravity in the Bay of Bengal and the ultimate objective of liberating Singapore. The Chiefs of Staff were strongly rebuked:

> I very much regret that the Chiefs of Staff should have proceeded so far in this matter and reached such settled conclusions upon it without in any way endeavouring to ascertain and carry the views of the civil power under which they are serving. They had certainly the duty of informing me as Minister of Defence, and making sure I understood the importance they attach to the issue.[18]

Churchill also accused the Chiefs of Staff directly in his minute of not wanting to discuss the plans with the Americans as they were afraid the division between them and the rest of the War Cabinet, including himself, would be revealed. At this time, Churchill was not well again and was often seen to be drinking heavily, perhaps in response to the stress of the frustrating news from Italy of Cassino and Anzio and the impending landings in Normandy. Brooke vented his frustration to his diary on 20 March 1944:

> One of the worst of Cabinet meetings with Winston in one of his worst moods. Nothing that the Army does can be right and he did nothing but belittle its efforts in the whole of the Cabinet. I cannot stick anymore meetings like it! He has now produced an impossible document in which he is overriding our opinions and our advice!

And the next day:

We discussed at the COS how best to deal with Winston's last impossible document. It is full of false statements, false deductions and defective strategy. We cannot accept it as it stands, and it would be better if we all three resigned rather than accept his solution.[19]

Entirely demoralised by Churchill's intransigence regarding Operation Culverin and the accusations levelled at them, the three Chiefs had seriously discussed resigning, a momentous step for a nation's top military team to contemplate in a time of war. A week later, they submitted their response to Churchill, claiming on the one hand that they had had insufficient time to completely compare the Bay of Bengal strategy with the Australian strategy and on the other that their first impression was that there would likely be insufficient resources for the Bay of Bengal strategy, which would not bring about the defeat of Japan any more quickly.[20] Churchill received this jointly signed minute without comment.

In Washington, the Americans were having similar debates on strategy with representatives from all commands and on 14 March the decision was reached by the Joint Chiefs of Staff to favour Nimitz's Pacific advance to the Marianas and the Palaus rather than MacArthur's advance to the Philippines, although the JCS left the question of Luzon or Formosa undecided. A week later, the JCS formally rejected Mountbatten's plans presented by his mission in Washington and affirmed their own strategy, requiring Mountbatten to assist the Pacific advance indirectly by capturing Myitkyina to enable an increase in the tonnage of supplies being airlifted to China. Meanwhile, the Americans were endeavouring to meet another target agreed in Cairo to deliver 10,000 tons a month to the Chinese by air.

A further staff conference on 8 April with Churchill, the Chiefs of Staff and senior officers of the Southeast Asia Command ended with the Joint Planning Staff being asked to examine the possibilities of establishing air bases on a number of different islands from November 1944 onwards from where the British could apparently 'obtain great advantage at small cost', according to Churchill.[21]

During April 1944, the Chinese were reluctant to attack from the Yunnan province in China into Burma to help open the Burma Road. Therefore Marshall on 13 April decided to withhold supplies being airlifted to the Yunnan force and reallocated them to US forces. On being informed of this, two days later the Chinese asked for the resumption of airlifted supplies, to which the Americans agreed, but it was not until 21 April did Chiang Kai-Shek order his troops into Burma and it was not until mid May that this physically happened.

This was an example of the United States using the supply of material to get its own way on strategy but Marshall was rightly determined that the Chinese should support American efforts to keep the aid flowing to them.

On 3 May, Mountbatten himself complained of the lack of clear-cut directive in a telegram to the Chiefs of Staff. Mountbatten was caught in the middle of a battle between British and American strategy over the use of limited resources for operations in northern Burma to open the Burma Road, Churchill and his own Chiefs of Staff regarding future operations and all while a greater part of his forces were besieged at Imphal and Kohima. On 17 March the Americans had granted Mountbatten's request for thirty transport planes to be diverted from operations over the 'hump' to help drop supplies to the besieged troops but a month later, he was forced by the continuing siege to request extra aircraft. Churchill's response in a minute to Ismay on 5 May was that the telegram from Mountbatten was 'most serious' and complained about the American tactics of forcing the British to accept their strategy by controlling shipping, landing craft and aircraft resources. With no firm British plans and the Americans dictating strategy in the Pacific and Burma, Churchill lamented, 'What with our own differences and the uncertainty of American action, we are not unfolding a creditable picture to history.'[22]

With American Pacific plans more certain and in the knowledge that a British fleet was not required until 1945 at the earliest, British planners worked hard to develop alternative plans for its fleet. These plans had the objectives of liberating parts of the Empire such as Singapore and Hong Kong rather than the defeat of Japan. At the beginning of May, the British had three options, two of which were around a fleet being based in Australia with Australian troops to operate on the left flank of MacArthur's SWPA:

(i)   Operation Culverin – Sumatra and on to Singapore
(ii)   A Middle Strategy – advance to Amboina, Borneo and Singapore
(iii) A modified Middle strategy – direct to Borneo then Singapore via north coast of New Guinea.

All aspects of these plans were extensively studied, including detailed assessments of the base facilities in Australia and India and the requisite fleet trains needed in each region but no decision was reached.

As the fighting in India continued, the Chiefs of Staff decided on 6 May that Mountbatten be allowed to retain seventy-nine transport aircraft from the Mediterranean theatre for operations until 31 May with the United States to make up the difference from the China airlift if replacement planes had not arrived by then. In a minute of 7 May regarding a proposed staff conference, Churchill decried the large organisational tail in India supporting the small force fighting at Imphal and Kohima and again raised the subject of a potential amphibious landing at Simalur. Churchill was firmly against the resumption of ground operations in Burma:

> We are to plunge about in the jungles of Burma, engaging the Japanese under conditions which though improved are still unfavourable to us, with the objective of building a pipeline or increasing the discharge over the 'hump'.[23]

At the conference on 8 May, Churchill again expressed his reluctance to accede to American strategy as this would interfere with his other plans such as Operation Culverin.[24]

From the beginning of May, operations had begun on the ground and in the air to relieve the besieged towns of Imphal and Kohima. Enjoying air superiority, the RAF squadrons based in India were able to harass the Japanese supply lines as well as dropping supplies by air to the besieged troops. As the battles at Kohima and Imphal hung in the balance, on 9 May Churchill demanded that aircraft be taken from airlift duties if necessary if the aircraft from the Mediterranean could not be retained longer to support Mountbatten's troops.[25]

The American commanders in the China–Burma–India theatre reported on the British reluctance to mount any operations at all in northern Burma, with the result that on 3 May the US Joint Chiefs of Staff ordered Stilwell to capture Myitkyina. In a surprise operation by Merrill's Marauders on 17 May, the Americans seized Myitkyina airfield after a 65-mile trek through the jungle and then invested the town, beginning an eleven-week siege before the Japanese forces withdrew on 3 August. Myitkyina airfield would provide an important staging post for aircraft ferrying supplies to China and eliminated the hazard of having to fly over the Himalayas in one bound. Stilwell's operation surprised both the Japanese and the British, as Churchill laconically commented after the war.[26] Stilwell was disparaging of both the British and Chinese in a telegram to Marshall on 25 May:

> 'The British simply do not want to fight in Burma or reopen communications with China,' wrote Stilwell. 'In short, I do not believe the British help is worth what we are paying for it.' As for the Chinese, 'the choice seems to be to get realistic and insist on a quid pro quo,' advised Stilwell, 'or else

restrict our effort in China to maintaining what American Aviation we can, the latter course allows Chiang Kai-Shek to welsh on his agreement. It also lays the ultimate burden of fighting the Jap Army on the USA.'[27]

In order to better defend its territorial gains of 1942 in China and the Pacific and forestall any American landings on the coast of China, the Japanese Imperial GHQ decided to force a decision in China. The subsequent offensive in China for 1944 was called Operation Ichigo with the objectives of forcing a land corridor through to French Indo China, controlling the railroads through central China, and eliminating the Fourteenth Air Force bases receiving supplies over the Himalayas. On 17 April Japanese forces crossed the Yellow River and an offensive towards Heng-Yang began on 27 May against limited Chinese resistance. Changsha fell on the 19 June 1944 followed by Heng-Yang on the 8 August, but the rapid advance required the Japanese to pause for thirty days to resupply.

On 3 June 1944, Mountbatten finally received his revised directive from the Combined Chiefs of Staff instructing him to concentrate on the airlift and opening the Burma Road to support the Chinese; disagreements between the British and Americans over its wording had delayed its issue. In the first British success of the Burma campaign, after nearly ten weeks of fighting, the Imphal siege was finally broken on 22 June with the arrival of the 2nd Division from India; the Japanese, lacking artillery, anti-tank weapons and food, were heavily defeated and by July had fallen back in disarray as far as the Chindwin River.

Discussions between Churchill and his Chiefs of Staff on the war against Japan were held over to 10 July but again deferred to 14 July when the same arguments were repeated, with Churchill promising to give a decision in a week. It was not until 8 August that discussion was resumed, Churchill perhaps unwilling to have a direct confrontation with his Chiefs of Staff. During the procrastination by Churchill, another issue had come to the fore and that was the future operations in Burma. Of Mountbatten's two plans, Operation Vanguard for the capture of Rangoon and Operation Champion in northern Burma, Mountbatten believed he had adequate resources for the Rangoon operation if given the go ahead but all parties still agreed that an Operation Culverin-type landing could not be mounted until the next year. Deliberations, at times contentious, continued well into the night and resumed the next evening. It was finally agreed to mount the Rangoon operation, which would require American support in terms of shipping and offer a fleet for the Pacific which, if turned down, would be offered to MacArthur. A telegram advising of this was duly sent to Washington on 12 August and thus, after over six months of sometimes bitter debate, British strategy for the war against Japan had finally been decided after the strategic situation in Burma had provided an alternative to the Chiefs of Staff strategy so despised by Churchill and his own Operation Culverin objected to by the Chiefs of Staff.

Anvil/Overlord

Eisenhower and Montgomery examined the initial Overlord plan devised by COSSAC and expressed great dissatisfaction with it, demanding the assault force be increased from three to five divisions. Regarding the timing of the assault, the ideal moon and tide conditions in May were on 5 May, which was far too early for Churchill. The next most suitable date was 3 June, which was more preferable as it gave another month to prepare. However, as this was different to what had been agreed at Trident, Churchill requested the date be changed in a telegram to Roosevelt on 6 January 1944, claiming that the Overlord commanders thought they had a better chance on the later date.[28]

After the Tehran conference, the US Joint Chiefs of Staff were not impressed to hear that Montgomery had been given command of the ground forces in Operation Overlord; although the Americans had respect for his demonstrated qualities as a general, after having been under his command in Sicily they feared that he would delay or postpone to such an extent that any favourable opportunity regarding the weather for launching Overlord would be lost. However, in this respect, they were mistaken as once Montgomery became involved in Overlord, he became a determined champion of the assault, obtaining the additional divisions and adhering to the date set by the Combined Chiefs of Staff.[29]

With the confirmation at Trident of 1 May 1944 as the date for the cross-Channel operation, the build-up of forces in the UK under Operation Bolero continued at a faster pace. From 1 January, nine more US divisions arrived in the UK, making a total of twenty by D-Day. This flow of men was also matched by the corresponding increases in tanks, aircraft and supporting materiel.

Churchill, on 2 February, then proposed an operation to assist the French resistance by landing 5,000 commandos at Bordeaux soon after D-Day to cause havoc in the south of France, a plan subsequently called Operation Caliph. Churchill's enthusiasm was not shared by the Joint Planning Staff, who recommended that Caliph only be mounted in the event that the diversionary landings in the south of France, Operation Anvil, were cancelled.

The US plans to mount an operation in the south of France on or about D-Day as discussed and agreed at Trident and reaffirmed in Cairo now began to be a cause of further friction between the Americans and British; the operation would continue to be a contentious issue in both the Mediterranean and the cross-Channel plans almost up until the day it was finally launched. The primary reason for the disharmony was the decision to increase the cross-Channel assault from three to five divisions with two divisions for the follow-up forces, which exacerbated the existing shortage of landing craft and limited future operations. Operation Anvil was to be mounted with a two-division assault and this made further demands on scarce shipping.

Eisenhower, backed by the British Chiefs of Staff, on 21 January had requested a five-division assault for Overlord that would be delayed to June and ideally a three-division landing (with a minimum of two) for Anvil. An extra month of preparation for Overlord would also make a further month's production of landing craft available. If these requirements could not be met, wrote Eisenhower, landing craft should be withdrawn from the Mediterranean after leaving enough for a one-division lift when the Germans were significantly weaker. The British Chiefs of Staff supported Eisenhower fully in a telegram of 26 January to the Joint Chiefs of Staff.

The Joint Chiefs of Staff disagreed, however, and urged that Overlord take place in May as agreed at Sextant in view of Stalin's promise to mount a simultaneous attack and that Anvil should be undertaken with a minimum of two divisions. Eisenhower and Marshall saw Operations Overlord and Anvil as being inextricably linked and this belief that Anvil was a diversion needed for Overlord underpinned American strategic thinking. The perceived need for Anvil would fuel Anglo-American strategic debate for the next six months.

The British Chiefs of Staff considered the American response for several days and came around to the view that operations in Italy would be more fruitful than Anvil and offered a better diversion than this operation, despite having accepted the operation at Trident and Sextant. On 4 February, a telegram was duly sent to the Americans querying the wisdom of Anvil at all as the landings in the south of France were 500 miles from Normandy and pointing out that as the Germans had not withdrawn to a line north of Rome as envisaged, all the Allied divisions were needed for the fighting in Italy, which was to be pursued with the utmost vigour. The British also disagreed with the US serviceability rates and estimated that after the requirements for Overlord were taken from Italy there would only be sufficient landing craft for one lift.[30] Meanwhile, fighting in Italy had not yet achieved a breach of the Gustav Line and the Anzio beachhead remained isolated.

The Joint Chiefs of Staff in their reply disagreed with all the British points except for one, namely that while Overlord had a target date of 31 May, some latitude to 2 June was permitted to take into account moon and tide conditions. The debate over the numbers of landing craft and shipping required for the proposed operations had now escalated to the point where US and British planners disagreed on how many men each vessel carried and the serviceability rates of the craft. Marshall sent a telegram to Eisenhower on 7 February with the American view:

> As to this, the British and American planners here yesterday afternoon agreed that there is sufficient lift to stage at least a 7-Division OVERLORD and at the same time a 2-Division ANVIL on the basis of May 31st. This is an apparent disagreement with the British planners in London, or Montgomery, I don't know which.[31]

In view of the importance of determining available shipping for Overlord, Churchill had cabled Roosevelt the previous day asking for Marshall or the US Chiefs of Staff to come to London for a meeting with Eisenhower to resolve the differences. Regarding preferred strategy, a complete reversal of previous British and American thinking had now arisen with the American insistence on Operation Anvil, as wryly commented on by General Marshall in the same telegram to Eisenhower:

> Judging from the discussions and differences of opinion at the present time, the British and American Chiefs of Staff seem to have completely reversed themselves and we have become Mediterraneanites and they heavily pro-OVERLORD.

The meeting suggested by Churchill was turned down by Roosevelt on 9 February as his Chiefs of Staff were too busy preparing plans for the Pacific theatre. To resolve the issues, the President suggested that the plans and recommendations of the Combined British and American planners in Washington be accepted. The Americans were clearly wary of another session with Churchill and the British Chiefs of Staff. Despite this, several more junior American officers were quickly sent to London to clarify the load-carrying capabilities of the landing craft and they duly reported back to Washington on the lack of British enthusiasm for Operation Anvil. Eisenhower met with the Chiefs of Staff on 10 February and it was decided that top priority had to be given to shipping for Operation Overlord and any unallocated be used in the Mediterranean in an operation to be decided later.

The relative failure at Anzio in January had hughlighted the major pitfalls of an amphibious landing and many senior British officers, including Churchill, were even more apprehensive about Operation Overlord. Eisenhower, too, was now wary of launching Anvil with anything less than two divisions but was faced with the competing but greater needs of Overlord. After having thoroughly examined the landing craft inventory, Eisenhower decided on a redistribution of landing craft between Overlord and Anvil which left only enough in Italy for Anvil and precious few for maintenance of the Anzio beachhead.[32] When this was discussed by the British Chiefs of Staff on 19 February following the failure of the New Zealand attack at Cassino, they admitted that operations in Italy had not gone to plan and recommended abandoning Anvil altogether as considerable German forces were already being tied down in Italy, where they could be 'bled and burnt'.[33] Eisenhower, while in favour of Anvil, also proposed that if Anvil was abandoned or post-poned, this would also allow Overlord to be strengthened to better ensure its success. The Chiefs of Staff were concerned that both Anvil and Overlord were both being skimped and informed the Joint Chiefs of Staff of this, along with Eisenhower's personal view that Anvil may 'no longer be practicable owing to the developments in the situation in Italy'.[34] While this was being considered in Washington, Wilson, in a telegram to all the Chiefs of Staff on 22 February, had also requested that Anvil be cancelled as the offensive to liberate Rome was in a 'position of considerable difficulty' and the diversion of troops would seriously reduce the strength of the Allied forces fighting in Italy.[35] A compro-mise was then proposed following discussions between Eisenhower and the British Chiefs of Staff that the Italian campaign should have absolute priority for the next four weeks, after which the situation would be reviewed.[36] The review after a month was subsequently agreed to by the Joint Chiefs of Staff and operations could continue in Italy; a decision did not have to be taken until 20 March for the movement of assault shipping for Anvil.

Churchill was increasingly apprehensive about Operation Overlord and in mid February wrote to the Chiefs of Staff reviving Operation Jupiter and a flanking operation from the Balkans if it was unsuccessful. Montgomery was firmly of the opinion that Anvil should be abandoned and wrote to

Eisenhower to tell him just that on 21 February. The landing craft issue continued to dominate planning and in order to force a decision at least on the Italian operations, Churchill summoned the Chiefs of Staff and Eisenhower to a meeting on 29 February at which the general agreed to let twenty-six landing craft stay in Italy to supply the Anzio beachhead and be available for future Italian operations.[37]

The Polish issue was still very much at the forefront of Churchill's thinking as the Soviet armies entered eastern Poland on the heels of the retreating Germans. As Roosevelt surmised in a long telegram to Churchill, Britain was very conscious of its treaty obligations to Poland, which tended to cloud the bigger picture of maintaining harmony between Russia, America and Britain for the conduct of the war along the principles agreed upon at Tehran.[38] Churchill, of course, was still unaware of the agreement over Poland struck between Stalin and Roosevelt at Tehran. Since the German announcement of the discovery of the Polish officers murdered at Katyn, the Russians had worked hard on their version of events, which culminated in a report published in January 1944. Sir Owen O'Malley revisited his despatch of May 1943 and once again demolished the Russian case in another report to Eden.[39] O'Malley suggested the British consult a neutral Swiss advisor who had been part of the original German forensic investigative committee. On reading this, Churchill initialled a comment by Eden that the British should definitely not do this, evidently concerned about lending any weight to the German accusations or creating further difficulties with Stalin.

With the introduction of the P-51D Mustang long-range fighter as an escort, the VIII Bomber Command (redesignated the Eighth Air Force on 22 February 1944) had resumed deep daylight raids in December 1943 with the Ninth Air Force, which had completed its transfer to the UK. In conjunction with the RAF, a 'Big Week' (Operation Argument) of raids was launched at the end of February to both bomb aircraft construction facilities and engage the Luftwaffe fighters in combat. The Fifteenth Air Force also joined the attack from its Mediterranean bases. In six days of continuous operations, the Allies claimed more than 500 German fighters shot down with the loss of nearly 100 experienced German pilots. Although the effects of the bombing were not significant, the Allies succeeded in establishing aerial superiority over much of France.

In London, conditions similar to that of the Blitz were experienced during March 1944 when the Luftwaffe renewed air raids at night for a short time with small numbers of aircraft, perhaps more to boost the morale of German civilians than damage targets. The Combined Bomber Offensive had created a significant change in the Luftwaffe, which was forced to switch all its bomber production to fighter construction. This change added to the momentum created by the Luftwaffe's failure to develop a heavy bomber to replace the Heinkel 111 and thus the Luftwaffe was transformed into a defensive air force rather than one with offensive capabilities.

In order to assess the progress of the Italian campaign in view of the imminent decision on shipping for Anvil, the Chiefs of Staff asked Wilson for an appreciation of the situation in Italy. In his subsequent report, General Wilson declared on 22 March that with an offensive due to begin on 15 April, he was strongly opposed to withdrawing any troops from Italy for Anvil before the capture of Rome and as the Anzio bridgehead and the main force could not link up before 15 May at the earliest, Anvil should be postponed. Wilson outlined three possible future landings in his telegram – Anvil, Po Valley and Istria – as well as putting all resources into the current Italian position, but favoured a continuation of operations in Italy.[40] Two days later, a British Joint Staff Planning paper recommended that Anvil be cancelled altogether. Following another meeting with Eisenhower, a telegram was duly sent to the US Chiefs of Staff asking for the operation to be reconsidered.[41] Eisenhower had also sent his own message the day before to Marshall with the same recommendation because of the large number of German divisions already being tied down in Italy. The issues of Anvil and Italy along with Wilson's pessimistic telegram were discussed at a Combined Chiefs of Staff meeting on 24 March and, much to the surprise of the British, a postponement of Anvil to 10 July was agreed with the shipping no longer required for Anvil to be sent to the UK for Overlord and additional landing craft to be diverted to the Mediterranean for Anvil from the Pacific. This postponement of Anvil meant it would no longer be a diversionary landing for Overlord as envisaged at Sextant. The Americans, however, did not believe that the capture of Rome was worth the effort required and thought that once the Anzio beachhead had linked up with the main armies, then a defensive line should be formed in order to pin down the maximum number of German divisions in Italy.[42] This position drew the battlelines for the next Anglo-American round of debate over Mediterranean strategy as once the stalemate was broken at Cassino, the Americans wanted Anvil to be launched in July and the British a continuation of the Italian offensive with an advance to Rome. The British had at least won a temporary reprieve for the Italian campaign – until the Anzio bridgehead and the main army had linked up, there would be no diversion of resources for Anvil. Anzio, the operation to break the stalemate in Italy, had in itself become largely the cause of the stalemate in Italian operations in early 1944 as reinforcements from the Cassino area were transferred to the beachhead, which reduced the strength of the Allied armies at the Gustav Line. Worse, the existence of the Anzio beachhead because of its ongoing shipping requirements was imperilling future operations, at least from the American point of view. All now depended on better weather and a coming offensive to regain the initiative in Italy.

Another invitation by Churchill on 25 March to Roosevelt for a meeting in Bermuda was also turned down. Churchill was increasingly tired and weary, even depressed, about the increasingly aggressive messages and intransigence of Stalin over Poland and a dispute over two merchant seamen found guilty of affray who had been imprisoned in Siberia. The Chiefs of Staff remained opposed to Churchill's strategy for the Far East. The Anzio landings had stalled along with the entire Italian theatre. There were increasing difficulties in Parliament for Churchill with the Conservative Party losing another seat in the House of Commons to an independent candidate with the West Derbyshire by-election of 17 February and a government amendment to the Education Bill being defeated by one vote on 28 March. Churchill made this an issue of confidence in his own government and when the amendment was reintroduced three days later, it passed with a majority of more than 400.

With preparations for Operation Overlord going all-out, Churchill admitted to Roosevelt on 1 April, 'I harden for it as it gets nearer.' Ten days later Churchill further claimed, '… he did not agree with the loose talk on both sides of the Atlantic about the unduly heavy casualties we shall sustain.'[43]

This was hypocritical of Churchill as he had been saying similar things in private for many months. Meanwhile, a heavy bomber offensive against German supply lines and railways north of Rome had commenced from airfields in North Africa.

The war of words between the British and American Chiefs of Staff continued over a definite date for the postponed Operation Anvil and the allocation of resources in order to provide Wilson with a new directive for operations as he had requested. When the British failed to provide an alternative date and Wilson had postponed the start of the Italian offensive by a month to 14 May (much to the dismay of both Churchill and the Americans), the Americans warned on 30 March that they could not continue any build-up for Overlord and reinforce the Mediterranean when there was no fixed date for Anvil.[44] The British took umbrage at this, regarding it as an attempt to make them accept the American arguments for Mediterranean operations by threatening to with-hold resources.[45] A draft British directive to Wilson with a target date for Anvil of 10 July with no mention of preparations sent to the Joint Chiefs of Staff was returned on 4 April with alterations that the British found 'quite unacceptable'.

Churchill claimed on 5 April that the Dodecanese campaign was ruined by the decisive battles in Italy, the decisive battles in Italy were ruined by the with-drawal of the seven best divisions for Overlord and now the climax of the Italian campaign would be ruined by the proposed landing in the south of France.[46]

According to Dill in Washington, Marshall was digging his heels in and would not change his position. The American view was that Anvil was still essential to support Overlord and once the Normandy beachhead was established then this should be the next priority. On 8 April, the Americans urged that the initiative should not be handed to the Germans in the Mediterranean but later the same day reluctantly accepted the proposed British directive in a telegram which effectively cancelled Anvil as support for Overlord but used the promised allocation of extra shipping to try to force the British hand by refusing to despatch it from the Pacific to the Mediterranean.[47] This was again viewed very poorly by the British, who were convinced the Americans were trying to browbeat them into a strategy they did not think was correct in a theatre where they had the larger forces and overall responsibility. Preparations were in progress for the renewed offensive at Cassino and the British did not want to see any troops withdrawn to prepare for Anvil. The threat of reduced shipping was reviewed by the British Joint Planners, who came to the conclusion that without the extra shipping from the Pacific, a two-division lift for the Anvil amphibious operation was no longer possible. Following a Chiefs of Staff meeting with Alexander the day before, Churchill took up the issue in a telegram crafted by the entire Chiefs of Staff Committee to Marshall on 12 April in a further attempt to get the promised Pacific landing craft. Churchill's views were that an amphibious operation in the south of France was unlikely to succeed in influencing the main battle in northern France as it was too far away and the advance would be opposed by the Germans, that deception might achieve the pinning of the German forces in southern France, and that without the landing craft from the Pacific only a one-division amphibious operation in the future would be possible. Continuing, Churchill said that according to Ultra decrypts the Allies were fighting thirty-four German divisions in the western Mediterranean (twenty-five in Italy and nine in the south of France), which was a substantial contribution to the likely success of Overlord.[48] Marshall's reply on 12 April was firm and pointed out that the current preparations for an amphibious operation (Anvil or another) would give the Allies more options in Italy. Regarding the transfer of landing craft, Marshall stated that the landing craft were needed in the Pacific for 'an operation in the effectiveness of which we have complete faith', i.e. unlike the current Italian offensive.

On 16 April the British Chiefs of Staff sent a revised directive for Wilson to the Joint Chiefs of Staff with an explanatory message to Dill that the preparations for an Anvil-type amphibious operation could not take precedence over the continuation of the Italian campaign once the Anzio bridgehead was joined with the main armies, and without the landing craft from the Pacific, an Anvil-type operation was 'terminated'. Despite the attraction of the extra landing craft, the British would not be forced into adopting a strategy they believed to be wrong.[49] The British position had changed in response to American pressure from not wanting Operation Anvil before the union of the beachhead with the main armies to one of not wanting any amphibious operation at all so as not to weaken the offensive in Italy, with its prize of Rome. Churchill and his Chiefs of Staff were well and truly committed to Italy.

Marshall's telegram was a red flag to a bull, as indicated by Churchill's reply in a strongly worded telegram on 16 April:

> What I cannot bear is to agree beforehand to starve a battle or have to break it off just at the moment when success, after long efforts and heavy losses, may be in view. Our forces in Italy are not more than those of the enemy. They comprise seven or eight different races, while the enemy is all German. The wet weather has hitherto restricted the full use of our superiority in artillery, in armour, and in the air.[50]

Churchill had previously asked Roosevelt on 4 April that the US maintain landing craft production at maximum levels in order to have sufficient for future operations against Japan. This was turned down by Roosevelt as the Americans believed the carry-over of existing production of landing craft for Overlord would be sufficient for future plans; on 14 April Churchill expressed his regret to Roosevelt about this decision as the US would 'certainly want them even if they did not give any to us'. Roosevelt did not reply and instructed his staff not to reply or acknowledge this telegram.[51] Churchill's telegram to Marshall had made the same complaint about lack of landing craft; evidently the Prime Minister's relationship with the Americans was at a low point at this time. In order to break the impasse, Marshall, in a telegram of 18 April, informed Churchill that the Combined Chiefs of Staff had accepted the revised British directive to General Wilson in order to reduce any further delay in Mediterranean operations. Marshall urged that everything be thrown into operations in Italy, which would be the first priority as there would be no Operation Anvil to support Overlord and every effort in terms of deception and threats should be made to ensure the German divisions in the south of France stayed there.[52] The British had once again prevailed in the Battle of strategy, with the Americans to continue the Italian campaign at the cost of having to forego the extra shipping from the Pacific. Somewhat mollified by this small victory, Churchill on 22 April duly followed up his own February proposal for an operation in the south of France near Bordeaux, Operation Caliph, and this was recommended by the British Joint Planners the same day. While Churchill was implacably opposed to Operation Anvil, he was quite prepared to champion an amphibious operation of his own design with extra forces suddenly available and not required in Italy.

During this part of 1944, Churchill continued to suffer from fatigue and weariness. Overlord was looming, his relationship with Stalin was poor and there were no meetings scheduled with Roosevelt, who was not being as pleasant or co-operative as in the past. Britain's position in the war as the nation leading the fight against Germany was in the process of being overtaken by its more powerful Allies. Operation Overlord was imminent and Churchill had dreaded this for a long time. Once more Rommel would be the protagonist, which did not bode well for the Allied troops that would make the assault. The British and Churchill had managed to avoid mounting a Second Front in both 1942 and 1943 on the grounds that it was not feasible, or would not be successful, or there were other operations or theatres such as the Mediterranean that offered better, less risky and more immediate returns while satisfying Roosevelt's political objectives – yet there was stalemate in Italy.

In a telegram to Roosevelt on 23 October 1943, Churchill had expressed doubts about Overlord, although admittedly he was trying to encourage Roosevelt to attend the Tehran conference: 'I do not doubt our ability in the conditions laid down to get ashore and deploy. I am however deeply concerned with the build-up and with the situation which may arise between the 30th and the 60th days.'[53]

In February 1944, four months before D-Day, Churchill had further doubts about the operation and its possible very high casualty rate, which could mean the loss of another generation of men as in the First World War: 'Why are trying to do this? Why do we not land in friendly territory, the territory of our oldest ally, Portugal?'[54]

To be fair, Brooke also had grave fears about Operation Overlord and if the two most senior British directors of strategy had cause for concern, then the operation was indeed perilous:

> I am very uneasy about the whole operation At the best it will fall so very far short of the expectations of the bulk of the people, namely all those who know nothing about its difficulties. At the worst it will be the most ghastly disaster of the whole war. I wish to God it were safely over.[55]

However, Churchill did not have similar qualms about sending the Canadians into Dieppe in 1942 and this time very heavy naval and air bombardments were planned in support of Overlord as aerial supremacy over Normandy had been achieved, allowing Royal Navy warships to operate under their protective umbrella. With the stalemate at Anzio, Attlee wrote to Churchill on 8 March with his concerns about Overlord becoming a similar operation with the beachhead surrounded by strong German troops. Churchill, in a minute to the Chiefs of Staff about Attlee's warning, agreed: 'As you know, I am in sympathy with their general tenor.'[56]

While Churchill had accepted the inevitability of Operation Overlord, he was still less than enthusiastic about it, telling Cadogan in April that 'this battle has been forced upon us by the Russians and the United States military authorities'.[57] As late as May 1944, Churchill admitted to a gathering of the Dominion Prime Ministers that he was much more in favour of the Mediterranean strategy:

> He was bound to admit that if he had his own way the lay-out of the war would be different. His inclination would have been in favour of rolling up Europe from the South-East and joining hands with the Russians. However it had proved impossible to persuade the Americans to this view. They had been determined at every stage on the invasion in North West Europe and had constantly wanted us to break off our Mediterranean operations ...
>
> ... he himself had opposed the opening of this campaign in 1942 and 1943 but now was in favour of it and all his military advisors supported him in this.[58]

This statement by Churchill went to the heart of the differences between British (i.e. Churchill's) and American strategy. The peripheral Mediterranean strategy was always preferred by and was uppermost in Churchill's mind, and had the decision been solely his then Operation Overlord may well have not even been mounted in 1944. At the same Prime Minister's conference, Churchill had admitted that the Americans were suspicious of his motives regarding the Balkans, and the Americans had all along said, '... that we were leading them up the garden path in the Mediterranean. His reply had been that, in return, we had provided them in the garden with nourishing vegetables and refreshing fruits.'[59]

When what was hoped to be the final battle in Italy was about to commence, Churchill sent a telegram to Roosevelt on 29 April claiming that the purpose of the offensive, Operation Diadem, was solely to destroy German forces and was not about liberating Rome or even seeking the siege of Anzio beachhead lifted.[60] Since the Allied Armies had been struggling to reach Anzio following the January landings and such a union had been driving British plans for the last three months, this was a strange statement for Churchill to make. Roosevelt did not bother to reply.

In Poland, the Red Army was advancing towards Warsaw from the territory occupied in 1939. The Russians complained to the British that the Polish Underground was obstructing the fighting in their progress to 'liberate' Poland. Churchill expressed his concerns to Eden:

> I fear that very great evil may come upon the world. This time at any rate we and the Americans will be heavily armed. The Russians are drunk with victory and there is no length they may not go.[61]

Just before midnight on 11 May, the Italian offensive was renewed. Monte Cassino was finally captured on the 18th and the Fifth Army at last broke through the Gustav Line. There was, however, no corresponding attack from the Anzio bridgehead until 23 May and it was two more days before it finally linked up with its parent Fifth Army. In the attack from Anzio, VI Corps made a thrust towards Valmontone in the Alban Hills in an attempt to cut off the main line of communication of the rapidly retreating Germans as originally planned in January. General Clark then ordered the bulk of this force, the US 1st Armoured Division and three infantry divisions, to advance northwards to Rome and on 4 June, American troops entered the city to a delirious welcome from its inhabitants. However, this reduced the strength of the blocking force to a single division, the 3rd Division, which was not strong enough to reach Valmontone and as a result most of the German Army to the south was able to withdraw without difficulty over the course of 2 and 3 June to a new line of defences north of Rome, the Trasimeno Line. A major opportunity to trap the German forces, which was the main objective of the Anzio landings in the first place, was missed. Clark seems to have been driven by his original doubts about the whole Anzio plan, a belief that his Fifth Army had done the lion's share of the fighting to facilitate the breakthrough and he was certainly attracted by the prestige of capturing Rome.[62] In late May, two more German divisions were sent to Italy from Istria making a total of twenty-two divisions, which was regarded as the culmination of the Allied efforts to pin as many German units in Italy as possible to aid the landings in Normandy. The Allied strategic objectives for the Italian campaign had now been achieved but the British Chiefs of Staff and Wilson were already making plans for a continuation of the campaign.

Following a speech in the House of Commons on 24 May in which Churchill had praised the Spanish dictator, the fascist General Franco, for preserving Spain's neutrality during the North African operations, Roosevelt contradicted Churchill a week later and stated publicly that Spain's neutrality had been 'less than satisfactory'. Eleanor Roosevelt had commented earlier in the day that 'Mr Churchill has thought the same way for 60 years and doesn't want to change.'[63] The possibility of Spain entering the war on Germany's side or letting German troops enter Spain had been a constant concern of the Americans rather than the British and Spain had refused to not supply tungsten to Germany despite Allied pressure. Substantial payments (totalling approximately £10 million) were funnelled by MI6 to Spanish agents as bribes to senior Spanish generals early in the war to ensure that Spain remained neutral. Roosevelt later felt that Spain should be treated the same way as Italy, i.e. as an ally of Germany.

A left-wing aircraftman in the RAF commented to his pen friend in the United States, 'Congratulations on Mrs Roosevelt's reprimanding of Churchill on his praising of Franco. This is typical of this two-faced Tory. He'll go as soon as the next election comes.'[64]

The last British general election had been in 1935 as the election of 1940 had been postponed because of the war and therefore the British people had not had the opportunity to express themselves regarding pre-war events or the war itself. Churchill's leadership had not been tested at the polls as he had been appointed Prime Minister on Chamberlain's resignation.

At the Chiefs of Staff meeting of 20 May, a report from the Joint Intelligence Committee was examined which stated that Churchill's pre-Overlord conditions of a reduction in German fighter aircraft strength and fewer than twelve full strength German divisions in France had been met. Operation Overlord could now proceed, all that was required was for the weather to play its part. Churchill revealed his fears to his wife Clementine on the eve of D-Day: 'Do you realise that by the time you wake up in the morning, twenty thousand young men may have been killed?'

From mid year, the once resilient Germany economy could no longer cope with the effects of Allied bombing and reached a tipping point. All spare capacity had been taken up and measures to lessen the impact of the bombing such as the relocation and camouflage of factories were exhausted at the same time as the fighter force had been significantly weakened as a result of the daylight American raids, which now had fighters as escorts while over enemy territory.

The Combined Bomber Offensive ended on 1 April 1944 in order for the Strategic air forces to come under the control of the Supreme Commander, Eisenhower, for Operation Overlord. For the next fifty days, the British and American strategic and tactical air forces systematically bombed the railway communication hubs and marshalling yards in the whole of northern France under the Transportation Plan in order not to focus any particular attention on Normandy. The plan had been opposed by Churchill and some members of the War Cabinet because of the estimated high level of casualties to French civilians. The number of targets was eventually scaled back and a limit put on the projected French deaths of 10,000 in number. An area bounded by the Loire and Seine Rivers was almost isolated with bridges destroyed, rail junctions bombed and telephone and power networks put out of service. With air superiority achieved over the skies of northern France, the bomber forces were able to fly to targets in Normandy largely unhindered. In response to this growing Allied dominance and in order to combat the Combined Bomber Offensive against Germany, many German fighter squadrons had been withdrawn altogether from the north of France. The success of the Transportation Plan and Allied air superiority would make the movement of any German forces to the invasion beaches to conduct a counter-attack much more difficult. Heavy bombers also continued to strike at German oil production facilities, ball bearing factories and aircraft assembly plants in this period before D-Day to keep up an unrelenting assault on German aircraft production.

The build-up in England under Operation Bolero saw Devon and Cornwall crowded with American troops and a few days before D-Day, all farming activity was suspended in order for military traffic to use the roads:

> The build-up of the invasion forces prior to D-Day is something I shall never
> forget. American troops and military equipment were everywhere. They

were camped on Crinnis Beach and the Golf Course, and in the surrounding woods and fields. Pentewan Beach was used for practice embarkation and disembarkation. Large ships with opening bow doors were moored in the bay, and DUKWS, amphibious tanks and landing craft were constantly shuttling between the beach and the ships. As the big day approached, army lorries, tanks, bren gun carriers and jeeps towing field guns lined the roads nose to tail. We went down to Holmbush to witness the spectacle. The troops all seemed in high spirits, and were even more generous than usual with their 'candy'. One American officer even gave one of the local boys a steel helmet, with his lieutenant's silver bar on the front. I wonder if the lieutenant and his mates made it home?

Then Cornwall became a different place overnight. By the morning all the troops had gone, but overhead there were many gliders, mostly towed by Dakotas, and I believe, some by Lancasters, going out to join the fray. From then on, we were relatively unaware of military activity, apart from newspaper and radio reports.[65]

On the morning of 6 June 1944, five Allied divisions – two British, two American and one Canadian – began their long awaited cross-Channel assault on German-occupied France on a stretch of coastline from Ouistreham to Sainte-Mère-Église. Preceded by a massive naval and air bombardment and supported by amphibious tanks, the Allies had established themselves ashore by the end of the day. Only in the American Omaha sector were the landings in any great danger of failure owing to the beach defences being largely intact after a shortened naval bombardment, inaccurate air force bombing and the loss of many amphibious tanks in the rough seas. Casualties were much lower than Churchill or the Chiefs of Staff had expected, with fewer than 1,300 British and American soldiers reported killed and less than 3,000 wounded, with 1,300 men missing. Although the casualties were serious, the English Channel was certainly not filled with corpses as Churchill had believed. Montgomery's plan of staking out large tracts of high ground by armoured columns penetrating inland on D-Day or the next day before any German counter-attack was not successful. The town of Caen, a D-Day British objective, was not captured until six weeks later because an advance by insufficient British forces was stopped by a limited counter-attack by the 21st Panzer Division.

The news of the long-awaited Second Front and return to the Continent was received joyously by most of the nation, which now saw an end in sight to the war:

So at last it has begun, this mighty assault which will liberate Europe from the Nazi grip and bring Germany to her knees. Four years since our overwhelming disaster at Dunkirk. Four years since the capitulation of France and now we are back. But the position is vastly different, Germany is broken and bleeding along the Russian Front, her troops are being pushed back relentlessly from Rome and now in the west she is being engaged by a vastly superior force; the high officials in Berlin must view the future with gloom indeed.[66]

Caen became the focus of fierce fighting for the British Second Army and dominated Montgomery's plans. By the middle of June, the Allies were well established ashore but occupied a limited beachhead, which had been roped off by German reinforcements including Panzer divisions rushed to Normandy. Because of faulty tactics and a convoluted command structure, the much-feared massed German Panzer attack on the beaches never materialised as the Panzer divisions had to be committed hastily to the front line in response to Allied attacks and then found themselves unable to disengage. An entire Panzer Korps was recalled from Russia, weakening significantly the German Army there. On 23 June, after waiting to see the outcome of the British and American landings, the Russians began a massive offensive against Army Group Centre as promised by Stalin. In a few days, the Red Army had destroyed many German divisions and began an advance which would end in Berlin.

British operations in June to encircle Caen (Operations Perch and Epsom) were, however, unsuccessful and Churchill began to have concerns about a stalemate developing in Normandy. A major break-out operation was planned by both the British and the Americans using heavy bomber support, which had been utilised for the first time in the support of ground operations during the capture of Cherbourg and the northern half of Caen. A first attempt by the Americans in early July to break out of the Bocage to Saint-Lô was unsuccessful, and on 18 July the British attempt to break out in Operation Goodwood with three armoured divisions was defeated by the Germans. A second American attempt, called Operation Cobra, was this time successful and two armoured divisions broke through the German lines and thrust south-westwards in an attempt to cut off the left wing of the German Seventh Army. The thrust advanced slower than anticipated and most German units were able to evade the American cordon, but those that did not were caught by Allied fighter-bombers, which wreaked havoc amongst the long lines of retreating German vehicles and soldiers. Operation Cobra did sever the Seventh Army connection to the coast near Avranches, which created a gap through which the Americans launched General Patton's Third Army to seize the ports of Brittany as per the Operation Overlord plan. Hitler, disappointed by the performance of the German commanders and Panzer divisions in the Normandy campaign, then intervened and ordered a massed Panzer attack to the coast and Avranches from around Mortain. This attack, Operation Luttich, was poorly co-ordinated and eventually defeated by Allied airpower and armoured divisions repositioned to block the German advance. With Patton's army advancing rapidly eastwards behind the German front lines and the concentration of German units in the west for Operation Luttich, the German forces were left strung out in a large salient, which offered the Allies the opportunity to encircle all the German forces in Normandy. After several attempts, the encirclement was completed at Falaise on 19 August by the First Canadian Army coming from the north and Patton's Third Army from the south. Despite the initially slow progress by the Allies, Montgomery's forces had destroyed an entire army in fewer than ninety days and the road to Paris was open, a victory beyond the wildest expectations of the Overlord planners, Churchill and Brooke.

OPERATION DRAGOON

Churchill's renewed pursuit of Operation Caliph had an unexpected result once the Americans were informed of the British proposal in a telegram of 27 April. At a meeting with two hostile American officials the previous week, Churchill had been reminded of the American bitterness resulting from the British attitude to Anvil. The chief American concern was that German forces could suddenly withdraw from either the south of France or Italy and redeploy to northern France. Churchill was confident that the coming offensive operations in Italy would tie down the German forces there but suddenly had doubts about the south of France. This compelled the Chiefs of Staff to write a minute to Churchill, reminding him of the reasons for the British refusal to undertake Anvil and the part he had himself played in this.[1] Churchill's renewed interest in an amphibious landing, along with a telegram from Wilson suggesting possible future operations, prompted the Americans to renew their promise of extra assault shipping to be made available from the Pacific. Wilson returned to London in early May to discuss his plans and four possible options were then developed for landings in the Mediterranean to take place between mid August and mid September; Wilson was not keen on a landing in the Atlantic such as for Operation Caliph. The Americans were advised of these options, which were contingent on the successful coming offensive in Italy, and on 8 May the extra assault shipping (nineteen LSTs) was approved. Following the success of Operation Diadem and the German withdrawal from the Gustav Line, on 17 May Wilson forwarded more detailed plans of the four future options to the Chiefs of Staff. Wilson was now in favour of Operation Anvil or a similar operation in the Toulon area.[2] Wilson's headquarters was also preparing plans for operations on the Dalmatian coast and Istria should the opportunity present itself. Operation Caliph was also still being pressed by Churchill, who decided on 8 June that the options should be discussed at a Combined Chiefs of Staff meeting scheduled for the 11th in London.

Meanwhile, General Alexander, as the Commander-in-Chief of the Allied Armies in Italy, had his own ideas about the conduct of the Italian campaign and, emboldened by the withdrawal of the apparently demoralised and weakened German forces northwards, signalled Wilson (with a copy to the Chiefs of Staff) on 7 June about his plans to advance into the Po Valley before preparing to advance either into the south of France or towards Istria, the Ljubljana Gap and Vienna.[3] By this time, the Allies were successfully ashore in Normandy and Rome had been liberated on the eve of D-Day following the rapid German retreat. Marshall and the other Chiefs of Staff travelled to Britain to see the Normandy beaches for themselves and to consult with their British counterparts on the next steps.

Despite meeting regularly over the next four days, the Combined Chiefs of Staff decided to not take a decision until the advance of the Allied armies in Italy neared the Pisa-Rimini line. A telegram from the Combined Chiefs of Staff was however sent to the British Chiefs of Staff confirming the importance of another landing of three divisions as soon as possible in order to assist the fighting in France with a target date of 25 July. Furthermore, the Combined Chiefs of Staff ordered the advance in Italy to halt at the Pisa–Rimini line. Marshall was still strongly pro-Anvil but the Combined Chiefs Staff at this point were not favourably disposed towards the operation due to the perceived strength of the German defences on the south coast and in the Rhone Valley.[4] Marshall was also fully aware that Roosevelt had promised such an operation to Stalin in Tehran and therefore was committed to carrying it out. Three options were now being seriously considered by Wilson, including landings in the south of France, Istria or in the west coast of France. As a result of this telegram, plans started to be made to withdraw divisions from the fighting in Italy in preparation for a landing.

Of growing concern to Eisenhower and Marshall at this time was the lack of a deep water port through which forty divisions already assembled in the United States could be rapidly passed to reinforce the battle in France. Cherbourg had not yet been captured but when this was achieved the port would most likely be unusable for several months. After the meetings in England, Marshall then flew on to Italy to talk with Wilson, who accepted the Allied need for a deep water port but also informed Marshall he was considering an attack through the Balkans as suggested by Alexander. A north-eastern advance was proposed towards Austria and the Hungarian border after an amphibious landing at Trieste. This operation would require twenty Allied divisions to be retained in Italy and would hopefully compel the Germans to send yet more troops from other theatres to face this new threat.[5] Wilson thought Anvil was not feasible until at least the middle of August if he was to first comply with a previous Combined Chiefs of Staff directive to destroy the enemy forces south of a line from Pisa to Rimini.[6]

Debate continued for several days between the British Chiefs of Staff and Wilson and Alexander on future operations. Wilson sent a detailed telegram to Eisenhower and the Chiefs of Staff on 19 June with details of the proposed advance to the north-east from the Italian Po Valley and pointed out several disadvantages of the Anvil landing, including the fact that it could not be launched before 15 August.[7] The preferred British strategy, as before, was to continue the offensive in Italy in anticipation of future operations and they were strongly opposed to the withdrawal of any forces for other amphibious operations that would weaken the Italian front before at least the Pisa–Rimini line was reached. Alexander reinforced this position by cabling Churchill on 19 June claiming optimistically that he could destroy the remaining German forces in Italy provided his forces were left intact, thus opening the way for an advance to Vienna unless Italy was strongly reinforced.[8] Once more Churchill (and Alexander) saw an opportunity for a successful Italian campaign to have a dramatic impact on the war; they were in favour of another amphibious landing provided it was to develop operations in Italy and not France.

However, Eisenhower sent a telegram to Marshall the next day with comments on Wilson's telegram, adding that he was against Wilson's plans and now was the time for the Combined Chiefs of Staff to step in and direct that Anvil be undertaken at the earliest possible moment in order to secure a deep-water port:

> To speculate on possible adventures in south central Europe in the coming autumn, to my mind has no, repeat no, reference to current operations in this theatre. In spite of our brilliant successes in Italy, the enemy has been moving sizeable formations out of south France into the OVERLORD area. Both the enemy and ourselves now consider OVERLORD the vital operation. It is imperative that we obtain and maintain superiority over him, and this must be done in France as quickly as we can. We need big ports.[9]

Admiral King, on 20 June, ordered a large part of the Overlord naval task-force to the Mediterranean, much to Churchill's indignation. Churchill cabled Roosevelt a day later and Eisenhower subsequently countermanded the order. Marshall, who was also not keen on what he saw as another potential diver-sionary action by the British, directed Eisenhower to make his objections about British plans to the Combined Chiefs of Staff, which he duly did on 23 June. Eisenhower's forces, following three days of severe gales in the English Channel which prevented the unloading of ships for several days and nearly destroyed the American artificial harbour, needed a port more than ever. In his telegram, Eisenhower incorporated Wilson's likely date of 15 August for the earliest start of the operation but stated that he regarded Anvil as essential to capture a deep-water port as quickly as possible which would provide the most direct route to the battle in northern France: 'France is the decisive theatre. The Combined Chiefs of Staff took this decision long ago. In my view, the resources of Great Britain and the US will not allow us to maintain two major theatres in the European war, each with decisive missions.'[10]

The relative importance of the Mediterranean and cross-Channel strategies in the eyes of the British and the Americans was once again coming to a head. If Operation Anvil was to be launched in August, it would require divisions to be withdrawn almost immediately from the fighting in Italy in order to prepare for the landings, which was the last thing the British wanted at that point in the campaign as the Germans were retreating in some disorder. The Joint Chiefs of Staff then requested in a telegram to their British counterpart followed by a memorandum on 24 June to the Combined Chiefs of Staff that every effort should be made to launch Operation Anvil with three divisions by 1 August, adding that Wilson's proposal for an advance into northern Italy and the Balkans was unacceptable.[11] A draft directive for Wilson was also attached and forwarded to London. This predictably was not well received and Churchill immediately sent a telegram to Roosevelt warning that the War Cabinet would have to be consulted over these grave issues and the decisions required.

Churchill and his staff had discussed options for Italy and the Mediterranean in the Chiefs of Staff meeting of 22 June. It was decided against Operation Caliph but Churchill, buoyed by the optimistic reports from Italy, now argued in favour of an advance through the Balkans to Vienna; Brooke was broadly in favour of this operation but saw the difficulties posed by mountainous ter-rain and poor weather as the advance would be pushing through the Alps in winter. If Anvil went ahead, it would take away seven divisions from the forces in Italy, leaving only fifteen, which could lead to a further Italian stalemate. In contradiction of Eisenhower, any landings in the south of France were seen by the British as being too late and too far away from Normandy to affect the battle there significantly.[12] In the last month Churchill, Wilson and Alexander had all contemplated further operations from Italy into the Balkans, the south of France, Istria and the Dalmatian coast as the next stage after reaching the Po Valley in northern Italy. The British clearly had no intention of halting on the Pisa–Rimini line.

Piqued at the apparent intransigence of the US Chiefs of Staff, the British Chiefs of Staff replied on 26 June that in their view the best way of assisting the Normandy campaign was to continue the battle in Italy and destroy the German forces there. There was no need for a landing in the south of France as they were not convinced of the need for a large port as the Overlord require-ments could be met by smaller ports and keeping the shipping earmarked for Anvil operating off the Normandy coast. An advance up the Rhone Valley would be effectively too late to threaten anything that summer. Furthermore, the immediate withdrawal of forces for Operation Anvil on 15 August would imperil the fighting in Italy, which was also 'unacceptable' to the British.[13] The US Chiefs of Staff fired back next day, declaring again that the new British proposal was unacceptable. Going further, the British arguments were described as not logical and appeared out of keeping with the existing military situation and requirements.[14] The Americans, particularly Marshall, were out-raged that the British were going back on a previous agreement that once the Pisa–Rimini line was reached, the Italian campaign would go on the defen-sive to allow other operations such as Anvil to proceed. The British had also agreed to further amphibious operations in the talks after D-Day in London and were now reneging on this as well. The British Chiefs of Staff thought that the Americans had missed the point that they wanted to destroy German forces in Italy and push on towards Germany. Realising that the dispute would undoubtedly go to the heads of government for resolution, the Chiefs of Staff still drafted a reply anyway.[15] The British and American Chiefs of Staff were in complete disagreement with each other, which was a most deplorable situation at that stage of the war, according to the Americans, when a quick decision was needed.

An Ultra decrypt had revealed to the British that the Germans were plan-ning to prevent at all costs an Allied breakout into northern Italy and beyond and were digging in along the Apennines north of the line from Pisa–Rimini. The British used this new information in their memorandum of reply as they felt this vindicated their opposition to the withdrawal of any troops from Italy as the Germans clearly felt more threatened there than in the south of France; therefore the British strategy was the more correct of the two.[16]

Despite Churchill's threat, the War Cabinet did not consider the issue in this period and neither did the Defence Committee but some ministers were involved in discussions at Chiefs of Staff meetings. Following an appeal to Roosevelt to examine the matter himself, Churchill sent a very long telegram to the President on 29 June arguing against the diversion of landing craft to Anvil from Overlord and the subsequent deprivation of the offensive powers of the Allied armies in Italy; it was again suggested that the small Channel ports were capable of handling the necessary supplies for Overlord. The telegram was largely a copy of Churchill's own notes on 'Operations in the European Theatres' written on 28 June to summarise the issue and was a long-winded message that perhaps did not help the British cause.[17]

On 29 June, Roosevelt replied to Churchill with a telegram written by the Joint Chiefs of Staff emphasising that Anvil should go ahead as agreed and requested that Eisenhower should be supported. Roosevelt also made it clear that the Americans regarded Italy as a diversion:

> My interests and hopes centre on defeating the Germans in front of Eisenhower and driving on into Germany, rather than limiting this action for the purpose of staging a full major effort in Italy. I am convinced we shall have sufficient forces in Italy with Anvil forces withdrawn to chase Kesselring north of Pisa–Rimini and maintain heavy pressure against his army at the very least to the extent necessary to contain his forces. I cannot conceive of the Germans paying the price of ten additional divisions, estimated by General Wilson, in order to keep us out of Northern Italy.

Roosevelt also had a personal consideration in the light of the impending presidential elections: 'Finally, for purely political considerations over here, I should never survive even a slight setback in "OVERLORD" if it were known that fairly large forces had been diverted to the Balkans.'[18]

Once again the importance of Operation Overlord to the Americans as the main strategy for the defeat of Germany was emphasised by Roosevelt, who reminded Churchill that a definite plan of attack had been agreed on at Tehran by Britain and Russia so any cancellation would need the consent of the latter. The President requested that a new directive be given to Wilson by 1 July so as to not delay further. Wilson had to some extent undermined the British position by writing in a telegram to Eisenhower on 24 June that he had the necessary forces available and was able to launch Anvil by 15 August as long as he was given the requisite shipping and a directive to do so.

Despite his declining health, Roosevelt was seeking re-election for a record fourth term as President. Having already set a new precedent by standing for a third term, this was not as unexpected as in 1940. The war was now going relatively well for the United States and Roosevelt campaigned on this success with a plan for a strong post-war United Nations in which America would play a leading role.

On 30 June, the British Chiefs of Staff came to the conclusion that they had no choice but to reluctantly approve Operation Anvil, even though they believed it would harm future operations in Italy.[19] Churchill, as always, refused to take no for an answer and cabled Roosevelt back on 1 July with an emotional appeal that offered no new arguments but claimed that by splitting the Mediterranean campaign into two parts it would be the first major strategic mistake by Roosevelt and himself in the war:

> What can I do, Mr President, when your Chiefs of Staff insist on casting aside our Italian offensive campaign, with all it dazzling possibilities, relieving Hitler of his anxieties in the Po Basin and when we are to see the integral life of this campaign drained off into the Rhone valley in the belief that it will in several months carry effective help to Eisenhower so far away in the north?[20]

Churchill's Mediterranean strategy had been struck a mortal blow and in these telegrams the essential differences between the Americans and the British can again be seen. The Mediterranean strategy had always been preferred by Churchill for the possibilities it opened up if successful, to the east, the west or straight through the Ljubljana gap to Vienna, while American strategy had firmly focussed on a cross-Channel operation since 1942. The Americans clearly did not value the 'nourishing vegetables and refreshing fruits' that Churchill claimed the Mediterranean strategy gave them. Roosevelt repeated a day later his request for a directive to be given to Wilson, saying that when the fighting was renewed in Italy, the Germans would merely withdraw to another defensive position. Wilson received his orders from Eisenhower for Anvil the same day. Marshall and the US Chiefs of Staff had finally got their way to restore the highest priority to the cross-Channel French campaign at the expense of Anvil and the Mediterranean campaign. Following the allocation of units to Anvil, the Italian front was by no means denuded as there were still nineteen Allied divisions (fifteen infantry and four armoured divisions plus six independent armoured brigades) in the Mediterranean. This was a considerable force for Alexander to plan future operations with, although the success or otherwise of these depended on the strength and numbers of the German divisions that remained in Italy.[21] Alexander had requested twenty divisions for future offensives and as fifteen divisions were considered necessary to hold Italy, the Italian theatre was not being cruelled as claimed by Churchill and the Chiefs of Staff. To offset the loss of the Anvil force, three more American divisions including a mountain division were sent to Italy, so Alexander still commanded a sizeable force, though replacements for casualties remained a problem.

The CIGS, Brooke, was in private more realistic and perspicacious, concluding in a diary entry that as the balance of contributing forces in the war changed with the greater build-up of US troops and material, then the Americans would play a commensurately more significant role in determining Allied strategy and therefore Britain must accept their decision:

> The Americans now begin to own the major strength on land, in the air and on the sea. They therefore consider that they are entitled to decide how their forces are to be employed. We shall be forced into carrying out an invasion of southern France but I am not certain that this need cripple Alexander's power to finish crushing Kesselring.[22]

The Americans were clearly in the ascendancy as the dominant partner in the Anglo-American partnership. In recognition of the larger part being contributed by the Americans in Normandy, Churchill and Roosevelt had already agreed long before D-Day that command of the forces there would be taken over by Eisenhower on 1 September. Churchill, too, was conscious of the changing of the guard, so to speak, writing later that July 1944 saw the rapid expansion of the American forces in Europe and the Far East, making their number greater than those of the British forces for the first time.[23]

The thoughts of the Allies were already turning to future world organisations and the post-war conditions to be imposed on Germany, which was to be divided into several zones of control. The British War Cabinet had already drafted Terms of Surrender documents for Germany and it was widely expected the war in Europe would be over by the end of the year. In the east, Soviet armies were entering Rumania and Bulgaria as communist cells and resistance movements that had been set up in Yugoslavia, Greece and Italy were openly engaging the Germans; even France had an active communist party at this time. British and American relations with Stalin were at such a low ebb at this point that Roosevelt had recalled his special representative, Harriman, from Moscow and Churchill considered doing the same.

V-Weapons

In England, the long-suffering civilian population was subjected to a new horror after D-Day on a scale unknown since the Blitz when Hitler launched his vengeance weapon, the V-1 flying bomb, on London. More than 2,000 civilians were killed and nearly 5,400 injured in the first sixteen days of the attacks. The V-1 missile warhead caused tremendous blast damage and many civilian casualties were caused by flying glass and debris. Almost 500 houses were being destroyed each day with another 21,000 being damaged.[24] A 6-year-old boy recalled at that time:

> Some of the Mums in our road went out and did part-time jobs, so the arrangement was that the Mums who were home would leave their front doors open so we kids playing in the road could run into the first open door near to where we were playing, and dive under the steel Morrison table shelter in the dining room, dog and all. The mothers who were off work would just naturally look after all of the street's kids who played together …
>
> A few minutes after the wailing stereophonic 'Alert' warning sirens, we heard a loud droning noise, which got even louder as one of these heartless flying automata roared up from a south easterly direction.
>
> Then, if the deafening pulse engine cut out on the approach, there was a heart-stopping 7 to 12 second silence. This terrible silence was followed by a huge bang as it exploded just before it hit the ground or on rooftops. Lucky folk like us not too close to the blast just had their windows blown in and ornaments knocked off their mantelpiece. We kept our window curtains closed even on the hottest of summer days which prevented glass from the windows flying into our rooms.[25]

At the peak of the bombardment, more than 100 V-1s a day were launched at England and although many were shot down by fighter aircraft and anti-aircraft guns or hit barrage balloons, the constant sound of the air raid sirens day and night posed a great strain in people. Once the V-1s reached London, their interception and destruction over the city only caused more damage when they exploded, so a gun-line of anti-aircraft guns was set up south of the capital to bring down the missiles in more open countryside:

> June 18th 1944
>
> We've gone back to 1940 days again. Preparing for the night is quite a performance. Gas turned off, tea tray ready, chairs, knitting and books in the hall, suitcase packed with spare clothes and money![26]

In considering the British response, Churchill asked the Chiefs of Staff to look very seriously at using the RAF to destroy 100 small German towns and the use of gas to drench cities.[27] Gas was fortunately ruled out as being ineffective against V-1s and it was considered that its use in Europe at the current time would be militarily to the disadvantage of the British because of likely German retaliation.[28] Churchill, however, continued to ask the Chiefs of Staff for further options for its use.

Three months later, England was subjected to an even more terrifying weapon, the V-2 rocket. The first two V-2 rockets struck Chiswick and Epping on 9 September. There was no warning as the rockets travelled faster than the speed of sound and only the explosion of the warhead announced their arrival; there was little that anyone could do to protect themselves as the British air defence system was equally powerless against the missiles. As people could not remain in their air raid shelters or the Underground all the time just in case a V-2 came over, they were forced to carry on and hope for the best, which added to the stress of the time:

> The missile would leave a crater up to 45 feet in diameter and 20 feet deep, large enough to accommodate a double decker bus. Fired from launchers in Holland, they travelled through a huge arc, entering space before finally descending silently on to their target on the other side of the North Sea. Since no evasive action could be taken, the loss of life at any incident in a populated area was high. One of the worst single incidents occurred when a V-2 fell on a shopping centre in New Cross. One hundred and sixty-eight persons are known to have died. On one occasion I was travelling home on a trolleybus when the street shook with an explosion. The bus stopped, the overhead power lines had gone dead, and I had to get off and finish my journey on foot. As I walked along the road, I was passed by ambulances, rescue

tenders and fire engines. Half a mile later, I came upon the scene. The missile appeared to have landed in Barnby Street, its rows of little Victorian houses reduced to heaps of rubble from which dust and smoke was rising. It was a shocking sight; nearly all the houses had been reduced to debris, along with some more in an adjacent street. The main road was cordoned off and I had to make a detour to get home. The number of dead listed in this incident was 27 with many more seriously injured.

The Civil Defence workers and the Fire Brigade are, to me anyway, some of the bravest people of the war, faced with the grim task of recovering the victims from the debris, often when their own lives are in danger. No post traumatic counselling was available then. It's hard not to sound as if I am exaggerating, but it was a simple fact in those days that every moment could be your last. Life had become a deadly game of chance and it is difficult to describe the tension under which we lived. Realisations could only come about through personal experience. For a total of 190 days and for 24 hours a day we were vulnerable, whether at home on the street or at work. Indeed, the only places which afforded any degree of safety were the deepest stations of the London underground. It was only the belief that the war was likely to end within months that enabled us to keep going. Morale in London was not high at the time, and these latest attacks were almost the last straw. We had already endured nearly 5 years of conventional aerial bombardment.[29]

Others managed to find some humour in the threat from the new robotic weapons:

July 8th 1944

Do these bombs frighten me? Oh no, look at it this way. When it's got to England, it's got to find London. When it's found London, it's got to find Bethnal Green. When it's found Bethnal Green, it's got to find Widow's Walk. Then it's got to find No. 5 and chances are, I'd be at the pub anyway![30]

Perhaps unsurprisingly in the strength of their convictions, Churchill and his Chiefs of Staff had not given up on trying to get Anvil cancelled while the Americans remained equally determined to stage it. General Devers, as commander of the US Services of Supply in the Mediterranean, had refused to reallocate the supplies and equipment that had already been gathered for the landing during the debate over whether Anvil should proceed or not and had instructed the commander of the newly created US Seventh

Army to continue planning for the southern France assault. Devers would ultimately command the French and American armies in Operation Anvil. In Normandy in early July while the US First Army was struggling through the hedgerows north of Saint-Lô, the need for another landing in the south of France was very apparent. In Italy, General Wilson's latest Italian offensive had run its course and another quiet period had developed following the withdrawal of the troops designated for Anvil, primarily the US VI Corps that had fought at Anzio, although two new American divisions had arrived to take their place. General Alexander then had a total of nineteen divisions at his disposal but the British still firmly believed this was not adequate to destroy the Germans in Italy and to pose any sort of threat to Germany by an advance into northern Italy.

Churchill made his opinions of the Americans clear in a vitriolic minute to the Chiefs of Staff on 6 July, which was prompted by the need for a firm decision on how many divisions Alexander would have for any future offensive:

> Alexander is to have his campaign. If the Americans try to withdraw the two divisions still left with him, I shall ask you to send the 53rd Division from the United Kingdom to bridge the gap. I hope you realise that an intense impression must be made on the Americans that we have been ill-treated and are furious. Do not let any smoothings or smirchings cover up this fact. After a little, we shall get together again; but if we take everything lying down then there will be no end to what will be put upon us. The Arnold–King–Marshall strategic team is one of the stupidest strategic teams ever seen. They are good fellows and there is no need to tell them this.[31]

The Chiefs of Staff meeting that evening saw another heated exchange between Churchill and Brooke when the Prime Minister criticised the performance of both Alexander and Montgomery before Brooke leapt to their defence, accusing Churchill of always running down his generals.[32] Churchill was certainly in a querulous mood, wanting to let Roosevelt know in a telegram his feelings about the Anvil operation; his humour was not improved by renewed discussion on the proposal to send details to Washington of the plan to base naval forces in Australia to advance in SWPA as part of the British strategy to defeat Japan. The Prime Minister continued to expound his views that in the Southeast Asia Command; his preferred operations were for the seizures of the island of Simalur and the tip of Sumatra to set up air bases as a prelude to the recapture of Singapore. According to Churchill, this had to be done by the British in order to wipe clean the shame of the disaster there in 1942. The meeting was described as 'deplorable' by Eden and, according to Cunningham, Churchill was too tired and in no state to discuss anything, being the worse for alcohol.[33] Churchill continued to be greatly concerned about the British being relegated to a secondary role in the Pacific.

On 16 July, Churchill proposed another meeting of the Big Three to Roosevelt and then Stalin, this time in Scotland. Stalin turned down the invitation on 28 July due to the rapid military advances westwards of the Red Army. Roosevelt also declined, citing Stalin's non-attendance and the coming presidential election. A day later, with the Far Eastern strategy still undecided, Churchill ordered Mountbatten back to England for talks, promising a decision within a week.[34]

At a Chiefs of Staff meeting on 26 July, a prescient paper was discussed that analysed Britain's post-war security, concluding that Russia was the only threat to Britain in the foreseeable future after the defeat of Germany. A hostile Russia could only be resisted by the British and Americans together and ironically Germany was regarded as one of the only countries that had the geographical location, resources and manpower to stop the Soviets. The greatest threat was perceived to be a rearmed Germany in an alliance with Russia, to which a grouping of Western European powers along with the United States was seen as the only solution.[35]

In order to reduce the V-1 missile attacks on Britain, the British were naturally keen to clear the launch sites in the Pas-de-Calais and sent a telegram to the US Chiefs of Staff on 30 July on this subject.[36] In Poland, a broadcast by Radio Moscow urged the Polish in Warsaw to rise up against the Germans as the liberating Russian armies were nearing the city. The inhabitants of Warsaw duly revolted but the Red Army halted and initially refused to assist or even allow British or American supplies to be dropped from the air. Churchill was anxious to take some action but Roosevelt did not want to offend Stalin at this point as the Americans were contemplating the use of airfields in Russia for the bombing of Japan.

In Italy, on 3 August, Alexander's army finally reached Florence on the much sought after Pisa–Rimini line but then had to pause for three weeks before the next planned offensive. As Roosevelt had predicted, another line of German defences, the Gothic Line, now confronted the Allies. Churchill made one last attempt to resuscitate operations in Italy by attempting to get Operation Anvil postponed or cancelled again. Eisenhower, according to Churchill, apparently was now considering cancelling Operation Anvil (rechristened

Operation Dragoon) and the Prime Minister immediately made plans to visit him. Churchill got the Chiefs of Staff to send a telegram to the Joint Chiefs of Staff on 4 August asking that Dragoon be reconsidered and to use the forces allocated for it to land on the coast of Brittany to capture a port and help bring the Normandy campaign to an end.[37] At the same time Churchill again tried to engage Roosevelt in the debate, proposing the Brittany landings in a telegram that did not mention Eisenhower's 'suggestion'. One of Churchill's arguments was that the Brittany landings would be unopposed compared with those in the south of France. However, by 5 August Eisenhower had apparently changed his mind again (if he had ever changed it in the first place) and remained steadfast in the face of Churchill's attempts over the course of a whole afternoon to persuade him to cancel Anvil. Churchill then wrote a telegram to Hopkins in a further effort to further influence Roosevelt. Hopkins' reply was non-committal while the Joint Chiefs of Staff were firmly against any late change to strategy on the eve of a major operation, which could only lead to the utmost confusion everywhere. The Americans confirmed their position in a paper of 8 August which the British Chiefs of Staff reluctantly accepted at their meeting the following day.

On 12 August, Roosevelt finally relented to Churchill's repeated requests and invited Churchill to Quebec again, where they would meet without Stalin for a conference code-named Octagon in September. The principal matters requiring discussion and decisions were the future of operations in Italy and what part Britain could play in the war against Japan.

On 15 August, the US Seventh Army with three American divisions in the assault landed largely unopposed in southern France between Cannes and the Isle of Hyères after an intense sea and air bombardment of the coast. Seven newly equipped French and one mixed British and US airborne division provided the follow-up forces. Before the Allied landings, the German OKW had considered pulling back the eleven German divisions in southern France to a defensive line closer to the German border, but failed to act. The landings were directly opposed by three German divisions and when the Germans learned that the Allied landings were in considerable force, the units south of the Loire were ordered to withdraw toward Germany. The Allied forces were able to move quickly inland against sporadic resistance amid local uprisings by the French underground, the Maquis. By 11 September, the Seventh Army had linked up with Eisenhower's troops in the north of France but the German divisions retreating before them had also reached the safety of the main German armies in France and Germany.

Churchill claimed that Operation Anvil was too late to assist the Normandy campaign and the diversion of troops from Italy for the landings was responsible for Alexander's next offensive being unable to strike a formidable blow at the Germans and very possibly reach Vienna before the Russians.[38] In a telegram to Smuts later, Churchill was more pointed in this criticism, referring to the opposite outcomes as to what had been intended by the 'abortion' of Operation Anvil. Two and half to three German divisions of the rearguard had been able to join the forces in northern France whilst three other German divisions including a Panzer division had been transferred from the German Italian front line to northern France.[39]

Alexander's armies resumed their offensive against the Gothic Line on 26 August, the day after de Gaulle had triumphantly entered Paris. In terms of future strategies, Churchill was now very much in favour of a drive through the Ljubljana Gap to Vienna, which as well as putting additional pressure on Germany, would forestall any advances by the Russians in the Balkans. Following meetings with the Yugoslav partisan leader Tito on 12 and 13 August when plans for landing in Istria were discussed, Churchill met with Wilson on 21 August in Rome to further discuss the operation and instruct planning to continue. The main driver of the operation was an acknowledgement at last by Churchill and Wilson of the difficulties the mountainous Italian terrain posed for any further overland advance northwards.[40]

Churchill on 28 August telegraphed Roosevelt with his intentions:

I have never forgotten your talks to me at Tehran about Istria, and I am sure the arrival of a powerful army in Trieste and Istria in four or five weeks would have an effect far outside purely military values. Tito's people will be waiting for us in Istria. What the condition of Hungary will be then I cannot imagine but we shall at any rate be in a position to take full advantage of any great new situation.[41]

By reminding Roosevelt of a previous discussion regarding a landing in Istria, Churchill cleverly avoided the plans being dismissed as another one of his peripheral and diversionary operations and put them on the agenda for the upcoming conference in Quebec. However, Roosevelt's reply ignored the subject of Istria altogether.

Far East

After the reverses of 1942 the Americans were making sound progress in their campaign in the Pacific in 1943. General MacArthur's forces in the South West Pacific Area had control of most of New Guinea while Admiral Nimitz in the Pacific had captured the Mariana Islands. However, on 11 July 1944, Marshall, at a meeting of US Joint Chiefs of Staff, stated that it would be necessary to invade the industrial heartland of Japan as blockade and strangulation would take too long to defeat the country. This was accepted by Britain on 29 July with the proviso that any such invasion did not interfere with any operations to defeat Germany first.[42] The British wanted to take a more active part in the Pacific campaign now that the war with Germany was nearly over and Churchill in particular remained anxious to regain the territories of Singapore and Hong Kong. The furore over future strategy in the Far East between Churchill and his Chiefs of Staff had not been forgotten by the Prime Minister, as he reminded them in a minute:

> To sum up, our policy should be to give naval assistance on the largest scale to the main American operations but to keep our own thrust for Dracula [renamed Operation Vanguard] as a preliminary operation or one of the preliminary operations to a major attack on Singapore. Here is the supreme British objective in the whole of the Indian and Far Eastern theatres. It is the only prize that will restore British prestige in the region ...[43]

British manpower was exhausted but a naval fleet could be contributed as the war in the Mediterranean was over and the Italian fleet was now operating with the Royal Navy, although the Russians had claimed a number of warships as reparations after the surrender of Italy. The Americans believed they had adequate resources in the Pacific and did not rush to accept the British offer, stating that they were not keen on having a different fleet with its unique supply problems in the Pacific; the British accordingly offered a fully self-supporting fleet, which was politely acknowledged by the Americans.

Mountbatten's Southeast Asia Command remained the only problematic theatre for Britain and America. Little progress was being made on the ground in northern Burma to open the Burma Road, while the Japanese were still advancing into eastern China. The Japanese drive into India had, however, been halted at Kohima and Imphal. Regarding Burma as a British problem, the Americans announced that the numbers of combat aircraft in the theatre were at their highest and no more would henceforth be sent. The airlift of supplies to the Chinese continued over the Himalayas (the 'Hump') but by September 1944 the receiving airfields in China were being threatened by the Japanese advances in Operation Ichigo. Following the vague orders in the directive of 3 June 1944 from the British Chiefs of Staff to Mountbatten (and approved by the Americans) to give priority to the Chinese airlift and 'to press advantages over the enemy', Mountbatten considered his options with what resources were available in Burma once the sieges of Kohima and Imphal were lifted.[44] Two plans were devised by Mountbatten and submitted to the Chiefs of Staff before he attended a conference in London in early August to discuss them. One plan was to capture Mandalay by means of overland and airborne assaults and the other was an amphibious and airborne assault on Rangoon.[45] Mountbatten did not think an overland offensive all the way to Rangoon could be supplied successfully from India. After considering the plans for two days, the British Chiefs of Staff proposed requesting assistance from the United States for the Rangoon operation as soon as possible. The problem the British had was a lack of resources to conduct the Rangoon landings (Operation Vanguard) as Germany had not yet been defeated and no troops were to be transferred from Europe until this was achieved. In the fierce debate with the Americans over the use of resources for the global war, any resources allocated for the British Mediterranean theatre always came at the expense of the Far East. The Mandalay attack (Operation Champion) was privately regarded as being too difficult by the British in terms of the jungle terrain and disease.[46] Churchill had already again voiced his opposition to such an operation in a minute of 24 July: 'Nothing can be worse than having our armies bogged down in northern Burma and I have no intention whatever of giving way to the US Chiefs of Staff in this matter. The troops are ours and we have the military direction of troops in this theatre.'[47]

The Americans believed that their forces in the region should withdraw to allow the British to reconquer their territory and therefore Marshall in September refused to send any more reinforcements.[48] The United States remained committed to sending aircraft to China for the provision of supplies with the objective of keeping the Chinese in the war. There were no American infantry divisions in the region, only one regiment (Merrill's Marauders). There were, however, already a total of 149,014 American troops manning the lines of communications and the twenty air groups stationed in the India and Burma region.[49] When the US Chiefs of Staff reviewed Mountbatten's proposed plans, they favoured the Mandalay operation as it coincided with other

Pacific operations and would provide a larger buffer zone for Myitkyina and its valuable airfield. In mid August, the British asked if the north Burma operation could be suspended until sufficient forces for the Rangoon operation became available but the Combined Chiefs of Staff urged that the Southeast Asia Command conduct the Mandalay offensive as soon as possible to be followed by the Rangoon operation later in 1945. This predictably did not go down well with Churchill and the strength of his resentment regarding this decision can be seen in the following telegram to the Prime Minister of Canada:

> We are thus committed to a long drawn out struggle in the jungles and the swamps against an enemy who has superior lines of communication to those we possess. The wastage from sickness and disease amounted during the campaign of 1944 up to 30th June alone to 282,000 in addition to a loss of killed, wounded and missing of approximately 40,000. Clearly therefore we should make every effort to liquidate this highly undesirable commitment, if it can by any means be done.[50]

Octagon conference

Churchill and his staff left for Quebec on 5 September to use the same conference facilities that had been used for Quadrant at the Octagon conference, which ran from 12 to 16 September. Roosevelt and Churchill officially met only twice, once to review the progress of the war and the second time to discuss the final report produced by the Combined Chiefs of Staff, which began their meetings the day before the first plenary meeting on 13 September. The Combined Chiefs of Staff only met five times and, unlike the mutual suspicions and hostility between the British and Americans which characterised the Trident and Quadrant conferences, Octagon was relatively harmonious. It was believed that Germany was close to collapse and victory was possible before the end of the year.

The most significant military issue to be resolved at the conference was again regarding the campaign in Italy. Two other outstanding issues of secondary importance were Burma and the role British forces would play in the Pacific. Churchill opened the first plenary session by stating that everything that the Allies had touched had turned to gold and there had been an unbroken run of military successes over the previous seven weeks. The Americans were congratulated somewhat sarcastically by Churchill on Operation Dragoon having cleared large parts of south and west France; Roosevelt was alert to this sarcasm and reminded Churchill that Stalin deserved some of the credit – a reference to the fact that the Americans had to threaten to raise the subject with Stalin to overcome British intransigence toward the operation. Future operations from Italy were then raised by Churchill who, again on the basis of not wanting armies idle for any length of time and looking for 'fresh fields and pastures new', proposed operations towards Vienna and, failing that, Trieste. Churchill then wasted no time in seeking an answer on the contentious issue of a British fleet and directly offered Roosevelt a fleet for the main operations against Japan. Roosevelt accepted the offer without any other detail as to when or where.

The issues regarding the European theatres were quickly dealt with by the Combined Chiefs of Staff in the first two days. As the American units that had been withdrawn from Italy for Anvil had weakened the Allied armies in Italy, the British were extremely concerned to know if the US Fifth Army (of four infantry and one armoured divisions) would be withdrawn for use in the north-west European campaign or whether it was available for future operations in Italy once the River Po basin was reached, which might include a drive to Vienna when the Italian forces in Germany were destroyed. Marshall had previously indicated that if the Italian front bogged down again, the Fifth Army would be better employed in France.[51]

The final report of the Chiefs to Roosevelt and Churchill stated that it had been agreed not to move the Fifth Army before the results of Alexander's current offensive in Italy were known and Wilson could retain the landing craft that had been used in Operation Anvil for future amphibious landings such as in Istria if required, provided the plans were submitted before 10 October as the landing craft had been allocated to the Far East. Eisenhower was to assume command of Italy over Wilson. In north-west Europe, Eisenhower's proposed northern thrust was approved by the Combined Chiefs of Staff into Germany through the Ruhr Valley, Operation Market Garden and Arnhem being the first operation. The Supreme Allied Commander was also directed to open the ports of Rotterdam and Antwerp before the weather worsened.

The majority of the conference discussions were taken up by the war against Japan with regard to future operations in the Far East and the Pacific. The two on again/off again operations in Burma had been renamed after the British believed they might have been compromised. Operation Vanguard, the amphibious assault on Rangoon, was renamed Operation Dracula while the overland Operation Champion was redesignated Operation Capital. At the opening session of the conference, Churchill had admitted that the contribution of the British Empire was at a peak whereas that of its ally was ever increasing.[52] With the war against Germany still in progress, Britain had no more troops to spare for Burma. Therefore Churchill wanted to only use the minimum force for Operation Capital so as to have maximum strength for Operation Dracula if this was to be mounted on 15 March before the onset of the monsoon season. The British requested two light infantry divisions from Marshall, who later politely refused. Churchill warned of the consequences if Operation Dracula was not executed as planned, which would leave British troops exposed to unnecessary sacrifices and being ravaged by disease in northern Burma.[53] The final offensives approved by Churchill and Roosevelt for Burma were remarkably similar to those of previous conferences. The Rangoon amphibious assault was to take place before 15 March 1945. The overland offensive in northern Burma was to be carried out so as ensure the security of Myitkyina and the air supply route to China. If Operation Dracula was not undertaken, Operation Capital was to proceed regardless. Regarding the question of the participation of a British fleet in the Pacific campaign as being purely political, Admiral King was initially strongly opposed to the idea but was eventually persuaded by the other Chiefs of Staff as Roosevelt had already accepted Churchill's offer of the fleet in the first plenary session. King resented sharing the glory of success with the British, believing the US Navy could do the job alone and that the Royal Navy was 'a liability'. It was agreed in principle that a self-supporting, balanced fleet was to be provided by the British without any specific tasks being set for it, something that was to be studied later.[54]

A directive was duly issued to Mountbatten by the Combined Chiefs of Staff on 16 September for the two operations in Burma. However, Operation Dracula was then postponed on 2 October 1944 at a staff conference by Churchill to after the next monsoon (the end of October) in 1945 as the war was continuing in Europe because of the continued strong German resistance and there were insufficient LSTs under British control in Italy for the operation without having to go cap in hand to the Americans. A suggestion of withdrawing three divisions from the fighting in France was not approved by Montgomery and two Indian divisions could not be spared from Italy either.[55] The US Joint Chiefs of Staff were informed of this decision on 5 October. One of the last acts of Octagon by Roosevelt and Churchill was to approve and sign the Morgenthau Plan for a demilitarised and de-industrialised post-war Germany which would virtually reduce it to an agrarian economy. In view of the warnings about the threat to the security of Western Europe from Russia, this was short-sighted of Churchill, who later denounced the plan, as did Roosevelt, when it leaked into the press. Roosevelt and Morgenthau may have used Britain's financial debt to the United States as leverage in their discussions beforehand with Churchill in order to gain his initial approval of the plan.

After the Octagon conference, Churchill met again with his Mediterranean commanders on 8 October in Naples on his way to another meeting with Stalin in Moscow in order to brief him on the decisions taken in Quebec. Roosevelt was unable to travel because of the upcoming presidential elections. As this was two days before the deadline for the submission of plans for the use of landing craft in the Mediterranean before their transfer to the Far East was to begin, Wilson was instructed to send his plans for Istria to the Combined Chiefs of Staff in Washington. This was despite Churchill having been advised the day before that no landings were possible before the early spring of 1945.[56] As the October offensive by Alexander had once again bogged down in the face of renewed German resistance and bad weather, he was not keen to see more of his divisions diverted to other operations and asked for three extra divisions to be sent to Italy. After listening to Alexander, Churchill replied that in a message to Roosevelt he would blame the stalemate in Italy on the lack of two divisions and would request two or three extra American divisions to be sent; this message was duly sent on 10 October whilst Wilson forwarded his plans for a landing in Trieste for some time in February.[57]

Roosevelt's response of 16 October was an unequivocal refusal to divert American reinforcements on their way to France to Italy as the battle in Germany was the main effort. This was considered at the Chiefs of Staff meeting of the 21st and Wilson was instructed to prepare plans for a smaller, hopefully unopposed, landing of one division south of Fiume before advancing north along the Dalmatian coast. The revised plans (Operation Sunstar) were sent by Wilson on 24 October with a February target date, which concerned Churchill as relations with Tito had started to deteriorate as the Russian advance westwards neared the Balkans and Churchill believed the Partisans might occupy Trieste first.

The US Joint Chiefs of Staff unusually took their time replying and it was not until 17 November that they indicated that they were not in favour of Wilson's proposals. This setback to Churchill's plans was considered at the Chiefs of Staff meeting on 20 November, when it was decided that the withdrawal of units for Operation Sunstar would endanger the Italian front and therefore Wilson should be urged to continue winter operations in Italy.[58] The Ljubljana Gap to Vienna strategy favoured by Churchill was now also defunct.

The German Army in Italy did not withdraw to the Alps as anticipated and with the onset of winter, the Italian campaign once more settled into a stalemate in the northern Apennines short of the Po Valley.

Victory in the Far East

Phase two of the Japanese Operation Ichigo began at the end of August with the 11th Army driving southwards down the railway from Heng-Yang and the 23rd Army northwards from Canton. The important air base at Kweilin was captured on 10 November and Liuchow a day later. As well as threatening to halt the Himalayan air supply route, Ichigo removed all American hopes of using Chinese air bases to bomb Japan and the American B-29 forces were redeployed to the newly captured Saipan in the Marianas. This development, along along with Russia's anticipated entry into the war against Japan, further reduced the importance of the Chinese as an ally to both the British and the Americans. In December 1944, two Chinese divisions from Stillwell's army in Burma had to be sent back to China, despite Mountbatten's protests, to defend Chungking, Chiang Kai-Shek's capital, and Kunming, the destination airfield for the airlift of supplies.

Mountbatten met with Churchill, who was on his way to Moscow, on 20 October and potential future operations and their difficulties were discussed. As a result, Dracula was postponed again to December 1945 but the advance from north Burma, Operation Capital, was ordered to proceed as soon as possible as directed at Octagon by the Combined Chiefs of Staff.[59] As this offensive had been postponed or cancelled so many times, Churchill could no longer delay this offensive which was an obligation to the Americans as they were providing so much support in the European theatre.

Following the defeat of the Japanese forces besieging Imphal and Kohima, two separate British corps began a pursuit of the weakened Japanese forces, which were soon forced to pull back to a line behind the Irrawaddy River from Indaw to Mandalay, vacating most of Burma. The overextended Japanese forces had suffered high casualties in the battles at Kohima and Imphal and also were badly afflicted by disease and starvation. The Allies had air superiority and were able to deploy tanks in their advance, the Japanese having few tanks and anti-tank weapons. The British were able to establish bridgeheads over the Chindwin River at Kalewa and Sittaung, although the supply of these advanced troops was a major problem compounded by the monsoon and sickness. Mountbatten gave his directive to the British forces in Burma on 19 November for Operation Capital, which could not begin until the monsoon had ended. The operation was launched from the bridgeheads across the Chindwin River into north-east Burma towards Mandalay on 29 November 1944. The objectives were to clear the Japanese forces from northern Burma, reopen the Burma Road supply route to China and tie down the Japanese forces to prevent their transfer to the Pacific theatre. A follow-up attack by a second army corps from Kalewa on 4 December found that the Japanese had largely withdrawn back across the Irrawaddy River, which necessitated the plan to be revised. On 16 December, General Slim's Fourteenth Army linked up for the first time with Stilwell's army at Indaw which had been captured the week before by the British 36th Division placed under Stilwell's command to augment the weak Chinese forces. Stilwell had in the meantime been recalled to Washington due to differences between himself and Chiang Kai-Shek but the operations of his army continued; on 28 January 1945, the Burma Road was finally reopened to vehicles when the Ledo Road link through Myitkyina was finished.

At the Yalta conference in early 1945, a directive was given to Mountbatten to liberate Burma at the earliest date.[60] The war against Japan was expected to last another eighteen months after the defeat of Germany and would require an invasion of Japan itself which was not an attractive prospect given the fanatical Japanese defence of the Mariana Islands.

The next British offensive, Operation Capital Extended, was renewed on 14 January 1945. During February and March, the Fourteenth Army fought a major battle in central Burma and finally captured Mandalay on 20 March, shattering the Japanese forces and compelling them to retreat into the Shan states of Burma and Thailand. Slim ordered his forces to exploit their victory by advancing south along the Irrawaddy River and Sittang River valleys towards Rangoon. In April, the Indian IV Corps, spearheaded by an armoured brigade, advanced almost 200 miles southwards and reached Pegu, which was only 40 miles north of Rangoon, by the end of the month.

However, with overland supply lines strained to the limit by the rapid advances and the monsoon imminent which would make most roads impassable and supplies by air difficult, Slim asked for Operation Dracula to be reinstated and to take place before the monsoon began in early May. On 2 April, Mountbatten issued the appropriate orders for Rangoon to be captured by an amphibious landing not later than 5 May. The Japanese evacuated Rangoon after fighting a rearguard action at Pegu and the city was occupied on 2 May 1945 by an Indian division that was successfully put ashore by landing craft. Thus after two years of prevarication and the failed Arakan campaign of 1943, the British were able to recapture Burma, largely by an overland campaign which Churchill had always militated against. However, since 1942, there had been significant developments in the Burma campaign. The Japanese forces in 1944 were overextended and poorly supplied in contrast to the British forces. Actions elsewhere in the Pacific theatre had disrupted the movement of replacement troops for the Japanese divisions in Burma, which were short of 40,000 men.[61] The achievement of aerial supremacy in Burmese skies by the RAF based in India allowed troops to be resupplied by air drops and Japanese lines of communication to be bombed and harassed at will. By waiting until the Japanese forces had withered on the vine because of the actions of the Americans in the Pacific, the British arguably achieved victory with the minimum of casualties. However, this was not a deliberate strategy of Churchill's and he had remained steadfastly opposed to all operations in the jungle, despite the obligations to America to open the Burma Road. Churchill had been opposed to even undertaking Operation Capital in late 1944 and only agreed to it on the basis of having postponed previous plans so many times there was no longer any excuse to remain on the defensive.

Churchill's Second Moscow Visit

The advance of the Soviet armies into Eastern Europe was raising concerns in the Foreign Office and War Cabinet about the likely post-war political situation. Communists were playing a large part in the organised resistance to German occupation of Italy, Rumania, Yugoslavia, Greece and Bulgaria. On 4 May 1944, Churchill had asked for a paper to be prepared for the War Cabinet about British options to restore the Greek government in Greece. The previous month, on 6 April, Greek troops in Cairo had mutinied and declared their loyalty to a rival Communist Committee of National Liberation in the Greek mountains that was in opposition to the Greek government-in-exile in Egypt. The crew of a Greek destroyer at Alexandria had followed suit. Following the almost bloodless resolution of the mutiny, Eden suggested to the Soviet Ambassador that the Soviet Union should regard Rumania as mainly their concern while the situation in Greece could be left to Britain.

This was agreed to by Stalin and the proposed plan was put to Roosevelt for his blessing. After some correspondence with Churchill, Roosevelt reluctantly approved this measure temporarily but warned of the dangers of creating post-war spheres of influence. In communications with the British, Stalin was careful that all decisions were approved by the US as well. The Greek situation continued to worsen as the Germans increasingly looked like vacating Greece and the negotiations between the Greek king and the communists did not go smoothly as the communists manoeuvred for political power without any elections. Churchill minuted on 6 August regarding the possible future need to send British troops to Greece to support the incumbent government. In his view, the Greek people had to be given the opportunity to decide between the incumbent monarchy or a republic in a future plebiscite.

With the August Warsaw uprising in mind and following the Octagon meetings in Quebec, Churchill offered on 27 September to go to Moscow again in order to brief Stalin on the latest Anglo-American decisions and to try to find a solution to the Polish problem; Stalin accepted this suggestion and invited Churchill three days later. Churchill told a Cabinet Secretary that the only reason he was going was to reassure Russia that, despite the second Quebec conference, Britain and America still regarded Russia as an important ally and were not excluding it from their plans.[62] Churchill, Eden, Brooke and Ismay arrived on 9 October in Moscow and Churchill and Eden met with Stalin and Molotov that night. Churchill wasted no time in bringing up the question of Poland, suggesting that a meeting take place between London-based representatives of the government-in-exile and the de facto government set up by the Russians, the Lublin Committee. Stalin agreed to this and the discussion moved on to the armistice terms for Germany's allies. Churchill added Greece to the countries for discussion because of its importance to the British and reminded Stalin of the informal arrangement already in place between the Soviet Union and Britain for the affairs of Greece and Rumania. Then in a quite remarkable incident, Churchill wrote on a piece of paper the suggested percentages of predominance in the affairs of each country post-war that Britain and the Soviet Union should have.[63] Churchill called this a 'naughty' document and showed it to Stalin, who approved it with a tick of a blue pen. The top two countries on the list made by Churchill were Rumania and Greece and thus in order for the British to secure a continuation of their free hand in Greece, Churchill was forced to do the same for Stalin over Rumania. In a matter of minutes, the post-war fate of the other Eastern European countries was decided, although the Red Army would make any percentages meaningless in countries which it overran. Churchill was well aware of how this crude diplomacy would be regarded in the future and suggested the paper be burnt but Stalin asked Churchill to keep it. Unable to destroy the evidence, Churchill attempted to explain it in a telegram to the War Cabinet, although there is no record of any subsequent discussion. No reference was made to it either in a statement Churchill gave to the House of Commons on 27 October on his return to England.

Following the arrival of the London Polish representatives, the talks between the parties to the Polish dispute began on 13 October and quickly reached an impasse. Molotov became frustrated at the stance adopted by the London Poles over the proposed redrawing of the eastern boundary and let it slip that Roosevelt supported Stalin's demands. This was news to both Churchill and Harriman and a considerable shock to the Poles, who had been assured by Roosevelt in discussions in Washington as late as June 1944 that the USA had not agreed to any settlement.[64] Later that day Churchill, Eden and Harriman met with Stalin and the representatives of the Lublin government, and Churchill learned first-hand from Stalin of the private agreement with Roosevelt that had been kept secret in order not to lose the votes of Polish voters in America. The London Poles obstinately clung to their demands for the pre-war frontiers and Churchill became increasingly exasperated, alternately cajoling and pleading for them to accept what was being offered as the best deal they would get. Churchill sent a telegram to Roosevelt on 18 October summarising the progress of the Moscow visit and politely pointed out that he now knew of Roosevelt's pact with Stalin.[65] Roosevelt promptly replied, asking that no announcement be made for about two weeks for reasons Churchill 'would understand'. The US presidential elections were to be held on 7 November and Roosevelt would leave no stone unturned to help his re-election. One of Roosevelt's special emissaries, James Earle, who had been working in the Balkans, had returned to Washington in May 1944 and tried to convince Roosevelt that the Russians were responsible for the Katyn massacre. Roosevelt would have none of it and when Earle sought permission to publish his views in March 1945 he found himself swiftly posted to Samoa.[66] It would take until 1990 for the Russians to finally admit responsibility for this war crime.

Not surprisingly in this atmosphere of betrayal, the Polish talks duly foundered on the proposed boundary between Russia and Poland and the future power-sharing arrangements of any new government. One positive outcome of the visit was, however, the Soviet confirmation of their intention to enter the war against Japan three or four months after the defeat of Germany following the build-up of forces and supplies in the region.

RACE TO BERLIN/TUBE ALLOYS

With the appointment of Eisenhower as the Supreme Commander of the Allied Expeditionary Force in Europe, the strategic decisions for the rest of the war in Europe were largely devolved from Churchill and Roosevelt to the general. Eisenhower, of course, still obeyed the directions of the Combined Chiefs of Staff who approved his operational plans but few grand strategic decisions remained to be taken. For the Allies, there was the knowledge that they were going to win the war and the only uncertainty was as to when.

Following the destruction of the German Seventh Army in Normandy, the Allies slowly pursued the remnants of the shattered divisions that managed to retreat across the River Seine and reorganise into the semblance of an army. The British continued their thrusts towards the north of Holland while Patton's forces drove across France towards Germany. The rapid advance created supply issues for the Allies; Eisenhower could afford to give supplies to either Montgomery or Patton but not both. Montgomery came up with an uncharacteristic audacious plan to seize the bridges over the Rhine in Holland, and thereby bypass the much vaunted defences of the German Siegfried Line to enter Germany through the Ruhr Valley, hastening the end of the war. Operations in Holland would also have the added benefit of destroying many of the V-1 launch sites. Much to Patton's dismay, the British plan was approved but the airborne Operation Market proved to be 'a bridge too far' when the ground forces in Operation Garden were unable to link up with the British paratroops dropped to seize the last bridge over the Rhine at Arnhem; the paratroops were forced to withdraw with heavy losses back across the river. Churchill was not dismayed by this outcome or the ensuing criticism of Montgomery; as he said in a telegram to General Smuts, 'The battle was a decided victory, but the leading division, asking, quite rightly, for more, had a chop. I have sustained any feeling of disappointment over this and I am glad our commanders are capable of running this kind of risk.'[1]

The Allies were still lacking a major port close to the operations in north-west Europe, and following the failure to seize the Rhine bridges a rapid end to the war was no longer in sight. After their liberation in the controversial Operation Dragoon, Marseille and Toulon in southern France became the main ports for the flow of American reinforcements into the battle. By the end of the campaign, more than a third of American supplies had come through these two ports. Plans were made for the capture of the port of Antwerp, which was in Montgomery's British 21st Army Group area of operations; responsibility for the mission was given to the First Canadian Army. Antwerp was liberated on 4 September, the day after the liberation of Brussels, but the port was unusable as it was still in range of German artillery in the River Scheldt estuary.

The launching of Operation Market Garden had allowed the German defenders around the Scheldt time to build their defences. After a campaign dogged by bad weather, stiff German resistance and the German flooding of the estuary which channelled the advance along particular well-defended roads, the estuary was finally cleared on 8 November 1944, allowing the port of Antwerp to become operational.

Eisenhower ordered two of the Allied armies in north-west Europe to make two thrusts against Germany, directing First US Army (FUSA) in the north against Aachen and the Third Army in the south through the Alsace region. Aachen was not entered until 20 October and the Americans lamented that had they been given priority earlier instead of the 21st Army Group, they could have walked into the city in September.[2] From Aachen, the first city in Germany to be captured, FUSA then had to advance in atrocious weather through the Hürtgen Forest, which provided many suitable positions for defence and to ambush the Americans. On 8 November, Patton's Third Army began its offensive in appalling weather towards the Saar region and the city of Metz after having carefully husbanded and built up its supplies for the preceding two months. After experiencing difficulties crossing the swollen Moselle River, the advance of Patton's army was checked at Metz by a series of fortifications and strongpoints that proved difficult to eliminate and it was not until 21 November that the city surrendered, although some fortifications continued to hold out for several more days. With the onset of winter, it became clear that the war was not going to end by Christmas as some had forecast, much to the disappointment of many people:

> Germany it seems will not be defeated this year and the end of the war may not come until the summer of 1945. It is a bitter disappointment for all of us that this conflict should be prolonged when we all expected an ending in the autumn of this year.[3]

On 12 December, Eisenhower discussed his plans for the continued advance into Germany with Churchill and the Chiefs of Staff. The first phase of his plans was an advance to the Rhine and the second phase an advance into the heart of Germany after crossing the river. In the second phase, two thrusts were to be made into Germany, the main one to the north by Montgomery and the other to the south by the Americans. Brooke urged that one thrust be made the main attack with the other relegated to the supporting role.[4]

After D-Day, attacks by the Allied strategic air forces had resumed on Germany; its economy, until then surprisingly resilient, went into a dramatic decline in the second half of 1944, having reached a tipping point where damage could no longer be repaired. Heavy bombers began an offensive on 8 June against oil facilities and synthetic oil-producing plants. In August, the Russians occupied Rumania and cut off supply from the Ploesti oil fields. Oil was the Achilles heel of the German war economy and this action produced rapid results; by the end of June, German aviation fuel output had been cut by 90 per cent. Fuel shortages affected everything from training flights for new pilots to the movement of Panzer divisions. The attacks on the synthetic oil plants also curtailed the production of nitrogen and methanol, which caused a precipitate decline in the production of explosives. The synthetic rubber industry also suffered from the attacks on oil facilities. In the second half of 1944, 481,400 tons of bombs were dropped on Germany as compared with 150,700 tons in all of 1943.[5] The production of most other weapons such as U-boats and tanks was similarly affected. Despite the attentions of the Allied bombers in Operation Pointblank, German aircraft production actually doubled from December 1943 to July 1944, by which time more planes were being turned out than could be supplied with fuel and brought into action at the front. German monthly fighter production peaked at 3,375 planes in September 1944, then declined gradually until by January 1945 production had virtually stopped except on the new jet fighters because of the fuel shortage.[6] In conjunction with the damage to the military and industrial facilities, the civilian economy also broke down because of the disruption to transport systems. Goods could not be distributed from the factories as the transport infrastructure was destroyed and there was a shortage of coal for both domestic heating and to power factories. The Allied bomber offensive was finally reaping its rewards and had brought the German military machine to its knees.

British Greek Operation

Having readied a force for an expedition to Greece to forestall any moves by the EAM and ELAS communist guerrilla groups to seize power when the Germans left, the force was deployed on 14 October and British paratroops landed on an airfield outside Athens and proceeded to occupy the city. The rest of the British troops arrived by boat to a joyous welcome from Athenians and on 16 October the Greek government returned from exile, having been waiting nearby in Italy, where a peace agreement had been signed with the communists. However, there were shortages of food and as the Germans had destroyed many railways and roads as they withdrew, civil discontent and unrest quickly developed. With the limited British force unable to patrol the whole country, it was feared that the communist groups would try to take power by force and plans were made by the Greek government to disarm the guerrillas, which had been originally armed by the British to fight the Germans or had seized weapons from the Italians on their surrender. A demonstration on 3 December turned violent and the British ordered the communists to leave Athens and Piraeus, only for them to try to seize power in Athens by occupying police stations and government offices. On 5 December, Churchill, after discussions with Eden (but not the War Cabinet), authorised the British troops to restore order in Athens by any reasonable means and prevent communist reinforcements arriving in the city. If Churchill could not prevent Eastern Europe falling under Russian influence, he was determined to at least save Greece. The British, having reinforced Greece in 1941 to deter a German invasion and only succeeding in precipitating just such an action which saw the Greeks suffer under the subsequent German occupation for three years, were then firing on the Greeks on their return. The departure of the Germans from Greece did not bring relief or aid, only more bloodshed. There was a furious reaction from the western press, both in Britain and particularly in America, where some newspapers declared that the British action in Greece

falsified the cause for which America went to war and had violated the principles of the Atlantic Charter. *The Times* newspaper in England in particular
led the criticism of the British policy in Greece. The public opposition to
America's involvement in the war before Pearl Harbor reappeared, more for-
cibly than ever.

The new American Secretary of State, Edward Stettinius, issued a press
release on Italy that was widely seen as also referring to British actions in
Greece, containing a sentence to the effect that the US expected foreign governments to resolve their issues democratically, particularly in the liberated
territories of the United Nations governments.[7] A British naval reservist commented in a letter to his wife:

> What an awful business this is in Greece, isn't it? And Mr Stettinius getting
> cross with England ... As for the Greeks, it's a pity ... I can think of nothing
> more annoying than to be killed fighting the people we have liberated.[8]

Significantly, amidst this furore, not one negative comment came from the
Russians, who were no doubt enjoying the discomfort of the British caused by
the communists in Greece, being secure in the bargain struck by Churchill and
Stalin in Moscow in October.[9] Other English socialist supporters expressed
their dismay privately:

> The situation in Greece is not at all pleasing at the moment. I take an
> extremely bad view of the use of British troops to quell them both. In
> my opinion, it is quite obvious Churchill won't tolerate the idea of a Left
> government anywhere when the whole of Europe seems to be moving to
> the Left.[10]

As a result of the situation in Greece, Churchill faced another no-confidence
motion in the House of Commons on 8 December, which in a telegram
to Roosevelt he blamed on Stettinius' press release; Churchill offered to
resign but the motion was again soundly defeated by 279 votes to 30. In the
Mediterranean, American landing craft involved in the transport of supplies to Greece were ordered not to participate in the operation by Admiral
King, without Roosevelt's knowledge. Churchill was infuriated by the lack
of American support and fired off a telegram to Hopkins warning that he
saw 'signs of our drifting apart', knowing that Roosevelt was likely to see it.
American public opinion was then further inflamed by the leaking to the press

by the State Department of the telegram from Churchill on 5 December to Wilson urging action in Athens after it was mistakenly sent to the Americans. Roosevelt, on holiday at Warm Springs, informed Churchill in a telegram drafted by the State Department that he could not support the British action because of the weight of public opinion in America but hoped the situation could be rectified so that he could stand with Churchill 'shoulder to shoulder' in the future. In perhaps his most difficult telegram of the war to Roosevelt, Churchill's response complained of American ambivalence: 'The fact you are supposed to be against us, in accordance with the last sentence of Stettinius' press release, as I feared, has added to our difficulties and burdens.'[11]

The British action in Greece saw Anglo-American relations reach their lowest point in the war. While Churchill was gravely concerned at both the lack of American support and criticism of British policy, with Roosevelt away it was largely the State Department that was leading the American disapproval. Nevertheless, this was another occasion when Roosevelt did not support Churchill and this episode served to confirm that Britain was now the junior partner in the alliance.

On 16 December, the Germans launched a major counter-attack straight at the weaker centre of Eisenhower's forces through the Ardennes region, which they had previously advanced through in 1940. The German intentions were to recapture the port of Antwerp after splitting the Allied armies into two and then destroy each part separately. The first essential objective was to capture the bridges over the River Meuse for the advancing Panzer divisions to use. The Germans had been able to amass Panzer and infantry divisions for the attack without the knowledge of Allied Intelligence units or code-breaking departments; preparations had also included the construction of a new rail spur to the assembly areas which went unnoticed by Allied photo reconnaissance. The Germans were at last suspicious that their signal communications were being intercepted and therefore all messages and instructions for the counter-attack were delivered by hand, making the Allied surprise complete. Two Panzer armies fell on the four American infantry divisions of VIII Corps defending a 135km front line in the Ardennes sector in what became known as the Battle of the Bulge. The Germans made steady but not spectacular progress and the Americans managed to hold the important road hub at Bastogne, which was surrounded just after reinforcements from the 101st Airborne Division arrived by road. Some elements of the American 99th Division, a green unit, put up valuable resistance but more than 7,000 men from the 106th Division were taken prisoner after being in action for only five days – one of the largest

American capitulations of the war. Churchill suggested that Montgomery command all forces north of the Ardennes and Bradley the south so as to better co-ordinate the Allied response to the German attack, which was agreed to by Eisenhower on 20 December. This was something Montgomery had been after for the past two months.

As the fighting intensified in the Ardennes, Churchill, suitably embarrassed by his leaked telegram, flew to Athens in the early hours of Christmas Day in order to facilitate talks between the Greek protagonists in the civil war. Churchill needed to resolve the problems he had a major part in creating as quickly as possible in order to rehabilitate Anglo-American relations. The fighting in the Ardennes no doubt provided a welcome distraction for the American press from the events in Greece.

After progress was made in Athens over the course of three days of talks, Churchill flew back to England. There, in further talks, the exiled Greek King, who had refused to return until the Greek people held a plebiscite to decide whether they wanted a republic or a monarchy, agreed to make an archbishop the Regent of Greece in order to give the Regent the authority to negotiate a peace and form a Greek government until elections could be held. The archbishop was not a supporter of the communists and Churchill was confident they would be excluded from any provisional government. The communists committed to a ceasefire on 4 January and an uneasy truce persisted for a year; more than 200 British soldiers and more than 2,000 Greeks were killed in the fighting. In 1946, a civil war broke out again between the government and communists which lasted for three years until eventually defeated by the government. This post-war instability required the presence of British troops until 1950, although they did not take part in any active operations after the end of the Second World War.

Bad weather in the Ardennes had grounded Allied aircraft since the start of the German offensive and this cleared on Christmas Day; many Allied fighter-bombers were able to take to the air and wreak havoc on the supply columns of the Panzer divisions. The German offensive then lost impetus when the armoured spearheads were deprived of fuel following the disruption of their supply lines and being unable to find Allied fuel dumps. There were insufficient reserves of fuel to support the operation because of the damage to fuel production by Allied bombers and the offensive had relied on capturing Allied fuel supplies. Many tanks had to be abandoned and their crews returned to their start lines on foot. A relief force from Patton's Third Army reached Bastogne on 27 December and Montgomery's delayed counter-attack began on 3 January. Following a critical letter from Montgomery on 29 December, Eisenhower had drafted a letter demanding Montgomery be replaced or he would resign. Churchill and Brooke went to meet first with Eisenhower on 3 January and then Montgomery before leaving on 5 January after having made Eisenhower reconsider. The same day, Moscow officially recognised the Lublin Committee as the National Government of Poland, much to the disappointment of Churchill and Roosevelt. Roosevelt had been corresponding with Stalin following the Dumbarton Oaks conference to resolve issues regarding the proposed United Nations and took the opportunity to express his disappointment to Stalin over Poland.

There had already been complaints in the US press about the minor contribution of the British forces in defeating the German attack in the Ardennes and Churchill cabled Roosevelt on 6 January expressing support for Eisenhower and praising the gallantry of the American forces. Then, at an ill-judged press conference on 7 January, Montgomery implied he had been running the Ardennes battle and the British troops had made a massive contribution. Although the text was innocuous and had been cleared by Churchill and Brooke, Montgomery's presentation was disastrous. In the ensuing uproar, Churchill was forced to make a statement in Parliament that it had been an American battle, but Anglo-American relations were further damaged. A soothing, congratulatory telegram was sent to Bradley by Churchill, who was privately distressed at the timing of this controversy as it overshadowed the Germans' defeat at the same time he was trying to convince Roosevelt to meet him at Malta on the way to Yalta for another meeting with Stalin.

Even as the Ardennes offensive was petering out, the Combined Chiefs of Staff were pondering their next operations. Hitler, as he had done in Normandy with the failure of Operation Luttich, had left much of his army in the west where they could be engaged by the Allies rather than withdrawing across the River Rhine, the next natural line of defence. In order to co-ordinate actions with Russia, Churchill cabled Stalin on 6 January enquiring as to when the next Soviet offensive would begin. Stalin's reply was to the effect that the Red Army had decided to accelerate its next offensive to no later than mid January in order to assist the fighting in the west. Eisenhower planned a series of advances to destroy all German forces in the west before crossing the Rhine and moving deeper into Germany by means of two thrusts. The British doubted there were sufficient resources to mount both offensives and wanted priority to be given to the offensive by Montgomery's 21st Army Group to the north. Meanwhile, on 22 January, the Russian advance reached the River Oder, the proposed new western boundary of Poland, and crossed into Germany itself.

Yalta

In a gloomy review of the war in December, Churchill had asked for another meeting with Roosevelt, who claimed he did not feel a similar need and indeed thought the war was going according to plan, there being no more broad questions of strategy to be discussed. Roosevelt had been trying to organise a meeting of all three Allied leaders for six months and was a little put out that Churchill had met Stalin in Moscow again. Preferring to wait until after his inauguration and with Stalin insisting on meeting in the Crimea, in late December Roosevelt finally got agreement on another meeting of the three Allied leaders (to be code-named Argonaut) for early February at Yalta to discuss Poland, post-war Germany and the future United Nations organisation.

Roosevelt and Churchill and their respective Chiefs of Staff met at Malta for a few days of preliminary talks before going on to Yalta in the Crimea. Roosevelt had initially declined to meet with Churchill so as not to be seen to be ganging up against Stalin. The Combined Chiefs of Staff also met several times and at their meeting on 1 February, a row broke out between Marshall and Brooke over the relative merits of Eisenhower and Montgomery. Marshall had met with Eisenhower on his way to Malta and heard Eisenhower's opinion of Montgomery plus how Churchill and Brooke kept trying to influence his plans. At a closed session, Marshall let rip and frankly expressed long pent-up frustrations with Montgomery and the British way of determining strategy.[12] Brooke naturally defended his protégé, Montgomery, and initially refused to approve Eisenhower's plans, but did so later.

The Yalta conference, held from 4–11 February 1945, was largely a political meeting with only one strategic military decision made. As this was only the second meeting of the Big Three powers, the official discussions between Roosevelt, Churchill and Stalin were dominated by the issues of the post-war dismemberment and occupation of Germany, reparations for the Allies and the problem of Poland. Talks on the structure and voting rights of the proposed United Nations were also continued from the meeting at Dumbarton Oaks the previous year following the Moscow declaration of 1943 regarding the creation of such a world body by the four major powers of Britain, the USA, the Soviet Union and China. However, China was not represented at Yalta and any discussion of the Far East is notably absent from the minutes of the conference plenary sessions. Stalin only agreed to the United Nations when two Russian republics, the Ukraine and White Russia, were added to the list of original members, thereby ensuring more votes for Russia. Regarding Poland, Churchill agreed to potential new members of the Polish government being vetted in all practicality by Moscow prior to free elections being held and the eastern boundary of Poland was settled as the Curzon Line. Stalin backed up Russian diplomacy by reminding the conference participants that the Red Army was fielding 180 divisions against an estimated eighty German divisions and enquired as to how many the Allies had in the battle. The reply from Marshall was that seventy-eight Allied divisions were fighting seventy-nine German divisions.

The most significant military talks were between Stalin and Roosevelt on 8 February on the conditions under which the Soviet Union would enter the war against Japan. Churchill and Stalin in Moscow in October 1944 had previously discussed the timing of the Soviet entry into the war against Japan, which would be two or three months after Germany had surrendered. The Soviets had then supplied their political and military demands for entry through Harriman on 15 December.[13] Roosevelt requested beforehand that only he and Stalin discuss these conditions while Churchill was merely to be kept informed. Stalin asked for the southern portion of Sakhalin Island to be returned to Russia along with the Kurile Islands plus a lease of a warm water port at Port Arthur. As there had to be something for the Soviet people's national interests, Stalin also demanded transit rights through Manchuria along with the use of the Chinese eastern railways through Manchuria to the ports. After Roosevelt responded that the Chinese would need to be consulted, Stalin demanded a written agreement signed by the Big Three before they left Yalta, to which Roosevelt agreed. This was all done without the involvement or approval of the Chinese, who were later persuaded by the Americans to accept the terms as the price of Soviet participation in the war against Japan.

The Combined Chiefs of Staff considered Eisenhower's plans for the final offensive against Germany which had already been discussed with the British. The plan, as before, was to destroy as many German forces possible west of the River Rhine, establish two bridgeheads over the river and then advance into Germany with two thrusts, the main one being the British thrust to the north of the Ruhr while an American thrust further south towards Frankfurt and Kassel would have the primary objective of drawing forces away from the northern thrust.[14] This was discussed and agreed at the Combined Chiefs of Staff meeting on 30 January; Brooke, having again pointed out that there was not sufficient strength for two major operations, wanted Montgomery to seize a Rhine crossing as quickly as possible without waiting for the Americans to close up along the length of the river further south.[15] Berlin was not mentioned and this plan was incorporated into the final report presented to Roosevelt and Churchill.[16]

Regarding the Italian theatre, prior to the Yalta conference, the British Chiefs of Staff had approved at their meeting in Malta on 30 January the transfer of three divisions to Eisenhower for the battle in Germany with a further three more when the situation in Greece would allow. Churchill had reluctantly previously conceded at a staff conference on 23 January that there was no longer a possibility of an advance from Italy to Vienna – a 'right-handed thrust into the armpit of the Adriatic' – and therefore the importance of the Italian theatre was greatly reduced.[17] The transfer of three divisions and two fighter groups from the Mediterranean theatre was also confirmed with the objective for the Italian theatre being reduced to simply holding as many German divisions there as possible. By 1945 the Germans had twenty-eight understrength infantry and mountain divisions in Italy (including four Italian fascist divisions) to prevent an Allied breakthrough. Veteran units were moved to Eastern Europe, their place being taken by inexperienced units as the construction of further defensive lines continued. Churchill's grand Mediterranean strategy had served its usefulness and was finally dead.

The US regarded the Yalta conference as largely successful – an agreement had been reached on the proposed United Nations when the extra votes requested by Stalin were agreed to by the Big Three. This was despite Roosevelt having been very unwell, sitting motionless for long periods with his mouth hanging open without participating.[18] Russia would receive considerable reparations from a defeated Germany, territory from China as a reward for entering the war against Japan, while Stalin was satisfied with the resolution of the Polish question. Churchill, for his efforts, had obtained promises from Stalin regarding the future of Poland.

On his return to England from the Crimea, Churchill told the House of Commons on 27 February of the agreement reached on the future of Poland, although this had been effectively settled in Moscow the previous year. Churchill stated that Stalin had guaranteed the independence of Poland and that he, Churchill, had every confidence in the good faith of the Russians. Some MPs were not so confident and drafted an Amendment lamenting the treatment of Poland and the failure to ensure that democracies had been installed in countries liberated from Germany, but this was subsequently defeated along party lines. However, the British were so concerned about the impact of the Yalta announcement on the Polish that all Polish warships were suddenly recalled to port while the commander of the 2nd Polish Corps fighting in Italy requested that his troops (many of whose homes were now part of Russia) be withdrawn from the front line, a request which was denied.

After a little over a week after the final session at Yalta, it became clear that Stalin was not going to honour the Yalta decisions regarding Poland and would act with impunity in Eastern Europe. British nominees for the present Polish government were rejected and the Soviets reneged on their promise to allow observers into the country for elections. In Rumania, a Soviet-backed government had been rapidly installed.

A British fleet finally entered the Pacific and was given the designation Task Force 57. The fleet took part successfully in the operations for the capture of the Okinawa Islands in March 1945. The British ships had far less refrigeration and air conditioning than American vessels and so required more frequent replenishment. The armoured flight decks of the British aircraft carriers did, however, prove far more resilient than those of the American carriers against strikes by Japanese suicide planes. A US Navy liaison office aboard HMS *Indefatigable* commented, 'When a kamikaze hits a US carrier its six months repair at Pearl. In a Limey carrier, it's "Sweepers, man your brooms".'[19]

Crossing the Rhine

The First Canadian Army began a major offensive, Operation Veritable, on 8 February from the Nijmegen bridgehead. Thus nearly six months after its capture in Operation Market Garden, the bridgehead was at last used for operations against Germany. Simultaneously, the American 12th Army Group advanced on a broad front and captured Cologne on 7 March. Initial stiff German resistance crumbled in the face of Allied air superiority and a lack of fuel; by 21 March, the Allies were on the west bank of the Rhine, having eliminated all pockets of German resistance trapped by their rapid advance. The railway bridge at Remagen over the Rhine was partially destroyed but still usable and the Americans quickly threw two divisions across it to make a bridgehead on the far side. However, as the main thrust was to be made by

Montgomery, Eisenhower did not want the Remagen bridgehead exploited and ordered that it be built up slowly to contain nine divisions in order to provide a diversionary attack for the British effort further north. The FUSA commanders were not happy at this restriction, pointing out they had already made a diversion for the 21st Army Group – they had crossed the Rhine.

In England, there was a great deal of civil unrest as the end of the war neared; the nation's workers, having heeded Churchill's calls for every man and woman to contribute to the war effort for more than four years, now sought to improve their own pay and working conditions:

From the *Daily Telegraph* of 13 March 1945:

> It is difficult not to ask what the feelings of our fighting men in Germany and Burma are likely to be when they hear of some of the recent strikes that have disfigured the Home Front. In London 9000 dockers, on Tyneside 4000 transport workers, in Manchester several hundred gas workers, in Birmingham 3000 aircraft workers, at a Durham colliery 1600 miners; in all these diverse industries and places men have been deliberately sabotaging the nation's business while their comrades at the front are laying down their lives.[20]

On 23 March, after a great deal of preparation, Montgomery began his great operation to cross the Rhine at Wesel and Rees (Operation Plunder), which was supported by a massive air and artillery bombardment and two airborne divisions being dropped the next day behind the German positions in the front line. The British and American troops under Montgomery's command made steady progress and by 27 March the bridgehead was some 35 miles wide and 20 miles deep. Patton's Third Army made its own crossing of the Rhine at Oppenheim on 23 March against little opposition. The planned advance from the Remagen bridgehead did not begin until 25 March, more than two weeks after the railway bridge was captured. The bridge eventually fell into the Rhine River on 17 March but the possession of the bridgehead had enabled pontoon bridges to be quickly built across the river in anticipation of its collapse.

With the American forces also across the Rhine and making rapid advances eastwards against little opposition, the end of the war was in sight as the Allied armies marched into Germany from both the east and the west. Many small German towns and villages experienced for the first time the destruction and horrors of war. This was regarded as poetic justice by many:

At last Germany is being made to suffer the untold miseries that she, in her lust for domination, has made so many nations suffer. Her people are realising now what it means to have their houses destroyed by shells and all their furniture and food and clothes burned to ashes and their towns and villages occupied by armies of another nation. A great exodus has begun from East Germany as the Russians advance and millions of men, women and children are trudging towards Berlin and the west.[21]

A tide of refugees moved westwards in front of the advancing Red Army and included Germans that were living in the territories to be ceded to Poland along with British and American prisoners of war who left their camps when their guards fled before the arrival of the Russians.

Eisenhower's immediate concern was how and where to affect a link up with the Russians while continuing to destroy as much of the German Army that resisted as soon as possible. On 2 April, Eisenhower issued his orders for the final advance to Berlin. The drive into the heart of Germany to link up with the Russians would be carried out by the American armies once they had completed the Ruhr encirclement, while Montgomery's army group was given the mission of capturing northern Germany and preventing the Russians from entering Denmark. Berlin was to be bypassed by the British and Americans and left to the Russians, who at that time were only 40 miles from the city compared with the more than 200 miles of the 21st Army Group.

The British Chiefs of Staff were furious when they found out about Eisenhower's revised intentions after receiving a copy of a telegram sent four days earlier to Stalin in order to co-ordinate the final offensive to Berlin in which the American declared that his plans were for his main thrust to now be to the south of Berlin in order to link-up with the Russians near Leipzig and Dresden.[22] This plan was quickly agreed to by Stalin, who had already set in motion his own plans for the advancing Soviet armies to get to Berlin first when the Americans got their bridgehead over the Rhine at Remagen. In his prompt reply to Eisenhower on 1 April, Stalin stated the Red Army would also aim its main blow at Leipzig and Dresden in order to link up with the Americans.

In a strongly worded telegram to the US Chiefs of Staff in Washington, the British Chiefs of Staff argued that Eisenhower had deviated both from the plan for Germany agreed at the meeting in Malta before the Yalta conference by reducing the importance of the largely British northern thrust and from protocol by contacting Stalin directly, which was the prerogative of only

Roosevelt, Churchill or the Combined Chiefs of Staff. Churchill rebuked his Chiefs of Staff in a minute on 31 March for parts of their telegram, which he claimed to have not seen before its despatch, but expressed his concern at Berlin being bypassed and about the main effort now to be made to the south of Berlin. The British Chiefs of Staff's relationship with Eisenhower was becoming increasingly strained as they strived to continue to get their way on strategic decisions as they had done earlier in the war.

Eisenhower believed that the American 12th Army Group could provide a single more concentrated thrust to the south of Berlin to link up with the Russians and isolate the capital. He claimed that Berlin was no longer a particularly important objective. Churchill spoke on the scrambler telephone to Eisenhower and complained that he was mistaken regarding the insignificance of Berlin and the need to not advance further east than the River Elbe. Churchill was convinced that it was imperative for the British and the Americans to advance as far east as possible, even though this would be in contravention of the zones of occupation agreed at Trident. The more German territory the Russians held, Churchill believed the more difficult it would be to negotiate with them in the future as relations inevitably deteriorated. Churchill and Eisenhower also exchanged terse telegrams. Churchill:

> Why should we not cross the Elbe and advance as far eastward as possible? This has an important political bearing as the Russian armies of the south seem certain to enter Vienna and overrun Austria. If we deliberately leave Berlin to them, even if it should be within our grasp, the double event may strengthen their conviction, already apparent, that they have done everything.[23]

As this Battle of words continued, Eisenhower complained in private to Marshall about how Churchill and the British had opposed Anvil, had opposed the destruction of German forces west of the Rhine and now wanted an advance to Berlin before the current encirclement had been completed.[24] Marshall and the US Chiefs of Staff were completely supportive of Eisenhower in this renewed exchange of hostilities between the British and the Americans. British currency with the Americans was now completely exhausted, as Churchill himself had realised in an earlier minute to the Chiefs of Staff: 'We have only a quarter of the forces invading Germany and the situation has thus changed remarkably from the days of June.'[25]

As was his habit when the Americans did not see the British point of view, Churchill went directly to Roosevelt on 1 April, denying there was any lack of confidence in Eisenhower and asking that more time be taken to consider the next step. Churchill also took the opportunity to put forward his view that Berlin 'remains of high strategic importance' and that the Allies should capture it rather than the Russians, who were already about to enter Vienna. This should be done in order to not give the Russians the impression that they had contributed more to the defeat of Germany which might lead to grave difficulties in the future.[26] Roosevelt at this time was very ill, something that Churchill was apparently not aware of or sensitive to, having even made a comment to the effect that he was writing personally to the President rather than having his staff answer communications as appeared to be the case with many of Roosevelt's telegrams; American military matters were in fact largely being dealt with by Marshall at this time because of Roosevelt's ailing condition.

Roosevelt's 'reply' on 4 April also fully supported Eisenhower's final plans and a day later a suitably mollified Churchill replied that he considered the matter closed but continued to make his point in another telegram the same day:

> All this makes it more important that we should join hands with the Russian armies as far to the east as possible and if circumstances allow, enter Berlin. I may remind you that six weeks ago we proposed and thought we arranged provisional zones of occupation in Austria but that since Yalta we have received no confirmation of these zones. Now that they are on the eve of taking Vienna and very likely the whole of Austria, it may well be prudent for us to hold as much as possible in the north.[27]

As a world power, Britain was now completely eclipsed by America and Churchill was forced to accept that it was now an American-led war. In a later telegram to Marshall, Eisenhower said that he would gladly change his plans to achieve a political objective if so directed by the Combined Chiefs of Staff. As well as destroying Germans and linking up with the Russians, Eisenhower was increasingly concerned about friendly fire incidents after Russian fighters had attacked American planes over Kustrin. Yet more difficulties with Stalin had arisen when Stalin had accused the Allies of negotiating secretly with the Germans as he believed this was the reason for the spectacular advances of the British and Americans. Stalin knew the Allies were negotiating in Berne with a German general for the surrender of the German forces in Italy; at this point Stalin mistrusted the British and Americans as much as they mistrusted the Soviets.

The American encirclement of German Army Group B in the Ruhr was successful by the end of the first week in April with more than 320,000 German soldiers being taken prisoner. One American division was directed towards Berlin by FUSA in its enthusiasm but this was halted by Eisenhower. The general was in fact conducting the closing stages of the campaign purely on the basis of military expediency and without any thought for the post-war political situation. Despite his dalliance in Vichy French politics in North Africa and the Italian and French intrigues in Europe, Eisenhower was now only concerned with ending the war as quickly as possible. In response to a telegram from Eisenhower outlining the procedure to be followed when the Western armies met the Red Army, Churchill wrote a minute to the British Chiefs of Staff on 7 April urging that the advance should be continued until contact, when the armies should rest and then any major disputes settled later by the three governments. The Combined Chiefs of Staff agreed and accordingly instructed Eisenhower on 20 April to advance to contact with the Russians and then halt.

President Roosevelt finally succumbed to his long illness and passed away on 12 April 1945. Churchill believed he had lost a friend as well as perhaps the greatest ally Britain ever had and without whom the country could never have defeated Germany. However, Churchill declined to attend Roosevelt's funeral, delegating this to Eden, so the two men were not as close as he would have history believe. While Churchill claimed that Parliamentary duties kept him in England, it is odd that he did not take the opportunity to meet with the new President, Harry Truman, with whom there was now the challenge of forging a new working relationship. However, the war was unmistakeably nearly at an end, much to the relief of the war-weary civilians of Britain:

> It is interesting this spectacle in Germany, this slow crushing, between two mighty armies in the west and in the east, of a nation of 80m people who thought that the world was theirs for the plundering, that all people other than their own were fit only for exploitation and slavery. The Germans are learning a lesson now which they will not forget for many years to come and we enter upon the last pages in the story of Hitler and his Nazi regime as we wait impatiently for each news bulletin with reports of the progress of the conquering armies; for we have had enough of war and we are anxious for peace.[28]

Churchill then claimed in one of his first telegrams to Truman that he wanted to see the Allies occupy as much territory as possible to ensure that there would be enough food for all of Germany as the most productive food area with the least population was in the Russian zone.[29]

By April, it was already clear that much of the Yalta agreement regarding Germany and Poland was in tatters. In Poland, political opponents of the Russian-backed government had been arrested and fifteen candidates nominated for inclusion in the formation of a new government had disappeared. In Rumania, the Russians had taken over and installed their own government but Churchill ordered that British missions there should not interfere in order to honour his infamous percentage agreement with Stalin. In Germany, British and American forces had advanced much further than their agreed zones because of the limited German resistance as the Germans preferred to use their last reserves against the Russians; some Germans even hoped that the British and Americans would become embroiled in a conflict with the Russians. As the Red Army shock troops began their conquest of Berlin suburb by suburb and neared the city centre, Hitler committed suicide on 30 April in the bunker of his Berlin headquarters and Admiral Dönitz became the new German leader. Surrender negotiations began on 6 May and the surrender was finally signed a day later.

On 8 May, on what became Victory in Europe Day, Churchill in a radio broadcast declared the end of the war in Europe. Following the broadcast, the Prime Minister appeared on a balcony of the Ministry of Health building in Whitehall and addressed the massed cheering crowds below. At one point he said, 'This is your victory!' The crowd roared back, 'No, it's yours!'[30]

So we jumped on a train from our nearby Clapham Junction station to Victoria and were astounded to see such huge, swirling crowds. We tried desperately to make our way to Buckingham Palace and staggered shoulder to shoulder with the crowds. What an incredible sight. A wave of humanity confronted us. Impassioned emotions would never be as high again. London was aflame with human exhilaration. Bonfires blazed continuously over London and the sky was alight with the glow of victory. No more suffering and hardship; peace had finally descended upon us and everybody was at one with each other regardless of race, creed and status. Survival and freedom were all that mattered. We had waited so very long for this and in our wildest dreams had never envisaged a night like this.

Mum and I finally reached Buckingham Palace with much effort and laughter and joined in the masses converging on the Palace and celebrating outside. Hundreds of people all waving flags were crowding in front of the

Palace and drifting in from Piccadilly and Regents Street and thronging down the Mall. They sang their hearts out with many of the war songs particularly the Vera Lynn favourites and London was deafened once again, not from the bombs and artillery fire, but from the depths of human feeling in utter, utter relief that their beloved city of London which had endured so much was free. Dear old London; this was its finest hour. Fireworks streaked through the sky instead of searchlights and bombers. The pent up spirits of the long, weary war burst out and the whole of London was ablaze with celebration.

No more suffering; peace at last; survival and freedom were all that mattered. London was submerged in jubilation and screams of relief from humanity. People climbed on anything they could, statues, buildings, cars, and every lamp-post was scaled. Noisy dustbin lids were banged and the hysterical crowds were totally beyond any order. Nothing mattered, only freedom. The ultimate heights of pent up human emotion were as they had never been and will probably never be again.

I was 15, and, as mentioned earlier, was deeply embedded with my mother in those swirling masses outside the Palace. The royal family together with Sir Winston Churchill came out on to the balcony of Buckingham Palace many times, joining in all the jubilation and joy looking utterly exhilarated and thoroughly overwhelmed as we all were in that incredible atmosphere.[31]

Nine months later, there was a spike in the number of children born in Britain.

Potsdam and Tube Alloys

On 18 September 1944 during their meetings in Washington, Churchill and Roosevelt had discussed the atomic bomb and agreed that its development would continue in secret. At Churchill's instigation, the British and Americans continued to share information and in October 1944 a proposal was made by Professor Lindemann for key British scientists and personnel to work in the American factories alongside the development team.[32]

Churchill had to let his Chiefs of Staff know about the project as the Air Chief Marshal had been ordered to bomb certain targets in Germany. They were initially briefed in November 1944 and again in January 1945 but Churchill insisted that no one else be told.[33] The January briefing came only after a query from the Chancellor of the Exchequer, John Anderson, who was managing the Tube Alloys project, as to whether the atomic bomb should be included in discussions about new weapons being held by the Chiefs of Staff in mid January. In March 1944, the subject of the atomic bombs had been raised as a possible discussion for the War Cabinet in another minute by Anderson but Churchill did not agree and no briefing was held.[34]

Churchill gave the British approval to use the atomic bomb on 2 July before a formal decision was to be made by the Combined Policy Committee in Washington rather than the Combined Chiefs of Staff.[35] This committee met on 4 July and noted that the use of the atomic bomb had been approved by the British and American governments. This decision by Churchill was made without referring the use of this weapon to the War Cabinet.

At the Yalta conference, Stalin, Churchill and Roosevelt had agreed to meet following the surrender of Germany to determine the post-war borders in Europe and continue the discussions that had begun at Yalta, particularly the secret talks about the entry of Russia into the war with Japan. The nature of the Polish government was still unresolved and similar doubts regarding the influence of the Soviets were beginning to emerge in the Russian-occupied countries of Rumania, Czechoslovakia, Bulgaria and Austria; Yugoslavia was also now under the influence of the Russian-backed Tito. After Germany's surrender, on 1 June the Allied leaders arranged to meet over the summer for a 'Triple conference' at Potsdam just outside Berlin, where they assembled from 17 July to 2 August.

General Election of 1945

The long-delayed British general election was to be held on 5 July; it had been ten years since the previous election. Churchill resigned on 23 May and became leader of a caretaker government at the request of the King for the duration of the campaign. The national coalition government was dissolved and members of the War Cabinet that had worked together as a team for many years became once again political opponents on the hustings. After a poorly regarded opening campaign speech, Churchill toured the countryside to be met by cheering crowds wherever he went. Churchill and the Conservative Party believed the country could not be left to the Labour Party to run in the uncertainty of post-war Europe and the emerging menace of the Soviet

Union, but had few other policies. The results of the election would not be known for three weeks to allow for the votes of the servicemen and women overseas to be collected and collated. On 15 July, Churchill went to Berlin for the victors' conference at Potsdam. Out of courtesy, although Churchill and the Conservative Party leaders were convinced they had won the election, Churchill took Attlee with him as an observer.

Meanwhile, the war against Japan continued. An invasion of the southern island of Japan, Kyushu, was planned for 1 November after an extensive aerial bombing campaign and naval blockade. Operations against the Tokyo mainland itself were to begin in 1946. These operations would require an anticipated 5 million fighting troops and, given the great resistance put up by the Japanese when the Americans attacked the islands of Okinawa and Iwo Jima earlier that year, a very high number of American casualties were expected. Therefore every effort would be made to induce Japan to surrender before any invasion by intensifying the strategic bombing campaign which would include all types of bombs including the new atomic devices.[36]

A prototype atomic bomb was successfully tested on 16 July 1945. Churchill was ecstatic at the news as the British and the Americans now had a weapon to defeat Japan and redress the balance of power with the Russians. Relations with the Soviet Union had sunk to such a level that the British Chiefs of Staff had contingency plans drawn up in case of conflict breaking out with the Russians: Operation Unthinkable. On 24 July at Potsdam, Truman gave the news of this test to Stalin, who did not offer much in the way of reaction and significantly did not ask a single question. Stalin had learned to keep a poker face in dealing with the Allies and the development of a Russian atomic bomb was also in progress, helped by information from Soviet spies in America.

On 25 July, Churchill and Attlee returned to England for the results of the election. The Conservative Party suffered a decisive defeat, retaining only 213 seats to the Labour Party's 393 seats:

July 26th 1945

We got a real shock when we heard that our Conservative member had been beaten by 12000 votes – we simply could not believe it … The general opinion was that the soldier's vote had swung the election. Some thought that England would go down in the world's opinion, that no-one would believe in her stability and that Russia would rejoice since it would suit Stalin.[37]

Churchill resigned once more and repaired to Chequers for the last time. Attlee returned to Potsdam as the new Prime Minister, prompting Stalin to remark that he had much to understand about democracy. Only a few months previously, Stalin, when discussing the political systems of Britain and Russia with Churchill, had said that having only one political party was a much better system.

Following the Potsdam meeting, an ultimatum was given to Japan on 26 July, only for it to be rejected two days later as being 'unworthy of public notice'. The Americans only had enough raw materials for two bombs and the cities of Hiroshima and Nagasaki were the targets. The medieval capital of Kyoto had been originally selected as a target but was saved by the intervention of Truman and Stimson; Nagasaki was subsequently chosen as the substitute. Nagasaki was on the southern island and Hiroshima was on the mainland; Hiroshima was an important port and military supply depot as well as headquarters for the army defending southern Japan. The first bomb was dropped on Hiroshima on 6 August and the second on Nagasaki three days later. Churchill's successor, Attlee, knew very little about the atomic bomb but had to assume responsibility once they were dropped.

The Russians honoured their commitment to the Allies and declared war on Japan on 8 August, the news of the Hiroshima bomb having made Stalin realise that the war against Japan was going to end sooner rather than later and if Russia was to seize any Japanese territory, it would have to be done quickly. On 10 August, the Japanese government offered to begin surrender negotiations, which were finalised on 14 August. The surrender ceremony was led by General MacArthur and was held in Tokyo Bay on 2 September.

The Second World War was finally over but Churchill, having not been Prime Minister at the start of the war, was not in office at the end either to see the victorious culmination of all the British and American grand strategic plans. Churchill's own constituency seat of Epping had been subdivided before the election and as Epping itself was not polling well (being subsequently lost to Labour), his political instincts did not desert him and he had opted to stand in the new seat of Woodford, which he duly won. It may well have been that the votes of the men and women in the armed forces who had to implement Churchill's war strategies ultimately counted against him.

Churchill himself was silent on his feelings after being rejected at the polls but no man could not fail to be depressed at such a result. In his history of the Second World War, Churchill writes only of his despair at the loss of the power to shape the future and the goodwill earnt in so many countries. There is no reference to the attitude of the British people or any indication of what Churchill's future plans were for the nation. A glimpse of his emotional state was provided by his wife, Clementine, in a letter to their daughter:

> I cannot explain how it is but in our misery we seem, instead of clinging to each other to be always having scenes. I'm sure it is all my fault but I'm finding life more than I can bear. He is so unhappy and that makes him very difficult. He hates his food (hardly any meat) ... I can't see any future.[38]

But the British general public did not forget Churchill, who would have one more term as Prime Minister. It took two general elections before he took office for a second time in 1951 at the age of 77, this time as one elected by the British people.

16

CHURCHILL THE LEADER

Planning

After Churchill restructured the Military Co-ordination Committee in May 1940 to set up the Defence Committee, the new streamlined machinery for planning the strategy for the war placed Churchill at its head as both the Prime Minister and Minister of Defence. In August 1940 Churchill made a further change and required the Joint Planning Committee to report directly to him as the Minister of Defence, as well as to the Chiefs of Staff Committee, in order to draw up plans in accordance with his instructions. This was because, after a year of war, Churchill could not recall a single plan being initiated by the committees.[1] The reality was that new ideas did come almost exclusively from Churchill rather than the Chiefs of Staff Committee or the War Cabinet. Almost totally in Churchill's thrall, the War Cabinet rarely voted against an operation or came up with an alternative. Menzies described the War Cabinet as being full of yes-men and Churchill as acting like a dictator. The War Cabinet was consulted when important decisions such as the decisions to send troops to Greece or for Anzio needed to be made but this was perhaps when Churchill was more anxious to apportion any future blame or consequences if the venture failed. Politically, Churchill was well aided by Eden, Attlee and Halifax in the War Cabinet, although as the war progressed, this met less and less to the point where it was not even consulted on major issues such as the decision to drop the atomic bomb on Japan or to send British troops to Greece a second time. Halifax, Churchill's only rival for the position of Prime Minister, having proposed peace negotiations in May 1940, was shunted off to Washington in early 1941 as Britain's Ambassador where, given the propensity for Roosevelt and Churchill to contact each other directly, he was largely redundant.

The Chiefs of Staff were not always happy with these arrangements, as Brooke commented in his diary in August 1943 after returning from Quebec:

> Winston made matters almost impossible, temperamental like a film star, and peevish like a spoilt child. He has an unfortunate trick of picking up some isolated operation and without ever having looked into it, setting his heart on it. When he once gets in one of those moods he feels everybody is trying to thwart him and to produce difficulties. He becomes more and more set on the operation brushing everything aside, and when the planners prove the operation to be impossible he then appoints new planners in the hope that they will prove that the operation is possible.[2]

Fortunately, as the head of the British war machine, Churchill's imaginative mind was an endless source of ideas to offset the shortage of them from the Chiefs of Staff. Even at the Admiralty in the first nine months of the year when Churchill, as First Lord, chaired meetings to discuss problems, he would always provide several potential solutions. If decisions were required, Churchill took them immediately. If one possible solution was unsuccessful, he promptly came up with another. Churchill certainly regarded it as a major sin to sit back and do nothing but accept the inevitable.[3] One Cabinet Secretary, John Colville, wrote:

> He is always having ideas which he puts down on paper in the form of questions and despatches to Ismay and the Chief of Imperial General Staff. Sometimes they relate to matters of major importance and sometimes to quite trivial matters.[4]
>
> Churchill scrutinises every document which has anything to do with the war and does not disdain to enquire into the most trivial point.[5]

Churchill was almost the only source of ideas for British military initiatives and strategies, which flowed from his imagination in a series of minutes, memoranda and papers. In order to improve the flow of paperwork, Churchill used labels to prioritise his minutes with phrases such as 'Action this Day' or 'Report progress in a week', and the minutes often became not so much discussion points but directives. Minutes from Churchill beginning with the phrase 'Pray tell me ...' became known as 'prayers' by the Cabinet secretaries as they invariably requested more information or pointed out some shortcoming. In an effort to then reduce the paperwork that these instructions created, Churchill tried to have summaries produced on single sheets of paper as the Chiefs of Staff and planners, for example, would produce several papers within a matter of days on the same subject, which then had to be reduced to aide-memoires. Churchill in fact had so many ideas that the problem for the Chiefs of Staff Committee was winnowing out the bad ones and reducing the flood of alternatives to a few practicable options. Such was Churchill's fecundity that this process imposed enormous demands and long hours on the Chiefs of Staff and the officers and secretaries of the various Planning and Intelligence committees assisting them that were part of the war planning machinery. To address the most urgent problems such as the U-boat threat and the night air defence of Britain, Churchill also set up committees, which he then presided over. Other committees and planning teams examined future plans and analysed possible German strategies with their available resources, e.g. oil reserves.

The examination of Churchill's ideas through the development of plans for operations that were never carried out wasted a great deal of time and energy of all the Chiefs of Staff committees involved. A by no means comprehensive list of such operations includes:

Caliph – Bordeaux 1944
Culverin – Sumatra 1943 and 1944
Anakim – Burma 1943
Buccaneer – Burma 1943/4
Stumper – raid on battery near Trondheim 1941
Truncheon – raid on Livorno 1941
Thresher – raids on Norwegian coast
Jupiter – Norway 1941–44
Whipcord – Sicily 1941
Accolade – Dodecanese 1943
Ajax – landing Murmansk 1941
Ascot – raid Bodo 1941
Brimstone – capture of Sardinia 1943
Bullfrog – Burma 1943
Champion – Burma 1943
Firebrand – Corsica 1943
Musket – Taranto landing 1943

Pigstick – Burma amphibious landing 1944
Sledgehammer – France 1942–43
Tarzan – Burma 1943/4

The number of cancelled plans for the campaign in Burma is further evidence of the unenthusiastic attitude of Churchill towards this theatre.

Because of the concentration of power in Churchill's hands, it was essential that he should be supported by a strong and capable military staff. This Churchill eventually found in the Chiefs of Staff with the appointment of Alan Brooke as CIGS in December 1941 and his eventual promotion to chairman of the Chiefs of Staff in March 1942. Their relationship was not always harmonious as Brooke was prepared to stand up to Churchill and had the ability to make him eventually see reason most of the time. Churchill himself was not averse to argument and sometimes looked for it as a way of testing his ideas; as he said after the war, 'All I wanted was compliance with my wishes, after reasonable discussion.'[6]

A common complaint from Brooke was that Churchill often advocated diversion of forces, whereas the Chiefs of Staff preferred concentration.[7] For example, always looking for the great outflanking strategic opportunity, Churchill persistently put up the idea of troops landing in Norway (Operation Jupiter) until very late in the war.

The brunt of responding directly to Churchill's fertile mind fell on Brooke, who recorded that Churchill had ten ideas every day, only one of which was good and he did not know which one it was:[8] 'In all his plans he lives from hand to mouth; he can never grasp a whole plan, either in its width (i.e. all fronts) or its depth (long term projects).'[9]

Roosevelt also made a very similar remark, saying that the Prime Minister had 100 ideas a day of which four were good.[10] Churchill's relationship with Brooke was particularly difficult when the war was not going well, when the Americans would not do what he wanted or Stalin was sending aggrieved telegrams. At other times, their relationship ran smoothly, as one Cabinet minister observed of Churchill and the Chiefs of Staff:

> On military matters he is instinctively right as he is wrong on foreign affairs. As a war minister, he is superb, driving our own Chiefs of Staff, guiding them like a coach and four, applying whip and brake as necessary, with the confidence and touch of a genius.[11]

Nevertheless, Brooke had the most interaction of anyone with Churchill and his strategic thinking. By the end of the war, Brooke, following their long history of working together, was quite ambivalent in his opinion of Churchill, 'Churchill knows no details, has only got half the picture in his mind, talks absurdities and makes my blood boil to listen to his nonsense. I find it hard to remain civil.'[12]

Brooke, however, also had great admiration for Churchill and described him as:

> … a genius mixed with an astonishing lack of vision – he is quite the most difficult man to work with that I have ever struck but I should not have missed the chance of working with him for anything on earth![13]

In an argument with Menzies in 1941 when he told Churchill that he needed assistance to run the war, the Prime Minister proclaimed that his advisors were devoid of ideas and he had to run things himself.[14] Sometimes the strain of being the sole source of strategic ideas and having to justify their merits with the Chiefs of Staff left Churchill exhausted (as well as them), as he lamented with his wisecrack about the need to place an advertisement in the newspaper for ideas if no one else would provide them. Not all of the ideas put forward by Churchill were his own, however. Many came from the scientific advisor on his personal staff, Professor Lindemann (the future Lord Cherwell), and Churchill was not above putting his signature to the draft letters from Lindemann.[15]

While Churchill dominated the War Cabinet and the Chiefs of Staff, Ismay claims that Churchill did not once overrule his military advisors on a purely military matter.[16] This is simply not true, for example during the debate over future operations in Burma when the Chiefs of Staff contemplated resigning – a serious step for a country at war. The planning for the Anzio landings was also done almost entirely outside of the Chiefs of Staff Committee when Brooke declined to go to the meeting of the Commanders-in-Chief in North Africa.

Churchill had a great interest in new weapons and military technology, anything in fact that might give the British an advantage. Lindemann would often provide suggestions for new weapons and their applications, as well as supplying critiques of Chiefs of Staff military proposals and reports for Churchill to use in meetings. Before the war, Churchill sat on a Royal Navy committee looking at the development and trials of radar for warships and one of his first actions as First Lord of the Admiralty in 1939 was to push for its installation.

Radar, especially airborne radar, would go on to become an important tactical weapon in the defeat of the U-boats in the Atlantic and came into its own during the Battle of Britain. The Germans, to their cost, never realised at the time the significance of the chain of radar stations around the coast of England, nor how far advanced British technology was compared with their own.

For the future landings on the Continent, Churchill supported the concept of the floating harbours devised by Combined Operations, which eventually became to be known as Mulberry in the D-Day landings. In a famous minute of 30 May 1942, Churchill suggested some improvements to the design of the pier system and urged Mountbatten to provide solutions to problems that had arisen, which were eventually found. A more bizarre idea from Combined Operations that caught Churchill's imagination was for an artificial airfield code-named 'habbakuk'. These were to be constructed on icebergs to provide temporary floating airfields for use in northern Norway. Later the habbakuk idea was extended to floating runways made of wood and steel that could be towed to where they were required and the concept was offered to the Americans for use in the Pacific Ocean. Churchill even suggested bubble machines be used to calm a rough sea to enable the habbakuks to be used by aircraft. The habbakuk idea was paid lip service by both the British and American Chiefs of Staff and quietly dropped; increases in the range of bomber aircraft made the need for them redundant, as did the more widespread use of aircraft carriers.

The advent of war saw some of Churchill's pre-war ideas on weapons rapidly disproved. His thinking that the anti-aircraft armament of modern warships would defeat air power was rapidly dispelled by the sinking of the *Prince of Wales* and *Repulse* days after Pearl Harbor and the *Hermes*, *Dorsetshire* and *Cornwall* a few months later. Naval warfare in the Second World War would come to be dominated by aircraft and their carriers. Similarly, Churchill's pre-war claims that the 'submarine was mastered' proved to be completely wrong; Churchill himself later admitted that nothing terrified him more than the threat posed by the German U-boats.[17] It was not until mid 1943 that the Allies gained the upper hand in the Battle of the Atlantic and the official British historian of the war at sea later lamented that victory over the U-boats could have been achieved six months earlier if Churchill had intervened in the struggle between Coastal Command and the advocates of Bomber Command's strategic bombing campaign for the allocation of long-range aircraft.[18]

In 1940, after the fall of France, Churchill looked at ways to take the offensive to Germany. With the Army rebuilding after Dunkirk and the Royal Navy stretched in meeting its commitments of defending Britain from invasion and securing the sea lanes, the bombers of the RAF provided the only way to hit back at Germany from England. Churchill seized on this and ordered the bomber force to be increased in size. However, this could only be done slowly in 1940 as the manufacture of bombers competed with the higher priority production of fighter aircraft for engines, tools and assembly workers. The strategy of hitting back then expanded in July 1940 when Churchill saw the bomber force as the only way to win the war by destroying German military production and demoralising civilians. This view was enthusiastically adopted by Air Chief Marshal Harris at Bomber Command, but by 1942 Churchill was of the opinion that the bombing offensive was only 'experimental' and conventional Army operations would still be required to win the war. Nevertheless, Harris continued the offensive relentlessly and was supported in this by Churchill. Before the Casablanca conference, the British Chiefs of Staff recommended that the bomber force should have 3,000 American and British heavy and medium bombers operating from the United Kingdom by the end of 1943.[19] This resulted in the Combined Bomber Offensive directive for the strategic bombing of Germany, which as well as setting military objectives also had the objective of undermining civilian morale. At Chequers one weekend in June 1943, while viewing RAF footage of the bombing of German cities and the tremendous damage caused, Churchill is reported to have said, 'Are we beasts? Are we taking this too far?'[20]

Churchill had become one of the tyrants he had warned against pre-war but despite this moment of introspection, the bomber offensive continued with the American planes by day and the RAF by night for the remainder of the war as a 'twenty-four-hour service', as Churchill once joked to American news reporters. As the American bomber groups and RAF squadrons based in England were joined by aircraft operating from Italy, the tonnage of bombs dropped on Germany increased dramatically every three months. With the success of Operation Pointblank, the strength of the Luftwaffe diminished rapidly in 1944, which with improvements in Allied target finding and navigation led to greater and more widespread destruction of the German industry in the bomber offensive. By early 1945, the German economy had virtually collapsed altogether and although the full effects of this were not always felt by the German Army units in the front line before they were overrun, Allied air power was decisive in the war in Western Europe.[21] As the destruction of Germany continued, Churchill wrote on the 1 April of the destruction and shortage of housing:

If we come into control of an entirely ruined land, there will be a great shortage of accommodation for ourselves and our Allies; and we shall be unable to get housing materials out of Germany for our own needs because some temporary provision will have to be made for the Germans themselves. We must see to it that our attacks do not do more harm to ourselves than they do to the enemy's immediate war effort.

Some 20 per cent (900,000) of German homes were destroyed or severely damaged and there were 7.5 million homeless people in Germany by the end of the war. Churchill's experimental strategy was ultimately a war-winning one although he was more modest after the war, claiming that the air offensive played a major part only in the economic collapse of Germany rather than its defeat on the battlefield.

From forecasting in 1938 that tanks would not play an important part in any future conflict as anti-tank gun technology would defeat them, Churchill was forced by the Germans' use of tanks in the blitzkriegs in France and Greece and their importance in the desert fighting in North Africa to quickly revise his thinking. Following the evacuation of the BEF from Dunkirk with the loss of its equipment and faced with imminent invasion, it was vital that tanks be replaced as soon as possible. Therefore British industry in the early years of the war continued to largely produce the same types of tanks as it had before the war with the exception of 500 of the new A22 Churchills that Churchill ordered in July 1940 to be built by March 1941. However, tanks were not placed on the production 'high priority list' at that time. In November 1940, Churchill urged that 'At this stage in Tank production numbers count above everything else. It is better to have any serviceable tank than none at all.'[22]

A dilemma faced the War Office and the manufacturers of tanks as the demands for greater output conflicted with both the development of existing types and the introduction of new models as production inevitably would fall off while any changes to production were made. In his minute of November, Churchill also expressed his doubts about the wisdom of plans to switch any future emphasis from heavy infantry tanks to lighter cruiser tanks. Once Prime Minister, Churchill retained a special programme that was independent of the War Office and Ministry of Supply to build a monster tank, the so-called Stern tank. It was not until 1943 that this project was finally abandoned but Churchill continued to believe that larger, more heavily armoured tanks were needed.

In 1941, as the threat of invasion receded, Churchill set up a Tank Parliament to bring together manufacturers, the War Office and the commanders of tank units to decide on how current issues could be resolved and what future developments were needed to meet the Army's requirements of 1942 and 1943. The Tank Parliament only met four times from May to June 1941 and its functions overlapped with that of Tank Boards already in existence. First set up in June 1940, there were four different Boards in two years until the fifth Tank Board was set up in September 1942, which remained in place until the end of the war. One early finding of the Tank Parliament was that more armour was needed on British tanks to negate the firepower of German anti-tank guns and, as a consequence of the increased weight, tanks would require a more powerful engine to maintain the same mobility. Following the British tank losses in Libya during Operation Battle Axe, at the end of Operation Crusader in 1941 and then in Rommel's counter-attack in early 1942, criticism of the lack of firepower and poor reliability of British tanks became more commonplace, not least from General Auchinleck in North Africa. Churchill remained an advocate of heavy tanks:

> I am not at all sure that speed is the supreme requirement of tanks, certainly not all tanks. Armour and gun power decide the matter when ever tank meets tank. Anti-tank weapons are advancing fast in power, and thin-skinned animals will run ever-increasing risks.[23]

Following questions in Parliament about the poor performance of British tanks, a Select Committee on National Expenditure was set up to report on their production. When the report was produced in August 1942, Churchill wrote that it was an indictment of all at the War Office, Ministry of Supply and himself as Head of Government while the committee '... have certainly rendered a high service in bringing this tangle of inefficiency and incompetence to my notice'.

The British tanks were certainly being outgunned by improved German tanks and a programme began to replace the obsolete 2-pounder gun with the 6-pounder. However, another problem also became apparent – the lack of an effective high-explosive shell for the 6-pounder guns as armour-piercing shells could not effectively destroy anti-tank guns or soft targets. In order to supplement British production and re-equip tank units on schedule, Britain had been purchasing M3 Grant tanks with cash from the United States before the advent of Lend-Lease and there were favourable reports about the 75mm main gun of these tanks. Following the loss of Tobruk in June 1942, the first Sherman/M4 tanks with the same 75mm gun were supplied by the United States directly to

Egypt in time for the battle at El Alamein. There was widespread approbation for the Sherman and its 75mm gun (particularly from Montgomery) that fired a better high-explosive round than the 6-pounder and so the British began to look very closely at adopting the Sherman as their main cruiser tank until the next home-designed tank, the Cromwell, could be produced in numbers.[24] A new, more powerful engine based on the Merlin aircraft engine, the Meteor, had been developed for the Cromwell, which would be fast and equipped with a British-made 75mm gun that used American ammunition. The Crusader and Valentine tanks would cease production in 1943. A warning bell was rung in a Tank Supply Policy paper that the Sherman may have reached the limit of its development and might be unacceptable on a battlefield in 1944. Churchill duly minuted:

> We shall, I am sure, be exposed to criticism if we are found with a great mass of thin skinned tanks of medium size, none of which can stand up to the German guns of 1943, still less than those of 1944 … The warthog must play his part as well as the gazelle.[25]

This policy of using Shermans was nevertheless approved by the Defence Committee with the added measure of retaining the Churchill infantry tank in service for another year. Thus the Sherman tank with only 25mm of extra armour and an engine of 50 more horsepower than the M3 Grant tank of 1941 was adopted as the main British battle tank until enough Cromwells could be produced to equip the British armoured formations.

With the conclusion of the North African campaign in 1943 and the difficult terrain in Sicily and Italy being unsuitable for large armoured formations, by mid 1943 Britain had for the first time since Dunkirk sufficient tanks for its requirements with the flow of Shermans into the country from the United States. In May 1943, Churchill had ended the debate about the main gun by ordering that tank units be equipped with a mix of 75mm and 6-pounder guns. The Cromwell, even though a prototype had first been demonstrated to the War Office in the summer 1942, was not produced in large numbers until early 1944 and was not well received by the crews of the veteran divisions to which it was issued. A second Select Committee report was produced in March 1944, which was again critical of British tank production and development. This time Churchill was not appreciative of the Select Committee's work and he came under pressure to answer questions in Parliament and respond to the new report. In a House of Commons debate, Churchill declared, 'The next time that the British Armies take the field, in country suitable for the use of armour, they will be found to be equipped in a manner at least equal to the forces of any other country in the world.'[26]

In the meantime, the Germans had upgunned both their Panzer Mk IV and assault guns again and introduced a new tank in mid 1943, the Panther, designed to replace the Mk IV. Following the D-Day landings, the Allied Shermans and Cromwells came up against the new German tanks and in the ensuing campaign the Allies lost almost three times the number the Germans lost in combat. There was also widespread criticism of the Shermans and Cromwells from the tank regiments in the field.[27] Efforts by the British to upgun the Sherman with a 17-pounder gun were successful and resulted in the Sherman Firefly tank, although these remained in short supply and none were available to the Americans. The Cromwell was found to be undergunned and was quickly phased out in early 1945, being replaced by the Comet. Shermans remained in service until the end of the war, making up in numbers what they lacked in performance.

Churchill had misgivings in 1943 about the widespread adoption of the medium Sherman but Britain had little choice as to that point in the war it had been unable to manufacture a reliable tank with a good high-explosive firing gun. However, as Churchill himself said, as Head of Government he had to take responsibility for the situation. Churchill was correct in his understanding of the interaction of the factors of armour, firepower and speed in tank design but his preference was for heavy, slow-moving infantry models; the British were too far behind with the technology to produce anything to match the better German types. Such was the superiority of German anti-tank guns that even the warthogs were vulnerable. The statement made by Churchill to the House of Commons was found to be untrue, as he suspected at the time he made it. Certainly Churchill and later Montgomery were at pains to stop any public debate about British tanks in case this led to a deterioration in morale among the crew members in France. Fortunately for Churchill, the great Allied victory in Normandy largely silenced the vocal critics of British tanks.

While at the Admiralty in 1939, Churchill came up with an idea for giant machines to tunnel their way towards enemy lines while digging a trench behind them to be used by attacking infantry and even tanks. The Royal Navy was charged with developing the prototype machines and the programme was continued by Churchill when he became Prime Minister, despite the lessons of modern war demonstrated by the German blitzkrieg in France. A prototype machine weighing 131 tons successfully performed some trials in 1941 in soft loam soil but the War Office did not share Churchill's enthusiasm and the project was cancelled in 1943. The idea for these machines showed that Churchill was firmly wedded to the First World War concept of fighting against static lines and positions. The project, code-named White Rabbit No. 6 in an ironic reference to *Alice in Wonderland*, was very reminiscent of how tanks were developed in the First World War by the engineers of the Royal Navy.[28]

On becoming Prime Minister, Churchill ordered a small engineering workshop to be set up to develop new weapons outside of the regular War Office and Ministry of Supply channels. The project was administered by Professor Lindemann and was known as the 'MDI'. One of the first weapons developed was the 'sticky bomb' for use by infantry against advancing tanks and more than a million were eventually manufactured. A variety of other weapons were produced with varying degrees of success – these included the spigot mortar, which became the forward firing anti-submarine 'Hedgehog' system, credited with destroying thirty-seven U-boats, and the PIAT, the British soldiers' standard anti-tank weapon after D-Day. Churchill recognised genius in others and was prepared to back their ideas and projects in order that the British forces could hopefully gain a technological advantage over their opponents.

Advised by Lindemann, Churchill was quick to seize on the potential of the atomic bomb project when it was drawn to his attention. Original research conducted by the British and Canadians was shared with the United States, which quickly took the lead in its development. By mid 1942, it had become apparent that the Manhattan Project, as it was code-named by the Americans, was so far ahead that the entire project would have to be carried out jointly in the United States as Britain did not have the resources to set up full-scale manufacturing. After transatlantic arguments about the exchange of information, Churchill took the matter up with Roosevelt at the May 1943 Trident conference and complete collaboration was assured. The development continued apace, although with Britain very much the junior partner, until the prototype was tested in July 1945. Instead of the British suffering the effects of 'perverted science', as Churchill had warned regarding Germany in a speech of 1940, it was the Allies who unleashed the power of the atom on the Japanese in order to successfully induce their surrender.

Though the struggle for strategy and plans with Churchill left the Chiefs of Staff, and particularly Brooke, fatigued, bruised and battered, it was a successful combination. The Chiefs of Staff were able to dissuade Churchill of his wilder plans and ideas while adhering broadly to the agreed Anglo-American strategy, although their preference too was for the Mediterranean peripheral strategy and Italy. These restraints imposed by the Chiefs of Staff kept Churchill focussed and were one of the reasons that Britain survived and won the war under his leadership, according to one Cabinet Secretary.[29]

Routine

Churchill tended to rise late in the morning after working for a few hours in bed and reading the newspapers. Lunch was usually eaten late followed by meetings, after which Churchill often took a nap before having a bath and dinner. Many regular meetings did not start until after dinner in the evening and often dragged on to late into the night as Churchill argued and cajoled those present into seeing his point of view. Invariably, Churchill would go off at tangents and it would be difficult at times to get him back on to the subject at hand. All of these activities were accompanied by alcoholic beverages, which sometimes got the better of Churchill, particularly in 1944, causing meetings to become even more unproductive. Churchill would often stay up to 1 or 2 a.m., dictating to his staff, who were rostered to be available for such duties day and night, even when he was taking a bath. This lifestyle was very difficult for anyone to keep up with, especially as no one else had the luxury of late morning starts and afternoon naps. As committee and Cabinet members were often extremely tired, this partially explains the impression of the conduct of meetings in 1941 recorded by Menzies; ministers were often probably too tired to offer much input or argue with Churchill, knowing that to do so might cause the meeting to drag on for another hour or so before a decision would be reached. The War Cabinet did not generally discuss day-to-day military affairs as this was left to the Defence Committee and the Chiefs of Staff, which added to the reluctance of Cabinet members to enter into any late-night debate.[30]

By modern standards, Churchill's health regime was far from being a model regime in terms of diet, exercise and addictions. He became Prime Minister at the age of 65 and had a heavy dependence on alcohol and tobacco. Cigars came to be part of the Churchill wartime image and were ever-present in his mouth whether they were actually being smoked or not. Churchill certainly consumed alcohol heavily, with most activities being accompanied by a whisky and soda on top of what was consumed at meals. Churchill once famously boasted that he had drunk a bottle of champagne a day for most of his life. There are many references by contemporary politicians, military officers and diplomats to Churchill's drinking habits, but as he had a drink in hand most of the time this became a part of his character and way of life. Churchill reportedly usually drank the same exact amount every day and so built up a tolerance despite the amount consumed being greater than most people would imbibe.[31] Alcohol does not seem to have affected his performance or conduct of meetings until early in 1944 when the arguments over Burma and Anvil were at their height, the Anzio landing stalled and relations with Stalin were poor, although there were reports of Churchill being the worse for wear in 1940, particularly from Kennedy. In the 1940s, most men smoked cigarettes and the majority of meetings were conducted in a haze of smoke so Churchill's dependence on alcohol was perhaps not dissimilar to that of nicotine in other people.

Of more concern were the three potentially life-threatening illnesses that Churchill suffered during the Second World War alone. He had a minor heart attack in Washington in 1941 and two bouts of pneumonia in 1943, one in February and a very serious recurrence following the Tehran conference in December. The heart attack was no doubt due to the stress at the time of US entry into the war and the subsequent illnesses a result of fatigue from the amount of effort that Churchill expended in directing the war for Britain. Few men would have had the energy, strength and constitution to perform this task for nearly six years of war with hardly a break. Even men such as Brooke felt it necessary to take leave every now and then.

War Strategy

Before the outbreak of war, Churchill was proven completely correct in his predictions in international politics regarding the consequences of the rise to power of Hitler and the resurrection of Germany. However, Churchill's predictions and beliefs regarding military strategy proved to be more flawed. Before the war, Churchill severely underestimated the importance of modern aircraft and their effectiveness against ships as well as the future of tanks; he also believed that the Japanese would never risk attacking the fortress of Singapore.

Ultimately, Churchill's military strategies largely failed Britain during the war and arguably prolonged it unnecessarily. While not responsible for the British declaration of war with France to save Poland (although he strongly supported it) and certainly not responsible for the state of the British Army before the outbreak of war (something he campaigned vigorously against), he was certainly culpable in the misfortunes that befell Britain in the first three years of the war and the continuation of the Mediterranean strategy that ultimately became a dead end.

Norway

Churchill was impatient for action against Germany, having proposed the mining of Norwegian territorial waters as early as September 1939. Offensive action was his motto, defence was a necessary evil and inaction a heresy. In a minute to the Admiralty in December 1939 regarding proposed action in the Baltic Sea, Churchill said, 'I could never become responsible for a naval strategy which excluded the offensive principle and relegated us to keeping open the lines of communication and maintaining the blockade.'[32]

After the war, it was proved from captured German documents that it was the *Altmark* incident that prompted Hitler's final decision to invade Norway. This had been ordered personally by Churchill and as a consequence, German troops descended on the country. Had Germany not made its plans as a result of the capture of the *Altmark*, the mining of Norwegian territorial waters as proposed by Churchill (who had merely borrowed the idea from similar actions in the First World War) would have almost certainly produced the same outcome. Thus Churchill caused the German invasion of Norway, which was probably something he was not displeased with given his reaction to the indifference of the country and Sweden to fighting for a free Europe and the plight of Finland. Churchill's culpability does not stop there because as Chairman of the Military Co-ordination Committee and the First Lord of the Admiralty, Churchill had a great hand in the direction of the campaign and its subsequent ignominious defeat. Even he described the campaign as ramshackle and considered himself lucky to survive in Cabinet after what was a major political and military catastrophe.

Fortunately, there was a much larger political scalp to be had in the guise of Chamberlain, who had severely misjudged the political and military ambitions of Hitler and Germany, unlike Churchill. Having claimed 'peace in our time' after the Munich conference of 1938, Britain and France had then gone to war over a distant Poland, despite Chamberlain's ultimatum (without providing a tiny bit of support to Poland) before he had presided over the Norwegian fiasco. Churchill modestly accepted responsibility for Norway during the debate in the House of Commons but such was the mood of Parliament, which had its sights set on Chamberlain, that even this admission only brought opposition taunts about him using himself as an air raid shelter to protect the government.[33]

France 1940

Thus on the day of the German attack on France, Churchill found himself elevated to the highest political office in the land to fight a war which he had predicted for a long time and for which Britain was woefully unprepared, despite his warnings and tireless campaign for rearmament throughout the 1930s. It was a position that Churchill believed was his destiny, for he thought he knew a great deal about the business of war and was sure he would not fail. As an earnest student of British history, Churchill believed he had the opportunity to become a member of the pantheon of great British leaders and strategists such as his relative, the Duke of Marlborough. Therefore it was a huge shock to Churchill for the War Cabinet to be contemplating entering into peace negotiations with Germany after only two weeks of fighting in France; Churchill's first act as Prime Minister, had he agreed to such an idea, would have been to ignore 900 years of Britons resisting foreign invasions and surrender to Germany. It is no wonder that this was unacceptable to Churchill, who rallied support from wherever he could find it, most notably at a meeting of the full Cabinet rather than the War Cabinet on 28 May after Halifax had discussed peace negotiations:

> I am convinced that every man of you would rise up and tear me down from my place if I were for one moment to contemplate parley or surrender. If this long island story of ours is to end at last, let it end only when each one of us lies choking in his own blood upon the ground.[34]

Thus having finally received the backing of the War Cabinet to not seek peace terms, Churchill's next problem was to keep the French fighting as long as possible. Churchill rejected an appeal to the United States as not being the right moment, for he believed the Americans would think better of such a plea if

Britain made a bold stand against Germany first and so better command their respect and admiration.[35] However, the involvement of the USA in this period engendered the notion in the British that America would have to enter the war if Britain was to survive. In France, the rapid German advance created an unfolding disaster and Churchill made repeated visits to the country to try to determine for himself the real situation and force the French into some sort of counter-attack. Given that the French did not know the real situation on the ground, they must have been bemused by Churchill's visits which, although essential for meetings of the Supreme War Council, merely served as distractions. The newly appointed General Weygand seemed to offer some hope of a counter-attack and Churchill eagerly seized upon it, to the incredulity of the British commanders of the BEF who had been forced to conform to a French withdrawal on their right flank, which had in turn uncovered the Belgian Army on their left in the north. The French continually appealed to Churchill for more aircraft to combat the German dominance of the skies and Churchill was perfectly willing to send them until stopped by a plea from Dowding on 16 May to preserve the fighter force for the coming defence of Britain.

Even after the almost miraculous evacuation of the BEF from Dunkirk, Churchill was within days planning to send more troops and aircraft to France to keep it fighting. Perhaps the far greater number of troops rescued from Dunkirk than anticipated enabled Churchill to contemplate running the risk of losing a few more to this end. The despatch of additional British troops was seen as madness by almost everyone except Churchill, as was his idea to create a redoubt in Brittany for future operations. Even the French were not keen on this last idea and fortunately the future CIGS, Brooke, who was commanding the forces still in France at the time, was able to convince Churchill to change his mind. A second evacuation from France then took place of the remaining troops of the BEF and the very recently arrived reinforcements, one division of which did not even leave its train on arriving in France. This time the evacuation was orderly without the loss of equipment and the Luftwaffe missed another easy target. Churchill later even deliberately misinterpreted a telegram from Roosevelt to Reynaud regarding future American aid in an attempt to persuade France to keep fighting. The French and British armies in France were ultimately defeated by their adherence to the First World War doctrine of the Maginot Line and by the modern weapons and aircraft of the German blitzkrieg. With France lost, Britain was left alone facing a rampant Germany and the Battle for Britain would begin.

Peace Negotiations

Always offensive minded and conscious of his place in history, Churchill had no truck with the suggestions of Halifax in late May that Britain and France explore peace proposals through the United States or Italy directly, using the flawed argument that Britain would receive no better terms after Dunkirk than if she was later invaded and forced to surrender. Britain in 1940 had been defeated in France but had not been vanquished and would have received far better terms in June than if forced by military action to accept an unconditional surrender later. Imbued by visions of death or glory for himself and the nation, Churchill was determined that Britain would never surrender.

While Britain drew breath and waited for the German onslaught, Churchill looked at how Britain could go on the offensive with what meagre resources were available. The SOE was set up with Churchill's famous exhortation 'to set Europe ablaze'. The Combined Operations office was created to plan and launch small raids on the Continent. If Britain could not challenge Germany directly, it would do so by subterfuge and guerrilla tactics.

The disposal of the French fleet became a burning issue for Churchill for if it was incorporated into the German and Italian fleets, the Royal Navy would be seriously challenged for control of the seas. With the failure of the French fleet to sail to America or scuttle itself, Churchill ruthlessly ordered the Royal Navy to destroy the French warships in the harbour at Oran. Englishmen bombarded Frenchmen; for the British ships it was like shooting fish in a barrel with the French ships at anchor and unable to manoeuvre in the harbour. Many Frenchmen have not forgiven the British for this action to this day which did, however, demonstrate to the rest of the world, particularly the United States, Churchill's determination to carry on the war. Roosevelt, finally convinced that Britain was not going to seek peace terms, authorised the First World War vintage destroyers requested by Churchill to be traded with Britain for Atlantic bases as a consequence of this action.

Even though the Battle of Britain had not been won and the immediate threat of invasion not yet eased, Churchill felt confident enough to reject further peace overtures from the King of Sweden in early August, along with other approaches from Europe and America.

The first anniversary of Churchill becoming Prime Minister coincided with the arrival of Hess in Scotland. This was a last attempt at peace by Hitler, who was anxious to secure Germany's western flank before invading Russia. Hess was given short shrift by Churchill and was eventually locked up in an asylum so that all access to him was strictly controlled. Hitler went ahead with the invasion of Russia, giving Britain and Churchill an unintended but hugely important lifeline. The Red Army would spend the next four years fighting the greater part of the Germany Army (180–200 divisions), which was to the enormous benefit of Britain and America.

Battle of Britain

German plans for the invasion of Britain were dependent on the Luftwaffe gaining aerial supremacy over the RAF before the invasion fleet sailed, a condition which the small and understrength German Navy was no doubt happy to see met first. The naval actions off Norway had sunk or put out of action half the Kriegsmarine's destroyers so that only five were available for any invasion. The Royal Navy had assembled more than thirty destroyers at ports on the south coast and had already contributed significantly to the defence of Britain through its action in Norway without realising it. In the ensuing air battles over England, the RAF won a great victory, although it was almost brought to its knees by the high number of pilots that became casualties. Dowding's memorandum of 16 May and the refusal to send more aircraft to France after Dunkirk as Churchill had proposed preserved just enough men and aircraft to stave off the Luftwaffe. This victory was helped enormously by the decision of the Germans to begin bombing British cities instead of RAF facilities in retaliation for raids on Berlin. These raids were specifically ordered by Churchill as a means of hitting back at Germany and appear to have been more motivated by revenge than to ease the pressure on the exhausted RAF. Nevertheless, the outcome for the civilians of both Germany and Britain was that they and their homes were now in the front line. The English cities and their unprepared local councils experienced death, destruction and the misery of homelessness on a hitherto unknown scale, London being heavily bombed on seventy-one occasions including on fifty-seven consecutive nights in the second half of 1940.[36] There was little discussion in the War Cabinet of Churchill's change of policy in the bombing of Germany until 11 September, when the possibility of reprisals for indiscriminate attacks on London against twenty German cities was raised after the Prime Minister had ordered the raids on military targets in Berlin.[37] In the German air raids on Britain between 1940 and 1945, 60,595 civilians were killed by bombs and rockets. In Germany, at the hands of the

USAAF and the RAF, the equivalent figure of civilians was more than 500,000 killed because of the greater size and intensity of the British night raids, which were later augmented by American daylight raids.[38]

At the end of September, having won the aerial battle in the skies over England, Britain still stood alone, protected by the moat of the English Channel which was a physical barrier to the German Army but not the Luftwaffe, which now made almost daily raids on English cities in the eight-month-long Blitz.

Greece

The question as to what Germany and its allies might do next was partially answered by the Italian invasion of Egypt from Libya on 13 September and Greece from Albania on 28 October 1940. Churchill and the Defence Committee on 31 October approved the despatch of British aircraft from the beleaguered Middle East Command to help the Greeks and troops to occupy the islands of Crete and Lemnos. These British reactions to Italy's aggression prompted Hitler to order plans to be made for the invasion of Greece within days of the arrival of aircraft; Hitler was furious with Mussolini for not informing him of his intentions and that Germany's achievement by diplomatic means of access to the Rumanian oilfields at Ploesti had been imperilled by the arrival of British aircraft in Greece. Britain raised the stakes in February 1941 when the War Cabinet approved the sending of a larger force to Greece. Even as the situation worsened, a formal agreement was signed by Eden and the Greek government on 4 March, the day before the first troops left Egypt.

Churchill's strategy of sending more troops was made up of several different elements. Britain had extended to Greece a pact guaranteeing support in April 1939 and this was reinforced on 4 March 1941 so Britain was obliged to come to the assistance of the Greeks, who were determined to fight in any case; the failure to do so by Britain would be poorly regarded by countries such as the United States. Another part of Churchill's strategy was to create a bloc against Germany by forming an alliance with Greece and Turkey. The Chiefs of Staff were also concerned about Turkey becoming a German ally or being used by the Germans as a jumping off point for operations against the Middle East through Syria. Lastly, the Lend-Lease Bill was proceeding through the

American Senate and House of Representatives and the British could ill afford any negative public opinion of its actions or even inactions in Greece. However, Churchill completely misjudged German intentions, which were to secure its south-eastern borders diplomatically and then invade Russia. The sending of British aircraft in early November to Athens changed German plans and caused it to invade Greece, principally to protect the Ploesti oilfields. Turkey, after losing much of its empire in the First World War, was certainly not going to join the next conflict and remained neutral throughout, despite Churchill's repeated attempts to bring it into the war. Yugoslavia was coerced into signing the Tripartite pact with Germany and British efforts (at Churchill's instigation) to trigger a coup in the country after the pact was signed were successful, but that strategy too led to invasion by Germany. Once Yugoslavia was occupied, this gave the German Army a route with which to turn the Aliakmon Line in Greece being manned by British and Greek forces and the result was another British military humiliation and evacuation. This was followed by yet another evacuation from Crete. Many hundreds of British and Dominion lives were lost in these invasions, thousands of men were taken prisoner and once again all their equipment was lost. As in France and Norway, the British failed to learn the lessons of the overwhelming air support that the Germans gave their ground forces and the need for fighter aircraft to combat this. Militarily and politically, Churchill's strategy was a disaster as Turkey remained steadfastly neutral, two countries had been invaded and the British suffered two more heavy defeats. Churchill had tried to position Britain as the defender of democracies against German aggression for Roosevelt, which only resulted in another military defeat. Churchill did, however, have the consolation that the Lend-Lease Bill had passed through Congress, thus assuring Britain's survival with this lifeline from America which was the real objective of the Greek debacle.

North Africa

If the disasters in Greece and Crete were not enough, Rommel's newly arrived divisions in North Africa had smashed through the British defences in Libya, weakened as a result of the transfer of units to Greece. By 10 April, the Germans had laid siege to Tobruk and Egypt was once again threatened. With the passage of the Lend-Lease legislation, suddenly the evacuation of the British and Dominion troops in Greece was not as important as preventing the further German advances in Libya towards Egypt, judging from Churchill's directive of 18 April. Rommel's arrival in the Middle East was primarily to support the beleaguered Italians in Libya and it was only later following the rapid German advances that the opportunity of advancing to the Suez Canal became apparent.

Following the defeats and humiliating evacuations from Norway, France, Greece and Crete in the first two years of war, the British Army was in no position to wage war directly against Germany. Although the Army was being increased in size to fifty-five divisions largely as a result of Churchill's efforts on the Land Forces Committee, it also needed great quantities of rifles, tanks, artillery guns and ammunition, large quantities having been lost during each evacuation. Having averted the threat of invasion by winning the Battle of Britain, there was nowhere in 1941 that the British could take on the might of the German Army of more than 200 divisions even if it had a large enough army to do so. Fortunately Britain found an ally that was capable of matching and defeating the bulk of the German Army in the form of Russia from June 1941. Therefore Churchill and Britain adopted the only strategy they could, which was to wage a peripheral war against Germany and Italy while working with the United States for its eventual entry into the conflict. The Italians had taken the initiative in the Mediterranean by invading Greece from Albania, Egypt from Libya and Somaliland from Ethiopia, so for the first two years Britain was largely reacting to the presence and offensives of firstly the Italians and then the Germans rather than following any strategy. The Mediterranean provided the only arena where it was possible to engage the Axis in a limited ground campaign with the possibility of a future strike at the soft underbelly of Germany and this was where Britain opted to send some of its precious few divisions. However, rather than going on the offensive and taking the fight to Germany, of even more concern to Britain at this time was the protection of the Middle East and the sea lanes to the Far East via the Suez Canal from an opportunistic Italy. Therefore it fell to the unfortunate General Wavell in the Middle East to provide forces in 1941 to protect Egypt and British interests in East Africa as well as provide expeditionary forces to Syria and Greece. Although Wavell received several divisions from the Australians, Indians and the New Zealanders, there were never enough troops in the Middle East command to accomplish all of the objectives required by Churchill.

Having already misjudged the mood of the Vichy French when the September 1940 attempt by de Gaulle and an Anglo-French task force to seize Dakar had to be abandoned when the French resisted, Churchill would attempt the same in Syria in 1941. The coup in Iraq fermented by German agents prompted Churchill to demand further military action of Wavell, whose overstretched forces were already dealing with the battles in Greece and Crete while trying to force Rommel back from Tobruk. However, a scratch force of British, Free French and Australian troops entered Syria in June 1941 to rapidly put down the Iraqi coup. Once again, de Gaulle's assumption that Vichy French forces would not resist proved to be wrong and bitter fighting ensued. After a short campaign of five weeks, the Vichy French signed an armistice and Free Frenchmen took over the administration of Syria. Therefore, after nearly two years of war against Germany, Britain's only successful land operation was against the French. Churchill reorganised the Middle East command, bringing in Auchinleck to replace the taciturn Wavell, who was given command of the ABDA forces in the Far East.

After more than two years of war, Churchill's interventionist strategies had led to disasters, evacuations and German invasions of Norway, Greece and Yugoslavia. In North Africa and the Middle East, Churchill had been forced to send scarce troops to the region to secure Egypt and Syria to block the Axis initiatives, as Britain was very much on the defensive.

Britain and America

Following Roosevelt's re-election in November 1940, the US President and Churchill set about establishing stronger military ties between the two countries and planning for the possibility of future joint involvement in the war. At some point before the election, Roosevelt had decided that if he was re-elected, the United States would have to enter the war against Germany and more than likely Japan in the future, and that he was the man to lead the country; indeed this may well have prompted his decision to stand for re-election for an unprecedented third term. Provided Britain did not succumb to the Axis, it would provide a base and jumping-off point for future operations against Germany. American and British officers in plain clothes met in Washington in the first quarter of 1941 and agreed joint plans known as ABC-1, which gave priority to defeating Germany first. In the Atlantic Ocean, the active role of the US Navy gradually increased throughout the year as it took on more and more responsibility for patrolling and escorting convoys, initially to and from Iceland, which US troops occupied in July 1941 to relieve the British garrison.

Churchill was naturally anxious to establish a personal relationship with the man who would be the architect of Lend-Lease and Britain's potential ally and saviour; eventually the two met at Placentia Bay in August 1941, ironically one of the ex-British bases that Churchill had leased to the Americans in exchange for the fifty vintage destroyers. While military planning by the respective Chiefs of Staff continued in the background, Churchill tried to impress Roosevelt by suggesting the drawing up of the Atlantic Charter that declared their joint nations' interest in a future world free of aggression. Churchill was warned not to even raise the subject of American entry into the war with Roosevelt, who was grappling with political and public opposition to the conflict at the time. America's ambitious rearmament programme was nearly scuppered by an amendment to the Selective Service Act, which was only passed by one vote during the historic Placentia meetin. Despite one article of the Atlantic Charter being tantamount to a declaration of war, the conference ended without this or even a planned date for entry by the United States, which was frustrating for Churchill. If there was a formal strategy to get the United States onside, it was not working at the rate Churchill would have liked. Both Churchill and Roosevelt required 'an incident' to change public opinion and propel the United States into the war.

The United States was the only possible source of salvation for Britain and despite Churchill's best efforts and most earnest desire, America would not come into the war until there was a justifiable cause to sway public opinion. With an increasingly bellicose Roosevelt escalating the war in the Atlantic and having placed an oil embargo on Japan in an attempt to curb its aggression, the conflict became truly global with the Japanese attack on the United States on 7 December 1941 at Pearl Harbor. This did not come as a surprise to Churchill and Roosevelt with the United States already on a war footing, the only unknown factor being where Japan would strike. The US Congress declared war on Japan the next day but despite all the previous manoeuvres, plans and expectations of Churchill, the United States did not declare war on Germany. It took Hitler's stupendous declaration of war on the United States on 11 December to bring it into the war against Germany, even though the campaign in Russia was still in progress. Now Britain's eventual victory over Germany was assured. To these good tidings for Churchill was added the news from the Middle East that the Operation Crusader offensive by Auchinleck's newly formed Eighth Army had succeeded in lifting the siege at Tobruk on the same day as the Japanese struck at Pearl Harbor.

In the aftermath of Pearl Harbor and the fateful German declaration of war, Churchill and his Chiefs immediately rushed to the United States. They were fearful that, in view of the Japanese attack, the Americans would demand action against Japan and change the 'Germany first' policy, although these fears proved unfounded. However, the carefully made plans for a defensive stance in the Pacific were rendered redundant by the rampaging Japanese forces in the Far East. Malaya, Burma and the Dutch East Indies were all invaded and occupied in the space of ten weeks, while India itself was threatened. The Philippines were also invaded but held out until 6 May 1942. The prized British possession of Hong Kong was captured along with Singapore, the supposedly impregnable fortress that Japan would not risk attacking, according to Churchill and others pre-war.[39] Churchill called the loss of Singapore the greatest defeat in British military history when addressing the US Congress in May 1943, yet the British leader had gambled that the Japanese would not attack and diverted the men and material necessary for building defences in Malaya to North Africa and Syria. In a matter of days, two of Churchill's pre-war assumptions regarding the ability of warships to defend themselves against aircraft and the impregnability of Singapore were proven wrong. While Singapore had long been neglected, there were opportunities to bolster its defences in 1941 which Churchill did not take, so he must bear the responsibility for its fall.

The success of Japan meant that the first strategic issue for Britain and the United States after Pearl Harbor was how to bolster the defences in the Far East and Pacific lest India should be invaded, despite the commitment of both countries to a 'Germany first' policy.

Operation Torch, North-West Africa

With Britain still rebuilding and re-equipping its Army, as was the United States, Anglo-American strategy against Germany had to be carefully examined as Roosevelt in particular could not afford any political failures. In determining joint strategy, Churchill hoped to bend the Americans to his will and to a great extent succeeded for the next year. Churchill's vision of how the war should be conducted differed markedly to that of the Americans. They were determined to set the strategic agenda and a memorandum by General Marshall provided the basis for discussions in early April 1942 for Allied strategy against Germany. Roosevelt and Marshall took a more global view than the British and firmly believed that as the Russians were the only Ally actively fighting Germans, then the British and Americans needed to mount a landing in France that year, Operation Sledgehammer, even if it was sacrificial, in order to draw away German forces from Russia. Churchill and the British Chiefs of Staff were horrified at this proposal. Mid 1942 was the nadir of British fortunes in the war. To the previous defeats and evacuations of 1940 and 1941 at the hands of the Germans were added the defeats by the Japanese in the Far East, all of which had again seen the British Army lose thousands of men killed or taken prisoner along with valuable equipment. British soldiers were becoming casualties or prisoners of war almost as rapidly as new divisions were being created. Churchill was not prepared to risk a direct confrontation with German troops at this point and he and his Chiefs of Staff believed that Britain did not have the resources in 1942 to make any landing in France successful and permanent. Accordingly, the British accepted Marshall's plan in principle which had enough latitude in their minds to avoid committing themselves to Operation Sledgehammer.

The arrival of Molotov in London and then Washington convinced Roosevelt more than ever of the need for some sort of operation, if not a Second Front, as soon as possible to assist Russia in 1942. Churchill used Mountbatten to explain to Roosevelt in Washington in June why a Second Front or even Operation Sledgehammer was not possible in 1942. At this point, the first crisis in Anglo–American relations arose with Roosevelt threatening to make the Pacific a priority after this apparent change of British heart. Sufficiently alarmed, Churchill and his Staff flew to Washington for a series of vigorous but inconclusive meetings with the Americans. Roosevelt had suggested to the US Chiefs of Staff that they reconsider the North African operation, Gymnast, as an alternative but they bitterly opposed this on the grounds that this would delay any build-up in the United Kingdom and as a consequence, any landing under Operation Roundup in 1943. The talks were interrupted by the news of Rommel's capture of Tobruk and Churchill was forced to return to England without a decision to face a Parliamentary no confidence motion that was ultimately easily defeated. Roosevelt then sent Marshall and Hopkins to England to thrash out an agreement with the British Chiefs of Staff for action in 1942. Both to assist the Russians and for his own political benefits with mid-term elections in November, Roosevelt wanted American troops in action somewhere in 1942. Churchill was aware of Roosevelt's motivations and astutely let Marshall make a futile attempt to change the British position, which had been endorsed by the War Cabinet. When no agreement could be reached, Roosevelt then ordered Marshall to agree on some action with the British and the only other real alternative besides putting American troops into the Middle East under British command was Operation Gymnast in north-west Africa. Thus Churchill won this Battle of strategy by shrewdly exploiting the differences between Roosevelt and Marshall and the Americans found themselves committed to operations in north-west Africa and the Mediterranean. The British strategy of a peripheral war against Germany in 1942 would be followed more for domestic American political reasons than any other. The responsibility for the Allies embarking on their Mediterranean strategy lies with Roosevelt and not Churchill. Once again, the next proposed British operation would be against the Vichy French.

Before Pearl Harbor, Britain had suffered consecutive defeats in reacting to Axis offensives and Churchill had no strategy against Germany other than his peripheral strategy and to get the US into the war. Once that was achieved, from 1942 onwards, Churchill had two strategic imperatives. The first imperative was to keep the focus on 'Germany first' and not allow any major diversion of resources to the Pacific, and the second was to ensure that a Mediterranean strategy was pursued rather than any landings in France, which Churchill was convinced could not succeed.

Having decided on the course of operations for the remainder of 1942, Churchill suggested a meeting with Stalin to inform him of the more glamorously renamed Operation Gymnast, Operation Torch, and explain the decision not to launch a Second Front that year. Churchill was given an understandably frosty reception but Stalin eventually warmed to the plan in the hope that it would divert German divisions from the Eastern Front and provide a route for the British and Americans to attack the soft underbelly of the Axis. Later, Churchill was forced to admit to the British Chiefs of Staff that he had led Stalin to believe there would be Second Front in 1943. Churchill also promised the Russians a renewed bomber offensive against Germany and a raid in force on the French coast. That raid duly took place at Dieppe in August 1942, Churchill having said to Stalin he was prepared to lose 10,000 men. For Churchill, the decision to launch the raid was a win-win situation for all the Allies except for the Canadians. If the raid succeeded, it would boost Allied morale and compel the Germans to bring in more troops to defend the coastline. If it failed, the raid would have demonstrated to both the Americans and Russians the difficulties of making a landing on the Continent such as proposed for Operation Sledgehammer or a Second Front. Deprived of naval support, fail it did and out of a force of 4,912 Canadian personnel, 907 were killed, 586 wounded and 1,946 taken prisoner.

After vigorous debate about the landing sites for the north-west African operation and the forces allocated to them which was only settled by the Chiefs of Staff of both nations being forced to refer the issue to Roosevelt and Churchill, Operation Torch was launched on 8 November 1942. A likely consequence of the British and American action was for the Germans to occupy Vichy France, although Churchill had played this down to Roosevelt. The Torch landings were successful, although a third of the total Allied assault force remained idle at Casablanca after its capture, remote from Tunisia. On 13 November, the switch of the allegiance of the Vichy Forces to Free France was negotiated and German forces promptly overran the rest of mainland France. The Americans and British advanced slowly to the east as the Germans rushed reinforcements into Tunisia and managed to block the Allied advances. By 4 December, the Germans and the bad weather had caused a temporary halt to the campaign; the Germans had won the race to build up forces in Tunisia as feared by Churchill and had transferred enough units to build an entire new Panzer army. The campaign would not be over by Christmas as planned.

However, British and American thoughts were already turning to post-Torch operations and the two nations met at Casablanca in January, each armed with reports on their preferred strategy for the war in 1943. The same differences of grand strategy as in 1942 quickly arose, with Marshall wanting to launch Roundup in the autumn of 1943 into France while the British preferred an invasion of Sicily with the objective of knocking Italy out of the war. Roosevelt and Churchill both did not want to see their North African armies idle for any length of time with the Russians being left as the only nation fighting Germany. Therefore the quickest and easiest way of continuing the fight against the Axis was for the Allies to invade Sicily, which was the strategy finally agreed upon. This would see a continuation of the Mediterranean strategy from which Marshall feared the Americans would never disentangle themselves once committed. Marshall also pointed out that if the invasion of Sicily was undertaken, Operation Roundup would not be feasible until 1944. With Roosevelt preferring operations in the Mediterranean and not supporting Marshall, the decision was taken to invade either Sicily or Sardinia. Thus operations continued in the Mediterranean as desired by Churchill and Brooke at the behest of all at Casablanca, thus relieving Churchill of his commitment to Stalin.

Better weather saw the resumption of the slow advances by the British and American forces and the Axis forces in Tunisia finally surrendered on

12 May 1943; the North African campaign lasted five months longer than planned and saw no German Army units diverted there from Russia. This delay once and for all effectively scuppered any landings in France that year, much to Churchill's relief. From Britain's point of view, the entire coastline of North Africa was now under their control and Egypt was secure; the only remaining threat in the Mediterranean was from the Italians. By mid 1943, the war was going a lot better for Britain since the dark days of twelve months earlier. Britain was victorious in North Africa, had not been invaded and now had powerful Allies in Russia and America. The Germans had been defeated at Stalingrad while the Japanese, having suffered reverses at Midway, Guadalcanal and in Papua New Guinea, were now on the defensive. The prospects of the Allies winning the war were a lot brighter than at any time before.

Sicily

The major decisions taken at Casablanca were then reviewed and in order to forestall any American moves to give priority to the Pacific, Churchill and his staff 'gate-crashed' a conference of the Far East commanders in Washington in May 1943 at what became known as the Trident conference. After vigorous debate between the Chiefs of Staff, operations in the Mediterranean were allowed to continue while the British were forced to commit to a cross-Channel operation on the Continent for May 1944 for which seven divisions would be transferred to Britain from Italy. Most importantly, Trident approved the Combined Bomber Offensive to reduce the industrial and military power of Germany as well as undermining the morale of the German people; Anglo-American work would also continue on the atomic bomb project.

Churchill, fearful of further recriminations from Stalin and mindful of his promise regarding a Second Front, was determined that the next operation would be mainland Italy and immediately went from Washington to Algiers to put his point of view to Eisenhower, who preferred to wait to see how the Sicilian landings faired. The American and British armies landed on Sicily on 10 July without the next step in the Mediterranean strategy even having been decided. Less than a week after the successful landings, Roosevelt and Churchill agreed to another meeting to discuss future strategy at the conclusion of the Sicilian campaign. Tension had arisen between the British and Americans over a British 'stand-still' order for shipping and the Italians had made genuine approaches regarding peace negotiations. Before this meeting at Quebec took place, the Combined Chiefs of Staff directed Eisenhower on 26 July to plan for the invasion of the Italian mainland and later approved Operation Avalanche for an amphibious landing at Salerno.

The Quadrant conference in Quebec in mid August affirmed the decision for operations against the Italian mainland but this time the objectives had been extended by Churchill to liberating Rome as a continuation of the Mediterranean strategy. Debate at this conference became acrimonious when the Americans queried the British resolve in Burma and for the cross-Channel operation; American suspicions were correct – Churchill was opposed to both. However, after the British renewed their commitment to Overlord, which was to be given overriding priority, more harmonious meetings resumed. Nevertheless, the Mediterranean strategy would continue as Churchill's preferred course, one that offered 'glittering prizes'.

Italy finally surrendered in secret on 3 September, the day British troops crossed the Straits of Messina to land unopposed on the foot of Italy as the Germans had withdrawn northwards. The Germans reacted swiftly to the well-telegraphed Italian public surrender on 8 September by implementing plans to occupy Italy that were completed overnight. The airborne component of the Salerno landings the next day had to be cancelled but two British and one American divisions landed without a supporting naval bombardment on 9 September to be met by German rather than Italian forces. The German counter-attack was only repelled with strong naval and air support and nearly reached the landing beaches. Churchill's idea of the landings delivering another blow to Italian morale had been negated by the timing of the Italian surrender and the quick occupation of the country by German troops. The beachhead was forced to fight for its very survival rather than cutting off any German troops further south. On 16 September, the beachhead and the advancing Eighth Army linked up and two weeks later the port of Naples was captured while the Germans simply withdrew to yet another prepared line of defences on the Volturno Line. Despite the major objective of eliminating Italy from the war having been achieved, the Americans were inextricably committed to the war in the Mediterranean. Following the Italian surrender, Churchill became obsessed with seizing the weakly garrisoned Italian Dodecanese Islands in the Aegean Sea, ordering a stretched Middle East Command to provide the forces to take the islands. This was another of Churchill's pet projects – an operation to capture Rhodes called Operation Mandibles had been previously cancelled but would now finally be realised. A ruse to capture Rhodes was forestalled by German troops on the island but British troops landed on Kos, Leros and Samos. The Germans reacted strongly to the loss of these islands; Kos was recaptured by the Germans on 3 October and many British soldiers were taken prisoner. On 12 November, the Germans mounted a small amphibious operation against Leros and a further 3,200 British soldiers were taken prisoner. Within weeks the British were forced to abandon all the other islands they had seized while the Americans were able to occupy Corsica and Sardinia without firing a shot. Churchill was furious at what he saw as lost opportunities or prizes and blamed the Americans for not giving the Middle East command the small extra forces required. Churchill had presided over another military disaster just when the war was going the way of the Allies. At Churchill's personal insistence for the Middle East Commander-in-Chief 'to be bold and dare', more than 5,000 men were taken prisoner. At a point when the tide of war had appeared to have turned for Britain, this foolhardy venture which was not linked to any agreed Anglo-American strategy was an unnecessary setback.

Churchill had requested that American troops help in the Dodecanese at a critical point in the Italian campaign, but then became steadfastly opposed to the withdrawal of any divisions from Italy for Overlord. Churchill tried to delay the return of the seven veteran divisions by claiming there were only eleven Allied divisions to face fourteen German divisions. This plea was ignored by the Americans as there were in fact twenty Allied divisions in Italy on 1 November. Eisenhower was, however, permitted to retain landing craft for future operations until 15 December.

The three Allied leaders, the Big Three, finally agreed to meet for the first time in November in Tehran. At the conference, Stalin, having repeatedly been told of 'jam tomorrow' and then finding out that the Second Front had been repeatedly postponed, adopted an aggressive attitude towards Churchill. The three leaders agreed on a diversionary landing in the south of France at the same time as Overlord or even before it. The Russians made a surprise announcement that they would go to war with Japan after the defeat of Germany, as hoped by Churchill. Changes in high command were also made at this time, Eisenhower being appointed the Supreme Commander for Overlord and Wilson for the Mediterranean, making Italy now a largely British responsibility. With shipping still available for a short time, another amphibious operation was possible to break the deadlock in Italy where the Allies were being held on the Gustav Line at Cassino. Churchill seized on this opportunity and threw himself into the detailed planning of the operation whilst convalescing in the Middle East after a second bout of pneumonia. Operation Shingle, a three-division assault on Anzio, was launched on 22 January and once successfully ashore the American commander, General Lucas, opted to build up his forces before attempting any breakout to seize the Alban Hills to try to cut off or induce the retreat of the Germans on the Gustav Line to the south. This delay allowed the Germans to assemble a strong force for a counter-attack. The breakout attempt from Anzio was easily contained when it was made and the subsequent German counter-attack drove the Americans and British back to their last lines of defence but was ultimately unable to eliminate the beachhead altogether. Anzio had turned into another Salerno where the beachhead was forced to fight for its very survival rather than threatening the German strategic position in Italy. As the beachhead was reinforced by sea with troops from Cassino, the two armies there were correspondingly weakened and were in turn unable to break the Gustav Line. With new stalemates at both Cassino and Anzio, Churchill was less than impressed that his Mediterranean strategy had stalled again but was relieved that it had not ended in another Gallipoli.

As D-Day came nearer, Churchill's fears regarding the potential casualties and success of the operation grew. An alternative operation to support D-Day, Operation Caliph, to seize the port of Bordeaux was proposed for a time by Churchill. As time came for assembly of troops for Operation Anvil, the British became more and more opposed to it as the operation would divert strength from the Italian theatre, which was still not making progress quickly enough with Rome not captured, the Anzio beachhead isolated and the line Pisa–Rimini not reached. After many exchanges of telegrams, on 25 March the British, to their surprise, managed to get the Anvil landings postponed to after D-Day, on 10 July. This decision was followed by the news of the Americans retaining available shipping in the Pacific as it was no longer needed in the Mediterranean. This provoked a predictable outcry from the British and although they did not secure the use of the contested landing craft, Italian operations were once more made a priority. Churchill was, however, more than happy to support the diversion of troops for amphibious operations if they were of his own design (e.g. Operation Caliph). Having committed to the Anzio landings at the urging of Churchill, it would have been strategically unsound by the Allies to leave the beachhead to be destroyed by the Germans and Churchill was right at this point to insist that there be no weakening of the forces in Italy while the beachhead was threatened.

In mid May, the British and American offensive against the Gustav Line in southern Italy was renewed and this time broke through. A few days later, a limited offensive from Anzio began but instead of cutting off the German forces to the south, the bulk of the vanguard headed for Rome. The eternal city was liberated on 4 June, nearly six months later than planned, but the retreating German forces were able to bypass the weak American blocking force and take up new prepared positions to the north of Rome – the Trasimene Line. This was exactly as feared and predicted by the Americans.

Burma

Once the Japanese offensive in Burma that ejected the British from the country by the end of May had lost its impetus and India was no longer threatened, the British India Command consolidated its position along the India–Burma border at the end of 1942. At the Casablanca conference in January 1943, the Combined Chiefs of Staff ordered that a limited advance was to be made in northern Burma along with an amphibious operation to retake Rangoon, Operation Anakim, which was to be launched no later than November 1943. An operation to recapture Akyab in the Arakan Peninsula had already been planned and this started in December 1942, only to end in a demoralising retreat a few months later. A planned offensive by the Chinese and British in northern Burma did not take place as the Chinese had not moved from Yunnan province into position, and as a result the Japanese were able to move units to attack the flanks of the British troops in the Arakan Peninsula.

The Casablanca orders for Burma were reissued at the Trident conference and the British were again to commence operations in northern Burma plus capture Akyab when the monsoon finished in November of that year. Widespread flooding in India in the monsoon season then caused the postponement of these plans and by the time of the Quadrant conference, the British had yet to propose any new plans. The monsoon season was about to end with the British unprepared to launch any attacks in the coming dry season but Churchill remained strongly opposed to any operations at all in the jungles of northern Burma. Thus by the end of 1943, because of flooding, a lack of resources and a delay in planning caused by the creation of the Southeast Asia Command, the British had not mounted any operations in Burma. At the preliminary Sextant meetings in Cairo before Stalin, Roosevelt and Churchill met for the first time, Roosevelt had privately promised Chiang Kai-Shek that an amphibious assault, Operation Buccaneer, would be launched in conjunction with an operation in northern Burma, Operation Tarzan, both of which would largely be British offensives; Churchill was very unhappy at the prospects of such undertakings. On their return to Cairo, debate about Operation Buccaneer dominated the Anglo-American meetings until Roosevelt decided against it, overriding his own Chiefs of Staff once more in the process. Churchill saw this as meaning a reduced commitment to Burma and was pleased as all available resources could then be concentrated in the Mediterranean. The broken promise to the Chinese, however, signalled the dwindling importance of China as an ally.

The cancellation of Operation Buccaneer left a planning and operational vacuum in the Southeast Asia command for the coming year and Churchill then took issue with the strategy determined at Sextant for the Pacific to be the main effort of the war against Japan and the Southeast Asia Command to become a subsidiary theatre. Churchill claimed that he had not heard of the proposal and that there had not been sufficient time to consider it. Given Churchill's close management of all meetings with Roosevelt and his scrutiny of all documents, this claim is incredible. Churchill wanted to regain the colonies of Singapore and Hong Kong to restore British prestige and saw Operation Culverin, another favourite project, as an important first step in this process. Strategic planning meetings with Mountbatten in London and Washington were eclipsed by a new Japanese offensive in Burma on 8 March 1944. Following the arrival in Washington of another planning mission at the same time as Mountbatten's, one from Stilwell, Mountbatten's deputy, the Americans believed that the British were still going to mount Operation Culverin. This charge was denied by Mountbatten but Churchill was determined to regain lost prestige with operations to liberate Malaya and Singapore. Churchill then proposed another amphibious operation against the island of Simalur and consequently a major disagreement between Churchill and his own Chiefs of Staff arose, the latter going as far as contemplating resignation. The American Chiefs of Staff then rejected Mountbatten's plans at the time British troops were besieged at Kohima and Imphal. The Americans decided to launch their own operation given the prevarication and lack of enthusiasm on the part of the British for operations in Burma and the only American infantry regiment in the country marched through the jungle to seize the airfield at Myitkyina before laying siege to the town.

America refused to commit any more troops or aircraft to the Far East, believing Burma was a British responsibility, but Churchill was still extremely unwilling to order any offensive in the north of the country. This reluctance on the part of Churchill was despite the directives from the Combined Chiefs of Staff agreed at several Allied conferences to mount operations in northern Burma with the object of opening the Burma Road. Churchill and Britain had a moral obligation to meet the request of their American ally in ensuring the flow of aid to China in order to keep it in the war as the Americans were now supplying the bulk of men and equipment for the war in Europe. Churchill had been prepared to do anything previously to keep France in the war but was reluctant to help the Chinese, to whom he did not attach the same importance as America. At the Octagon conference of September 1944, Mountbatten was given another directive to mount Operation Capital in northern Burma and Operation Dracula against Rangoon. Claiming insufficient shipping, Churchill then postponed Dracula twice to December 1945 but reluctantly had to order Operation Capital to go ahead as the British had agreed to carry out such an offensive in northern Burma since Casablanca in early 1943 and had run out of excuses. Against the Japanese forces exhausted by the battles of Kohima and Imphal, Operation Capital in November 1944 was very successful and a follow-up operation in early 1945 allowed General Slim's army to advance overland across Burma to within 40 miles of Rangoon. Slim then requested an amphibious assault on Rangoon, which was successfully carried out by one division lifted in the only landing craft available. Burma was at last liberated but this was more due to the weakening of the Japanese forces by American operations against Japanese lines of communication in other theatres rather than any deliberate strategy adopted by Churchill. Despite Churchill's fears, following intensive planning, training and the use of aircraft for both supply and harassment of Japanese communications, British troops were able to operate successfully in the jungle.

D-Day and Operation Dragoon

Despite Churchill's considerable trepidations (and those of Brooke), the D-Day landings were successful although the American landings in the Omaha sector met considerable opposition. Meticulously planned and given an enormous amount of naval gunfire and heavy bomber support, the Allies were well established ashore by the end of the day. However, the major objective of Caen was not captured on D-Day as planned and fighting continued there for another six weeks before the British completed its capture. Following the failed German counter-attack at Mortain, the British and Americans were able to encircle the entire German Seventh Army and won a great victory at the end of August with the Germans in full retreat to the River Seine and beyond; Paris was liberated on 25 August. The American strategy for a cross-Channel landing as one of the proposed knock-out blows aimed at Germany had been completely vindicated.

Despite the success of Overlord, the Allies still needed a deep-water port through which to send follow-up divisions and supplies for the build-up, but the British were once again opposed to an Operation Anvil, now renamed Operation Dragoon. Churchill and his commanders in the Mediterranean were once again considering an alternative amphibious landing, this time in the Trieste area with the object of advancing from the Balkans to Vienna. Eisenhower and Marshall were against this 'diversionary' operation and angry telegrams were exchanged between the Chiefs of Staff, with the Americans labelling the British proposals 'unacceptable'. As was his habit, Churchill took the issue to Roosevelt, who strongly supported his commanders, claiming that Stalin would have to be consulted if Anvil was postponed as it had been agreed at Tehran. Churchill was forced to concede and planning for Operation Anvil continued as before. The balance of power between the British and Americans had changed and the latter were now providing the greater part of the resources for the war. Churchill and Britain had now been superseded by the Americans both in terms of the determination of strategy and contribution to the war effort. Churchill, however, made a last attempt to try to stop Operation Anvil by claiming that Eisenhower was against the operation. Always hopeful that the Italian campaign could be exploited, Churchill then became enamoured of another peripheral operation, this time a landing in Istria (Operation Sunstar) which was energetically pursued for the next three months until being finally cancelled in November as the withdrawal of troops from Italy for the operation would have dangerously weakened the Italian front. The Allied troops in Italy trying to break into the Po Valley repeatedly came up against new German defensive lines and the campaign ultimately fizzled out. It was the Germans who continued to pin down British and American troops in Italy rather than the other way around.

As if fighting against Germany and Japan was not enough, Churchill then got Britain involved in Greece, where there was a strong possibility that the Greek communists, having been originally armed by Britain to fight Germany, would try to seize power. Having readied a British force since September, on 5 December Churchill ordered it to be deployed in Athens and the immediate vicinity following the seizure of public buildings after a wave of civil unrest. From having despatched troops in 1941 to save Greece from an invasion which happened anyway, three years later British troops were firing on Greeks. Churchill did not put this intervention to the War Cabinet. Embarrassed by the leaking of a telegram regarding Greece to the American press, Churchill was forced to fly to Athens and try to negotiate a peaceful solution at the very time the Americans were fighting for their lives in the German Ardennes offensive.

A final dispute with the Americans arose over the advance to Berlin but British objections to a change of plans were largely ignored by an ailing Roosevelt and the Joint Chiefs of Staff. Churchill believed that the British and Americans should advance as far east as practicable in Germany (beyond the boundaries of the previously agreed zones of occupation) to ensure that the Soviets occupied as little German territory as possible to strengthen British and American post-war negotiations. Churchill would have liked to see both Berlin and Vienna occupied by fast-moving British or American troops but was given short shrift by Roosevelt and Marshall, who again supported Eisenhower. The Russians gratefully occupied Berlin and American and Russian troops met at the River Elbe on 25 April 1945.

Conclusion

After becoming Prime Minister, having averted the threat of invasion, Churchill's strategy had been more one of containment of potential German plans and reacting to actual Italian military operations in the Mediterranean. This had resulted in the ill-fated Greek expedition and against the Vichy French in Syria; both campaigns by Churchill overextended the British forces but the Greek campaign was more driven by the political considerations of Lend-Lease and the consequential negative American and world public opinion if Britain had not stood by its treaty obligations.

British and American strategy in the European war essentially came down to two alternatives. One alternative was the peripheral Mediterranean strategy and the other was the direct assault on the French coast. The British could not afford another disaster in 1942 (and nor could Churchill politically) if Operation Sledgehammer was launched to assist the Russians and therefore chose to not risk it. At Roosevelt's insistence for action in 1942, the Americans were committed to the Torch landings in north-west Africa. Although Eisenhower decried this decision, after the war he admitted that the British were right not to mount Operation Sledgehammer in 1942.[40]

Having suffered defeat after defeat, the British Army was not in the best condition to take on the German Army in a cross-Channel landing in 1942, especially when the RAF had not established aerial dominance over northern France. Britain, with its population of 48 million compared with the 131 million of the US, was struggling to raise and equip enough divisions to meet the competing requirements of a global conflict and simply could not afford to lose more men in an operation that did not have a good chance of success, just for the sake of aiding Russia.

Operation Torch was no Second Front but once committed, as Marshall feared, it proved impossible for the Allies to extricate themselves. A major landing in France (Operation Roundup) was planned and agreed to take place in 1943 but the resistance put up by the Germans in North Africa ensured the Tunisian campaign lasted six months longer than expected until mid 1943, when it was too late to switch men and equipment to England to make a landing on the Continent in sufficient force from England that year. The only chance of launching a decisive blow at Germany in 1943 would have been if this was decided at Casablanca and the shipping for a build-up in England subsequently organised for a cross-Channel landing in August or September. Following the efforts of Churchill, this was not the outcome as Roosevelt and Churchill preferred to not see their respective armies idle for any length of time, deciding that operations against Italy should continue with the invasion of Sicily in order to provide the most relief for the Russians. Subsequently the Italian mainland was invaded, even though Italy surrendered on the first day of the landings.

The decision to invade Sicily was made in the full knowledge that a cross-Channel landing would not then be possible in 1943. The invasion of Sicily was not what the Russians wanted or had been promised; they wanted that year a cross-Channel landing, a Second Front. The subsequent Sicilian campaign saw no German Army units diverted from Russia.

The war could have arguably ended twelve months earlier but Churchill's determination to mount a campaign through Italy into Germany and Hitler's tactics of reinforcing defeat in North Africa extended the north-west African campaign by a vital six months. This extension plus the demand for unconditional surrender announced at Casablanca certainly extended the war by a year, according to one of the American planners, General Wedemeyer.[41]

When Brooke angrily wrote in November 1943 that the war in Europe could have been over by the end of 1943, he was clearly frustrated and possibly exaggerating, but he too clearly believed it could have been ended sooner – if only the Americans had adhered to the Mediterranean strategy. The problem was deciding at what point had the Mediterranean strategy sufficiently weakened the Germans for a cross-Channel assault, which even Brooke agreed was necessary at some point.

A major objective of the Casablanca conference, the elimination of Italy from the war, had been achieved but the new objective of Rome had been added by Churchill, who would not give up on his peripheral strategy of striking at the underbelly of Germany until as late as October 1944, when amphibious landings at Trieste were being seriously considered in order to advance through the Balkans to Vienna. Churchill's desire for another Dardanelles-type strategy in the Mediterranean was really behind British strategy once America came into the war. The Americans finally refused to support any more operations they regarded as diversionary and even began to restrict the availability of shipping they controlled to ensure that the British adhered to the agreed strategy. If the Americans had not insisted on Operation Overlord in 1944, men and equipment would have been frittered away in the Mediterranean on operations of dubious potential. A decisive blow had to be aimed at Germany some time, despite Churchill's pessimistic views of Overlord and his preference for peripheral operations.

So could landings have been made in France in 1943 if this decision was taken at Casablanca? With the resources of men and equipment being poured into north-west Africa, victory there was only a matter of time despite Hitler's delaying tactics. Allied aircraft would then have been able to bomb Italy and force the eventual capitulation of Italy probably without even the invasion of Sicily, such was the growing feeling against the war in the formerly Axis country. Meanwhile, the transfer of forces to England could have achieved a sizeable force ready for invasion in late August or September had the Americans continued the build-up at the agreed rate. Such an operation would have undoubtedly drawn off German divisions from Russia as demanded by Stalin. Once ashore, would the Allied landings have been successful? This is a moot point and a detailed examination is beyond the scope of this book.

However, a significant factor in the success of Operation Overlord in 1944 was the Combined Bomber Offensive that after more than a year of operations had taken a considerable toll of German industry and brought the aerial dominance of the skies over Normandy that the Allies enjoyed. The impact of the bomber offensive would not have been felt in any landings in 1943 but the Germans would also have had a year less to improve their coastal defences of the Atlantic Wall. There is no reason why aerial superiority could have been achieved in 1943 once the decision was taken and adequate resources redeployed.

The invasion of Sicily showed that the Allies had enough landing craft in 1943 for a large amphibious assault, the problem being in 1944 that they were dispersed between the Mediterranean and the Pacific.

By 1944, the Germans had had plenty of time to build up their defences in France but in 1943 there were eight fewer German divisions in the west than in 1944. It is true that American troops gained valuable combat experience against Germans in Tunisia and Sicily in 1943 but several green divisions were successfully used in Overlord while some veteran divisions performed poorly, so the issue of combat experience is not significant. For most of 1943 there were sixteen divisions in the UK available for an assault on France rather than defence. With German troops forced to redeploy to France from their deepest penetration into Russia to face an Allied landing in 1943 (as they did in 1944) and the likely capitulation of Italy without an invasion, simultaneous blows by the Russians from the east and British and Americans from the west may well have ended the war sometime in 1944. Had Churchill strongly advocated a landing in France in 1943, there is no doubt it would have taken place as there would not have been the diversion of American resources to the Pacific theatre. It remains a subject of speculation as to how any landings in France in 1943 would have fared but experts such as Wedemeyer believed they would have been successful and the war could have ended a year earlier, provided the political question of unconditional surrender was resolved.

Certainly the consequences of the war ending a year earlier would have been enormous. With the benefit of hindsight, these consequences would have included the Red Army not overrunning Eastern Europe and Britain not being subjected to another Blitz from the V weapons. The greatest gain for the citizens of Europe would have been no further loss of life or damage to cities, homes and infrastructure. Berlin would have been captured by the British and Americans and the capital cities of Vienna and Prague would have been liberated instead of swapping one totalitarian regime for another.

Churchill's Mediterranean strategy ultimately proved to be a dead end. It saw few German Army units sent from the Eastern Front and merely served to engage and pin down twenty or so German divisions in terrain ideal for defence. It was Churchill himself who once pointed out that there were more German divisions engaged in fighting the Greek resistance and Yugoslav partisans than there were in Italy. Hitler's decision to defend Italy south of Rome while the winter defensive lines were prepared ultimately flipped Allied strategy on its head. While the Allies were trying to tie down the maximum number of German divisions in Italy, these German divisions were pinning down the armies of Britain and America, which allowed Hitler to focus resources on the Russian Front.

The ultimate results of the Mediterranean campaign were the elimination of Italy from the war, the securing of Egypt (and the vital Suez Canal) and the attrition of German units preventing their deployment elsewhere. The Germans employed in Italy no more than twenty-five divisions, which was less than 15 per cent of the total number of 200 divisions in the German Army. This statistic highlights the scale of the struggle on the Russian Front and the size of the burden carried by the Red Army. The Mediterranean campaign saw very few German divisions diverted from Russia but several were transferred from France. It was not until D-Day and the Normandy campaign that the Germans began a major redeployment of forces from Norway and Russia to the fighting in France, including the transfer of units such as the 2nd SS Panzer Korps from Russia, which certainly assisted the Russian offensive launched at the end of June. In late 1943, the British Chiefs of Staff were unable to prevent Churchill from being responsible for yet another British disaster in the Dodecanese Islands.

In the Far East, operations were hampered by both a lack of resources and British inertia. The Americans were finally forced to take matters into their own hands despite the orders to Mountbatten from the Combined Chiefs of Staff and use their own troops to capture Myitkyina in order to secure the Burma Road. The Far East is deserving of its soubriquet as the Forgotten Campaign as Churchill, wedded to the 'Germany first' policy, had no desire to carry out operations in northern Burma, no matter how much the Combined Chiefs of Staff and the Americans wanted them. Churchill ignored an obligation to an ally that had ensured Britain's survival and was contributing enormously in men and material to the war against Germany.

At the Trident and particularly the Quadrant conferences, Churchill and the British Chiefs of Staff complained about being forced to adhere to the rigid, fixed policy of the Americans. Marshall and the Americans had since 1942 always advocated a cross-Channel assault as one of the main ways of delivering a blow to Germany and winning the war. This became a cornerstone of Anglo-American strategy and the Americans, in view of their entry into the war and the great numbers of men and material they were contributing to defeating Germany, took a dim view of Churchill's lack of enthusiasm for it and the regular proposals for peripheral operations such as Operation Jupiter. The British conversely argued for a more flexible approach to strategy that allowed adjustments for changes in the strategic circumstances, such as the withdrawal of the seven divisions from Italy for Overlord or the withdrawal of the Anvil forces from the same country. Churchill was also deeply aggrieved by additional Allied units not being available for operations such as against the Dodecanese in 1943. The problem for the Allies was that there were limited resources even with America in the war and the best use of these had to be made, which is where the debate began as to what exactly was the best strategy to win the war. The lack of resources, notably in shipping, also influenced strategy as it took a minimum of three months to transfer it from one theatre to another and so plans had to be formulated well in advance. For example, the build-up of sufficient forces in Britain for a cross-Channel assault in early 1943 would have taken twelve months from America's entry into the war, i.e. the whole of 1942, had Operation Torch not gone ahead. Without having a fixed plan, the preparations for such landings would inevitably be delayed and an indeterminate strategy would continue. This is what the Americans feared with British 'flexibility' in the Mediterranean, the Americans ultimately requiring the British to make a commitment to Overlord which was designated as having an overriding priority. The Joint Chiefs of Staff did prove themselves capable of flexibility at times, for example when Anvil was cancelled early in 1944 in response to the stalemate in Italy when the Anzio beachhead was still isolated. The Americans did follow Churchill's peripheral Mediterranean strategy from 1942 until September 1943 and it was ultimately unsuccessful, although the British leader argued that the diversion of troops from Italy for Overlord and Anvil caused this to happen. While the British complained about the inflexibility of American strategy, they were very quick to demand the Americans adhere to the fixed policy of 'Germany first'. Indeed, Churchill had an unofficial policy towards Burma of doing the absolute minimum for so long that the delay had the unintended consequence of the Japanese forces in Burma withering on the vine because of American operations elsewhere in the Pacific. Churchill's poor opinion of the Chinese as an ally had a lot to do with this, believing they were not worth the effort to open the Burma Road despite the moral obligation the British had to the Americans to do so in return for US support against Germany. A lot of work was put in by Churchill and the Chiefs of Staff in 1942 and 1943 in order to prevent the diversion of resources to the Pacific on a large scale despite the considerable American public opinion in favour of such operations against Japan, something of which Roosevelt was always conscious. The British were right to be concerned about American adherence to 'Germany first' as the US Army planners used what they saw as diversionary operations in the Mediterranean and a lack of enthusiasm for a cross-Channel operation to justify sending troops to the Pacific, where there were in fact more divisions deployed until October 1943. In effect, faced with Churchill's intransigence towards Roundup, the Americans only paid lip service to Churchill's foremost strategy of 'Germany first' until after May 1943, when the build-up in the UK began in earnest.

A great deal of credit must go to Dill, head of the Joint Staff Mission in Washington, for maintaining relations between the respective Chiefs of Staff when they were close to breaking down; it was Dill's friendship with Marshall that provided a safety valve and a channel for each nation to get a better understanding of what the other was thinking through their frequent meetings.

Churchill's amphibious operations to outflank the enemy at Salerno and Anzio were both unsuccessful, while the operations in Norway, Greece and the Dodecanese all resulted in humiliating defeats and evacuations. Through his constant search for outflanking operations, Churchill eventually came in to conflict with his own Chiefs of Staff, who exhausted themselves ensuring Churchill and Britain kept to the strategies agreed with the Americans. Brooke commented after the war:

> And the wonderful thing is that 3/4 of the population of this world imagine that Winston Churchill is one of the strategists of history, a second Marlborough, and the other 1/4 have no conception what a public menace he is and has been throughout the war! It is far better that the world should never know and never suspect the feet of clay on that otherwise superhuman being. Without him England was lost for a certainty, with him England has been on the verge of disaster time and again ... Never have I admired and disliked a man simultaneously to the same extent.[42]

This was a harsh criticism but was from the man who worked most closely with Churchill in the war. Churchill may have believed he knew a lot about war but he was no Marlborough. Brooke's diary entry was not deleted after the war and is an apt description of Churchill's strategic thinking abilities, which were more akin to those of a menace than a genius.

As its military leader, Churchill ensured that Britain survived the threat of invasion in 1940 and remained as an island base for future operations against

Germany once the United States entered the war. In terms of military strategy, Churchill brought Britain defeat after defeat and it was only the entry of America into the war and its dogged efforts to ensure that Churchill adhered to the agreed strategy of a landing in France in 1944 that brought about the final defeat of Germany. Churchill's greatest contribution to the strategy for the defeat of Germany was the bomber offensive, albeit arrived at with the motive of revenge rather than as a strategy to systematically reduce the Nazis' capacity to wage war.

Churchill, Roosevelt and Stalin

An essential part of Churchill's strategy for Britain to survive and go on to defeat Germany depended on Churchill's relationship with the leaders of Britain's two main allies, America and Russia. Being half-American, Churchill was uniquely positioned to forge a strong alliance with Roosevelt, but the extent to which he achieved this is debateable. Roosevelt had clearly made up his mind that if Germany and possibly Japan were to be defeated, America would have to enter the war and he was the man to lead the country if re-elected for a third time, as he was in 1940. Roosevelt by 1941 had already agreed to American participation with the British in joint naval talks and the planning of strategy; he also organised Lend-Lease, ordered the enlargement of the Army and allowed the US Navy to play a more active part in the Atlantic, all before the attack on Pearl Harbor. Therefore despite all of Churchill's plans to woo Roosevelt, the President was already preparing the United States to enter the war but would only do so when America was given an excuse or an incident to polarise the majority of public and political opinion. Even after Pearl Harbor, it took the German declaration of war on America to finally bring America into the war in Europe.

In 1942, Churchill's astute understanding of Roosevelt's political motivations allowed Britain to refuse to undertake Operation Sledgehammer to assist the Russians and the President duly ordered American troops into north-west Africa at the start of the Mediterranean strategy. The next year, 1943, was about the struggle between Churchill's Mediterranean strategy and the more direct American plan to make an assault on the French coast. Churchill was able to persuade Roosevelt, who did not need much convincing, to become involved in operations against Italy by means of the simple argument of not wanting to have troops idle for any length of time in order to provide the maximum assistance to Russia, which would not be the case if the armies in North Africa were transferred to Britain for an operation into France. This argument was won at the cost of having to commit to Operation Overlord in 1944, about which Churchill was very apprehensive and would probably not have taken place at all if he had his way. It was also Roosevelt who spontaneously publicly announced the policy of unconditional surrender at Casablanca. By 1944, the United States had begun to outstrip the British contribution to the war and this enabled it to influence strategy more and more, and at least insist that the agreed joint strategy be implemented. In 1944 and to the end of the war, Churchill and Roosevelt met on fewer occasions than in previous years and by the time of the Yalta conference, the British leader was very much the junior partner in the alliance of the Big Three. Churchill's habit of sending frequent long telegrams to Roosevelt asking for changes to plans or resources for other operations cannot have endeared him to the American. Churchill was also not above asking Roosevelt to overrule his own commanders such as Eisenhower. Although Roosevelt was increasingly unwell, there was certainly a reduced exchange of telegrams as the war progressed to the point where he instructed his staff to not reply to a telegram of Churchill's. Roosevelt and the US Chiefs of Staff adopted a more global view to the prosecution of the war by relating British and American strategic actions to the effects they would have on Russia and China, whereas Churchill was not so concerned with Russia (particularly once it had demonstrated it could survive the German offensives) and had little time for China. Britain sent considerable aid to Russia and organised the convoys and escorts to transport this material but also postponed the convoys as necessary to give priority to British and American undertakings such as Torch and then Husky. Churchill's preoccupation with Poland was ultimately seen as potentially divisive of the Allies by Roosevelt. Poland was, after all, the *casus belli* for Britain but Roosevelt did not attach the same importance to Poland, urging Churchill to not imperil relations between the Allies over Polish issues. Roosevelt's secret agreement with Stalin on Poland permitted the Russians to retain the territory they had seized under the Soviet–Nazi non-aggression pact and Stalin must have regarded Churchill's attempts to reconcile the Poles and reach a negotiated solution with some amusement, if not contempt.

When it came to the Far East, the Americans realised that the British could not be relied on in Burma and were forced to mount their own operation to secure Myitkyina and the Burma Road. For the war against Japan, primarily

American forces were used in the Pacific island campaign with the British and the Australians being relegated to the South West Pacific Area; MacArthur did not want any Australian or British troops for the liberation of the Philippines either. Therefore, as much as Churchill believed that he had a friend in, and a close relationship with Roosevelt, as the war continued, this friendship proved to be more and more of an illusion. Perhaps Churchill in the end recognised this when he opted not to go to the US for Roosevelt's funeral.

In Churchill's relationship with Stalin there was no such mistaken impressions or illusion. Churchill was the self-confessed enemy of communism and thus Britain and Russia only became Allies by association when Hitler launched his invasion of Russia. Always acutely aware that the Red Army was fighting the bulk of the German Army, Stalin needed the British and Americans to do their share of the fighting and ease the pressure on his country. By not launching the Second Front, the Allies failed to do this in 1942 and as only a few German Army units were diverted to Italy from Russia in 1943, the Soviets were left to bear the brunt of the fighting for that year as well. Stalin quickly realised that Churchill's promises of 'jam tomorrow' were just that, empty promises. Thus when it came to settling disputes such as Poland, Stalin with his large army had no qualms about Polish or British concerns, especially when having the support of Roosevelt. The relationship between the two deteriorated to such an extent in 1943 that Stalin turned down repeated invitations to meet, if and when he finally replied to any telegrams from Churchill. Their relationship soured to the point that Roosevelt suggested that just he and Stalin meet without Churchill, much to the latter's indignation. When the three leaders met at Tehran, Stalin even subjected Churchill to a barrage of derogatory comments.

Stalin reportedly said about the British to an aide of the communist partisan leader, Tito:

> There's nothing they like better than to trick their Allies. During the First World War they constantly tricked the Russians and the French. And Churchill? Churchill is the kind of man who will pick your pocket for a kopeck if you didn't watch him. Yes, pick your pocket of a kopeck![43]

Stalin came to quickly appreciate the weakness of the British Army and its dependence on Roosevelt and American supplies to continue the war, which lessened Churchill's importance in his eyes while enlarging Roosevelt's. Stalin was careful to treat Roosevelt with respect in all their communications, which was reciprocated by Roosevelt. Roosevelt, who was guided by Hopkins in many matters, appeared to trust Stalin much more than Churchill. Churchill's secretary, John Colville, while considering Hopkins 'an honourable man and a sincere idealist', believed that he 'trusted the word and goodwill of Stalin to an imprudent extent, as did Roosevelt and the State Department'.[44]

By the end of the war, Churchill and Stalin's relationship had deteriorated to such an extent that the British had drawn up plans for possible hostilities with Russia: Operation Unthinkable. Stalin's Red Army came to dominate Eastern Europe post-war and had the British and Americans launched an invasion of France in 1943 that culminated in the defeat of Germany in 1944, Russia would not have been able to overrun so much of Eastern Europe before hostilities with Germany ended.

In many ways Chiang Kai-Shek was treated with the same indifference by Churchill, there always being promises of operations that were never launched. Roosevelt had believed in the potential of the Chinese since the 1930s but they never became formidable allies like the Russians, being preoccupied with their own civil war against the communists; the strength and fighting quality of their troops also left a lot to be desired, according to Stilwell. Churchill was correct in his assessment of the potential of China as an ally.

Churchill and the Ordinary Soldier

Following the military humiliations in Norway, France, Greece, Crete, Singapore and Tobruk, Churchill began to query the fighting abilities of the ordinary British soldiers. Churchill apparently feared that the current generation were not as good fighters as previous generations:

> In 1915 our men fought on even when they had only one shell and were under a fierce barrage. Now they cannot resist dive-bombers. We have so many men in Singapore, so many men – they should have done better.[45]

As the fall of Singapore looked likely, Churchill wrote a plan of defence for Wavell, the ABDA Commander-in-Chief, and ordered that men should 'perish at their posts'. Although the Chiefs of Staff duly sent the plan and in so doing demonstrated a lack of confidence in Wavell, the 'perish' instruction was deleted. Ultimately 85,000 British and Australian men surrendered to half their number of Japanese troops and were marched into captivity. Even Brooke was moved to comment along similar lines at the time: 'If the army cannot fight better than it is doing at present we shall deserve to lose our empire.'[46]

After the fall of Tobruk in June 1942, Churchill again doubted the fighting qualities of the British and Dominion soldiers, later writing that defeat was one thing, disgrace another.[47] Again, 33,000 men had surrendered to a numerically inferior force. It is hardly surprising that Churchill was set against Operation Sledgehammer that summer with this record of defeats for the British Army.

The major disgrace in these defeats was for the two men who had most to do with directing the war to be searching for scapegoats and finding one in the failures of the ordinary British or Empire soldiers. Brooke and Churchill had a responsibility to ensure that the soldiers they commanded were well trained, led, adequately armed and protected. It was all very well to rail against men unable to withstand attacks by dive-bombers but it was the responsibility of the theatre Commander-in-Chief to provide air cover and for the Chiefs of Staff and Churchill in turn to ensure that the Commander-in-Chief had adequate fighter aircraft. The soldiers would do their duty but relied on their generals and the strategists to send them into battles they at least had a chance of winning. In Norway, the British troops were hopelessly outnumbered and ill-equipped while in France and Greece the Allies had no answer to the German blitzkrieg of tanks and aircraft. Menzies realised this tendency of Churchill to blame others after the Greek campaign: 'He does not seem to realise that men without proper equipment, and with nothing but rifles, do not count in modern war – after all we are not living in the age of Omdurman.'[48]

In Singapore, the island's defences had been long neglected before the war but Churchill was preoccupied with the 'Germany first' policy and believed that the Japanese would never risk attacking the city, so repeated warnings about the state of the defences were ignored. Churchill himself wrote that Hong Kong could not be defended and was less than enthusiastic about the construction of defences in Malaya when there were other priorities elsewhere. Before the war, British generals had believed that soldiers could not live and fight in the jungle – a misconception that the Japanese exploited. Churchill must take the responsibility for Singapore and exhortations such as 'perish at your posts' were rank hypocrisy. Singapore was not the only time Churchill urged that British soldiers should fight to the death. Similar messages were sent to the commanders of forces at Calais in 1940 and Egypt in 1942, where the soldiers were expected to sacrifice themselves in order to atone for the strategic mistakes:

At Calais in 1940: 'Have greatest admiration for your splendid stand. Evacuation will not (repeat not) take place and craft required for the above purpose are to return to Dover.'[49]

A telegram to Auchinleck in June 1942: 'You have other 700,000 men on your ration strength in the Middle East. Every fit male should be made to fight and die for victory.'[50]

Another example of Churchill's unrealistic expectations of British soldiers is in his 1941 directive regarding the issuing of armour-piercing ammunition to every field artillery piece and anti-aircraft gun for their potential employment as anti-tank guns:

> Renown awaits the commander who first, in this war, restores the artillery to its prime importance upon the battlefield from which it has been ousted by heavily armoured tanks ...
>
> ... (b) When guns are attacked by tanks they must welcome the occasion. The guns should be fought to the muzzle ...
>
> ... (c) It may often happen as a result of the above tactics, especially when artillery is working with cruiser tanks, that guns may be overrun and lost. Provided they have been fought to the muzzle, this should not at all be considered a disaster but on the contrary, the highest honour to the battery concerned.[51]

This extraordinary directive harks back to the days of Napoleonic cavalry attacking cannons, except that the tanks of the 1940s had machine guns and cannons that fired high explosive as they advanced, rather than sabres or lances which could only be employed once they reached the cannons. Churchill expected untrained gunners to continue to engage approaching enemy tanks over open sights until they were right on top them, all the while under fire from the tanks. While the German Luftwaffe crews of 88mm guns sometimes operated in this role, they were often less than enthusiastic and sometimes had to be persuaded at gunpoint not to abandon their guns or debouch to the rear in the face of attacking tanks.

The ordinary British and Dominion soldiers were the men who had to carry out Churchill's strategies, whether they were strokes of genius, forlorn hopes or 'improvise and dare' missions and the architect of the strategy has to accept responsibility for its success or failure. In the Middle East, a left-wing debating society known as the Cairo Forces Parliament was set up in February 1944 to educate British soldiers and discuss current issues. However, this forum was short-lived when it was discovered that a motion that 'the Soviet system was the best system for winning the war' was overwhelmingly supported. The servicemen in all services and theatres would have the opportunity to express their opinion of Churchill's strategies and conduct of the war in the coming general election of 1945.

Churchill's direction of the war was based on ensuring Britain's survival and then protecting the Middle East, which led to the disaster in Greece and the setbacks in the desert campaign until the entry of the United States. After Pearl Harbor, Churchill's Mediterranean strategy was followed by the Allies until it finally petered out as Overlord succeeded. Given the ultimately flawed strategy pursued in the war by Churchill in the Mediterranean, what made him a great leader?

Churchill the Leader

When Churchill became Prime Minister, he believed he was uniquely qualified as a man who had both experience under fire and understanding of the strategies of previous battles and wars. He was also half-American, which gave him a better insight than most British politicians of the time into the minds of the American people. In 1940, Britain faced a German invasion across the English Channel after two humiliating defeats and evacuations. The British Army had been mauled and had lost much of its armour and artillery. It was impossible for Britain to challenge Germany directly and there were only a few ways the fight could be taken up to Hitler. Churchill created SOE and Combined Operations but these could initially only make pinpricks and minor raids on German-occupied Europe. Plans were put in place to build up the RAF bomber force but these would take time before sufficient numbers of aircraft could be assembled to deliver heavier blows. The major weapons Churchill first employed in the defence of Britain were those of leadership, oration and an attitude of defiance. It was appreciated by the Chiefs of Staff after the fall of France that the morale of British civilians and servicemen would be the decisive factor in the country's survival rather than military resources or equipment. The SOE and Combined Operations raids, although small, were a way of taking the offensive back to the Germans and were nevertheless good for British morale once they began. This was the same offensive spirit that Churchill had displayed since the first week of the war in September 1939 when he had urged the mining of Norwegian territorial waters. Churchill preferred offensive action, saw defence as a necessary evil and could not tolerate inaction. The Norwegian minelaying had not been initially approved by the War Cabinet, which still contained many of the politicians who had pursued the policy of appeasement of Germany, causing one MP to remark at the time, 'That the present War Cabinet was, with the exception of Winston himself, entirely devoid of the offensive fighting spirit and did not think they could last more than a few months.'[52]

From the outbreak of war, Churchill and even King George VI urged all of the British people to remain calm and united in the face of the war they were about to endure, a war that would only be won with the contributions from all the nation's citizens. In his speech on 3 September 1939, King George emphasised that a global struggle for freedom and peace was taking place and appealed to his people's sense of honour and duty to accept the challenge, 'I ask them to stand calm and firm and united in this time of trial.'

The same day, Churchill in a speech to Parliament, echoed this theme of the need for everyone's commitment to a global conflict to save the world from Nazi tyranny and all that was sacred to man. British and French peace efforts were faithful and sincere:

> This is of the highest moral value – and not only moral value, but practical value – at the present time, because the wholehearted concurrence of scores of millions of men and women, whose co-operation is indispensable and whose comradeship and brotherhood are indispensable, is the only foundation upon which the trial and tribulation of modern war can be endured and surmounted.[53]

While speaking in his usual eloquent and dramatic fashion, Churchill also warned of the many disappointments and unpleasant surprises in the task ahead. The nation's civilians were already partially prepared for war with the large-scale provision of air raid shelters for homes and the evacuation of women and children from the cities which was already in progress.

After the debacle in Norway, the politicians got the scalp of the appeaser Chamberlain and Churchill became Prime Minister after a two-horse race which only one wanted to win. In his first address as Prime Minister to the House of Commons on 13 May, Churchill famously offered as his strategy for the war against Germany nothing but a warning of the blood, toil, sweat and tears to come in the pursuit of victory, making a further appeal for national unity and commitment: 'Come then, let us go forward together with our united strength.'

Churchill himself set an example of the national unity required by establishing a coalition government that helped mobilise the country fully for war and endured to the defeat of Germany. In stark contrast to the previous Prime Minister, Churchill was all for immediate aggressive action in France and made frequent visits to exhort the French leaders to firstly counter-attack and then to continue the struggle in the face of defeat. After Dunkirk, Churchill in the House of Commons on 4 June again warned of the difficulties ahead, stating that wars were not won by evacuations alone. In perhaps his most brilliant speech, Churchill conjured up images of past British defenders of England such as the Knights of the Round Table, the Crusaders and how Napoleon was unable to invade in the nineteenth century:

> We shall defend our island whatever the cost may be. We shall fight on the beaches, we shall fight on the landing grounds, we shall fight in the fields and in the streets, we shall fight in the hills, we shall never surrender …'[54]

The speech was received with great cheers by almost all politicians, including those who were in opposition to Churchill. This peroration set the mood of Parliament and from there the mood of the British people. This was a fight to survive, a fight for a free Europe and a fight to preserve the Empire. Churchill closed the speech with a vision of the British Empire fighting on even if the British Isles were subjugated with the help of the New World, 'in God's time', which is the first public reference to potential American involvement. This would not be the last time that Churchill demonstrated the unique ability of inspiring people, even in the face of disaster.

In the War Cabinet there was a new energy and determination that emanated solely from Churchill. Even before Churchill had been made Prime Minister, Leo Amery had written of him in March 1940, 'I am beginning to come round to the idea that Winston with all his failings is the one man with real war drive and love of battle.'[55]

Amery was correct in his judgement. Following the fall of France and the entry of Italy into the war, on 18 June Churchill gave another patriotic and inspirational speech warning of the invasion and impending bombing attacks on British homes:

> What General Weygand called the Battle of France is over. I expect that the Battle of Britain is about to begin. Upon this battle depends the survival of Christian civilisation. Upon it depends our own British life, and the long

continuity of our institutions and our Empire. The whole fury and might of
the enemy must very soon be turned on us. Hitler knows that he will have to
break us in this Island or lose the war. If we can stand up to him, all Europe
may be free and the life of the world may move forward into broad, sunlit
uplands. But if we fail, then the whole world, including the United States,
including all that we have known and cared for, will sink into the abyss of
a new Dark Age made more sinister, and perhaps more protracted, by the
lights of perverted science. Let us therefore brace ourselves to our duties, and
so bear ourselves that, if the British Empire and its Commonwealth last for a
thousand years, men will still say, 'This was their finest hour.'[56]

Churchill warned that the survival of Britain and Christianity itself was under
threat and appealed to the country as a whole to prepare itself for the coming
fight to the death – a fight that every person could play a part in and become a
part of history to be lauded by future generations. It was the duty of the people
to take up arms or contribute in some other way, according to Churchill. Most
importantly, Churchill did not offer false hope or illusions to the populace
but was honest with them in a manner which appealed to the traditionally
stoic people. Churchill made it clear that government alone was not going to
win the war but needed the support of every man and woman in the country.
This was a sort of struggle that the British people with their backs to the wall
more readily identified with and could understand. There was no other choice,
according to Churchill, but the general public for the most part would not
know of the overtures for peace made by various parties in 1940 and 1941.
Hess, for example, was demonised as an insane Nazi thug by the British press
and then incarcerated by Churchill's government to ensure his silence.

For an anxious population which had been suddenly exposed to the horrors
of war and defeats in Norway and France, Churchill's speeches broadcast on
the radio provided reassurance that Britain was morally correct by going to
war with Germany and that it was a war the country would win: 'I heard most
of Mr Churchill's speech and it certainly was one to give more confidence
than I have heard recently on the wireless.'[57]

From British propaganda, the civilian population understood that it was only
a matter of time until they themselves were perhaps in the front line being
bombed by German aircraft or defending the beaches. However fearful they
were, they were encouraged by the military defensive preparations for the anticipated invasion and by Churchill's speeches that stimulated a national mood of
defiance and determination to survive. These speeches, both over the radio and

in Parliament, worked towards maintaining morale and the public approval of Churchill's government, thus keeping the Home Front united. In order to preserve morale, Churchill wrote to senior civil servants asking them to set an example of steadfastness and resolution while stamping on negative opinions from their staff; this letter was subsequently published in the newspapers.

The people of England were cheered by the daily but often exaggerated victories of the RAF over the Luftwaffe broadcast on the BBC news and many watched the swirling patterns of contrails against the blue summer sky that marked the aerial battles overhead. Soon bombs began to rain down on the British cities and then the ordinary person found themselves in the front line. Having heard of the fate of Guernica and Barcelona at the hands of the German and Italian Air Forces, it was finally their turn. Despite a high number of civilian deaths and a greater number of homelessness – a phenomenon for which there had been little or no preparation – the British people proved to be resilient and for the most part were not cowed by the Blitz. The slogan, 'Keep calm and carry on' set the national mood. Churchill, conscious of his role as Prime Minister and leader (and no doubt his future place in history), toured bomb-damaged areas and was occasionally seen to put himself almost in harm's way. In public, Churchill always displayed cheerful optimism and his 'V for Victory' gesture, cigar and bowler hat became synonymous with the British bulldog spirit of never giving up until the battle was won. When swamped by large crowds of people, Churchill hoisted his bowler hat into the air on the end of his walking stick as a sign of his presence for those who could not see him.

Churchill's speeches in 1940 and 1941 continued to identify with the ordinary person who had lost his home and yet appealed to patriotic sentiment for people to do their duty. As the Blitz worsened, Churchill coined the slogan, 'We can take it,' as a chant of defiance to the Germans to demonstrate that the British could survive the worst the Germans could throw at them. During the eight-month Blitz, the Ministry of Information made great use of propaganda such as posters, films and the BBC radio to inform and reassure the inhabitants of London. With the co-operation of King George, a new medal, the George Cross, was created in September 1940 for bravery displayed by civilians. The award and presentation of this medal provided further propaganda opportunities for the government through the newspapers and radio broadcasts of the day.

The British people came to believe that Churchill's leadership offered certainty against any weakness or compromise in the conduct of the war, though they were ignorant of the peace feelers from the Germans. Hitler and Vichy France were not to be trusted, it was to be:

> Victory at all costs, victory in spite of all terror, victory however long and hard the road may be; for without victory, there is no survival.

Churchill's ruthlessness at Oran, Dieppe and Greece all demonstrated his willingness to sacrifice men when required. These actions coupled with Churchill's inspirational speeches gave the population the resolve and the will to carry on, despite the bombings and military setbacks early in the war.

Thus it was Churchill's leadership of the nation rather than his military strategy in the first two years of war with all its disappointments and defeats until the Americans finally entered the war that was his real genius. With the United States as an ally, victory was assured and it was only a matter of time. As the war progressed through 1943, the spirit of national unity and individual contributions to the war effort began to evaporate with the prolonged effects of rationing and the growing number of casualties. There was increased industrial unrest and strikes became more and more common. Churchill himself was challenged by no-confidence motions in Parliament and although easily defeated, these served to remind him of his fallibility. Churchill somewhat dismissively referred to these events as the workings of 'the little people'. The Maldon by-election result was certainly a shock to the government and evidence of a shift in the mood of the nation, although for a sitting government to lose a seat in a by-election is a not uncommon occurrence. Popular social reforms such as those championed in the Beveridge Report were not made by Churchill, who opted to leave such major issues regarding post-war Britain to the electorate. With the success of D-Day and the campaign in Normandy, victory was tantalisingly close. Londoners were then subjected to another Blitz by Germany, this time by the V-1 and V-2 'vengeance' weapons, and civilian morale plummeted once more. Fortunately this menace diminished rapidly with the Allied advances into north-west Europe, which overran the missile launching sites. Predictions of a German collapse by the end of the year proved to be premature and the war ground on, both in Europe and the Far East.

In May 1945, Germany finally surrendered and the war was at last over; Britain was swept by a tide of relief and euphoric celebrations were held everywhere. Churchill would be acclaimed as the architect of Britain's greatest victory and rightfully took his place in the pantheon of the greatest wartime leaders the country has ever produced. But the British people, while seeing

Churchill as a leader in the time of war, did not see him as a peacetime leader and voted the Conservative Party out of office in the July 1945 general election, much to the shock of the great man, although he had had an inkling of what was to come. It was the first opportunity for the British to vote on the war following the disastrous policy of appeasement under Chamberlain and almost six years of conflict; the nation was tired of war and rationing while eager for social reforms such as free education and those promised by the Beveridge Report. Churchill had been so preoccupied with the direction of the war that he was not prepared for the peace with major policies. In fact, as the war against Japan was not over and tensions were rising with the Russians, Churchill campaigned for election as the leader Britain needed for yet more conflict to come; many Conservative MPs ran their campaigns on the basis of urging their electorates to vote for Churchill rather than themselves. The nation was weary and anxious for change, a mood that Churchill and the Conservative Party misjudged badly:

> Our revered and beloved Winston Churchill suddenly metamorphosed into a politician, and a Tory at that. Shock and disgust. The British working class and the returning soldiers voted in the Labour government by a sweeping majority, and we were thrilled and delighted that the miserable days of the 1930s were gone for good. The mines and the railways were nationalised, the National Health Service set up and the new Education system brought in. The slums were to be cleared, and everyone in need was to receive an allowance of National Assistance. Let nobody tell you those were grey and miserable days. There was still rationing and shortages of all kinds, but we were used to that any way, and nobody was dropping bombs on us. The future was bright.[58]

NOTES

Introduction

1 Jenkins, R., *Churchill*, Pan, London, 2002, p. 912
2 CAB 101/251 telegram Churchill to President Truman, 12 May 1945, TNA
3 Churchill speech in Fulton, Missouri, on 5 March 1946, Hyperion, New York, 2003, p. 413
4 Hansard, House of Commons (HC) debate, 23 January 1948

Chapter 1

1 BBC History WW2 People's War, Salisbury – Diary entry August–September 1939, www.bbc.co.uk/history/ww2peopleswar/stories/99/a2005499.shtml
2 Davis, H., speech, 29 May 1934, Geneva Disarmament conference
3 Hansard HC debate 22 July 1935, Churchill 1935 vol. 304 cc. 1499–562
4 Bullock, A., *Hitler: A Study in Tyranny*, Odhams, London, 1952, p. 135
5 Hansard HC debate 26 March, Churchill 1936, vol. 310 cc. 1435–549
6 Hansard HC debate 14 March, Churchill 1938, vol. 333 cc. 45–169
7 Hansard HC debate 5 October 1938, vol. 339 cc. 337–454
8 Black, C., *Franklin Delano Roosevelt: Champion of Freedom*, Public Affairs, New York, 2014, p. 481
9 Dunbabin, J.P.D., 'British Rearmament in the 1930s', *The Historical Journal*, XVIII, No. 3, 1975, pp. 587–609
10 Postan, M.M., *British War Production*, HMSO, London, 1952, p. 27
11 PREM 1/345, Churchill, W., Memorandum on Sea Power, 27 March 1939, TNA
12 CHAR 8/614/49 Churchill, W., 'How Wars of the Future will be Waged', *News of the World*, 24 April 1938, Churchill Archives Cambridge
13 Reynolds, D., *In Command of History: Churchill Fighting and Rewriting the Second World War*, Basic, New York, 2007, p. 118
14 CHAR 8/653/A-3 Churchill, W., 'Let the Tyrant Criminals Bomb', *Colliers*, 14 January 1939, Churchill Archives Cambridge
15 CAB 66-1-14 WP (39) 14 report by Land Forces Committee, 8 September 1939, TNA
16 Jenkins, R., *Churchill*, Pan, London, 2002, p. 552

Chapter 2

1 Titmuss, R.M., *The Problems of Social Policy*, HMSO, London, 1950, p. 103
2 Field, G., 'Nights Underground in Darkest London: The Blitz 1940–41', *International Labour*

and Working-Class History, No. 62, Class and Catastrophe: September 11 and Other Working-Class Disasters, 2002, pp. 11–49

3   BBC History WW2 People's War – Evacuation from Ilford to Somerset 1 September 1939 www.bbc.co.uk/history/ww2peopleswar/stories/49/a4885149.shtml

4   CAB 66-1-36 Admiralty report No. 1, 17 September 1939, TNA

5   CAB 65-1-20 War Cabinet minutes, 19 September 1939, TNA

6   Hansard HC debate 12 October 1939 vol. 352 cc. 563–603

7   Strange, J., *Despatches from the Home Front: War Diaries 1939–45*, Jak Books, London, 1994, p. 21

8   CAB 65-5-30 War Cabinet minutes, 2 February 1940, TNA

9   Churchill, W., *The Second World War vol. 1: The Gathering Storm*, Cassel, London, 1948, p. 389

10 CAB 66-4-12 Churchill note for War Cabinet, 16 December 1939, TNA

11 CAB 66-4-29 COS paper WP 179, 31 December 1939, TNA

12 Strange, op. cit., p. 28

13 Gilbert, M., *Finest Hour: Winston Churchill 1939–1941*, Heinemann, London, 1984, p. 139

14 CAB 99-3 Supreme War Council minutes 28 March 1940, p. 3, TNA

15 CAB 66-6-45 COS directive, 30 march 1940, TNA

16 CAB 66-6-47 COS Report, 4 April 1940, TNA

17 Derry, T.K., *The Campaign in Norway*, HMSO, London, 1952, p. 23

18 CAB 80-105 COS paper (40) 297 (S), 19 April 1940, TNA

19 Despatch 38011 The Norway Campaign 1940, supplement to the *London Gazette*, 10 July 1947, p. 3168

20 CAB 79-83 confidential annex to COS meeting 17 April 1940, TNA

21 CAB 83-3 Military Co-ordination Committee meeting minutes 19 April 1940, TNA

22 Ibid., 12 April 1940, TNA

23 CAB 65-12-30 confidential annex to War Cabinet meeting 21 April 1940, TNA

24 CAB 65-12-35 confidential annex to War Cabinet meeting 26 April 1940, TNA

25 CAB 65-13-3 confidential annex to War Cabinet meeting 6 May 1940, TNA

26 CAB 80-11 paper COS (40) 372 JP, 21 May 1940, TNA

27 WO 32-16325 Norway Auchinleck report, Appendix E, TNA

28 Derry, op. cit., p. 230

29 Lunde, H., *Hitler's Pre-emptive War: The Battle for Norway, 1940*, Casemate, Newbury, 2009, p. 542

30 WO 32-16325 Norway – Auchinleck report, Appendix K, TNA

31 Gilbert, op. cit., p. 245

32 Hamilton, N., *JFK Reckless Youth*, Random House, New York, 1992, p. 324

33 CAB 65-1-36 War Cabinet minutes, 4 October 1939, TNA

34 Field, G., 'Nights Underground in Darkest London: The Blitz 1940–41 , *International Labour and Working-Class History, No. 62, Class and Catastrophe: September 11 and Other Working-Class Disasters'* 2002, pp. 15

35 Smith, E., letter, 1 October 1939, Private Papers, D.16015, Imperial War Museum, London

36 Strange, op. cit., p. 19

37 CAB 65-1-63 War Cabinet minutes, 28 October 1939, TNA

38 Strange, op. cit., p. 28

39 Lazarides, M., *Time of Triviality: History of the Second World War*, vol. 1, no. 6, Purnell, London, 1966

40 Churchill, W., *The Second World War, vol. I: The Gathering Storm*, Cassell, London, 1948, p. 511

Chapter 3

1   Thompson, W.H., *Assignment Churchill*, Farrer, Strauss and Young, New York, 1955, p. 165

2   Kennedy, J., Diplomatic Memoirs, Joseph Kennedy Papers, Box 149, Kennedy Library, Boston

3   Kennedy, J., diary 1940, US Ambassador to GB, Joseph Kennedy Papers, Box 100, Kennedy

Library, Boston

4 Churchill. W, *The Second World War, vol. I: The Gathering Storm*, Cassell, London, 1948, pp. 526–7

5 Dilks, D., *The Diaries of Sir Alexander Cadogan 1938–1945*, Faber, London, 2010, p. 280

6 Gilbert M., *Finest Hour: Winston Churchill 1939–1941*, Heinemann, London, 1984, p. 327

7 Hastings, M., *Finest Years: Churchill as Warlord 1940–1945*, Harper Press, London, 2009, p. 3

8 Broad, R. and Fleming, S. (eds), *Nella Last's War*, Profile, London, 2006, p. 47

9 Ismay, Gen. H.L., *The Memoirs of Lord Ismay*, Heinemann, London, 1960, p. 116

10 Butler, J.R.M., *Grand Strategy vol. II Sept 1939–June 1941*, HMSO, London, 1957, p. 177

11 Gilbert, M., op. cit., p. 340

12 CAB 101-246 telegram Churchill to Roosevelt, 15 May 1940, TNA

13 CAB 65-7-19 War Cabinet minutes, 16 May 1940, TNA

14 CAB 65-7-46 War Cabinet minutes, 1 June 1940, TNA

15 Kennedy, J., diary 1940, US Ambassador to GB, April–May 1940, Box 100, Joseph Kennedy papers, Box 100, Kennedy Library, Boston

16 Gilbert, op. cit., p. 358

17 CAB 65-13-11 confidential annex to minutes War Cabinet meeting, 18 May 1940, TNA

18 G.4.3 Minute Churchill to Ismay 19 May 1940, Cherwell Papers, Nuffield College, Oxford

19 CAB 101-246 telegram Churchill to Roosevelt 20th May 1940, TNA

20 Colville, J., *The Fringes of Power*, Hodder and Stoughton, London, 1985, p. 138, diary entry 21 May 1940

21 CAB 65-13-17 War Cabinet confidential annex, 23 May 1940

22 Pownall, Sir H., diary entry 23 May 1940, Catalogue 1393, Liddell Hart Centre Military Archives, London

23 CAB 65-13-17 War Cabinet confidential annex, 23 May 1940, TNA

24 CAB 65-13-20 War Cabinet confidential annex, 26 May, 1940, TNA

25 BBC History WW2 Peoples War, Dunkirk by J. Millner, www.bbc.co.uk/history/ww2peopleswar/stories/16/a4045916.shtml

26 CAB 66-8-25 War Cabinet resume, 30 May–6 June 1940, TNA

27 Ismay, op. cit., p. 135

28 BBC History WW2 Peoples War, An Acton Teenager's War (part 2), www.bbc.co.uk/history/ww2peopleswar/stories/15/a3070315.shtml

29 CAB 65-13-21 confidential annex to minutes War Cabinet meeting, 26 May 1940, TNA

30 CAB 80-11, COS paper British Strategy in the Near Future, 26 May 1940, TNA

31 CAB 101-240 minute Churchill, 28 May 1940, TNA

32 CAB 65-13-24 confidential annex to minutes War Cabinet meeting, 28 May 1940, TNA

33 Danchev, A., and Todman, D., *War Diaries 1939–1945, Field Marshal Lord Alanbrooke*, Weidenfeld and Nicolson, London, 2001, p. 75

34 Strange, J., *Despatches from the Home Front: War Diaries 1939–1945*, Jak Books, London, 1994, p. 38

35 CAB 65-14-2 confidential annex to minutes of War Cabinet meeting, 2 July 1940, TNA

36 *Delphos Daily Herald*, 13 June 1940

37 CAB 99-3 minutes Supreme War Council meeting, 11 June 1944, TNA

38 Ibid., 12 June 1940, TNA

39 CAB 65-7-60 War Cabinet minutes, 13 June 1940, TNA

40 CAB 65-7-60 annex to War Cabinet minutes, 13 June 1940, TNA

41 Roosevelt, F., telegram to Reynaud, 13 June 1940, Roosevelt Map Room papers, Box 1, Correspondence with Churchill 1939–1940, F.D. Roosevelt Museum/Library, New York

42 CAB 99-3 Supreme War Council Meeting minutes, 13 June 1940, TNA

43 Gilbert, op. cit., p. 520

44 Danchev, op. cit., p. 82

45 Foreign Relations of US, Roosevelt telegram, 15 June 1940, *Peace and War: United States Foreign Policy, 1931–1941*, US Department of State, Washington, 1943, p. 552

46 CAB 65-7-60 War Cabinet minutes, 13 June 1940, TNA

47 CAB 65-7-81 War Cabinet meeting minutes, 28 June 1941, TNA

48 Bland, L., *Papers G.C. Marshall, vol. II 1 July 1939 to 6 December 1941*, Johns Hopkins University Press, Baltimore, 1986, p. 238

49 CAB 65-7-65 minutes War Cabinet meeting, 17 June 1940, TNA

50 CAB 101-240, minute Churchill to Beaverbrook, 8 July 1940, TNA

51 Butler, op. cit., p. 219

52 PREM 3/457 Cable Halifax to FO 2 July 1940, TNA

53 CAB 65-14-6 War Cabinet confidential annex, 5 July 1940, TNA

54 CAB 65-14-3 confidential annex to minutes of War Cabinet meeting, 3 July 1940, TNA

55 Ismay, op. cit., p. 153

56 Gilbert, op. cit., pp. 587–8

Chapter 4

1 Roosevelt, F.D., An Appeal to Great Britain, France, Italy, Germany, and Poland to Refrain from Air Bombing of Civilians, 1 September 1939, Public Papers and Addresses of Franklin D. Roosevelt, 1939, p. 454

2 CAB 65-7-74 minutes War Cabinet meeting, 24 June 1940, TNA

3 Halifax diary 19 June 1940 A7/8/4 University of York, York

4 Halifax diary 26 July A7/8/5 University of York, York

5 PREM 3-100-3 Peace mediation offer by the King of Sweden, 2 August 1940, TNA

6 AIR 14/775 directives, 25 August 1940, TNA

7 CAB 65-8-48 minutes War Cabinet meeting, 29 August 1940, TNA

8 CAB 66-11-32 munitions paper WP (40) 352 by W. Churchill, TNA

9 Gilbert op. cit. p. 775

10 Churchill, W., *The Second World War, vol. II: Their Finest Hour*, Cassell, London, 1949, p. 303

11 CAB 120-300 RAF Bombing Policy, Churchill minutes, 13 October 1940, TNA

12 Irving, D., *Churchill's War*, Focal Point, London, 2002, p. 343

13 BBC History WW2 People's War 10 January 1941, The Blitz, Portsmouth, www.bbc.co.uk/history/ww2peopleswar/stories/18/a2636318.shtml

14 BBC History WW2 People's War, Churchill and the Winds of the Almighty, www.bbc.co.uk/history/ww2peopleswar/stories/93/a2618093.shtml

15 Field, G., 'Nights Underground in Darkest London: The Blitz 1940–41, *International Labour and Working-Class History*, No. 62 *Class and Catastrophe: September 11 and Other Working-Class Disasters*, 2002, pp. 11–49

16 Titmuss, R.M., *The Problems of Social Policy*, HMSO, London, 1950, p. 343

17 Field, op. cit., p. 16

18 BBC History WW2 People's War website Grandma's War pt 1 www.bbc.co.uk/history/ww2peopleswar/stories/70/a3223270.shtml

19 BBC History WW2 People's War Diary Rev Dabill – A visit to London 18 December 1940 www.bbc.co.uk/history/ww2peopleswar/stories/28/a2005228.shtml

20 Titmuss, op. cit., pp. 259–60

21 Ibid., p. 261

22 Hansard HC debate, 6 June 1940

23 Hansard HC debate, 8 October 1940, Winston S. Churchill, War situation debate

24 Colville, J., *The Fringes of Power*, Hodder and Stoughton, London, 1985, p. 268

25 Belsey, J., and Reid, H., *The West at War*, Redcliffe Press, Bristol, 1990, pp. 74–5

26 Papers Averell Harriman, 15 April 1941, Library of Congress

27 BBC History WW2 People's War, Churchill and the Winds of the Almighty, www.bbc.co.uk/history/ww2peopleswar/stories/93/a2618093.shtml

28 CAB 101-240 minutes Churchill to Chief of Air Staff, 20 October 1940, TNA

29 CAB 65-9-42 minutes War Cabinet meeting, 30 October 1940, TNA

30 CAB 65-17-1 minutes War Cabinet meeting, 2 January 1941, TNA
31 CAB 65-18-5 minutes War Cabinet meeting, 7 March 1941, TNA
32 CAB 101-247 telegram Churchill to Halifax, 23 February 1941, TNA
33 Titmuss, op. cit., p. 299
34 O'Brien, T.H., *Civil Defence*, HMSO, London, 1955, Appendix 1
35 Herington, J., *Australians at War 1939–45, vol. III, Air War against Germany and Italy 1939–1943*, Australian War Memorial, Canberra, 1954, p. 175

Chapter 5

1 Halder, F., *War Journal*, vol. IV, Pt 2, 22 July 1940, Combined Arms Digital Research Library, Fort Leavenworth, Kansas, p. 127
2 CAB 80-16 Draft General Directive for the C-in-C Middle East, 16 August 1940, TNA
3 CAB 65-14-25 confidential annex to War Cabinet meeting minutes, 26 August 1940, TNA
4 CAB 69-1 confidential annex to Defence Committee meeting, 31 October 1940, TNA
5 CAB 127-14 telegram AO CinC (Longmore) to CAS (Portal), 31 October 1940, TNA
6 Long, G., *Australia in the War of 1939–1945, Series 1 Army vol. II Greece, Crete and Syria*, 1953, p. 6
7 Irving, D., *Hitler's War*, Focal Point, London, 2001, p. 342
8 US Army CMH Pub 104-4, *The German Campaign in the Balkans*, pp. 4–5
9 Smith, E., letter 19 November 1940, Private Papers, D.16015, Imperial War Museum, London
10 CAB 65-16-12 War Cabinet meeting confidential annex, 12 December, 1940, TNA
11 CAB 65-14-23 War Cabinet meeting confidential annex, 22 August 1940, TNA
12 CAB 66-13-46 Cabinet WP (40) 466, draft telegram Churchill to FDR, 8 December 1940, TNA
13 Churchill, W., *The Second World War, vol. III, The Grand Alliance*, Cassell, London, 1950, p. 53
14 Gilbert M., Finest Hour: Winston Churchill 1939–1941, Heinemann, London, 1984, p. 982
15 CAB 69-2 Defence Committee meeting, annex (41), 8 January 1941, TNA
16 Ibid., 2nd meeting 9 January 1941, TNA
17 CAB 66-13-11 Cabinet WP(40) 431, An advance by the Enemy through the Balkans and Syria to the ME, 1 November 1940, TNA
18 CAB 69-8 Confidential annex to Defence Committee meeting, 12 January 1941
19 PREM 4-31-1 memorandum Eden to Hopkins, 8 February 1941, TNA
20 FO 371/29792 telegram Churchill to Donovan 30 January 1941, TNA
21 CAB 65-21-3 confidential annex to War Cabinet meeting, 20 January 1940, TNA
22 CHAR 9/150A Churchill radio broadcast 9 February 1941, Churchill Archives Cambridge
23 CAB 69-2 minutes Defence Committee meeting, 10 February 1941, TNA
24 CAB 65-21-4 confidential annex to War Cabinet meeting, 3 February 1941, TNA
25 CAB 69-2 minutes Defence Committee meeting, 11 February 1941, TNA
26 CAB 65-21-8 confidential annex to War Cabinet meeting, 24 February, 1941, TNA
27 CAB 66-15-11 telegram Churchill to Eden, 24 February, 1941, TNA
28 Ibid.
29 Ibid.
30 CAB 65-21-9 minutes War Cabinet meeting, 27 February 1941, TNA
31 Ibid.
32 Broad, R., and Fleming, S., (eds), *Nella Last's War*, Profile, London, 2006, p. 104
33 *Canberra Times*, 4 March 1941
34 Long, op. cit., p. 18
35 CAB 65-22-4 minutes War Cabinet meeting, 6 March 1941, TNA
36 FO 954/33B/282 report on the mission by the Foreign Secretary of State for Foreign Affairs to the Eastern Mediterranean, February to April 1941, TNA
37 CAB 65-22-5 minutes War Cabinet meeting, 7 March 1941, TNA
38 PREM 3-206-3 telegram Eden to Churchill, 7 March 1941, TNA
39 Long, op. cit., p. 17

40 CAB 101/247 Churchill telegram to Roosevelt, 9 March 1941, TNA

41 PREM 4/17-2 Operation of Lend Lease, letter Churchill to Winant, 8 March 1941, TNA

42 CAB 65-22-3 confidential annex to War Cabinet meeting 5 March 1941, TNA

43 Gilbert, op. cit., p. 1043

44 CAB 69-2 minutes Defence Committee meeting, 27 March 1941, TNA

45 A5954 telegram Churchill to #162, 30 March 1941, Item 528/1, NAA

46 Broad and Fleming, op. cit., pp. 114–115

47 CAB 65-22-14 confidential annex to War Cabinet meeting, 17 April 1941, TNA

48 CAB 69-2 minutes Defence Committee meeting, 16 April 1941, TNA

49 Long, op. cit., p. 81

50 Ibid., p. 183

51 Playfair, Maj. Gen. I.S.O., *History of the Second World War: The Mediterranean and Middle East Vol. II: The Germans Come to the Help of their Ally (1941)*, HMSO, London, 1953, p. 147

52 CAB 69-2 Churchill to Eden telegram, Defence Committee meeting minutes, 5 March 1941, TNA

53 CAB 69-2 minutes Defence Committee meeting, 17 April 1941, TNA

54 Freudenberg, G., *Churchill and Australia*, Macmillan, Sydney, 2008, p. 269

55 Halder, F., op. cit., vol. VI, 10 March 1941 p. 20

56 Hankey papers

57 Hansard HC Deb 07 May 1941 Churchill vol. 371 cc. 867–950

58 CAB 65-22-12 confidential annex to Cabinet meeting 12 April 1941, TNA

Chapter 6

1 CAB 80-28 COS Paper (41) 255, United States–British Staff Conversations, 22 April 1941, TNA

2 Ibid.

3 CAB 101/247 telegram Churchill to Roosevelt, 4 May 1941, TNA

4 Churchill, W., *The Second World War vol. III*, Cassell, London, 1950, p. 375

5 Postan, M.M., *British War Production*, HMSO, London, 1952, p. 184

6 Ibid., pp. 128–9

7 Burgis, L., private papers, BRGS 2-13, minutes War Cabinet meeting 26 October 1942, Churchill Archives Cambridge

8 Morison, S.E., *History of the United States Naval Operations in World War II, vol. II Battle of the Atlantic*, Little Brown, Boston, 1947, p. 78

9 CAB 101-247-4 telegram Churchill to Roosevelt, 7 June 1941, TNA

10 CAB 80-57 COS Paper (41) 98 (O), Operation Exporter, 6 June 1941, TNA

11 BBC History WW2 People's War, Memories of Tobruk, www.bbc.co.uk/history/ww2peopleswar/stories/88/a4506888.shtml

12 Strange, J., *Despatches from the Home Front : War Diaries 1939–1945*, Jak Books, London, 1994, p. 69

13 Wavell, Sir A., Operations in the Middle East from 7th February, 1941 to 15th July, 1941, supplement to *London Gazette*, 3 July 1946

14 Ziemke, E.F., *Moscow to Stalingrad*, US Army CMH Pub 30-12, Washington, 1987, p. 20

15 Gilbert M., *Finest Hour: Winston Churchill 1939–1941*, Heinemann, London, 1984, p. 1118

16 Colville J., *The Fringe of Power: Downing St Diaries 1939–1955*, Hodder and Stoughton, London, 1985, p. 404

17 Halder, F., *War Journal*, vol. VI, 21 June 1941, Combined Arms Digital Research Library, Fort Leavenworth, Kansas, p. 160

18 Clark, A., *Barbarossa*, Cassel, London, 2005, p. 40

19 Ziemke, op. cit., p. 13

20 Halder op. cit., 14 June 1941, p. 154

21 CAB 101-247-4 telegram Churchill to Stalin, 20 July 1941, TNA

22 Ibid., 25 July 1941, TNA

23 CAB 66-18-26 telegram Churchill to Lord Privy Seal, 12 August 1941, TNA

24 Churchill, W., First draft Atlantic Charter, 10 August 1941, PSF files, Box 1, Atlantic Charter, Franklin D. Roosevelt Museum/Library, New York

25 Cab 65-19-25 minutes War Cabinet meeting, 4 September 1941, TNA

26 Sherwood, R., *Roosevelt and Hopkins*, Harper Bros, New York, 1948, op. cit. p. 363

27 Ibid., p. 311

28 Gilbert, op. cit., p. 1161

29 CAB 66-18012 telegram Churchill to Lord Privy Seal, 12 August 1941, TNA

30 CAB 65-19-20 confidential annex to War Cabinet meeting 19 August 1941, TNA

31 Wilson, T.A., *The First Summit*, University Press of Kansas, Kansas, 1991, p. 80

32 Ibid.

33 Sherwood, op. cit., p. 363

34 Wilson, op. cit., p. 108

35 Sherwood, op. cit., p. 236

36 Wing Ray, D., The Takoradi Route: Roosevelt's Prewar Venture beyond the Western Hemisphere *The Journal of American History*, vol. 62, No. 2 (September 1975), pp. 340–58

37 Strange, op. cit., p. 72

38 Morison, op. cit., p. 80

39 Ibid., p. 35

40 Postan, op. cit., p. 126

41 CAB 101-241 minute Churchill to Chief of Air Staff, 7 October 1941, TNA

42 CAB 80-60 COS (41) 232 (O) reply to PM's minute Operation Ajax, 15 October 1941, TNA

43 Roosevelt, F.D., *The Public Papers and Addresses of Franklin D. Roosevelt 1941*, Harper Bros, New York, 1950, p. 440

44 Stafford, D., *Roosevelt and Churchill: Men of Secrets*, Abacus, London, 2000, p. 76

Chapter 7

1   PAM 20-212 *History of Military Mobilisation in the United States Army 1775–1945*, US Army, Washington, 1955, p. 542

2   'Roosevelt as Friend of France', *Foreign Affairs*, 5 November 2014, www.foreignaffairs.com/articles/23798/john-mcvickar-haight-jr/roosevelt-as-friend-of-france

3   Alsop, J. and Kintner, R., *American White Paper – The Story of American Diplomacy and the Second World War*, Simon and Schuster, New York, 1940, pp. 30–31

4   Roosevelt, F.D., *The Public Papers and Addresses of Franklin D. Roosevelt, 1939 – War and Neutrality*, Macmillan, New York, 1941, p. 113

5   PAM 20-212 op. cit. p. 549

6   Ibid., p. 555

7   WO 99/3 Supreme War Council meetings minutes, 5 February 1940, TNA

8   Ibid., 28 March 1940 p. 20, TNA

9   Craven, W.F., and Cate, J.L. (eds), *Army Air Forces in World War II, vol. 6, Men and Planes*, University of Chicago Press, Chicago, 1955, p. 191

10 Ibid., *vol. 1 Air Corps Prepares for War*, p. 107

11 PAM 20-212, op. cit., p. 581

12 US Bureau Labor Statistics, Series D1-10 Labor Force and its Components 1900–1947

13 Danchev, A., and Todman, D., *War Diaries 1939–1945: Field Marshal Lord Alanbrooke*, Weidenfeld and Nicolson, London, 2001, p. 203

14 CAB 69-2 minutes Defence Committee meeting, 17 October 1941, TNA.

15 CAB 69-8 minute Churchill to Defence Committee, 21 October 1941, TNA

16 Kennedy, Sir J., *The Business of War*, William Morrow, New York, 1958, p. 182

17 CAB 69-2 minutes Defence Committee meeting, 2 December 1941, TNA

18 Bland, L., *Papers G.C. Marshall, vol. 2: 1st July 1939–6th December 1941*, Johns Hopkins University, Baltimore, 1986, p. 684

19 Strange, J., *Despatches from the Home Front: War Diaries 1939–1945*, Jak Books, London, 1994, p. 78

20 Rusbridger, J., and Nave, E., *Betrayal at Pearl Harbour*, Michael O'Mara, London, 1991, p. 138

21 Ickes, H., *The Secret Diary of Harold Ickes, vol. III The Lowering Clouds, 1939–1941*, Simon and Schuster, New York, 1954, p. 630

22 Stimson Diaries, 25 November 1941, Yale University Library, Manuscripts and Archives, roll 7, vol. 36, pp. 48–9

23 Winant, A., *Hearings before the Joint Committee on the Investigation of the Pearl Harbour Attack*, vol. 14, exhibit 21, US Government, Washington, 1946, pp. 1246–8, telegrams 6 December 1941

24 MacArthur, D., *Reports of General MacArthur, Japanese Operations in the SW Pacific*, vol. II, pt 1, CMH Pub 13-1, US Army, Washington, 1966, p. 50

25 Toland, J., *Infamy – Pearl Harbor and Its Aftermath*, Doubleday, New York, 1982, pp. 282–3

26 US Congress, *Hearings before the Joint Committee on the Investigation of the Pearl Harbour Attack*, vol. 20, Exhibit 176, US Government, Washington, 1946, pp. 4121–31

27 Costello, J., *The Pacific War 1941–1945*, Rawson Wade, New York, 1981, p. 138

28 Churchill, W., *The Second World War, vol. III – The Grand Alliance*, Cassell, London, 1953, p. 538

29 Roosevelt, F.D., message to Churchill, 8 December 1941, Map Room, Box 1, Franklin D. Roosevelt Museum/Library

30 Burgis, L., private papers, BRGS 2/10 minutes War Cabinet meeting 10 December 1941, Churchill Archives Cambridge

31 CAB 80-60, COS (41) 250 (O) Operation Gymnast, 11 November 1941, TNA

32 Churchill, op. cit., pp. 539–40

33 CAB 69-4 Churchill, Memorandum on the Future Conduct of the War, 22 January 1942, TNA

34 Danchev, op. cit., 7 December 1941, p. 209

35 Foreign Relations US, *The conferences at Washington 1941–2 and Casablanca 1943*, Arcadia conference minutes, Annex 1 to First COS meeting 24 December 1941, Department of State, Washington, 1968, p. 210

36 CAB 99-17 Washington conference documents, paper CR (JP 6), 16 December 1941, TNA

37 CAB 69-4 minute Churchill to COS Committee, 16 December 1941, Paper DO (42) 6, 1 February 1942, TNA

38 CAB 66-18-25 WP (41) 202, memorandum PM's meeting with Roosevelt, 20 August 1941, TNA

39 CAB 99-17 Washington conference documents American–British Strategy WW1, 22 December 1941, TNA

40 CAB 99-17 minutes Washington conference WW1, 5th meeting, 1 January 1942, TNA

41 Danchev, op. cit., 9 February 1942, p. 228

42 FRUS, *The conferences at Washington, 1941–1942, and Casablanca, 1943*, 'The First Washington conference December 1941–January 1942', notes by General Arnold of meeting 12 January 1942, US State Department, Washington, 1941–3, p. 194

43 FO 800-401 records of meetings Eden and Stalin, 16 and 17 December 1941, TNA

44 PREM 3-156-6 minute Churchill to Ismay, 10 April 1941, TNA

45 Kennedy, Sir J., private papers, diary for 1942, KENN 4/2/4, Liddell Hart Centre Military Archives

46 Rusbridger, J., 'The Sinking of the "Automedon", the Capture of the "Nankin": New Light on Two Intelligence Disasters in World War II', *Encounter*, vol. 375, No. 5, pp. 8–14

47 Nicolson, N. (ed), *Diaries and Letters of Harold Nicolson 1939–45*, Collins, London, 1967, p. 211

48 Burgis, L., private papers, BRGS 2/11 minutes War Cabinet meeting, 17 January 1942, Churchill Archives Cambridge

49 Matlof, M., and Snell, E., *Strategic Planning for Coalition Warfare, 1941 Encounter 1942*, CMH pub 1-3, Washington, 1953, p. 159

50 Editorial, *Times* newspaper, 14 February 1942, p. 5

51 Matlof and Snell, op. cit., p. 176

52 Churchill, W., *History of the Second World War, vol. IV – Hinge of Fate*, Cassell, London, 1951, p. 250

53 CAB 101-241 minute Churchill to Lord President of the Council, 7 September, 1941, TNA

54 CAB 101-242, minute Churchill to Chief of Air Staff, 13 March 1942, TNA

55 Stanley, P., 'Great in Adversity: Indian POWs', *Journal of Australian War Memorial*, no. 37, October 2002

56 CAB 101-248 telegram Churchill to Roosevelt, 15 April 1942, TNA

Chapter 8

1   CAB 79-19-8 paper JP (42) 243 of 7 March considered COS meeting 10 March 1942, TNA

2   Butler, J.R.M., *Grand Strategy* vol. III pt II, HMSO, London, 1964, p. 573

3   CAB 80-62 COS paper (42) 97 (O), Future Strategy and Planning, 13 April 1942, TNA

4   CAB 69-4 minutes Defence Committee meeting, 14 April, 1942, TNA

5   Danchev, op. cit., p. 248

6   CAB 69-4 minutes Defence Committee meeting, 14 April, 1942, TNA

7   Bland, L., *Papers G.C. Marshall, vol. III, 7th December 1941–31st May 1943*, 28 April 1942, Johns Hopkins University, Baltimore, 1991, p. 175, letter Marshall to Churchill

8   Churchill, W., *The Second World War, vol. IV: The Hinge of Fate*, Cassell, London, pp. 288–90

9   CAB 101-248 telegrams Churchill to Roosevelt April 1942, TNA

10 CAB 80-62 Operations on the Continent, 18 April 1942, TNA

11 Sherwood, R., *Roosevelt and Hopkins*, Harper Bros, New York, 1948, p. 541

12 Bland, op. cit., p. 183, memorandum to Roosevelt, Pacific V Bolero 6 May 1942

13 Roosevelt, F.D., memorandum to Marshall, King and JCS, 6 May 1942, Box 83, Safe File, Franklin D. Roosevelt Museum/Library

14 Ibid.

15 CAB 66-24-50 Eden memorandum (25th May 1942) on state of negotiations with Russia and records of meetings, TNA

16 Foreign Relations US, *1942 vol. III, Russia,* Department of State, Washington, p. 594, White House press release 11 June 1942,

17 CAB 65-30-20 confidential annex to War Cabinet meeting, aide memoire, 11 June 1942, TNA

18 Roosevelt memorandum, 6 May 1942, Box 83, PSF File, Franklin D. Roosevelt Museum/Library

19 Bland, op. cit., p. 161

20 Sherwood, op. cit., p. 586

21 CAB 101-248 telegram Churchill to Roosevelt, 28 May 1942, TNA

22 Mountbatten, L., letter to Roosevelt, 15 June 1942, Map Room papers Box 164 General Correspondence, Franklin D. Roosevelt Museum/Library

23 Danchev, op. cit., diary 13 June 1942

24 CAB 65-30-20 confidential annex to minutes of War Cabinet meeting 11 June 1942, TNA

25 CAB 101-242 minute Churchill to Ismay, 8 June 1942, TNA

26 Harvey, J., *The War Diaries of Oliver Harvey 1941–45*, Collins, London, 1978, p. 131

27 Stimson, H., letter to Roosevelt, 19 June 1942, PSF file, FDR Museum/Library

28 CAB 99-20 minutes Argonaut conference, Washington, 19 June 1942, TNA

29 Moran, Lord, *Winston Churchill: The Struggle for Survival*, Constable, London, 1966, p. 38

30 Foreign Relations US, *The conferences at Washington, 1941–1942, and Casablanca, 1943,* Department of State, Washington 1968, p. 434

31 CAB 99-20 memorandum Ismay to Combined Chiefs of Staff, 21 June 1942, TNA

32 Bland op. cit. pp. 246–8, Marshall memorandum to Roosevelt, 23 June 1943

33 Sherwood, op. cit., p. 596
34 Wilmot, C., private papers LH 15/15/1, interviews 14 April and 31 April 1948, Liddell Hart Centre Military Archives
35 CAB 79-56 Chiefs of Staff (O) Committee meeting minutes, 6 July 1942, TNA
36 CAB 65-31-3 confidential annex to minutes of War Cabinet meeting 8 July 1942, TNA
37 Gilbert, M., *Road to Victory*, p. 145
38 Bland, op. cit., p. 271, Marshall to Roosevelt, 10 July 1942,
39 Bland, op. cit., p. 276, Roosevelt to King, Memorandum 15 July 1942,
40 Army Services Forces, Statistical Review of WWII, Appendix H, War Department, Washington, 1946, pp. 121–2
41 Sherwood op. cit. pp. 603–5
42 CHAR 20-78 telegram Dill to Churchill, 15 July 1942, Churchill Archives Cambridge
43 CAB 99-19 minutes of Anglo American meetings, July 1942, TNA
44 Roosevelt, F.D., telegram to Hopkins, Marshall and King, 22 July 1942, Hopkins Papers, Sherwood collection, Box 308; Sherwood, p. 610
45 CAB 65-31-7 confidential annex to minutes of War Cabinet meeting, paper CCS 94, 24 July 1942, TNA
46 Bland, op. cit., p. 280, memorandum to Roosevelt, 28 July 1942
47 Matloff, M., and Snell, E., *Strategic Planning for Coalition Warfare*, 1941–1942, CMH Pub 1-3, US Army, Washington, 1953, pp. 283–4
48 CAB 101/242 minute Churchill, 23 July 1942, TNA
49 Stimson diary MS 465, 23 July 1942, Yale University
50 Butcher, H., *My Three Years with Eisenhower*, Simon and Schuster, New York, 1946, p. 29
51 CAB 79-22 JPS paper JP (42) 670, 14 July 1942, TNA
52 CAB 69-4 minutes of Defence Committee meeting, 13 July 1942, TNA
53 Foreign Ministry of the USSR, *Correspondence between the Chairman of the Council of Ministers of the USSR and the presidents of the USA and the Prime Ministers of Great Britain during the Great Patriotic War 1941–1945*, vol. I, Progress Publishers, Moscow, 1957, telegram Stalin to Churchill, 23 July 1942
54 CAB 65-31-7 confidential annex to minutes of War Cabinet meeting 24 July 1942, TNA
55 CAB 101-248 telegram Churchill to Roosevelt, 5 August 1942, TNA
56 PREM 3-76A-1 note Eden to Secretary of State, 29 July 1942, TNA
57 CAB 66-28-3 WP (42) 373 minutes and notes of Prime Minister's visit to Moscow, 23 August 1942, TNA
58 PREM 3 76A-12 notes of meeting with Stalin, 15 August 1942, folio 30-4, TNA
59 PREM 3 76A-11 telegram Churchill to Attlee, 16 August 1942, Reflex 112, TNA
60 CAB 65-31-20 confidential annex to War Cabinet minutes of meeting, 25 August 1942, TNA
61 Danchev, op. cit., p. 300, diary 13 August 1942
62 CAB 79-56 minutes COS meeting, 8 May 1942, TNA
63 CAB 65-30-20 confidential annex to minutes of War Cabinet meeting, 11 June 1942, TNA
64 CMHQ report 159 Operation Jubilee – Additional information on planning, Appendix A, Interview with Capt J. Hughes-Hallett, 29 September 1946, DHH, Ottawa
65 CAB 79-56 minutes COS meeting 6 July 1942, TNA
66 CMHQ report 100, Dieppe, Director History and Heritage, Ottawa, p. 26
67 CMHQ report 159, op. cit.
68 CAB 79-22 minutes COS meeting 20 July 1942, TNA
69 Danchev, op. cit., p. 282, 20 July 1942
70 CMHQ 100 op. cit. p. 29
71 CAB 79-22 minutes COS meeting, 12 August, 1942, TNA
72 PREM 3-76A-12 Record of first meeting with Stalin, 12 August 1942, p. 13, TNA
73 CMHQ report 83 Dieppe preliminary report, Director History and Heritage, Ottawa
74 CAB 120-66 Telegram Churchill to Ismay, Reflex 99, 15 August 1942, TNA

75 CAB 65-31-18 confidential annex to minutes of War Cabinet meeting, 20 August 1942, TNA
76 DEFE 2/324 Jubilee part 1, Report Operation Jubilee CB04244, p.8, TNA
77 DEFE 2/324 The Combined Services Raid on Dieppe, 19 August 1942, by Brigadier Mann, TNA
78 Hansard HC debate, 8 September 1942, WAR SITUATION Churchill, vol. 383 cc. 82–110

Chapter 9

1 Howe, G., *North-west Africa, Seizing the Initiative*, CMH Pub 6-1-1, US Army, Washington, 1993, p. 26
2 CAB 80-64 COS (42) 239 (O) Operation Torch Outline Plan, 22 August 1942, TNA
3 CAB 80-64 COS (42) 240 (O) Eisenhower letter, 22 August 1942, TNA
4 CAB 79-57 Paper JP (42) 763 Operation Torch Outline Plan, 23 August 1942, TNA
5 CAB 105-39 telegram JSM 365, Washington to London, 25 August 1942, TNA
6 Rockwell telegram US Navy Dept, 4 July 1942, Map Room Box 93, Franklin D. Roosevelt Museum/Library
7 CAB 79-57 minutes COS meeting, 21 August 1942, TNA
8 CAB 101-248 telegram Churchill to Roosevelt, 26 August 1942, TNA
9 CAB 79-57 minutes COS meeting, 26 August 1942, TNA
10 CAB 101-248 telegram Churchill to Roosevelt, 27 August 1942, TNA
11 CAB 59-57 minutes COS meeting, 29 August 1942, TNA
12 Roosevelt F.D., telegram 180 to Churchill, 30 August 1942, Map Room, Box 2, Franklin D. Roosevelt Museum/Library
13 CAB 79-57 minutes to COS second meeting, 31 August 1942, TNA
14 CAB 101-248 telegram Churchill to Roosevelt, 1 September 1942, TNA
15 Roosevelt 2 September telegram 182 to Churchill, Map Room, Box 2, Franklin D. Roosevelt Museum/Library
16 CAB 101-248 telegram Churchill to Roosevelt, 3 September 1942, TNA
17 Roosevelt to Churchill 2nd telegram 182 Map Room, Box 2, Franklin D. Roosevelt Museum/Library
18 Churchill, W., *The Second World War, vol. IV – The Hinge of Fate*, Cassell, London, 1951, pp. 483–6
19 CAB 79-57 minutes COS meeting, 15 September 1942, TNA
20 CAB 79-87 confidential annex to COS conference, 21 September 1942, TNA
21 Churchill W., telegram to Stalin, 30 September 1942 in Foreign Ministry of the USSR, *Correspondence between the Chairman of the Council of Ministers of the USSR and the Presidents of the USA and Prime Ministers of Great Britain during the Great Patriotic War of 1941–1945*, vol. 1, Progress Publishers, Moscow, 1957, pp. 170–3
22 Churchill, op. cit., p. 518
23 CAB 65-32-4, confidential annex to minutes War Cabinet meeting, 26 October 1942, TNA
24 CAB 101-248 telegram Churchill to Stalin, 13 November 1942, TNA
25 Howe op. cit. p. 173
26 Ibid., p. 258
27 Murray, W., *Strategy for Defeat: The Luftwaffe 1933–1945*, Air University Press, Alabama, 1983, p. 151
28 CAB 105/139 telegram Eisenhower to War Department, NAF 41, Review no. 25, 12 December 1942, TNA
29 Leton, B., Private Papers – The Descent of Man, D.19780, Imperial War Museum, London, p. 584
30 Howard, M., *Grand Strategy, vol. IV Aug 1942–September 1943*, HMSO, London, 1972, p. 337
31 PREM 4-499-4 draft policy paper by Churchill, 22 October 1942, TNA
32 CAB 66-30-13 paper by Churchill W.P. (42) 483 Policy for the Conduct of the War, 24 October 1942, TNA

33 CAB 80-66 paper American British Strategy, COS (42) 345 (O), 30 October 1942, TNA
34 CAB 101/242 minute Churchill to Ismay, 9 November 1942, TNA
35 Roosevelt to Churchill 9 November 1942, Map Room, Box 3, Franklin D. Roosevelt Museum/Library
36 CAB 80-65 minute Churchill COS (42) 399 (O), 18 November 1942, TNA
37 CAB 101-248 telegram Churchill to Roosevelt, 24 November 1942, TNA
38 CAB 66-31-23 WP (42) 543, Plans and Operations in the Mediterranean, Middle East and Near East, 25 November 1942, TNA
39 Broad, R., and Fleming, S. (eds), *Nella Last's War*, Profile, London, 2006, p. 218
40 CAB 80-66, note Churchill to Chiefs of Staff, COS (42) 429 (O), 3 December 1942, TNA
41 Danchev, A., and Todman, D., War Diaries 1939–1945: Field Marshal Lord Alanbrooke, Weidenfeld and Nicolson, London, 2001, p. 346
42 CAB 80-66 minute Churchill COS (42) 429 (O), 3 December 1942, TNA
43 Churchill, op. cit., p. 590
44 CAB 65-28-32 minutes of War Cabinet meeting 30 November 1942, TNA
45 Roosevelt to Churchill, 2 December 1942, Map Room box 3, Franklin D. Roosevelt Museum/Library
46 CAB 101-248 telegram Churchill to Roosevelt, 3 December 1942, TNA
47 CAB 79-58 JP (42) 990 Offensive Strategy in the Mediterranean, 5 December 1942, TNA
48 CAB 80-66 paper COS (42) 466 (O), American-British Strategy in 1943, 31 December 1942, TNA
49 Minutes FDR and JCS Meeting 10 December 1942, Map Room, Box 29, Franklin D. Roosevelt Museum/Library
50 CAB 80-66 COS (42) 475 (O) American–British Strategy in 1943, 25 December 1942, TNA
51 CHAR 20-85 telegram Dill to Churchill, 14 December 1942, Churchill Archives Cambridge
52 Matlof, M., and Snell, E., *Strategic Planning for Coalition Warfare, 1941–1942*, CMH Pub 1-3, US Army, Washington, 1953, p. 359
53 Howe op. cit. p. 330
54 Cab 66-31-27 WP (42) 547 Summary of Beveridge Report, 25 November 1942, TNA
55 Broad and Fleming, op. cit., p. 219
56 Strange, J., *Despatches from the Home Front War Diaries 1939–1945*, Jak Books, London, 1994, p. 105
57 Churchill, op. cit., pp. 861–2
58 CAB 80-67 COS (43) 4 (O) Assault Shipping and Landing Craft, 5 January 1942, TNA
59 CAB 105-55 telegram COS (W) 412, 29 December 1942, TNA
60 CAB 99-24 minutes 1st plenary meeting, 15 January 1943, TNA
61 MJ26-J13 diaries of William Mackenzie King, 6 December 1942, pp. 1059–60, Library and Archives Canada
62 FRUS, *The conferences at Washington, 1941–1942, and Casablanca, 1943*, US Government, Washington, 1943, pp. 559–560
63 CAB 120-76 telegram Churchill to War Cabinet Stratagem #56, 17 January 1943, TNA
64 CAB 65-33-10 minutes War Cabinet meeting, 18 January 1943, TNA
65 Ibid., minutes CCS 58th Meeting, 16 January 1943, TNA
66 Ibid., minutes second plenary meeting, Casablanca 18 January 1943, TNA
67 Ibid., CCS paper 166/1/D, 21 January 1943, TNA
68 Ibid., minutes third plenary meeting Casablanca 23 January 1943, TNA
69 Ibid., CCS paper 170/2, 23 January 1943, TNA
70 Ibid., CCS paper 165, 22 January 1943, TNA
71 Wedemeyer, A.C., *Wedemeyer Reports!*, Henry Holt, New York, 1958, pp. 191–2
72 Bryant, A., *The Turn of the Tide*, Reprint Society, London, 1958, p. 462
73 Churchill, op. cit., p. 615

Chapter 10

1   Churchill, W., *The Second World War, vol. IV – The Hinge of Fate*, Cassell, London, 1951, p. 666
2   Foreign Ministry of the USSR, *Correspondence between the Chairman of the Council of Ministers of the USSR and the presidents of the USA and the Prime Ministers of Great Britain during the Great Patriotic War 1941–1945*, vol. I, Progress Publishers, Moscow, 1957, telegram Stalin to Churchill, 15 March 1943
3   CAB 105-139 telegram NAF 144 Eisenhower to War Department, 11 February 1944, TNA
4   CAB 80-67 minute Churchill to COS, paper (43) 68 (O), 19 February 1943, TNA
5   CAB 101-243 minute Churchill to Ismay, 13 February 1943, TNA
6   Gilbert op. cit. p. 339
7   CHAR 20/107/51 telegram Alexander to Churchill, 27 February 1943, Churchill Archives Cambridge
8   Davison, J., Private Papers, letter 22 March 1943, D.17406, Imperial War Museum, London
9   Churchill, W., message to Roosevelt, 24 March 1943, Map Room, Box 3, Franklin D. Roosevelt Museum/Library
10 Bland, L., *Papers G.C. Marshall, vol. III 7th December 1941–31st May 1943*, Johns Hopkins University, Baltimore, 1986, p. 621
11 WILK 1/2A, journal 30 March 1943, Papers of Gerard Wilkinson, Churchill Archives Cambridge
12 WO 203-6453 Mountbatten, L., Report to the Combined Chiefs of Staff by the Supreme Allied Commander Southeast Asia 1943–1946, 30 July 1947, p. 24
13 CAB 79-60-19 minute Churchill in minutes COS meeting, 8 April 1943, TNA
14 CAB 79-60-27 minutes COS meeting 15 April, JP (43) 146 (final) Operation Anakim, 11 April 1943, TNA
15 CAB 65-38-4 confidential annex to minutes War Cabinet meeting 29 April 1943, TNA
16 CAB 79-60-25 minutes COS meeting, 13 April 1943, TNA
17 CAB 80-68 minute Churchill, 14 April 1943, TNA
18 CAB 101-243 minute Churchill to Ismay, 18 April 1943, TNA
19 CAB 105-42 telegram Washington to COS, JSM 879, 14 April 1943, TNA
20 Bryant, A., *The Turn of the Tide*, Reprint Society, London, 1958, p. 494
21 CAB 80-69 COS report on telegram JSM 886 23 April 1943, TNA
22 Harrison, G., *Cross-Channel Attack*, CMH Pub 7-4-1, US Army, Washington, 1951, p. 143
23 CAB 90-22 Churchill note Operation Anakim, COS (T) 8, 8 May 1943, TNA
24 CAB 80-69 COS (43) 235 (O) 3 May 1942, Operations from India 1943–44, TNA
25 CAB 90-22 note Churchill Operation Anakim, COS (T) 8, 8 May 1943, TNA
26 Ibid., minutes COS Committee meeting 10 May 1943, TNA
27 Ibid., minutes Churchill COS (T) 8, 8 May 1943, TNA
28 Ibid. p. 124
29 Ibid., paper CCS 235 Defeat of Axis Powers in Europe, 18 May 1943, TNA
30 Danchev op. cit., p. 405, 18 May 1943,
31 CAB 99-22 resolutions of Combined Chiefs of Staff, CCS 237/1, 20 May 1943, TNA
32 Ibid., minutes second plenary meeting 14 May 1943, TNA
33 Ibid., minutes Trident conference, CCS paper 242/6, 25 May 1942, TNA
34 CAB 65-38-8, confidential annex to minutes War Cabinet meeting , 21 May 1943, TNA
35 Churchill, W., *The Second World War vol. IV – The Hinge of Fate*, Cassell, London, 1951, p. 730
36 Cab 99-22 minutes Algiers meeting 29 May 1942, part IV, TNA
37 Ibid., minutes Algiers meeting 31 May 1943, TNA
38 Ibid.
39 BBC History WWII People's War, Strange Things on the Table, www.bbc.co.uk/history/ ww2peopleswar/stories/92/a1110592.shtml
40 Churchill, op. cit., p. 740

41 CAB 99-22 minutes Trident conference meeting, 3 June 1943, TNA

42 FO 371/34577 despatch no. 51 Sir Owen O'Malley to Eden, 24 May 1943, TNA

43 CAB 101/243 minutes Churchill to Eden, 28 April 1943, TNA

44 Roosevelt, F.D., telegram to Churchill, 28 June 1943, Map Room, Box 3, Franklin D. Roosevelt Museum/Library

45 Birtle, A., *Sicily: US Army Campaigns of WWII*, CMH Pub 72-16, US Army, Washington, 1993, p. 7

46 Bland, op. cit., p. 662

47 Garland, Lt-Col A. and McGaw-Smyth, H., *Sicily and the Surrender of Italy*, US Army CMH Pub 6-22-1, Washington, 1965, p. 182

48 Ibid., p. 218

49 Ibid., p. 241

50 Leton, B., Private Papers, The Descent of Man, D.19780, Imperial War Museum, London

51 CAB 66-39-40 draft Italian surrender document, Eden, 26 July 1943, TNA

52 CAB 101-249 telegram Churchill to Roosevelt, 30 July 1943, TNA

53 Davison, J., Private Papers, letter 2 August 1943, D.17406, Imperial War Museum, London

54 Garland and McGaw-Smyth, op. cit., p. 416

Chapter 11

1 CAB 101-243 minute Churchill to Ismay, 2 July 1943, TNA

2 CAB 101-249 telegram Churchill to Alexander, 2 July 1943, TNA

3 CAB 80-71 minute Churchill to COS (43) 379 (O), 13 July 1943, TNA

4 Stimson, H., *On Active Service*, Harpers, New York, 1948, pp. 430–2

5 CAB 80-71 minute Churchill to Ismay, Habbakuk, 19 July 1943, TNA

6 CAB 84-54-67 Post Husky Operations, JP (43) 253 Operation Avalanche, 19 July 1943, TNA

7 Danchev op. cit. Brooke diary 20 July, p. 431

8 CAB 105-43 telegram JSM to Chiefs of Staff, JSM 1104, 26 July 1943, TNA

9 CAB 99-23, minutes COS meeting (COS (Q) 8), 11 August 1943, TNA

10 Matlof op. cit. p. 212

11 Howard, M., *Grand Strategy, vol. 4, August 1942–September 1943*, HMSO, London, 1972, p.563

12 CAB 99-23 minutes COS (Q) 6th meeting 10 August 1943, TNA

13 Ibid., minutes COS (Q) 7th meeting 10 August, 1943, TNA

14 CAB 99-22 paper COS (Q) 8 (revised), 8 August 1943, TNA

15 Danchev, op. cit., p. 437, 6 August 1943, (see also minutes meeting COS (Q) 6 August and paper COS (Q) 3, CAB 99-23, TNA)

16 CAB 105-43 telegram Dill JSM 1133 to COS, 7 August 1943, TNA

17 CCS paper 303, 9 August 1943, Quadrant papers, Box 27, Map Room, Franklin D. Roosevelt Museum/Library,

18 CAB 99-23 paper CCS 303/1 16 August 1943, TNA

19 Danchev, op. cit., p. 443, 16 August

20 Bland, L., *Papers of G.C. Marshall, vol. IV June 1 1943–December 31 1944*, Johns Hopkins University, Baltimore, 1996, p. 108

21 CAB 99-23 Quadrant conference, Churchill minute Operation Culverin COS(Q) 29, 17 August 1943, TNA

22 CAB 69-5 minutes Defence Committee meeting, 28 July 1943, TNA

23 Slim, W., *Defeat into Victory*, Cassell, London, 1955, p. 162

24 Churchill, W., *The Second World War, vol. V: Closing the Ring*, Cassell, London, 1952, p. 81

25 CAB 99-23 final report to President and Prime Minister, CCS 319/5, 24 August 1943, TNA

26 Ibid., CCS Paper 303/3 17 August 1943, TNA

27 Foreign Relations US, *The conferences at Washington and Quebec 1943*, Department of State, Washington, 1970, p. 1262, Roosevelt to Eisenhower telegram, 2 September 1943

28 BBC History WW2 People's War, Delphine's War – Here Come the Yanks! www.bbc.co.uk/
   history/ww2peopleswar/stories/89/a4073889.shtml
29 Foreign Ministry of the USSR, *Correspondence between the Chairman of the Council of Ministers
   of the USSR and the presidents of the USA and the Prime Ministers of Great Britain during the Great
   Patriotic War 1941–1945*, vol. I, Progress Publishers, Moscow, 1957, telegram Stalin to Churchill,
   22 August 1943
30 CAB 99-23 Churchill minute, annex to minutes of CCS meeting, 9 September 1943, TNA
31 CAB 101-249 telegram Churchill to Hopkins, 3 August 1943, TNA
32 Bland, op. cit., p. 136, Marshall to Eisenhower, 22 September 1943

Chapter 12

1 CAB 101-243 minute Churchill to Ismay, 27 July 1943, TNA
2 CAB 99-23 annex minute by Churchill to Roosevelt, Quadrant plenary meeting, 9 September
   1943, TNA
3 Churchill, W., *The Second World War vol. V: Closing the Ring*, Cassell, London, 1951, p. 182
4 CAB 101-249 telegram Churchill to Wilson, 8 September 1943, TNA
5 Letter Alexander to Brooke 23 September 1943, Papers FM Brooke 6-2-18 Liddell Hart
   Archives, London
6 Letter Alexander to Brooke 17 October 1943, Papers FM Brooke 6-2-19 Liddell, Hart
   Archives, London
7 Leton, B., Private Papers – The Descent of Man, D.19780, Imperial War Museum, London, p. 616
8 CAB 122-871 report AFHQ German Strategy in Italy in the event of an Italian Collapse, 7
   August 1943, TNA
9 CAB 122-871 telegram Ismay to Commanders-in-Chief, Chieftel 22, 25 September 1943, TNA
10 Ehrman, J., *Grand Strategy, vol. V, August 1943–September 1944*, HMSO, London, 1956, p. 68
11 CAB 80-75 minute Churchill to Ismay, Operations in the Eastern Mediterranean, 4 October
   1943, TNA
12 Danchev, A., and Todman, D., War Diaries 1939–1945: Field Marshal Lord Alanbrooke,
   Weidenfeld and Nicolson, London, 2001, pp. 458–9
13 CAB 101-249 telegram Churchill to Roosevelt, 10 October 1943, TNA
14 Churchill, op. cit., p. 198
15 CAB 80-77 minute Churchill, Future Operations in the European and Eastern Mediterranean
   theatre (COS – Sextant 1), 20 November 1943, TNA
16 JN4-2-5, Papers Maj. Gen. Sir J. Kennedy diary, 17–20 October 1943, LHCMA, London
17 CAB 79-66-11 minutes of staff conference, 19 October 1943, TNA
18 Ibid.
19 CAB 79-88, confidential annex to COS meeting, 20 October 1943, TNA
20 CAB 101-249 telegram Churchill to Roosevelt, 23 October 1943, TNA
21 Danchev, op. cit., p. 462
22 CAB 65-40-6 Eisenhower telegram, confidential annex to minutes of War Cabinet meeting,
   26 October 1943, TNA
23 Ibid., telegram Churchill to Eden, 26 October 1943
24 Danchev, op. cit., p. 465, 1 November 1943
25 CAB 65-40-9 confidential annex to minutes of War Cabinet meeting, 4 November 1943, TNA
26 Churchill, op. cit., p. 199
27 Matloff, M., *Strategic Planning for Coalition Warfare 1943–44*, US Army CMH Pub 1-4,
   Washington, 1959, p. 264
28 Ibid. p. 278
29 CAB 66-42-40 memorandum Churchill, Manpower, 1 November 1943, TNA

30 JCS, minutes meeting 15 November 1943, Box 29, Map Room, Franklin D. Roosevelt Museum/Library,

31 Bland, L., *Papers of G.C. Marshall vol. 3 December 7, 1941–May 31, 1943*, Johns Hopkins University, Baltimore, 1991, p. 621, memorandum 30 March 1943

32 Sherwood, R., *The White House Papers*, vol. II, Eyre and Spottiswood, London, 1949, p. 744

33 Matloff, op. cit., p. 304

34 Stilwell, J., diary 23 November 1943, Stillwell Collection, Box 39, Folder 9, Hoover Institution Archives, Stanford University, Stanford

35 CAB 99-25 Sextant, minutes Combined Chiefs of Staff meeting 24 November 1943, TNA

36 Ibid., minutes COS 4th meeting 25 November 1943, TNA

37 Ibid., JS (Sextant) 9 paper – Entry of Turkey into the War, 25 November 1943, TNA

38 Danchev, op. cit., p. 481, 26 November 1943

39 CAB 99-25 minutes 182nd CCS meeting, 30 November 1943, TNA

40 CHAR 20-94A Letter Churchill to MacArthur, 23 July 1943, Churchill Archives Cambridge

41 CAB 99-25 Sextant/Eureka conference notes, 2nd Meeting, 29 November 1943, TNA

42 CAB 66-45-8 records of British–American–Russian conversations at Eureka, WP (44) 9, 7 January 1944, TNA

43 Foreign Relations US, *The Cairo and Tehran Conferences*, Department of State, Washington, 1961, p. 553, Bohlen Minutes, 30 November 1943

44 CAB 79-67 JIC Paper (43) 458, Effects of Bombing Offensive on German War Effort, 12 November 1943, TNA

45 CAB 99-25 minutes 2nd plenary session 29 November 1943, TNA

46 Foreign Relations US, *The Cairo and Tehran Conferences*, Department of State, Washington, 1961, p. 594–5, Bohlen Minutes, 1 December 1943

47 CAB 99-25 Sextant conference, minutes of 3rd plenary meeting, 4 December 1943, TNA

48 Ibid., paper COS (Sextant) 25, Operation Buccaneer, 3 December 1943, TNA

49 Ibid., minutes 4th plenary meeting, 5 December 1943, TNA

50 Matloff, op. cit., p. 372

51 Churchill, op. cit., p. 364

52 CAB 99-25 paper Sextant conference CCS 427, 6 December 1943, TNA

53 Churchill, op. cit., p. 366

54 Roosevelt, F.D., telegram to Chiang Kai-Shek, 5 December 1943, Box 10, Map Room Franklin D. Roosevelt Museum/Library

55 Chiang Kai-Shek telegram to Roosevelt 10 December 1943, Box 10, Map Room Franklin D. Roosevelt Museum/Library

56 Bland, L., *Papers of G.C. Marshall, vol. IV June 1, 1943–December 31, 1944*, Johns Hopkins University, Baltimore, 1996, p. 195

57 CAB 65-40-16 Confidential annex to minutes of War Cabinet meeting, 15 December 1943, TNA

58 Matloff, op. cit., p. 367

59 Matloff, op. cit., p. 397

60 BBC History WW2 People's War, Memories of when the Yanks came to Truro part 2, www. bbc.co.uk/history/ww2peopleswar/stories/24/a4090024.shtml

61 CAB 79-68-20 minutes to COS (O) meeting, 20 December 1943, TNA

62 CAB 80-77 paper COS (43) 795 (O), Preparations for War against Japan, 28 December 1943, TNA

63 Person-Hayes, G., *History of the Joint Chiefs of Staff in WWII*, Naval Institute, Washington, 1982, p. 572

64 Nicolson, N., *The Harold Nicolson Diaries 1939–1945*, Collins, London, 1967, p. 348

65 CHAR 20-130 telegram Churchill to Chiefs of Staff #FROZEN 736, 19 December 1943, CAC

66 Churchill, op. cit., p. 381

67 CAB 101-249 telegram Churchill to Roosevelt, 26 December 1943, TNA

68 CAB 80-78 minutes Operation Shingle conferences, 7 and 8 January 1944, TNA

69 Eisenhower, D., telegram NAF 577 to Combined Chiefs of Staff, 3 January 1944, Map Room, Box 103, Franklin D. Roosevelt Museum/Library
70 Blumenson, M., *Salerno to Cassino*, US Army CMH Pub 6-3-1, Washington, 1969, p. 304
71 Ibid., p. 355
72 Ibid., pp. 356–7
73 Danchev, op. cit., p. 527
74 Churchill, op. cit. p. 448
75 Laurie, C.D., *Anzio, The US Army Campaigns of WWII*, CMH Pub 72-19, US Army, Washington, n.d., p. 25
76 Moran, Lord, C., *Winston Churchill: The Struggle for Survival 1940–1965*, Constable, London, 1966, p. 188

Chapter 13

1 Slim, W., *Defeat into Victory*, Cassell, London, 1956, p. 162
2 Wavell, Field Marshal A., 'Operations in the India Command from 1st January 1943 to 20th June 1943 , *London Gazette*, 22 April 1948
3 CAB 80-80 minutes Churchill to Ismay, 2 October 1943, TNA
4 CAB 69-6 minutes of Defence Committee meeting, 19 January 1944, TNA
5 Churchill, W., *The Second World War, vol. V: Closing the Ring*, Cassell, London, 1951, p. 504
6 CAB 99-25, minutes 5th plenary session, 6 December 1943, TNA
7 CAB 69-6 minutes of Defence Committee meeting, 19 January 1944, TNA
8 Churchill, op. cit., p. 79
9 CAB 120-707 Telegram JSM Washington to COS, JSM 1519, 17 February 1944, TNA
10 Roosevelt, F., telegram to Churchill 25 February 1944, Map Room, Box 5, Franklin D. Roosevelt Museum/Library
11 CAB 80-80 paper COS (44) 183 (O) SEAC – Future Operations, 23 February 1943, TNA
12 CAB 79-89 confidential annex to minutes of 10 p.m. COS meeting, 25 February 1944, TNA
13 CHAR 20/188A/22 memorandum Churchill, 29 February 1944, Churchill Archives, Cambridge
14 CHAR 20/1881/45-49 memorandum COS, 8 March 1944, Churchill Archives, Cambridge
15 Ehrman, J., *Grand Strategy*, vol. V, HMSO, London, 1956, p. 448
16 CAB 79-89 confidential annex to minutes of COS meeting, 8 March 1944, TNA
17 Danchev, A., and Todman, D., War Diaries 1939–1945: Field Marshal Lord Alanbrooke, Weidenfeld and Nicolson, London, 2001, p. 532
18 CHAR 20/188B/136-140 Memorandum Churchill to COS, 20 March 1944, Churchill Archives Cambridge
19 Danchev, op. cit., p. 533
20 CHAR 20/188B/28-32, memorandum COS to Churchill, 28 March 1944, Churchill Archives Cambridge
21 CAB 78-21 Plans for the Defeat of Japan – Meeting 1, 8 April 1944, TNA
22 CAB 120-707 Churchill minute to Ismay, 7 May 1944, TNA
23 Ibid.
24 CAB 79-74-9 minutes Staff conference COS, 8 May 1944, TNA
25 Churchill, op. cit., p. 501
26 Ibid., p. 502
27 Bland, L., *Papers of G.C. Marshall vol. IV June 1, 1943–December 31, 1944*, Johns Hopkins University, Baltimore, 1996, p. 466, Stilwell telegram
28 Roosevelt, F., telegram to Churchill 6 January 1944, Map Room, Box 5, Franklin D. Roosevelt Museum/Library
29 Sherwood, R., *Roosevelt and Hopkins: An Intimate History*, Harper, New York, 1950, p. 811
30 CAB 105-58 telegram COS(W) 1126 to Washington, 4 February 1944, TNA

31 Bland, op. cit., p. 271
32 Ibid., p. 313
33 CAB 105-58 telegram COS (W) 1156 to Washington, 19 February 1944, TNA
34 Ibid.
35 CAB 105-153 telegram Wilson to CCS, MEDCOS 41, 22 February 1944, TNA
36 CAB 105-58 telegram COS (W) 1168 to Washington, 23 February 1944, TNA
37 CAB 79-71-10 minutes COS meeting Landing Craft in the Mediterranean, 29 February 1944, TNA
38 Roosevelt, F.D., telegram to Churchill 7 February 1944, Map Room, Box 5, Franklin D. Roosevelt Museum/Library
39 FO 371-34577 despatch no. 25 O'Malley to Eden, 11 February 1944, TNA
40 CAB 105-153 telegram MEDCOS 73 Wilson to COS, 22 March 1944, TNA
41 CAB 79-72-5 minutes COS meeting, 22 March 1944, TNA
42 CAB 105-45 telegram JCS Washington to COS, JSM 1593, 24 March 1944, TNA
43 CAB 101-250 telegram Churchill to Roosevelt, 12 April 1944, TNA
44 CAB 105-45 telegram JCS Washington to COS, JSM 1605, 30 March 1944, TNA
45 CAB 105-59 telegram British COS to JCS, COS(W) 1249, 31 March 1944, TNA
46 CAB 101-244 minute Churchill to Ismay, 5 April 1944, TNA
47 CAB 105-45 telegram JCS Washington to COS, JSM 1629, 8 April 1944, TNA
48 CAB 101-250 telegram Churchill to Marshall, 12 April 1944, TNA
49 CAB 79-73-12 appendix 1 to annex 1 of minutes of COS meeting, 15 April 1944, TNA
50 CAB 101-250 telegram Churchill to Marshall, 16 April 1944, TNA
51 Ibid., telegram Churchill, W., to Roosevelt, 14 April 1944, TNA
52 Bland, op. cit., p. 424 , telegram Marshall to Churchill, 18 April 1944
53 CAB 101/249 telegram Churchill to Roosevelt, 23 October 1943, TNA
54 Fraser, D., *Alanbrooke*, Hamlyn, London, 1983, p. 397
55 Danchev, op. cit., p. 554, 5 June
56 CAB 80-80 minute Churchill to COS paper (44) 246 (O), 12 March 1944, TNA
57 Gilbert, M., *The Road to Victory*, Heinemann, London, 1986, p. 745
58 CAB 99-28 annex to minutes of 4th meeting of Dominion Prime Ministers conference, 3 May 1944, TNA
59 Ibid.
60 Churchill, W., telegram to Roosevelt, 29 April 1944, Map Room, Box 6, Franklin D. Roosevelt Museum/Library
61 CAB 101-244 minute Churchill to Eden, 8 May 1944, TNA
62 Mathews, S.T., *Command Decisions: General Clark's Decision to Drive on Rome*, CMH Pub 70-1, US Army, Washington, 1987, p. 356
63 *New York Times*, 31 May 1944, 'Roosevelt critics Spain, taking issue with Churchill'
64 Poole, B., letter 1 June 1944, Private Papers, D.2119, Imperial War Museum, London
65 BBC History WW2 People's War, Ken Sweet's Memories, www.bbc.co.uk/history/ww2peopleswar/stories/53/a4565153.shtml
66 Leton, B., Private Papers – The Descent of Man, D.19780, Imperial War Museum, London, p. 629

Chapter 14

1 CAB 79-73-21 annex III to minutes COS meeting 25 April 1944, TNA
2 CAB 79-75 paper JP (44) 141, Mediterranean Planning, 23 May 1944, COS meeting, 25 May 1944, TNA
3 CAB WO 214-15 telegram MA1364 Alexander to Churchill, 7 June 1944, TNA
4 CAB 122-1246 telegram Combined Chiefs of Staff to Wilson and Eisenhower, 14 June 1944, TNA
5 CAB 79-76 JPS paper 161 (44) Exploitation from Northern Italy, 15 June 1944, TNA

6 Bland, L., *Papers of G.C. Marshall vol. IV June 1, 1943–December 31, 1944*, Johns Hopkins University, Baltimore, 1996, p. 481

7 CAB 122/1246, telegram B-12995 Maitland Wilson to Eisenhower, 19 June 1944, TNA

8 CHAR 20/167/26-27 telegram Alexander to Churchill, 19 June 1944, Churchill Archives Cambridge

9 Bland op. cit. p. 487

10 CAB 122-1246 telegram SCAF 53 Eisenhower to Combined Chiefs of Staff, 23 June 1944, TNA

11 Ibid., telegram JCS to COS JSM 111, 24 June 1944, TNA

12 CAB 79-76 minutes third COS meeting, 22 June 1944, TNA

13 CAB 122-1246 telegram COS (W) 130 to JSM, 26 June 1944, TNA

14 Ibid., telegram JSM 114 JCS to COS, 27 June 1944, TNA

15 CAB 79-76 minutes COS meeting, 28 June 1944, TNA

16 CAB 122-1246 memorandum re CCS 603/2 by British Chiefs of Staff, undated but 28 June 1944, sent as COS (W) 134, TNA

17 CAB 101-250 telegram Churchill to Roosevelt, 28 June 1944, TNA

18 Roosevelt, F.D., telegram to Churchill, 29 June 1944, Map Room, Box 6, Franklin D. Roosevelt Museum/Library

19 CAB 79-76 minutes COS meeting, 30 June 1944, TNA

20 CAB 101-250 telegram Churchill to Roosevelt, 1 July 1944, TNA

21 CAB 79-76 paper JP (44) 173, Courses of Action in the Mediterranean, 25 June 1944, TNA

22 Danchev, op. cit., p. 564

23 Churchill, W., *The Second World War: vol. VI, Triumph and Tragedy*, Cassell, London, 1954, p. 62

24 CAB 65-43-1 minutes War Cabinet, 3 July 1944, TNA

25 Spink, V., BBC History WW2 People's War, The V1 and V2, www.bbc.co.uk/history/ww2peopleswar/stories/70/a2732870.shtml

26 Strange, J., *Despatches from the Home Front: War Diaries 1939–45*, Jak Books, London, 1994, p. 146

27 CAB 65-43-1 minutes War Cabinet, 3 July 1944, TNA

28 CAB 79-77 paper JPS (44) 177, Chemical Warfare in Connection with Crossbow, 5 July 1944, TNA

29 BBC History WW2 People's War, Len Smith the V-2, http://www.bbc.co.uk/history/ww2peopleswar/stories/86/a3332486.shtml

30 Strange, op. cit., pp. 147–8, 8 July 1944

31 CAB 101-244 Churchill minute to Ismay, 6 July 1944, TNA

32 Danchev, op. cit., p. 567, 6 July 1944

33 Gilbert, op. cit., p. 848

34 CAB 79-77 minutes COS meeting, 17 July 1944, TNA

35 CAB 79-79 paper in minutes COS meeting, 26 July 1944, Security in W. Europe and the North Atlantic, 20 July 1944, TNA

36 CAB 79-78 paper JP (44) 192 Final – The Pas de Calais 30 July 1944, TNA

37 CAB 79-79 minutes COS meeting 4, August 1944, TNA

38 Churchill, op. cit., p. 90

39 CAB 101-250 telegram Churchill to General Smuts, 26 August 1944, TNA

40 CAB 80-86 minutes of meeting Churchill, Wilson and Brooke in Rome, 21 August 1944, TNA

41 CAB 101-250 telegram Churchill to Roosevelt, 28 August 1944, TNA

42 Matloff, M., *Strategic Planning for Coalition Warfare 1943–44*, CMH Pub 1-4, US Army, Washington, 1994, p. 488

43 CAB 101-244 minute Churchill to Ismay, 12 September 1944, TNA

44 CAB 79-75 minutes COS meeting, 3 June 1944, TNA

45 CAB 79-78 paper JP (44) 198, Operations in Burma, 2 August 1944, TNA

46 CAB 79-79 minutes third COS meeting, 9 August 1944, TNA

47 CAB 120-707 Churchill minute to Ismay, 24 July 1944, TNA

48 Matloff, op. cit., p. 478

49 Ibid.,. p. 519

50 CAB 101-250 telegram Churchill to PM Canada (McKenzie King), 26 August 1944, TNA

51 Bland, op. cit., p. 524

52 CAB 99-29 minutes Octagon conference, 1st plenary meeting 13 September 1944, TNA

53 Ibid., annex to minutes Octagon conference, 2nd plenary meeting 16 September 1944, TNA

54 Ibid., Octagon conference, CCS paper 680/2 Final Report, 16 September 1944, TNA

55 CAB 79-81 minutes COS meeting, 2 October 1944, TNA

56 Minute Ismay to Churchill, 7 October 1944, Papers of FM Brooke 6-2-19 Liddell Hart
    Archives, London

57 CAB 80-88 minutes Naples meeting, 8 October 1944, TNA

58 CAB 79-83-4 annex I to minutes COS meeting, 20 November 1944, TNA

59 CAB 80-88 minutes of meeting South East Area Command, 20 October 1944, TNA

60 CAB 99-31 minutes of Argonaut Yalta conference, Annex C, CCS paper 776/3, 9 February
    1945, TNA

61 CAB 79-28-18 JIC (45) 13 (O) paper Japanese Strategy in Burma, COS meeting, 16 January
    1944, TNA

62 Colville, J., *Fringes of Power*, London, Hodder and Stoughton, 1985, p. 523, 8 October 1944

63 FO 800/302 Miscellaneous Correspondence Sir Archibald Kerr, vol. V, 1944, pp. 227–35

64 Foreign Relations US, *The conferences at Malta and Yalta 1945*, Department of State, Washington,
    1955, p. 205, letter Mikolajczyk to Harriman, 16 October 1944

65 CAB 101-250 telegram Churchill to Roosevelt, 18 October 1944, TNA

66 US Congress, Hearings before Select Committee on Katyn Massacre, vol. 7, Washington, 1952,
    pp. 2200–6

Chapter 15

1   CAB 101-250 telegram Churchill to General Smuts, 9 October 1944, TNA

2   Beevor, A., *The Second World War*, Phoenix, London, 2013, p. 641

3   Leton, B., Private Papers – The Descent of Man, D.19780, Imperial War Museum, London, p. 653

4   CAB 79-84 minutes Staff meeting, 12 December 1944, TNA

5   *USAAF United States Strategic Bombing Survey, Summary Report: Europe*, Air University Press,
    Alabama, 1987, p. 25

6   Ibid., pp. 19–20

7   US Department of State, press release, 5 December 1944, State Department Bulletin,
    10 December 1944, vol. XI, no. 285, p. 722

8   Davison, J., Private Papers, letter 10 December 1944, D.17406, Imperial War Museum, London

9   Churchill, W., *The Second World War: vol. VI, Triumph and Tragedy*, Cassell, London, 1954, p. 255

10 Poole, B., Private Papers, D.2119, Imperial War Museum, London, letter 9 December 1944

11 CAB 101-150, telegram Churchill to Roosevelt, 15 December 1944, TNA

12 Pogue, F., *George C. Marshall: The Organiser of Victory 1943–45*, Viking, New York, 1973, p. 516

13 US State Department, *Foreign Relations of the US: The conferences at Malta and Yalta 1945*, State
    Department, Washington, 1955, p. 361

14 CAB 99-31 Argonaut Record of Proceedings, CCS 761/3 Strategy in NW Europe: Enclosure
    B, Eisenhower SCAF 180 telegram, 20 January 1945, TNA

15 Ibid., Argonaut Record of Proceedings, minutes CCS 182nd Meeting 30 January 1945, TNA

16 ibid., Argonaut Record of Proceedings, CCS 776/3 Report to the President and the Prime
    Minister, 9 February 1945, TNA

17 CAB 79-28 minutes Staff conference, 23 January 1945, TNA

18 Moran, Lord., *Churchill at War 1940–45*, Robinson, London, 2002, p. 272

19 *Daily Telegraph* Obituaries, Richard Reynolds, 4 July 2000, www.telegraph.co.uk/news/ obituaries/1346476/Commander-Dickie-Reynolds.html

20 Strange, J., *Despatches from the Home Front: War Diaries 1939–45*, Jak Books, London, 1994, p. 166

21 Leton, op. cit., p. 660

22 SHAEF telegram SCAF 252, Eisenhower to Stalin, 28 March 1945 Marshall Foundation, Virginia

23 CAB 101-251 telegram Churchill to Eisenhower, 31 March 1945, TNA

24 SHAEF telegram FWD18345, Eisenhower to Marshall, 30 March 1945, Marshall Foundation, Virginia

25 CAB 101-245 minute Churchill, 31 March 1945, TNA

26 CAB 101-251 telegram Churchill to Roosevelt, 1 April 1945, TNA

27 Ibid., telegram Churchill to Roosevelt, 5 April 1945, TNA

28 Leton, B., Private Papers – The Descent of Man, D.19780, Imperial War Museum, London, p. 665

29 PREM 3-398 telegram Churchill to Truman, 18 April 1945, TNA

30 Gilbert op. cit. p. 1347

31 BBC History WW2 People's War, Victory Celebrations – Joan Styan www.bbc.co.uk/history/ ww2peopleswar/stories/51/a2756351.shtml

32 PREM 3-139-8A minute Lord Cherwell to Churchill, 19 October 1944, TNA

33 CAB 127-37 minute Churchill to Chancellor of Exchequer, 21 January 1945, TNA

34 PREM 3-139-2 minute Chancellor of Exchequer to Churchill, 21 March 1944, TNA

35 CAB 126-146 telegram CANAM 350 Chancellor of Exchequer to Halifax, 2 July 1945, TNA

36 Stimson, H., 'The Decision to Use the Atomic Bomb', *Harpers Magazine*, vol. 194, no. 1164, February 1947

37 Broad, R., and Fleming, S. (eds), *Nella Last's War*, Profile, London, 2006, p. 289

38 Soames, M., *Clementine Churchill*, Cassell, London, 1979, p. 391

Chapter 16

1 CAB 101/240/4 minute Churchill M52, 31st August 1940, TNA

2 Danchev, A., and Todman, D., War Diaries 1939–1945: Field Marshal Lord Alanbrooke, Weidenfeld and Nicolson, London, 2001, p. 450

3 Gilbert, M., *Finest Hour*, Heinemann, London, 1984, p. 165

4 Colville, J., *The Fringes of Power*, Hodder and Stoughton, London, 1985, p. 143, diary entry 29 May 1940

5 ibid., p. 159, diary 16 June 1940

6 Churchill, W., *The Second World War: vol. IV, The Hinge of Fate*, Cassell, London, 1951, p. 78

7 Churchill, W., op. cit, vol. II, pp. 233–4

8 Keegan, J., *Churchill*, Weidenfield and Nicholson, New York, 2003, p. 128

9 Danchev, op. cit., p. 515

10 Moran, Sir C., *The Struggle for Survival*, Constable, London, 1966, p. 326

11 Harvey, J., (ed) *War Diaries of Oliver Harvey*, Collins, London, 1978, p. 279, 24 July 1943

12 Alanbrooke Papers, 5/9, entry of 10 September 1944, Liddell Hart Centre for Military Archives, London

13 Danchev, op. cit., pp. 450–1, 30 August 1943

14 Day, D., *Menzies and Churchill at War*, Angus and Robertson, Sydney, 1987, p. 167

15 Gilbert op. cit. p. 593

16 Ismay, Lord H., *Memoirs of Lord Ismay*, Heinemann, London, 1960, p. 165

17 Churchill, W., op cit., vol. II, p. 529

18 Roskill, S., *Churchill and the Admirals*, Collins, London, 1977, p. 139

19 CAB 80-66 paper COS (42) 466 (O) American–British Strategy in 1943, Annex I, 31 December 1942, TNA

20 Gilbert, op. cit., p. 437
21 *USAAF United States Strategic Bombing Survey, Summary report – Europe*, Air University Press, Alabama, 1987, p. 37
22 CAB 101-240 minute Churchill to Ismay, 24 November 1940, TNA
23 CAB 101-242 minute Churchill to Stafford Cripps, 8 March 1942, TNA
24 PREM 3-427-1 DC(S) (43) 22, Tank Supply Policy, 16 April 1943, TNA
25 Ibid., minute Churchill to Defence Committee (Supply), 23 April 1943, TNA
26 Hansard HC debate, 16 March 1944, Churchill, vol. 398 cc. 393
27 Napier, S., *The Armoured Campaign in Normandy, June–August 1944*, The History Press, Stroud, 2015, pp. 412–6
28 Fletcher, D., *The Great Tank Scandal*, HMSO, London, 1989, pp. 25–6
29 Gilbert, op. cit., p. 659
30 Martin, A., and Harding, P. (eds), *Dark and Hurrying Days: Menzies' Diary 1941*, NLA, Canberra, 1993, p. 161
31 James, R.R., *Churchill: A Study in Failure 1900–1939*, Weidenfeld and Nicolson, London, 1970, p. 306
32 CAB 101-239 minute Churchill to First Sea Lord, 11 December 1939, TNA
33 Hansard HC debate, 8 May 1940, vol. 360 cc. 1251–366
34 Dalton, H., *The Fateful Years: Memoirs 1931–1945*, London, 1957, pp. 335–6
35 CAB 65-13-24 Confidential annex to minutes War Cabinet meeting, 28 May 1940, TNA
36 Ray, J., *The Night Blitz 1940–1941*, Cassell, London, 1994, p. 264
37 CAB 65-9-9 minutes War Cabinet meeting, 11 September 1940, TNA
38 Gilbert, M., *The Road to Victory*, Heinemann, London, 1986, p. 765
39 PREM 1-345 Churchill, Memorandum on Sea Power, 25 March 1939, TNA
40 Eisenhower, D.D., *Crusade in Europe*, Hopkins University, Baltimore, 1997, p. 71
41 Wedemeyer, A.C., *Wedemeyer Reports!*, Henry Holt, New York, 1958, p. 169
42 Alanbrooke Papers, 5/9, entry of 10 September 1944, Liddell Hart Centre for Military Archives
43 Djilas, M., *Conversations with Stalin*, Penguin, London, 1969, p. 73
44 Colville, op. cit., p. 751
45 Nicholson, N. (ed), *Harold Nicholson Diaries and Letters 1939–1945*, Atheneum, New York, 1967, p. 211
46 Danchev, op. cit., p. 231, 18 February 1942
47 Churchill, W., op. cit., vol. IV, p. 343
48 Kennedy, J., *The Business of War*, William Morrow, New York, 1958, p. 115
49 Gilbert, op. cit., p. 405
50 CAB 101/248 telegram Churchill to Auchinleck, 22 June 1942, TNA
51 CAB 120/10 note by Churchill, 30 August 1941, TNA
52 Gilbert, op cit, p. 11
53 Hansard HC debate, W. Churchill speech, 3 September 1939, vol. 351 cc. 291–302
54 Hansard HC debate, 4 June 1940, vol. 361 cc. 787–98
55 Barnes, J., and Nicholson, D., eds *The Empire at Bay: The Leo Amery Diaries 1929–1945*, Hutchinson, London, 1988, p. 584, diary 14 March 1940
56 Hansard HC debate, 18 June 1940, vol. 362 cc. 51–64
57 Smith, E., letter 20 June 1940, Private Papers, D.16015, Imperial War Museum , London
58 BBC History WW2 People's War, Recollections 1939–1945 – Jennifer de Villiers www.bbc.co.uk/history/ww2peopleswar/stories/01/a9900001.shtml

BIBLIOGRAPHY

Archives and Collections

Churchill Archives Cambridge, private papers L. Burgis, BRGS 2-13

Churchill Archives Cambridge – Churchill Chartwell papers

Churchill Archives Cambridge WILK 1/2A, journal 30 March 1943, papers of Gerard Wilkinson

DHH Archives, Ottawa, CMHQ reports WWII #159 Operation Jubilee - Appendix A, Interview with Capt. J. Hughes-Hallett

FD Roosevelt Museum/Library, New York, President's Secretary's Files and Map Room files

Hoover Institution Archives, Stanford University, Stanford J. Stilwell, diaries Box 39, Folder 9

Imperial War Museum, London, private papers E. Smith D.16015, B. Leeton D.19780, J. Davidson D.17406, B. Poole D.2119

Kennedy Library, Boston, J. Kennedy papers and Diplomatic Memoirs, Box 149 and 100.

Library and Archives, Canada, diaries William Mackenzie King MJ26-J13

Library of Congress, papers Averell Harriman, 15 April 1941

Liddell Hart Centre Military Archives, London, private papers Sir J. Kennedy, KENN 4/2/4, JN4-2-5; Sir H. Pownall, Catalogue 1393; private papers C. Wilmot LH 15/15/1; papers of FM Brooke 6-2-18

Marshall Foundation, Virginia, SHAEF Telegram FWD18345 Eisenhower to Marshall, 30 March 1945

University of York, York, Lord Halifax diary 19 June 1940 A7/8/4

Yale University Library, Yale, Stimson Diaries roll 7, vol. 36

Publications

Alsop, J., and Kintner, R., *American White Paper: The Story of American Diplomacy and the Second World War*, Simon and Schuster, New York, 1940

Barnes, J., and Nicholson, D., eds, *The Empire at Bay: the Leo Amery Diaries 1929-1945*, Hutchinson, London, 1988

Beevor, A., *The Second World War*, Phoenix, London, 2013

Belsey, J., and Reid, H., *The West at War*, Redcliffe Press, Bristol, 1990

Birtle, A., *Sicily: US Army Campaigns of WWII*, US Army CMH Pub 72-16, Washington, 1993

Bland, L., *Papers GC Marshall, Vol. II, 1 July 1939 to 6 December 1941*, Johns Hopkins University Press, Baltimore, 1986

Bland, L., *Papers GC Marshall, Vol III, 7 December 1941–31 May 1943*, Johns Hopkins University, Baltimore, 1991

Blumenson, M., *Salerno to Cassino*, US Army CMH Pub 6-3-1, Washington, 1969

Broad, R. and Fleming, S., (eds), *Nella Last's War*, Profile, London, 2006

Bryant, A., *The Turn of the Tide*, Reprint Society, London, 1958

Bullock, A., *Hitler: A Study in Tyranny*, Odhams, London, 1952

Butcher, H., *My Three Years with Eisenhower*, Simon and Schuster, New York, 1946

Butler, J.R.M., *Grand Strategy Vol. II Sept 1939–June 1941*, HMSO, London, 1957

Butler, J.R.M., *Grand Strategy Vol. III Pt II*, HMSO, London, 1964

Churchill, W., *The Second World War: Vol. I:, The Gathering Storm*, Cassell, London, 1948

Churchill, W., *The Second World War: Vol. II, Their Finest Hour*, Cassell, London, 1949

Churchill, W., *The Second World War: Vol. III, The Grand Alliance*, Cassell, London, 1950

Churchill, W., *The Second World War: Vol. IV, Hinge of Fate*, Cassell, London, 1951

Churchill, W., *The Second World War: Vol. V, Closing the Ring*, Cassell, London, 1952

Churchill, W., *Never Give in! The Best of Winston Churchill's Speeches*, Hyperion, New York, 2003

Clark, A., *Barbarossa*, Cassel, London, 2005

Colville, J., *The Fringes of Power*, Hodder and Stoughton, London, 1985

Costello, J., *The Pacific War 1941-1945*, Rawson Wade, New York, 1981

Craven, W.F. and Cate, J.L. eds, *Army Air Forces in World War II, Vol 1: Air Corps Prepares for War*, University of Chicago Press, Chicago, 1955

Craven, W.F. and Cate, J.L. eds, *Army Air Forces in World War II, Vol 6: Men and Planes*, University of Chicago Press, Chicago, 1955

Dalton, H., *The Fateful Years: Memoirs 1931–1945*, London, 1957

Danchev, A., and Todman, D., *War Diaries 1939–1945 of Field Marshal Lord Alan Brooke*, Weidenfeld and Nicolson, London, 2001

Day, D., *Menzies and Churchill at War*, Angus and Robertson, Sydney, 1987

Derry, T.K., *The Campaign in Norway*, HMSO, London, 1952

Dilks, D., *The Diaries of Sir Alexander Cadogan 1938–1945*, Cassell, London, 1971

Djilas, M., *Conversations with Stalin*, Penguin, London, 1969

Ehrman, J., *Grand Strategy, Vol. V: August 1943–September 1944*, HMSO, London, 1956

Eisenhower, D.D., *Crusade in Europe*, Hopkins University, Baltimore, 1997

Fletcher, D., *The Great Tank Scandal*, HMSO, London, 1989

Foreign Ministry of the USSR, *Correspondence between the Chairman of the Council of Ministers of the USSR and the Presidents of the USA and the Prime Ministers of Great Britain during the Great Patriotic War 1941–1945*, Progress Publishers, Moscow, 1957.

FRUS (Foreign Relations US), *The Conferences at Washington 1941-2 and Casablanca 1943*, Arcadia conference minutes State Department, Washington, 1968

FRUS, *The Cairo and Tehran Conferences*, State Department, Washington, 1961

FRUS, *The Conferences at Malta and Yalta 1945*, State Department, Washington, 1955

FRUS, 1942 Vol III, Russia, State Department, Washington

Fraser, D., *Alanbrooke*, Hamlyn, London, 1983

Freudenberg, G., *Churchill and Australia*, Macmillan, Sydney, 2008

Garland, Lt-Col A., and McGaw-Smyth, H., *Sicily and the Surrender of Italy*, US Army CMH Pub 6-22-1, Washington, 1965

Gilbert, M., *Finest Hour: Winston Churchill 1939-1941*, Heinemann, London, 1984

Gilbert, M., *The Road to Victory*, Heinemann, London, 1986

Halder, F., *War Journal, Vol IV Pt 2*, Combined Arms Research Library, Ft Leavenworth, Kansas

Halder, F., *War Journal , Vol VI*, Combined Arms Digital Research Library, Ft Leavenworth, Kansas

Hamilton, N., *JFK: Reckless Youth*, Random House, New York, 1992

Harrison, G., *Cross-Channel Attack*, US Army CMH Pub 7-4-1, Washington, 1951

Harvey, J., *The War Diaries of Oliver Harvey 1941–45*, Collins, London, 1978

Hastings, M., *Finest Years: Churchill as Warlord 1940–1945*, Harper Press, London, 2009

Herington, J., *Australians at War 1939–45, Air, Vol III: Air War against Germany and Italy 1939-1943*, Australian War Memorial, Canberra, 1954

Howard, M., *Grand Strategy, Vol IV: August 1942–September 1943*, HMSO, London, 1972

Howe, G., *Northwest Africa: Seizing the Initiative*, US Army CMH Pub 6-1-1, Washington, 1993

Ickes, H., *The Secret Diary of Harold Ickes, Vol. 3: The Lowering Clouds, 1939–1941*, Simon and Schuster, New York, 1954

Irving, D., *Churchill's War*, Focal Point, London, 2002

Ismay, Gen, H. L., *The Memoirs of Lord Ismay*, Heinemann, London, 1960

James, R.R., *Churchill: A Study in Failure 1900–1939*, Weidenfeld and Nicolson, London, 1970

Jenkins, R., *Churchill*, Pan, London, 2002

Keegan, J., *Churchill*, Weidenfield and Nicholson, New York, 2003

Kennedy, Sir J., *The Business of War*, William Morrow, New York, 1958

Laurie, C.D., Anzio, *The US Army Campaigns of WII*, US Army CMH Pub 72-19, Washington, n.d.,

Long, G., *Australia in the War of 1939–1945: Greece, Crete and Syria.* Australian War Memorial, Canberra, 1953

Lunde, H., *Hitler's Pre-Emptive War: The Battle for Norway, 1940.* Casemate, Newbury, 2009

MacArthur, D., *Reports of General MacArthur: Japanese Operations in the SW Pacific*, Vol II, pt 1, CMH Pub 13-1, US Army, Washington 1966

Martin, A., and Harding, P. (eds), *Dark and Hurrying Days: Menzies' Diary 1941*, NLA, Canberra, 1993

Mathews, S.T., *Command Decisions: General Clark's Decision To Drive on Rome*, US Army CMH Pub 70-1, Washington, 1987

Matloff, M., and Snell, E., *Strategic Planning for Coalition Warfare, 1941–1942*, US Army CMH Pub 1-3, Washington, 1953

Matloff, M., *Strategic Planning for Coalition Warfare, 1943–44*, US Army CMH Pub 1-4, Washington, 1959

Moran, Lord, *Churchill at War 1940–45*, Robinson, London, 2002

Moran, Lord, *Winston Churchill: The Struggle for Survival 1940–1965*, Constable, London, 1966

Morison, S.E., *History of the United States Naval Operations in World War II, Vol II: Battle of the Atlantic*, Little-Brown, Boston, 1947

Murray, W., *Strategy for Defeat: The Luftwaffe 1933–1945*, Air University Press, Alabama, 1983

Napier, S., *The Armoured Campaign in Normandy, June-August 1944*, The History Press, Stroud, 2015

Nicolson, N. (ed), *Diaries and Letters of Harold Nicolson 1939–45*, Collins, London, 1967

O'Brien, T.H., *Civil Defence*, HMSO, London, 1955

Pearson-Hayes, G., *History of the Joint Chiefs of Staff in WWII*, Naval Institute, Washington, 1982

Playfair, Maj- Gen I.S.O., *History of the Second World War The Mediterranean and Middle East Volume II: The Germans come to the Help of their Ally (1941)*, HMSO, London, 1953

Pogue, F., *George C Marshall: The Organiser of Victory 1943–45*, Viking, New York, 1973

Postan, M.M., *British War Production*, HMSO, London, 1952

Ray, J., *The Night Blitz 1940–1941*, Cassell, London, 1994

Reynolds, D., *In Command of History: Churchill Fighting and Rewriting the Second World War*, Basic, New York, 2007

Roosevelt, F.D., *An Appeal to Great Britain, France, Italy, Germany, and Poland to Refrain from Air Bombing of Civilians, 1 September 1939*, Public Papers and Addresses of Franklin D. Roosevelt, 1939

Roosevelt F.D., *Press conference 3rd Feb 1939, The Public Papers and Addresses of Franklin D. Roosevelt: 1939 – War and Neutrality*, Macmillan, New York, 1941

Roosevelt, F.D., *The Public Papers and Addresses of Franklin D. Roosevelt 1941*, Harper Bros, New York, 1950

Roskill, S., *Churchill and the Admirals*, Collins, London, 1977

Rusbridger, J., and Nave, E., *Betrayal at Pearl Harbour*, Michael O'Mara, London, 1991

Sherwood, R., *Roosevelt and Hopkins: An Intimate History*, Harper, New York, 1950

Sherwood, R., *The White House Papers: Vol II*, Eyre and Spottiswood, London, 1949

Slim, W., *Defeat into Victory*, Cassell, London, 1955

Stafford, D., *Roosevelt and Churchill: Men of Secrets*, Abacus, London, 2000

Stimson, H., *On Active Service*, Harpers, New York, 1948

Strange, J., *Despatches from the Home Front: War Diaries 1939-45*, Jak Books, London, 1994

Titmuss, R.M., *The Problems of Social Policy*, HMSO, London, 1950

Thompson, W.H., *Assignment Churchill*, Farrer, Strauss and Young, New York, 1955

Soames, M., *Clementine Churchill*, Cassell, London, 1979

Toland, J., *Infamy: Pearl Harbor and Its Aftermath*, Doubleday, New York, 1982

USAAF United States Strategic Bombing Survey, Summary report – Europe, Air University Press, Alabama, 1987

US Army Services Forces, *Statistical Review of WWII: Appendix H*, War Department, Washington, 1946

US Army, *The German Campaign in the Balkans*, CMH Publication 104-4, Washington, 1953

US Army, *History of Military Mobilisation in the United States Army 1775–1945*, PAM 20-212, Washington, 1955

US Congress, *Hearings before Select Committee on Katyn Massacre, vol 7*, Washington, 1952

US Congress, *Hearings before the Joint Committee on the Investigation of the Pearl Harbour Attack, Vol 14, Exhibit 21*, US Government, Washington, 1946

US Congress, *Hearings before the Joint Committee on the Investigation of the Pearl Harbour Attack, Vol 20, Exhibit 176*, US Government, Washington, 1946

U.S. Department of State, *Foreign Relations of US, Peace and War: United States Foreign Policy, 1931–1941*, Washington, 1943

Wedemeyer, A.C., *Wedemeyer Reports!*, Henry Holt, New York, 1958

Wilson, T.A., *The First Summit*, University Press of Kansas, Kansas, 1991

Ziemke, E.F., *Moscow to Stalingrad*, US Army CMH Pubn 30-12, Washington, 1987

Journals

Black, C., 'Franklin Delano Roosevelt: Champion of Freedom', *Public Affairs*, New York, 2014, p. 481

Despatch 38011, 'The Norway Campaign 1940', *Supplement to the London Gazette*, 10 July 1947

Dunbabin, J.P.D., 'British Rearmament in the 1930s', *The Historical Journal*, XVIII, No. 3, 1975, pp. 587–609

Field, G., 'Nights Underground in Darkest London – The Blitz 1940-41', *International Labour and Working-Class History, Class and Catastrophe: September 11 and Other Working-Class Disasters*, No. 62, 2002

Lazarides, M., 'Time of Triviality', *History of the Second World War*, Vol 1, No. 6, Purnell, London, 1966

Rusbridger, J., 'The Sinking of the "Automedon", the Capture of the "Nankin": New Light on Two Intelligence Disasters in World War II', *Encounter*, Vol. 375, No. 5, pp. 8–14

Stanley, P., 'Great in Adversity: Indian POWs', *Journal of Australian War Memorial*, No. 37, October 2002

Stimson, H., 'The Decision to Use the Atomic Bomb', *Harpers Magazine*, Vol. 194, No. 1164, Feb 1947

Wavell, Sir A., 'Operations in the India Command from 1st January 1943 to 20th June 1943', *London Gazette*, 22 April 1948 Wavell, Sir A., 'Operations in the Middle East from 7th February 1941 to 15th July 1941', *Supplement to London Gazette*, 3 July 1946

Wing Ray, D., 'The Takoradi Route: Roosevelt's Prewar Venture beyond the Western Hemisphere', *The Journal of American History*, Vol. 62, No. 2 (Sept 1975), pp. 340–358

INDEX